MISSION AFTER PENTECOST

MISSION
in Global Community

SCOTT W. SUNQUIST
AND AMOS YONG,
SERIES EDITORS

The Mission in Global Community series is designed to reach college students and those interested in learning more about responsible mission involvement. Written by faculty and graduates from Fuller Theological Seminary, the series is designed as a global conversation with stories and perspectives from around the world.

MISSION AFTER PENTECOST

The Witness of the Spirit from Genesis to Revelation

AMOS YONG

Baker Academic

a division of Baker Publishing Group
Grand Rapids, Michigan

© 2019 by Amos Yong

Published by Baker Academic
a division of Baker Publishing Group
PO Box 6287, Grand Rapids, MI 49516-6287
www.bakeracademic.com

Printed in the United States of America

Library of Congress Cataloging-in-Publication Data
Names: Yong, Amos, author.
Title: Mission after Pentecost : the witness of the spirit from Genesis to Revelation / Amos Yong.
Description: Grand Rapids : Baker Academic, a division of Baker Publishing Group, 2019. | Series: Mission in global community | Includes index.
Identifiers: LCCN 2019003752 | ISBN 9781540961150 (pbk.)
Subjects: LCSH: Missions—Biblical teaching. | Pentecostal churches—Doctrines.
Classification: LCC BV2073 .Y66 2019 | DDC 266—dc23
LC record available at https://lccn.loc.gov/2019003752

ISBN 978-1-5409-6236-2 (casebound)

19   20   21   22   23   24   25   7   6   5   4   3   2   1

Dedicated to
Sue and Tony Richie,
kindred spirits in the *missio Dei*

Contents

Expanded Table of Contents

Series Preface

A mission leader in 1965, not too long ago, could not have foreseen what mission looks like today. In 1965 nations in the non-Western world were gaining their independence after centuries of Western colonialism. Mission societies from Europe and North America were trying to adjust to the new global realities where Muslim nations, once dominated by the West, no longer granted "missionary visas." The largest mission field, China, was closed. Decolonization, it seemed, was bringing a decline to missionary work in Africa and Asia.

On the home front, Western churches were in decline, and the traditional missionary factories—mainline churches in the West—were struggling with their own identities. Membership was then—and remains—in decline, and missionary vocations were following the same pattern. Evangelical and Pentecostal churches began to surpass mainline churches in mission, and then, just when we thought we understood the new missionary patterns, Brazilians began to go to Pakistan and Malaysians began to evangelize Vietnam and Cambodia. Africans (highly educated and strongly Christian) began to move in great numbers to Europe and North America. Countries that had been closed began to see conversions to Christ, without the aid of traditional mission societies. And in the midst of this rapid transformation of missionary work, the alarm rang out that most Christians in the world were now in Asia, Latin America, and Africa rather than in the West.

What does it mean to be involved in mission in this new world where Christianity has been turned upside down in less than a century?

This series is directed at this new global context for mission. Fuller Theological Seminary, particularly through its School of Intercultural Studies (formerly School of World Mission), has been attentive to trends in global mission for over half a century. In fact, much innovation in mission thinking and practice has emanated from Fuller since Donald McGavran moved from Oregon to California—as the first and founding dean of the then School of World Mission—to apply lessons about church growth learned in India to other areas of the world. Since that time many creative mission professors have provided global leadership in mission thinking: Ralph Winter (unreached people groups), Paul Hiebert (anthropology for mission), Charles Kraft (mission and spiritual dynamics), and Dudley Woodberry (Islamics), among others.

This series provides the most recent global scholarship on key themes in mission, written for a general audience of Christians committed to God's mission. Designed to be student, user, and textbook friendly, each volume contains voices from around the world speaking about the theme, and each chapter concludes with discussion questions so the books can be used for group studies. As the fields of mission are changing, shifting, or shrinking, the discussions connect the church and the world, East and West, North and South, the developed and developing worlds, each crossing cultural, political, social, and religious boundaries in its own way and knitting together people living and serving in various communities, both of faith and of other commitments—this is the contemporary landscape of the mission of God. Enjoy the challenges of each volume and find ways to live into God's mission.

Scott W. Sunquist

Amos Yong

Preface

It has taken me almost four years to write this book, working on and off, around teaching, administrative work, and other writing assignments. When I came to Fuller Seminary as professor of theology and mission and director of the Center for Missiological Research at the School of Intercultural Studies (SIS) in the summer of 2014, I said to myself: I now need to write a full-fledged missiology. As I set out to work on such a book, I built most immediately off work I had been doing in theological interpretation of scripture, with the result being perhaps more appropriately considered pneumato-missiological interpretation of scripture. Yet the book you hold in your hands could only have come about because of the welcome afforded to me by Fuller Seminary as a whole and by my colleagues in the SIS more specifically. It has been a wonderful learning experience working in the field of missiology, and I have learned a great deal about mission theology and mission studies from my faculty colleagues and students. As the manuscript goes to press, I am doubly welcomed—and honored—now to have been invited to serve as dean of the SIS and its sister, the School of Theology (SOT).

This dual decanal appointment is also a source of trepidation. Not only am I out of my element as systematician turned mission theologian, I am now wading into the field of biblical studies. Hence, this has turned out to be one of the most challenging books I have written so far, not least because the Old Testament canon spans almost two millennia and there has been no hope for me to digest the vast scholarship in the field, much less the detailed treatments of the texts that my own focused approached has identified for comment. I have learned a great deal about the world of ancient Israel through these last few years but surely still not enough to avoid what I am sure will appear to scholars who work in this arena—now including my new SOT colleagues,

indeed!—as very naive statements. In any case, I am extremely grateful to Rick
Wadholm for reading a previous draft of my manuscript, as he helped save me
from many egregious errors of scriptural interpretation, especially in the Old
Testament. Thanks also to the sixteen interlocutors whose comments grace
these pages, and especially to Federico Roth, Amelia Rebecca Basdeo-Hill,
and Bitrus Sarma, who each went the additional mile to provide corrective
perspective on various chapters of my text. The book is greatly improved as
a result of these colleagues' perspicacious and insightful contributions.

I appreciate also Scott W. Sunquist's friendship and constant decanal prayer
(as preceding dean of the SIS) for me and our faculty colleagues here, as well
as his comradeship in coediting the book series in which this volume is published. Jim Kinney and the Baker staff, especially Eric Salo, have also been
enthusiastic about this project and professional all along the publication way.
Ryan Davis in particular did yeoman's labor in his detailed copyediting of
the manuscript that made it more readable, correcting misplaced references
and smoothing over many other mistakes. All the persisting interpretation
and factual foibles are not to be charged to those named above but remain
my responsibility.

My graduate assistants Jeremy Bone and, previously, Hoon Jung, Nok
Kam, and Ryan Seow have helped at various stages of this four-year-long
writing project, getting research materials and indexing the book (Bone). Gail
Frederick, Alice Song, and others at Fuller's David Allen Hubbard Library
have helped with the acquisitions of books I have consulted.

My wife, Alma, is a constant supportive and loving presence by my side.
Over the last few years here in Southern California, we have lived with almost a full household at various points (with our children, their spouses, and
granddaughters all present). She nevertheless accompanies me regularly on
dinner dates, just the two of us, and her smiles, conversation, prayers, and
exhortations give me the encouragement to keep pressing into the vocation
of scholarship that has been our path now for the last three decades plus. To
say *Thank you, Alma!* insufficiently expresses the gratefulness I have to God
for such a caring life confidant.

I dedicate this book to Sue and Tony Richie. From what I can tell, Sue is
to Tony as Alma is to me: a continual source of love, joy, and strength for
her husband. And as our wives are to us as life companions, so Tony has
been walking with me as a fellow pentecostal theologian for at least the last
fifteen years. He first came upon my early work on pentecostal theology of
religions, saw the need, and joined me in what at that time was and still in
many respects remains a lonely journey, developing inimitably along the way
his own pentecostally inspired testimonial theology of interfaith dialogue.

What is unique to his accomplishments is Tony's location at the heart of the Holiness-Pentecostal Church of God, Cleveland, Tennessee, group of churches, which is relatively classically pentecostal in its orientation. That he has been able to lead denominational conversations about intra-Christian ecumenism and interfaith relations at a high level speaks to his own gifts as a pentecostal scholar, minister, and leader. In all these respects, and many more beyond his own groundbreaking contributions to pentecostal theology, Tony is a missionary in crossing established borders, breaking long-held conventions, and exploring new territory for the gospel's unfolding. I am grateful for such a colleague and friend, recalling with special fondness when the Richies have extended the warmest of Southern hospitality to the Yong family, including allowing us time away at their lakeshore cabin, with the gift of laughter as I tried to navigate their boat across the lake. Thank you, Sue and Tony. May your missionary journey from Knoxville, Tennessee, to the ends of the earth continue to be led and blessed by the divine spirit!

Abbreviations

AB	Anchor Bible
AJPS	*Asian Journal of Pentecostal Studies*
AsJT	*Asia Journal of Theology*
AUSS	*Andrews University Seminary Studies*
BBR	*Bulletin for Biblical Research*
BETL	Bibliotheca Ephemeridum Theologicarum Lovaniensium
BibInt	*Biblical Interpretation*
BibInt	Biblical Interpretation Series
BSac	*Bibliotheca Sacra*
BZAW	Beihefte zur Zeitschrift für die alttestamentliche Wissenschaft
CBQ	*Catholic Biblical Quarterly*
CTJ	*Calvin Theological Journal*
CurTM	*Currents in Theology and Mission*
EvQ	*Evangelical Quarterly*
ExAud	*Ex Auditu*
FAT	Forschungen zum Alten Testament
IBC	Interpretation: A Bible Commentary for Teaching and Preaching
Int	*Interpretation*
IRM	*International Review of Mission*
ITC	International Theological Commentary
JBL	*Journal of Biblical Literature*
JBPR	*Journal of Biblical and Pneumatological Research*
JBQ	*Jewish Bible Quarterly*
JETS	*Journal of the Evangelical Theological Society*
JPT	*Journal of Pentecostal Theology*
JPTSup	Journal of Pentecostal Theology Supplement Series
JSNT	*Journal for the Study of the New Testament*
JSNTSup	Journal for the Study of the New Testament Supplement Series
JSOT	*Journal for the Study of the Old Testament*
JSOTSup	Journal for the Study of the Old Testament Supplement Series

JTI	*Journal of Theological Interpretation*
LHBOTS	The Library of Hebrew Bible/Old Testament Studies
LNTS	The Library of New Testament Studies
NCBC	New Century Bible Commentary
NIBC	New International Biblical Commentary
NovTSup	Supplements to Novum Testamentum
NSBT	New Studies in Biblical Theology
NTS	*New Testament Studies*
OTL	Old Testament Library
RevExp	*Review and Expositor*
RTR	*Reformed Theological Review*
SBEC	Studies in the Bible and Early Christianity
SBLDS	Society of Biblical Literature Dissertation Series
SNTSMS	Society for New Testament Studies Monograph Series
StBibLit	Studies in Biblical Literature
SwJT	*Southwestern Journal of Theology*
TJ	*Trinity Journal*
TOTC	Tyndale Old Testament Commentaries
TynBul	*Tyndale Bulletin*
VT	*Vetus Testamentum*
WBC	Word Biblical Commentary
WTJ	*Westminster Theological Journal*
WUNT	Wissenschaftliche Untersuchungen zum Neuen Testament
ZAW	*Zeitschrift für die alttestamentliche Wissenschaft*

Introduction

On the Pneumatological and Missiological Interpretation of Scripture

This is an ambitious book that attempts to triangulate around three scholarly domains: theological interpretation of scripture, pneumatology and pneumatological theology, and missiology or mission studies. Our overarching objective is to contribute to theology of mission discussions and do so via a reading of scriptural references to the divine spirit. Our secondary goals are to develop pneumatological theology in a missiological venue and to enrich theological interpretation of scripture initiatives from pneumatological and missiological perspectives. Such a complex and complicated triadic and tri-directional thesis nevertheless considers the two ancillary aspirations—in pneumatology and theological hermeneutics—in effect as the "two hands" that drive the broader venture in missiology and missional theology.[1]

This introductory discussion situates our efforts along three registers: the contemporary mission predicament, recent developments signaling the revitalization of theology of mission as a subfield of missiology, and the emergence of what I am calling "pneumatological interpretation of scripture" as a

---

1. Here I play off the classical Irenaean trope of the Son and spirit as the two hands of the Father since I am attempting something similar in this book—namely, developing a missiological pneumatology and a theology, or better pneumatology, of mission as part and parcel of a more robustly articulated trinitarian missiology, or triunely conceptualized theology of the *missio Dei*, as will be clarified momentarily. For more on the "two hands" motif in trinitarian theology, see my *Spirit-Word-Community: Theological Hermeneutics in Trinitarian Perspective*, New Critical Thinking in Religion, Theology, and Biblical Studies (Burlington, VT: Ashgate, 2002), §2.1.

1

resource for mission theology today. A fourth and final section will introduce the method and argumentative trajectory of the two parts of the book. This introduction outlines the current historical-missiological-theological context both in the hopes that the crisis of mission[2] that many now experience also may be felt through the reading of this book and so that the missiological proposals sketched throughout and summarized at the end can also be more adequately appreciated in the present historical moment.

Are We in a Post-Mission Era?

Since John Gatu, the general secretary of the Presbyterian Church of East Africa, called for a moratorium on foreign missionaries and funds in 1971,[3] the crisis of modern mission has only intensified rather than alleviated over the last almost half century. We have no space here to provide any exhaustive analysis, so I will delineate the issues in terms of the passing away of the classical mission paradigm and reality, and the emergence of something new, the precise nature of which remains to be understood and hence adequately articulated. For our purposes, then, and in order also to be provocative in an appropriately pedagogical sense, I will simply call ours a *post-mission* era and sketch its primary features along three lines.

First, ours is a postcolonial reality.[4] Yes, we are a long way from complete equality among nations in the present globalizing context, and it does appear that even with the European nations giving way to national self-governance, new global powers (e.g., China) have arisen while the emergence of the neoliberal economic world order portends new imperial pressures and constraints. Nevertheless, the postcolonial turn means not just that people are (putatively) self-governing but also that sociopolitical, cultural, and ethnic voices across Asia, Africa, and Latin America are no longer presumed to be subservient to those of the (former) Euro-American masters. Indeed, the postcolonial resurgence signals what might be called the color-ing of the global conversation in that the dominance of white (European and Anglo-Saxon) peoples is

2. Michael W. Stroope overviews the contemporary "crisis in mission"; his entire first chapter effectively charts the emergence and deepening of this felt predicament. Stroope, *Transcending Mission: The Eclipse of a Modern Tradition* (Downers Grove, IL: IVP Academic, 2017), 23–24.

3. See Robert Reese, "John Gatu and the Moratorium on Missionaries," *Missiology* 42:3 (2014): 245–56.

4. The "post" in "postcolonial" (intentionally unhyphenated in the scholarly literature) is less a historical than a critical-ethical category, meaning we live in a sense *after* the time of the modern colonial enterprise but yet still amid its legacy and hence in need of comprehending and responding critically to its grip. See, e.g., Federico Alfredo Roth, *Hyphenating Moses: A Postcolonial Exegesis of Identity in Exodus 1:1–3:15*, BibInt 154 (Leiden: Brill, 2017), 21–23.

giving way—imperceptibly slowly in some contexts and not without a fight in all others—to reds, yellows, browns, and blacks, and these in variously hybridized forms. To the degree that the modern mission movement—like the modern theological academe—was forged from the colonial enterprise, it was a project of white supremacy and normativity.[5] In our postcolonial context, then, the interrogation of whiteness includes with it the questioning of Christian mission and its complicity in the subjugation of the peoples of the earth for the benefit of Euro-American Westerners (whites). If the postcolonial moment is in quest of the end of whiteness, does that not also mean that a mission paradigm facilitated by whiteness is coming to an end, if not already finished?

At another parallel level, ours is also a post-Western and post-Enlightenment reality.[6] Here I am distinguishing European colonialism as a socioeconomic and political project from the Western Enlightenment as an epistemological "discovery" and foundational construct. Although both the political and the epistemological projects presume and support each other, I focus here on the latter because of its, in a sense, ironic interface with the theological sphere.[7] If the Enlightenment rationality was the climax of the intellectual quest for certainty punctured variously in the early modern period by Descartes and his successors (e.g., Leibniz and Kant on the Continent; Berkeley, Locke, and Hume in England), then this contributed to an even more radical dualism in the field of theology, given its commitments to understanding the world as composed of both material and spiritual dimensions. The problem was and remains that these theological convictions were marginalized as private belief (fit only for religious adherents) by the Enlightenment-based intellectualistic and scientific (scientistic, actually) paradigm that claimed to be the basis for

5. On modern theology as a byproduct of colonialism, see, e.g., Willie James Jennings, *The Christian Imagination: Theology and the Origins of Race* (New Haven: Yale University Press, 2010); and Shawn Kelley, *Racializing Jesus: Race, Ideology, and the Formation of Modern Biblical Scholarship* (New York: Routledge, 2002), esp. chaps. 2–3. On modern missions also intertwined with colonialism, see Love L. Sechrest, Johnny Ramírez-Johnson, and Amos Yong, eds., *Can "White" People Be Saved? Triangulating Race, Theology, and Mission*, Missiological Engagements (Downers Grove, IL: IVP Academic, 2018).

6. Again, meaning not that we are no longer Western or that we have left the Enlightenment completely, but that we remain with(in) their effects. Similarly (and as will be further detailed momentarily), we are postmoderns, meaning only *after* the modern, but unsure about what that means and needing to engage our time more intentionally. (Note: I use *postcolonial, postmodern, post-Western,* and *post-Enlightenment* in a similar sense: being *after* in some respect but yet *within* and therefore needing critical and ethical perspective.)

7. Apologies for the density of this paragraph; its major themes are explicated in J. Andrew Kirk and Kevin J. Vanhoozer, *To Stake a Claim: Mission and the Western Crisis of Knowledge* (Maryknoll, NY: Orbis, 1999), part 1.

public and verifiable knowledge. Yet the result in both directions remains problematic in our late modern situation. On the one side, Enlightenment rationalism, logocentrism, and conceptualism were taken over by scientistic positivism, and this combination began to show its limitations with the two world wars in the West during the first half of the twentieth century, and its so-called iron cage of rationality has since further unraveled with the emergence of the postmodern and its affective, embodied, and interrelational modalities of knowing. On the other side, theological dualism, forced into this position by Enlightenment rules, has proffered an otherworldly sensibility that has functioned for a while to preserve the political, economic, and religious status quo with its promise of rewards in an afterlife, but this alignment is becoming largely ineffective when measured against the resurgence of indigenous religious traditions that see no bifurcation between the material and the spiritual orders of the world. In other words, classical Christian mission, initially allied with Enlightenment reason against the perceived irrationalities of the non-European and non-Western world, now finds itself being the nonrational outsider on multiple fronts: too spiritual for Enlightenment goods on the one side and too otherworldly for traditional Christian or any other good on the other side. In this case, then, the epistemological underpinnings of modern Christian mission have begun to evaporate and are in need of reconstruction if the enterprise is to be salvaged.[8] Hence, to reiterate in another key, if the post-Western and post-Enlightenment condition has overturned the rationalist and scientistic hegemony, does that also mean that a mission paradigm facilitated by that kind of ordering of the cosmos is also expiring, if not already extinguished?

Alongside the postcolonial and the post-Western/post-Enlightenment arc is the post-Christendom arc.[9] Here my focus is not just on how Christian mission abetted developments in the political and epistemological spheres but on how Christian faith itself has been decentered from the public square in almost every meaningful measure.[10] And it is not just that Christianity has

8. Initial efforts in this direction are charted by Peter J. Bellini, *Participation: Epistemology and Mission Theology* (Wilmore, KY: Emeth, 2010).

9. Alan Kreider, *Worship and Mission after Christendom* (Scottdale, PA: Herald, 2011). See also Yong, "Many Tongues, Many Practices: Pentecost and Theology of Mission at 2010," in *Mission after Christendom: Emergent Themes in Contemporary Mission*, ed. Ogbu U. Kalu, Edmund Kee-Fook Chia, and Peter Vethanayagamony (Louisville: Westminster John Knox, 2010), 43–58, 160–63.

10. Christian mission could contribute to the political precisely because it was also generated in part out of the political. Bryan P. Stone clarifies the mutuality, albeit via historical discussion of what he calls *Constantinianism* instead; see his *Evangelism after Christendom: The Theology and Practice of Christian Witness* (Grand Rapids: Brazos, 2007), chap. 5.

been decentered but that the so-called "naked" public sphere has been filled in now by multiple "spirits": those of many cultures (multiculturalism) and those of many religions (religious pluralism), just for starters. So the anxiety some feel derives from a loss of Christian vitality and authority in the public domain and simultaneously an overcrowding of this same space by many other voices and powers. Some Christians are therefore now motivated to restore the glory and power of the Christian message to such a pluralistic world, but the problem is that they do not recognize that the plausibility structures undergirding such argumentative forms no longer hold in this post-everything world. More exactly, the nature of the Christian or Christianity itself might mean something different, so that mission or witness in the way of Christ will no longer be as if from a self-obviously recognizable "church" and related institutions and organizations to the "world," understood in terms of other realities needing redemption. Thus, some have called for a mission from or at the margins, while others have acknowledged that after the dissolution of Christendom, mission proceeds not from the West to the Rest but from every-where to anywhere.[11] To return to our point, then: if the post-Christendom era is in quest of the end of Christian hegemony, does that also mean that a mission paradigm facilitated by such sociopolitical-economic power is erod-ing, if not already passé?

Yet amid all the discussion that we live in a kind of *post*-age, we are also still very much grappling with the legacies, technologies, and achievements of the modern West, indeed in many ways even benefiting from these. Hence, my own preferences in this regard are to refer to ours as a *late modern* rather than *postmodern* context,[12] not least because the latter designates negatively and vacuously rather than positively. Recognizing our late modern situation allows us to see that the postcolonial, post-Enlightenment, and post-Christendom forces that today raise serious questions about classical Christian mission are real, even if dynamically fluid, phenomena. Part of the question that this book seeks to grapple with is how to buttress, even galvanize, the Christian mission enterprise when it is being assailed from so many sides. The way forward, however, might be to bury a modernist project, even one that bears the name of *Christian mission*, in order that something new may arise out of its throes.

11. See Anthony J. Gittins, *Ministry at the Margins: Strategy and Spirituality for Mission* (Maryknoll, NY: Orbis, 2002); Samuel Escobar, *The New Global Mission: The Gospel from Everywhere to Everyone* (Downers Grove, IL: IVP Academic, 2003); and Allen Yeh, *Polycentric Missiology: Twenty-First-Century Mission from Everyone to Everywhere* (Downers Grove, IL: IVP Academic, 2016).

12. See my *Theology and Down Syndrome: Reimagining Disability in Late Modernity* (Waco: Baylor University Press, 2007).

Reimagining Mission Theology in the Twenty-First Century?
Scriptural and Pneumatic Threads

So Christian mission, if it is to survive at all in whatever comes after late modernity, will look very different and perhaps have to go by a different name. Almost thirty years ago, David Bosch attempted to chart some of the ways forward in his book *Transforming Mission*, with his own *emerging ecumenical missionary paradigm* tracking along thirteen distinct, even if interrelated, fronts.[13] Interestingly, Bosch came to the field of missiology as a New Testament scholar and devoted a large portion of his book—the entire first part, consisting of 165 pages—to early Christian perspectives on a mission theology. As a systematician myself, I see the need both for ongoing theological reflection and for further scriptural consideration. Yes, there is a sense in which, as Martin Kähler opined over a hundred years ago, "mission became the 'mother of theology,'"[14] but there is also an ongoing need for sound theological reflection to provide perspective on the swiftly changing nature of the missional undertaking. Scriptural engagement remains key to this important missiological-theological task since there are few reliable places Christians can turn to for guidance in faithful discipleship in times of rapid change.

It may be deemed fortunate, then, that the subfield of mission theology has exploded with scripture studies. There are now many full-length formulations of what we might call *biblical theologies of mission*,[15] even as there

13. David J. Bosch, *Transforming Mission: Paradigm Shifts in Theology of Mission*, 20th anniv. ed. (Maryknoll, NY: Orbis, 2011). Bosch's thirteen missiological trajectories included *mission as* (1) the church-with-others; (2) *missio Dei*; (3) mediating salvation; (4) the quest for justice; (5) evangelism; (6) contextualization; (7) liberation; (8) inculturation; (9) common witness; (10) ministry by the whole people of God; (11) witness to people of other living faiths; (12) theology; and (13) action in hope. The breadth and scope are evident, as are the limitations that I identify elsewhere, e.g., in Yong, "Pentecost as Facet of the Church-in-Mission or Culmination of the *Missio Dei*? A Pentecostal Renewing of Bosch's (Reformed) Mission Theology," *Missionalia: Southern African Journal of Theology* (forthcoming). Extending from this article, my book attempts to provide further scriptural (Bosch's part 1 treats only some of the New Testament books) and pneumatological consideration for much of what Bosch proposes, but also other notions that are absent or underdeveloped in his book.

14. Kähler, originally 1908, reprinted in *Schriften zur Christologie und Mission* (Munich: Chr. Kaiser Verlag, 1971), 189, cited in Bosch, *Transforming Mission*, 489.

15. E.g., George W. Peters, *A Biblical Theology of Missions* (Chicago: Moody, 1972); Lucien Legrand, *Unity and Plurality: Mission in the Bible*, trans. Robert R. Barr (Maryknoll, NY: Orbis, 1990); William A. Dyrness, *Let the Earth Rejoice! A Biblical Theology of Holistic Mission* (Pasadena, CA: Fuller Seminary Press, 1992); Roger E. Hedlund, *God and the Nations: A Biblical Theology of Mission in the Asian Context* (Delhi: ISPCK, 1997); Arthur F. Glasser, with Charles E. Van Engen, Dean S. Gilliland, and Shawn B. Redford, *Announcing the Kingdom: The Story of God's Mission in the Bible* (Grand Rapids: Baker Academic, 2003); and

are emerging efforts specifically in the Old Testament and mission more particularly.[16] The latter are especially of interest since a question has persisted
about Israel's witness to the nations, particularly whether there was ever a
more centrifugal aspect of this mission in which Israel actively sought to
reach out to its neighbors, or whether much of it was centripetal, nurtured
by the expectation that Yahweh would draw the nations to his people and his
temple within Israel.[17] We will take up this question in part 1 of this book,
even if our own compass will treat it from different angles and in response to
different concerns. Simultaneously, more recent New Testament scholarship in
this area has explored more accurately the nature of early Christian mission
and developed constructive mission-theological ideas in intensive dialogue
with these documents.[18] There are now also specific book studies amid the
larger testamental considerations that probe missiological aspects of these
early Christian materials.[19] The important point to be made is that there is
an abundance of scriptural interrogation in the present context.

Yet my own sense is that much of this work is motivated by an effort to
recall the glory days of modern mission, even if there is a realization that
we ought not to retrieve the worst elements of the colonial enterprise. If
this is close to being true, then rereading the Bible from the perspectives of
bygone days is probably not the prognosis for imagining a different future

---

Christopher J. H. Wright, *The Mission of God's People: A Biblical Theology of the Church's
Mission* (Grand Rapids: Zondervan, 2010).

16. E.g., Robert Martin-Achard, *A Light to the Nations: A Study of the Old Testament
Conception of Israel's Mission to the World*, trans. John Penney Smith (Edinburgh: Oliver &
Boyd, 1962); David Filbeck, *Yes, God of the Gentiles, Too: The Missionary Message of the
Old Testament* (Wheaton: Billy Graham Center, 1994); Walter C. Kaiser Jr., *Mission in the
Old Testament: Israel as a Light to the Nations* (Grand Rapids: Baker Academic, 2000); and
James Chukwuma Okoye, *Israel and the Nations: A Mission Theology of the Old Testament*
(Maryknoll, NY: Orbis, 2006).

17. Of course, things are actually more complicated than this binary description; e.g., Sieg-
bert Riecker suggests that there are four missional mandates for Israel in the Old Testament: to
mediate blessings to the nations, to mediate knowledge to non-Israelites, to mediate between
Yahweh and gentiles (this is Israel's priestly role), and to mediate hospitality to/for strangers.
Riecker, "Missions in the Hebrew Canon Revisited: Four Theological Trails instead of One
Confining Concept," *Missiology* 44:3 (2016): 324–39.

18. For more on mission in early Christianity and in New Testament perspective, respectively,
see on the one hand Scot McKnight, *A Light among the Gentiles: Jewish Missionary Activity in
the Second Temple Period* (Minneapolis: Fortress, 1991); and Eckhard J. Schnabel, *Early Christian Mission*, 2 vols. (Downers Grove, IL: InterVarsity, 2004); and on the other hand William J.
Larkin Jr. and Joel F. Williams, eds., *Mission in the New Testament: An Evangelical Approach*
(Maryknoll, NY: Orbis, 1998); and Dean Flemming, *Contextualization in the New Testament:
Patterns for Theology and Mission* (Downers Grove, IL: InterVarsity, 2005).

19. E.g., Michael J. Gorman, *Becoming the Gospel: Paul, Participation, and Mission* (Grand
Rapids: Eerdmans, 2015).

since the worry is that any missiological takeaway in that case will only perpetuate what is now a failed missionary enterprise. New approaches are thus needed for new times, even in the activity of missiological interpretation of scripture. For instance, perhaps we might need to reread the story of ancient Israel and the earliest Christians less from a modern missions point of view than from either a political or an ethnic/racial perspective, both of which are at least in part culturally produced.[20] The former political register is important both since the relationship between Israel and other nations is central to the drama of the Old Testament,[21] and since at the heart of the Christian missional undertaking in the twenty-first century is the issue of transnational relations between countries deemed at least formerly Christian (if not also still associated with the Christian religion) and those that have other religious affiliations if not commitments. The latter ethnic/racial site is particularly salient both since we need new understandings of the particularity of Israel as the chosen people of God and of the church as being grafted into that people, and since we now realize how deeply divided modern Christians are ethnically and racially and how modern Christianity is constituted by such divisions.[22] So, just along these two trajectories, considerations of ancient Israel living under the shadow of imperial Egypt, Assyria, Babylon, and Persia and of early Jewish-Christian relations unfolding within the Pax Romana are much more than mere historical curiosities. Because they are important for contemporary constructive missiology, especially given our own imperial times and racialized circumstances, both parts of this book will engage specifically with such scholarship for our missiological purposes.

Another line of mission-theological development, however, is consistent with and undergirds some of these mission trajectories outlined and may also provide pointers for next steps. Here I am referring specifically to pneumatological mission theologies, including my own extensive work in the arena of pneumatology over the decades.[23] More specifically, there are two interrelated fronts: first, the literature generated from the arena of pentecostal studies,

---

20. On this point, see Laura Nasrallah and Elisabeth Schüssler Fiorenza, eds., *Prejudice and Christian Beginnings: Investigating Race, Gender, and Ethnicity in Early Christianity* (Minneapolis: Fortress, 2010).

21. As we find in J. G. McConville, *God and Earthly Power: An Old Testament Political Theology, Genesis–Kings*, LHBOTS 454 (New York: T&T Clark, 2006).

22. See, e.g., Denise Kimber Buell, *Why This New Race: Ethnic Reasoning in Early Christianity* (New York: Columbia University Press, 2005).

23. For my own work in pneumatology applied to the field of missiology, see Yong, *The Missiological Spirit: Christian Mission Theology for the Third Millennium Global Context* (Eugene, OR: Cascade, 2014).

and also that related to biblical theologies of mission.[24] The emergence of pentecostal studies in academia during the past generation has brought with it pentecostal missiological formulations, much of it pneumatologically oriented.[25] It might be anticipated that such perspectives will continue to expand given pentecostal mission commitments and their further theological development. These proposals have come alongside and invigorated previously existing and parallel developments in the wider missiological sphere. Although the proposals were practically unheard of until more recently,[26] the last few decades have seen the gathering of momentum at the interface of pneumatology and mission theology, including but not limited to work in the area of spirituality and mission, ministry and mission praxis, and spiritual warfare and mission, among other related topics.[27] Some of this ferment has derived from charismatic renewal in the mainline Protestant churches and the resulting reconsideration of familiar topics from the perspective of the person and work of the divine spirit.[28] Understandably, these trends in what might be called the charismatization of mission theology are parallel and oftentimes convergent with pentecostal missiological efforts. Although some of these proposals have proceeded from classical missiological assumptions,

24. As in my prior work, I do not capitalize *pentecostal* when used as an adjective, only when used as a noun or as part of a proper name. The reason—that *pentecostal* relates as much to the day of Pentecost narrative as to the contemporary movement that goes by that name—will be further clarified in the next section of this introduction.

25. E.g., John York, *Mission in the Age of the Spirit* (Springfield, MO: Logion, 2000); Allan Anderson, *Spreading Fires: The Missionary Nature of Early Pentecostalism* (London: SCM, 2007); Gary B. McGee, *Miracles, Missions and American Pentecostalism* (Maryknoll, NY: Orbis, 2010); Wonsuk Ma and Julie C. Ma, *Mission in the Spirit: Towards a Pentecostal/Charismatic Missiology* (Oxford: Regnum, 2011); and Gary Tyra, *The Holy Spirit in Mission: Prophetic Speech and Action in Christian Witness* (Downers Grove, IL: IVP Academic, 2011).

26. E.g., Robert L. Gallagher, "The Forgotten Factor: The Holy Spirit and Mission in Protestant Missiological Writings from 1945–95," in *Footprints of God: A Narrative Theology of Mission*, ed. Charles Van Engen, Nancy Thomas, and Robert Gallagher (Monrovia, CA: MARC, 1999), 199–214.

27. Leading the way has been Harry R. Boer, *Pentecost and Missions* (Grand Rapids: Eerdmans, 1961); John V. Taylor, *The Go-Between God: The Holy Spirit and Christian Mission* (London: SCM, 2004); David F. Wells, *God the Evangelist: How the Holy Spirit Works to Bring Men and Women to Faith* (Grand Rapids: Eerdmans, 1987); and C. Douglas McConnell, ed., *The Holy Spirit and Mission Dynamics*, Evangelical Missiological Society Series 5 (Pasadena, CA: William Carey Library, 1997). See also Andy Lord, *Spirit-Shaped Mission: A Holistic Charismatic Missiology* (Waynesboro, GA: Paternoster, 2005).

28. For instance, as presented by Fuller Theological Seminary practical theologian Ray Sherman Anderson in *Ministry on the Fireline: A Practical Theology for an Empowered Church* (Downers Grove, IL: InterVarsity, 1993), which was released earlier and on a smaller scale under another title: *The Praxis of Pentecost: Revisioning the Church's Life and Mission* (Pasadena, CA: Fuller Theological Seminary, 1992); the argument goes from part 1, "Christopraxis," through part 2 on apostolic "Mission Theology," to part 3, "Orthopraxis."

the pentecostal and pneumatological perspectives informing these inquiries are also opening up new vistas and contributing to the implosion of the older paradigm.

Behind the feverishness of this pneumatological activity in mission theologies lies a more steady stream of pneumatological reflection in relation to work in the biblical theology of mission. This current was initiated in the first half of the twentieth century by English missionary-theologian Roland Allen (1868–1947). Two of Allen's books can be read as precursors to the present volume. His *Missionary Methods: St. Paul's or Ours* focuses on a range of Pauline mission strategies, not the least of which include the role of signs and wonders and engagement with the principalities and powers, while his *Pentecost and the World: The Revelation of the Holy Spirit in the "Acts of the Apostles"* explores further the work of God's spirit for Christian history and missionary undertaking.[29] Allen was a classically modern missionary in many respects, so what is being recalled here is less the *what* of his mission-theological prescriptions than the pneumatological elements of his missiological thinking and the *how* with which he attempted to discern such. In particular, Allen was led back to an engagement with scripture and with the works of the divine spirit in relation to mission amid the early twentieth-century period within which he was wrestling with next steps for the missionary enterprise from the West to the Rest. How might a reengagement with scripture today from such a day of Pentecost starting point and pneumatological perspective generate next steps for Christian mission in our late modern context?[30]

Mission after Pentecost: Toward a Biblical-Canonical and Triune *Missio Dei*

Although I am not a biblical scholar, I consider this book, as well as a growing portion of my efforts as a theologian, to be part and parcel of what is now an established track in biblical studies called *theological interpretation of scripture*. In brief, theological interpretation of scripture insists that while modernist approaches to the biblical canon (e.g., historical, grammatical, and

29. Roland Allen, *Missionary Methods: St. Paul's or Ours* (London: R. Scott, 1912); Allen, *Pentecost and the World: The Revelation of the Holy Spirit in the "Acts of the Apostles"* (Oxford: Oxford University Press, 1917).

30. Richard Bauckham asks a related question and deploys a similarly biblical exploration in response; my thoroughly pneumatological (and pentecostal) answer is meant to complement, not displace, his own. See Bauckham, *Bible and Mission: Christian Witness in a Postmodern World* (Grand Rapids: Baker Academic, 2004).

textual criticism) have their place, the church or believing community as the people of God has never only read their sacred texts from such "objective" vantage points but always engaged these documents from a faith perspective expecting to hear God (not just know *about* God) in the process.[31] To be sure, this does not collapse into an extreme form of late modern reader-response hermeneutic in which we simply allow our subjectivities to dictate how to understand and apply ancient texts to present life circumstances. Instead, the theological reading of scripture is traditioned by the reception history of these texts, creedal in some respects (i.e., according to the Nicene confession, except in non-creedal communities), and ecclesial or confessional in being shaped by specific communities of faith (e.g., Roman Catholic, Orthodox, or, among Protestants, the various Reformation and post-Reformation confessions or statements of faith). The point is that while some in the biblical studies guild might approach these ancient texts from a critical "outsider's" perspective, others, while benefiting from existing biblical scholarship in its many forms, can and do read scripture also from a theological posture of faith that invites interaction with biblical content as communicating God's word for human benefit.

My own journey into theological interpretation of scripture began from my specifically pentecostal location. Hence, much of my earlier work in interfaith encounter, disability, science, and political theology is done from an explicitly pentecostal perspective. This meant for me both taking into account what pentecostal churches and even "traditions" (pentecostal believers don't like to admit they are part of a tradition) believed and thought about these matters and also returning particularly to the pentecostal canon-within-the-canon, the book of Acts, for fresh scriptural reconsideration in topics that pentecostal Christians had not explored much before.[32] It ought to be observed that while I have my own notions of what such a pentecostal interpretation of scripture might or ought to look like, there are many versions of such, not just one,[33] but this also is consistent with other ecclesial and denominational traditions (e.g., there is not one mode of Wesleyan interpretation of scripture either).[34]

31. For an overview, see Craig G. Bartholomew and Heath A. Thomas, eds., *A Manifesto for Theological Interpretation* (Grand Rapids: Baker Academic, 2016).

32. Such a method is manifest in many of my books, although exemplarily, in my humble opinion, in Yong, *The Spirit Poured Out on All Flesh: Pentecostalism and the Possibility of Global Theology* (Grand Rapids: Baker Academic, 2005).

33. I outline three models in my "Unveiling Interpretation after Pentecost: Revelation, Pentecostal Reading, and Christian Hermeneutics of Scripture—A Review Essay," *JTI* 11:1 (2017): 139–55.

34. See Joel B. Green and David F. Watson, eds., *Wesley, Wesleyans, and Reading the Bible as Scripture* (Waco: Baylor University Press, 2012).

Along the way, however, I have begun to realize that while my own reading of Acts, and increasingly the Gospel of Luke with it,[35] was informed by my pentecostal spirituality and traditioning, these texts are owned neither by my pentecostal denomination nor even the global movement as a whole. Instead, these are Christian books that belong to the church ecumenical. Yes, my pentecostal situatedness was prompting retrievals of these texts in perhaps some unique senses, but nevertheless, to the degree that I worked as a systematic theologian seeking to think faithfully for the church catholic and not just for my pentecostal community, my self-identified pentecostal hermeneutic was not copyrighted by my fellowship or movement (as we like to envision ourselves, against those other so-called denominations perceived to be static) but was constituted by the New Testament itself, especially Luke and his book about the acts of the divine wind poured out on the day of Pentecost. From this perspective, then, what is pentecostal is less a late modern phenomenon related to those churches and movements that see their genesis as the Azusa Street revival in Los Angeles in the early twentieth century, as sizable and vital as such is across the world Christian landscape a century later. Rather, *pentecostal* denotes connections to and energies unleashed by the outpouring of God's spirit on all flesh on the day of Pentecost (Acts 2:17).

In other words, I have moved from a pentecostal interpretation of scripture to a theological but even more explicitly pneumatological and day of Pentecost approach to scriptural interpretation.[36] The proposal is that Christians, at least—those who are followers of Jesus the Messiah, meaning those also filled with the same spirit that anointed Jesus—can read scripture only after Pentecost. The controlling Christian vision therefore is Jesus the Christ, the Messiah anointed by the divine spirit, including his life, death, resurrection, ascension, and then giving of his spirit (Acts 2:33), not just to the church institutionally conceived (and effectively controlled in many cases), but to all flesh understood as the people of God gathered from every tongue, tribe, and nation (cf. Rev. 5:9 and 7:9).[37] Perhaps pentecostal Christians might gravitate instinctively toward such a pneumatological stance and toward the interpretation

35. See Yong, *Who Is the Holy Spirit? A Walk with the Apostles* (Brewster, MA: Paraclete, 2011), for my discussion of Acts-Luke, in that I read Acts sequentially but return every other chapter to the Third Gospel from that vantage point of the early Christian experience as recorded in the sequel volume.

36. This is the argument of my recent book *The Hermeneutical Spirit: Theological Interpretation and the Scriptural Imagination for the Twenty-First Century* (Eugene, OR: Cascade, 2017).

37. See Yong, "Kings, Nations, and Cultures on the Way to the New Jerusalem: A Pentecostal Witness to an Apocalyptic Vision," in *The Pastor and the Kingdom: Essays Honoring Jack W. Hayford*, ed. S. David Moore and Jonathan Huntzinger (Southlake, TX: Gateway Academic and The King's University Press, 2017), 231–51.

of scripture (I did!), but not all do, even as many other Christians, filled with the same spirit of God, if not manifest in quite the same ways, have also advocated for some kind of related pneumatological hermeneutic and thereby demonstrated that one does not have to carry denominational credentials in any particular movement in order to embrace such a post- or after-Pentecost interpretive stance.[38]

In this book, then, I spring off such a Pentecost-inspired and spirit-initiated approach to theological interpretation of scripture to ask missiological questions. I note, of course, that, as Roland Allen himself presumed and urged, the Pentecost narrative is itself essentially a missiological account, concerned as it is with the gift or economy of the spirit as enabling messianic witness from Jerusalem through Judea and Samaria to the ends of the earth (which would be Rome, considered from a Jerusalem-centric perspective). This is what Acts 1:8 says, being the effective table of contents for the book of Acts, also known historically as the "acts of the holy spirit."[39] In other words, while there are human characters—human missionaries—galore in the Acts account (e.g., Stephen, Peter, Paul, and others), the central missionary is divine. The spirit is sent out from heaven and sends out Jesus's disciples and followers to bear witness to the Father in the name of his Son (see §§5.4–5.5 below). If Acts is therefore also the birth of the church as the witnessing or missionary people of God, then it is this account that established the foundation for the entire New Testament as a witness to what happens in and through the divine spirit after Pentecost. Hence, the rest of the Christian testament does not just unfold out of the Pentecost event, but we know about these developments through the writings that appeared after and were inspired by and through that outpouring. And if for the moment we assume that the divine breath loosed at Pentecost is also the divine wind spoken of in the Old Testament,[40] then in that case we

38. E.g., Clark H. Pinnock, *Flame of Love: A Theology of the Holy Spirit* (Downers Grove, IL: InterVarsity, 1996); cf. Myk Habets, *Third Article Theology: A Pneumatological Dogmatics* (Minneapolis: Fortress, 2016).

39. Dating back to Oecumenius, a seventh-century church leader; see Daniel Marguerat, "The Work of the Holy Spirit in Luke-Acts: A Western Perspective," in *The Holy Spirit and the Church according to the New Testament: Sixth International East-West Symposium of New Testament Scholars, Belgrade, August 25 to 31, 2013*, ed. Predrag Dragutinović et al., WUNT 354 (Tübingen: Mohr Siebeck, 2016), 111–28, here 118. The astute reader will notice that I have resisted capitalizing *holy spirit* here and the *divine spirit* elsewhere; in the next section I will say more about why.

40. Although many scholars have used the term "Hebrew Bible," our own Christian theological readings incline us to retain the more traditional nomenclature of "Old Testament," which in fact best conveys the orientation from which those within the church have long read these ancient texts, albeit without any supersessionist hint (that the New Testament or new covenant has displaced the former or that the church has replaced Israel, which we will comment

might also assume that the *ruah Elohim* (sixteen times in Hebrew and five in Aramaic) or *ruah Yahweh* (twenty-seven times in the Hebrew) in the Old Testament is also a manifestation, before the incarnation and Pentecost, of the missionary deity breathing among, within, and through ancient Israel. In short, a pentecostal or pneumatological perspective on mission helps us recognize across the scriptural traditions what we might call a *missio spiritus*.[41] This is a "biblical, missional Spirit theology," as another scholar puts it,[42] a theological vision of the missionary God expressed in and through the work of the divine wind, whose witness blows from Genesis to Revelation.[43]

There is one more point to be made along these lines. The person of the holy spirit has been traditionally known also as the shy or hidden member of the Trinity, in large part because, as the scriptures themselves also declare, the divine wind calls attention not to itself but to the person of Jesus and the God he worshiped.[44] From that perspective, any pneumatological interpretation of scripture cannot be for its own sake but must be for the sake of understanding the God of Israel, manifest in Jesus. Hence, any exploration of the *missio spiritus* also cannot be merely a theoretical exercise in pneumatological missiology but must open up understanding of the *missio Dei* more broadly. In this vein, the *missio spiritus* is the one side of the coin of which the other is the *missio trinitatis*,[45] meaning that any further understanding of the work of the divine wind in mission enables deeper comprehension of the redemptive witness of the triune Father, Son, and spirit to save the world. There are

on further in the next section). For a defense of this position, see Christopher R. Seitz, *Word without End: The Old Testament as Abiding Theological Witness* (Waco: Baylor University Press, 2004), esp. chap. 6, "Old Testament or Hebrew Bible? Some Theological Considerations."

41. Which is not synonymous with a biblical pneumatology—e.g., Trevor J. Burke and Keith Warrington, eds., *A Biblical Theology of the Holy Spirit* (Eugene, OR: Cascade, 2014)—even if our own work will build on such extant endeavors.

42. Cornelis Bennema, "Spirit and Mission in the Bible: Toward a Dialogue between Biblical Studies and Missiology," *TJ*, n.s., 32 (2011): 237–58, here 253; see also K. Steve McCormick, "The Mission of the Holy Spirit: Pentecostal Fellowship," in *Missio Dei: A Wesleyan Understanding*, ed. Keith Schwanz and Joseph E. Coleson (Kansas City, MO: Beacon Hill, 2011), 92–99.

43. I sketch some aspects of *missio spiritus* in my essay "Christological Constants in Shifting Contexts: Jesus Christ, Prophetic Dialogue, and the *Missio Spiritus* in a Pluralistic World," in *Mission on the Road to Emmaus: Constants, Contexts, and Prophetic Dialogue*, ed. Stephen B. Bevans and Cathy Ross (Maryknoll, NY: Orbis, 2015), 19–33.

44. See Frederick Dale Bruner and William Hordern, *Holy Spirit: Shy Member of the Trinity* (Minneapolis: Augsburg Fortress, 1984).

45. E.g., Bård Mæland, "A Free-Wheeling Breath of Life? Discerning the *Missio Spiritus*," *IRM* 102:2 (2013): 137–47; cf. my own preliminary sketch of such a trinitarian or triune missiological approach in Yong, "Pluralism, Secularism, and Pentecost: Newbigin-ings for *Missio Trinitatis* in a New Century," in *The Gospel and Pluralism Today: Reassessing Lesslie Newbigin for the 21st Century*, ed. Scott W. Sunquist and Amos Yong, Missiological Engagements (Downers Grove, IL: IVP Academic, 2015), 147–70.

complications here that will be addressed throughout this volume. For the moment, however, the point ought to be clear: our efforts in pentecostal and pneumatological reading of scripture are missiological and vice versa, and the trajectory of such an intertwined exploration is for the further development of theology of mission (*missio Dei*), more specifically a trinitarian or, more accurately vis-à-vis the biblical witness, triune account of mission theology.[46]

Outline of the Book and Other Important Matters

It is now time to overview what this book is about. Briefly put, what follows is an exercise in theological interpretation of scripture bifocally mediated: pneumatologically and missiologically. The latter missiological optic provides the telos for the project: how to imagine Christian witness through a rereading of the Bible in the late modern world after the collapse, or while experiencing the demise, of the modern missionary enterprise. The former pneumatological lens, conversely, provides the scriptural starting points for engaging toward the horizon. This means that we will focus scripturally on passages regarding the divine wind or breath and ask of these missiologically relevant questions.

We will proceed mostly canonically. I say *mostly* because we will follow the canonical sequence carefully with only a minor exception in part 1 devoted to the Old Testament, the sacred Jewish scriptures known as the Tanakh.[47] There, in the second chapter, I treat Elijah and Elisha together, and thus 1–2 Kings together first (§2.5), before picking up on a unique episode at the end of 1 Kings that deserves stand-alone commentary (§2.6). In part 2, devoted to the New Testament, our transgressions of the canonical order occur at two places, both concerning what is known as the Johannine literature that I have gathered together in the final chapter of the book. First, we read Luke-Acts next to one another in chapter 5, despite the Fourth Gospel's situatedness between the two Lukan texts. Second, we read 2 Peter and Jude together in the seventh chapter, which is a fairly common scholarly practice in the biblical studies guild, despite the Johannine Epistles being inserted between them as

---

46. Substantive recent work in *missio Dei* is deeply trinitarian in the post-Nicene sense; e.g., John G. Flett, *The Witness of God: The Trinity, Missio Dei, Karl Barth, and the Nature of Christian Community* (Grand Rapids: Eerdmans, 2010); and Thomas Noble, "The Mission of the Holy Trinity," in Schwanz and Coleson, *Missio Dei*, 77–84. Our efforts are to return to the scriptural sources and to attend to its witness as much as possible on its terms, and so we seek to be cautious about imposing a post-Nicene trinitarian frame on the biblical materials, and therefore our goal is an effort in missiology with a *triune* theological inflection.

47. We follow in the footsteps of H. D. Beeby, *Canon and Mission* (Harrisburg, PA: Trinity Press International, 1999), although with much more exegetical robustness.

part of what has long been considered the Catholic or General Letters (James through Jude). Chapter 8 on the Johannine writings, then, discusses 1 John sandwiched between the Gospel and Revelation (with further explanation for this given in the introductory remarks there). I will grant that once the canonical sequencing is broken, there are many other ways to read these texts even with our bifocal approach, but this is the path I have chosen, with better or worse reasons given here and in the relevant chapter introductions to come, along with their attending implications.

A few more cautions and warnings need to be registered before we turn to the scriptural texts. If in former times one could proceed in the realm of biblical theology as if it were acceptable to just read off the surface of the text, in our late modern context we cannot proceed as if historical consciousness never dawned. Let me register here some linguistic, hermeneutical, theological, covenantal, and missiological caveats related to our second naivete.[48]

First, linguistically, I have opted to talk about the divine breath or wind in the two parts of this book following the linguistic terms found in the Old and New Testaments, and this means we will use *ruahic* (the adjectival version) and *ruahological* (related to the study of the *ruah* Yahweh or *ruah Elohim*) in the first half and *pneumatic* (again, adjectival) and *pneumatological* (concerning the study of the divine *pneuma*) in the second.[49] This is one means of helping us be attentive to the different conceptual domains about the breath or wind of God in the Jewish and Christian scriptures while working to understand them in relation to each other. While as a Christian reader of the scriptural canon I might be justified in deploying one set of terms pertinent to the relevant theological commitments—in this case *pneuma* and its variations—I am convinced that the post-Nicene conversation (on which more momentarily) can be enriched by a fresh reconsideration of the biblical data and hence am motivated to resound the full scope of these texts in this work. But a further important question that needs to be asked is, How will we know which references to *wind* or *breath*—from the Hebrew *ruah*—are divinely related? How might we distinguish a wind from God from the spirit of God, and is there a difference?[50] As I am not a Hebrew scholar, I have had

48. Meaning with the full awareness of historical criticism, albeit still motivated by theological concerns and commitments; for explication, see Mark I. Wallace, *The Second Naiveté: Barth, Ricoeur, and the New Yale Theology* (Macon, GA: Mercer University Press, 1990).

49. Pronounced "ru-ā-ic" and "ru-a-ō-logical" (the *h* is silent in *ruah*) and "noo-ma-tō-logical" (the *p* is silent in the *pn*).

50. Of course, *ruah* applies not only to God and human beings but also to other creatures (angels and demons, at least), as well as to natural phenomena, like the wind (surprise, surprise!). For delineation in the Qumranic literature that we otherwise do not comment on, see Arthur Everett Sekki, *The Meaning of Ruah at Qumran*, SBLDS 110 (Atlanta: Scholars Press, 1989).

to rely on the work of others.[51] Realizing that even this approach does not guarantee either accuracy or exhaustiveness of identification, I have come to accept a much more modest objective particularly in part 1: to merely sketch out some ways to read the Old Testament missiologically in light of references to the divine *ruah* as generally agreed upon in the biblical guild. Part of the result of this limitation is that whole portions of these ancient Jewish sacred writings, even whole books like Joshua, Ruth, Proverbs, the expansive Jeremiah,[52] and eight of the so-called Minor Prophets (and, I should note, a few New Testament letters: Philemon and 2–3 John) do not have their own sections of discussion in this book, as no explicit reference to the divine wind is identifiable in these texts. My only justification is that part 1 is not meant to be an exhaustive missiology of the Old Testament but is part and parcel of a ruahological and missiological theology of the biblical canon. In any case, remember that whenever allowed grammatically, I will use interchangeably *wind*, *breath*, and *spirit*; *ruah* in the Hebrew and *pneuma* in the Greek are literally "wind" and "breath."[53]

Second, hermeneutically, each chapter is divided into sections, each of which focuses usually on one book in that scriptural segment. The discussion is therefore exceedingly brief, bifocally directed by ruahological/pneumatological data and missiological concerns. In each case, the goal is to understand from such a ruahological/pneumatological point of entry the broader missiological implications of the text before attempting to chart relevant late modern applications. Methodologically, I have attempted to do my historical-critical homework, although much of this is relegated to the footnotes, and I try to keep the discussion in the main text bifocally driven by our overarching theological and missiological concerns. Ours is therefore an attempt to understand, as much as possible within a short space, the pneumatological texts in their

---

51. Principally Lloyd R. Neve, *The Spirit of God in the Old Testament* (Cleveland, TN: CPT, 2011)—so long as we note his own view that "there is no personalization of the spirit within the limits of the Old Testament" (124)—with supporting help from Leon J. Wood, *The Holy Spirit in the Old Testament* (Grand Rapids: Zondervan, 1976); and George T. Montague, *The Holy Spirit: Growth of a Biblical Tradition* (Peabody, MA: Hendrickson, 1994), part 1.

52. However, Andrew Davies observes the multiple manifestations of *ruah* in this prophet while querying why concerns about charismatic and ecstatic prophecy may have undermined a more explicit ruahology (Davies uses "pneumatology") in this book like other Old Testament literature of the seventh century BCE and in the years leading up to the Babylonian exile; see "Jeremiah," in Burke and Warrington, *Biblical Theology of the Holy Spirit*, 46–56. I note, however, that what readers might miss in my book is made up for with the discussion of Jude's pneumatology in chap. 7 below, which is strangely omitted from the Burke and Warrington volume.

53. Donald L. Gelpi was one of the first theologians I read who used the language of *divine breath* regularly to talk about the spirit; see *The Divine Mother: A Trinitarian Theology of the Holy Spirit* (Lanham, MD: University Press of America, 1984).

final narrative and literary form and on their own terms before exploring mission-theological extensions. This also means that while there is much to be gained from intertextual considerations that link earlier and later references to the divine wind or breath, time and space constraints in an already long book prohibit such excursionary elaboration.[54] The exceptions will be when discussing New Testament pneumatological references that explicitly cite or quote from the Old Testament (e.g., §§5.1, 7.1). Readers should of course make their own connections.

Third, theologically, we have already discussed the challenges of reading backward from New Testament pneumatology to Old Testament ruahology. Navigating these issues will be part of the burden of this book. Perhaps the even more important theological question in our biblically focused expedition is whether or not our presumptive trinitarian theme already establishes an alien conceptual frame on what we find even before we have started. What I mean is that pneumatology considered in trinitarian terms is arguably a post-Nicene and in that sense later theological conceptualization that is technically foreign to the biblical canon and in that sense only anachronistically applied as such.[55] If we were to be careful in our approach, we might avoid the word *Trinity* and its various linguistic permutations, although we might do well to consider *triadic* used adjectivally as a synonym.[56] Yet if we recall ours is an experiment in theological—now pneumatological—interpretation of scripture, we are in that sense wanting to be sensitive to the various horizons at work: how later theological developments provide interpretive lenses for reappreciating the scriptural message on the one hand and how reengagement with the biblical texts can transform in an ongoing manner our inherited theological formulations and traditions on the other hand. Additionally complicated

54. Thus, aside from cross-referencing backward and forward (via our sectional enumeration), we will in very few instances be able to glean from insights such as this one made—long before intertextual studies or approaches were in vogue—by an Old Testament scholar, that Jesus's agony, indeed "the burden of the world" that he carried, was borne from Israel's scriptures; see H. H. Rowley, *The Missionary Message of the Old Testament* (London: Carey Southgate, 1955), 8.

55. John R. Levison, *Filled with the Spirit* (Grand Rapids: Eerdmans, 2009), helps us to understand these challenges more than any other text I know; cf. Clint Tibbs, *Religious Experience of the Pneuma: Communication with the Spirit World in 1 Corinthians 12 and 14*, WUNT 2/230 (Tübingen: Mohr Siebeck, 2007); and Guy Williams, *The Spirit World in the Letters of Paul the Apostle: A Critical Examination of the Role of Spiritual Beings in the Authentic Pauline Epistles*, Forschungen zur Religion und Literatur des Alten und Neuen Testaments 231 (Göttingen: Vandenhoeck & Ruprecht, 2009).

56. E.g., John W. Yates notes that while Paul is not trinitarian in the Nicene sense, "in Romans 8 the language of God, Christ and spirit, pushes toward a triadic presentation of God." *The Spirit and Creation in Paul*, WUNT 2/251 (Tübingen: Mohr Siebeck, 2008), 180.

herein is that ours is a bifocal investigation, which in effect means that we are navigating three horizons: scripture, spirit, and mission. In what follows, then, as a recognition of these complex matters, except when quoting other sources, I have decided not to capitalize the *divine wind*, *divine breath*, or *divine spirit*, nor *holy spirit* or *spirit*, all used interchangeably, even if with different contextual connotations.[57] This will remind us that we are working in a kind of liminal space, after Nicaea historically but yet after Pentecost biblically. What N. T. Wright calls a "pneumatological monotheism" suggests that we are beyond any undifferentiated Hebraic *Shema* on the one side but also before any fully differentiated post-Nicene trinitarianism on the other side.[58] Missiologically, for us the result is, we hope, a triunely inflected *missio Dei* that not only informs contemporary theology of mission but also has the potential to transform received conversations in trinitarian theology.

From this triunely intimated set of sensibilities and inclinations, fourth, flows a further theological matter, one that concerns not just how to read the Old Testament but also how to understand the ongoing relevance of the covenant made with ancient Israel. While Wright's *pneumatological monotheism* is convergent with our own pneumatological-triune missiology, his earlier stance on the church as true Israel—and more recently the development of his view regarding the transformation of the covenant by the triune God of Israel[59]—may be less capable of recognizing how Messianic Jews can embrace Jesus as Christ and simultaneously lay claim to and grapple with how to live out an authentic (Old Testament–based) Jewish identity.[60] The wider issue at stake is that the historic trajectory of Christian theological understanding of the church as replacing Israel has depended on certain New Testament texts to the neglect of others, even while such a view has also marginalized (at best) and not known what to do with or how to read the Old Testament except as superseded by the New. Wright's perspective contrasts with that generated

57. John Goldingay also cautions that references to the divine spirit in the Old Testament are not always explicit even as we have to observe the parallels to the divine presence, favor, face, will, and so on, so it is right to be hesitant about capitalizing *spirit* as if from a New Testament or post-Nicene perspective; see "The Holy Spirit in the Old Testament," *ExAud* 12 (1996): 14–28.

58. For Wright, pneumatological monotheism involves "the spirit, understood as the outpouring of the personal presence and energy of the one true God, [that] enables his people to do what the *Shema* required, to love God with the heart, with the strength, . . . with the mind." *Paul and the Faithfulness of God*, Christian Origins and the Question of God 4 (Minneapolis: Fortress, 2013), 719–27, here 722.

59. See Wright, *Paul and the Faithfulness of God*, esp. chaps. 11 and 15.

60. For a Messianic Jewish response to especially the earlier Wright, especially of the period from and preceding the first two volumes of the Christian Origins and the Question of God series, see Stuart Dauermann, *Converging Destinies: Jews, Christian, and the Mission of God* (Eugene, OR: Cascade, 2017), 37–44.

over the last generation by post-Shoah theologians who have sought to think through the covenant with Israel as having ongoing significance even in the age of the church (both covenants thus running in parallel, in effect). The results have been a treatment of Jews either like people of any other or no faith needing to be converted away from Judaism and assimilated into the church, or as those who ought not to be evangelized or missionized (to put this in terms of the two ends of the spectrum).[61] Our own pneumatological perspective observes that the outpouring of the spirit at Pentecost is also at least in part a direct response to the disciples' question, "Lord, will you at this time restore the kingdom to Israel?" (Acts 1:6 ESV), so that the work of the divine wind involves, rather than leaves behind, the renewal of the first covenant.[62] The point is that the covenant with ancient Israel continues and that it is as those grafted into the trunk of the originally chosen and elect people of God that gentile believers will participate in the eschatological mission of the triune deity to save the world.[63] From this perspective, then, the obligation is to read Israel's sacred scriptures as having theological relevance for the church; this is surely the case from our christological and pneumatological perspective, but also pertains when we consider that the Old Testament records the covenant people of God's own theological self-understanding.

Last but not least, we descend from the theological stratosphere to the more mundane missiological realm. The question remains: What might we mean by *mission* in what is ostensibly, as urged in the first pages above, a post-mission era? And how even might we extract any kind of biblical missiology when our focus is on pneumatological texts and references? I agree that this pneumatological terrain is a new and relatively unexcavated site for concerns in mission theology. On the other hand, the wager of this book is that the result has the potential to revitalize a moribund enterprise in unanticipated ways. So, following out this dare, rather than focusing on the sending aspect of classical mission theology (which is uneclipsable at any rate in our modern context), my own pentecostal sensitivities suggest that the message of Pentecost is about the arrival of the spirit into a world full of particularities, differences, and others: of other tongues, languages, cultures,

61. As suggested by the title of Mark S. Kinzer's *Postmissionary Messianic Judaism: Redefining Christian Engagement with the Jewish People* (Grand Rapids: Brazos, 2005), even if the argument here does not call explicitly for a moratorium on the evangelization of Jewish persons.

62. Elsewhere I develop further such a spirit-ecclesiology vis-à-vis a nonsupersessionist theology of Israel; see Yong, *Renewing Christian Theology: Systematics for a Global Christianity*, images and commentary by Jonathan A. Anderson (Waco: Baylor University Press, 2014), chap. 7.

63. For more on an eschatological but yet nonreplacement theology of Israel, see my *In the Days of Caesar: Pentecostalism and Political Theology; The Cadbury Lectures 2009*, Sacra Doctrina: Christian Theology for a Postmodern Age (Grand Rapids: Eerdmans, 2010), §8.2.1.

peoples, and nations, of male-female, young-old, slave-free, and so on. From this perspective, the missiological call suggested is one that opens up to and engages others.[64] Our pneumatological-missiological hermeneutic therefore queries how the scriptures witness to the divine wind or breath enabling the people of God's interaction with others: other nations, religions, cultures, ethnicities, and political structures, often understood even in the more benign sense as "outside" the people of God or the church, but in reality as dismissed to the margins or subjugated to the underside of colonial modernity.[65] What are the implications and perhaps problems of such a pneumatological missiology focused on *otherness* in our post-mission world?[66] Responses will be suggested along the way, even as we anticipate a more synthetic summation in the conclusion. Readers are invited, however, to discern how our ruaho-logical and pneumatological approach shows us that the stark lines we have drawn between "us" and "others" are mostly conventions of habit rather than theologically or scripturally sustainable. This means not that all such distinctions are passé but that we are invited to be continuously open to how the divine breath might forge new relationships and identities in and through the redemptive *missio Dei*.

A final clarification: insofar as we are bridging between scriptural and contemporary horizons, I will occasionally use *missional* synonymously with *missiological*. On the one hand, contemporary *missional* movements are one expression of those seeking a new missiological pathway forward from what they are also discerning as the end of classical missionary ventures.[67] On the other hand, *missional* has been coined in part certainly to register worries that the missiological is too wrapped up with the earlier modern paradigm. I apologize to those missional theologians who believe it is better to displace the missiological with the missional. My goal is similar to theirs: to find a way

64. In contrast to any self-preservational missional hermeneutic and project, as Shawn B. Redford also resists in *Missiological Hermeneutics: Biblical Interpretations for the Global Church* (Eugene, OR: Pickwick, 2012), 65–66n75.

65. Frank Anthony Spina's book *The Faith of the Outside: Exclusion and Inclusion in the Biblical Story* (Grand Rapids: Eerdmans, 2005) is an exemplary study in this regard, but only one of his chapters—on the Samaritan woman in John 4—is directly related to ruahic and pneumatic texts that are the focus of my book (and even there he says little about the pneuma-tological aspects of that discussion).

66. This *otherness* theme is also extrapolated in one direction—vis-à-vis the encounter of religions—in my *Hospitality and the Other: Pentecost, Christian Practices, and the Neighbor*, Faith Meets Faith (Maryknoll, NY: Orbis, 2008).

67. The missional literature is now legion; my very selective sampling includes J. R. Wood-ward, *Creating a Missional Culture: Equipping the Church for the Sake of the World* (Downers Grove, IL: InterVarsity, 2012); and Gary Tyra, *A Missional Orthodoxy: Theology and Ministry in a Post-Christian Context* (Downers Grove, IL: IVP Academic, 2013).

forward *after* modern missions. Yet from the post-Pentecost site I inhabit, I believe the missiological reconnects to the witness of God's spirit. Our goal is the recovery and revitalization of not just an idea but a set of spirit-led practices that bear witness to the God of Jesus Christ. *Missional* and *missiological* in that respect are both subservient to the divine spirit's witness. Our concluding reflections will pick up on and expand this thrust in light of the foregoing pages.

Part 1

DIVINE WIND AND THE OLD TESTAMENT

Ruahic Witness across Ancient Israel

1

Torah and the *Missio Spiritus*

The Winds of Creational Mission

Introduction

As we anticipate the divine wind's wafting and even blustering back and forth in this chapter that covers such references across the first five books of the Bible, known more broadly as the Torah and also as the Pentateuch, it may be difficult to identify any consistent ruahological thread. In order to appreciate the apparently disparate connections across these books, we need to step back and be reminded about the overarching narrative of the Old Testament. This collection of thirty-nine scrolls is ancient Israel's sacred writings that provide the account of the people's self-understanding as the chosen people and nation of Yahweh. There are two sides to this election. On the one hand, "election does not cut Israel off from the nations. It situates that people in a relationship with them."[1] On the other hand, by extension, Israel is appointed to be a representative of Yahweh to the nations. So, consistent with other understandings of deities in the ancient world, God exists in a patron-client relationship with Israel: blessing their welfare, land, and work, and receiving their worship and obedience.[2] And part of this obedience involves representational witness to other peoples. Yet the reality is that part of the memory

---

1. Lucien Legrand, *Unity and Plurality: Mission in the Bible*, trans. Robert R. Barr (Maryknoll, NY: Orbis, 1990), 14.
2. Daniel I. Block, *The Gods of the Nations: Studies in Ancient Near Eastern National Theology*, 2nd ed. (Grand Rapids: Baker Academic, 2000), chap. 2.

of ancient Israel involved self-constitution over against others—for instance, groups like the "Canaanites," who may never have been a coherent historical people but rather were simply an aggregate of that which was not-Israel (e.g., Hittites earlier, Samaritans later) and whose land was deemed as preserved for Israel by its God.[3] From this perspective, we have to respect the narrative arc of these ancient texts while simultaneously reading between the lines, as it were, to discern redemptive—and missiological—threads related to Israel's vocation in relation to others around them.

The Torah is concerned to establish, at least in part, this priestly character of Israel's identity, not only with regard to the original moments of the constitution of the Torah's various parts (which may have extended over centuries), but also vis-à-vis their cumulative reappropriation during and after the exilic period into its final canonical form. The tabernacle, prototypical of the temple to come and consistent with the entire created world understood as the cosmic habitation over which God is enthroned, is not just for the worship of God but also for mediating God's presence to the world.[4] We see this priestly role and responsibility explicitly stated in Exodus: "If you obey my voice and keep my covenant, you shall be my treasured possession out of all the peoples. Indeed, the whole earth is mine, but you shall be for me a priestly kingdom and a holy nation" (19:5–6). Although we will return soon to this text (§1.4), two aspects of such priestly mediation are important for our missiological purposes.

First, God can raise up individual conduits, as the case may be, for such tasks, and here the deity of ancient Israel is no respecter of national or ethnic identity markers. God can choose "insiders" to Israel as he pleases upon whom to blow the divine wind—for instance, Bezalel and Oholiab, or Joseph, or Joshua—even as he can breathe through "outsiders" to the covenant people, like the Pharaoh or Balaam. Missiologically, we have to be attuned to the cosmic compass in order to discern from whence and to where the wind of God comes and goes.

Second, and now stepping "upward" toward the more macro plane, the divine wind comes both generatively, as when the breath enlivened the primordial waters in the creation account, but also destructively, as when, in the

3. It is at least in this sense that we ought to understand "the strongly anti-Canaanite tradition of the Old Testament." Niels Peter Lemche, *The Canaanites and Their Land: The Tradition of the Canaanites*, JSOTSup 110 (Sheffield: JSOT Press, 1991), 149.

4. See John H. Walton, *The Lost World of Genesis One: Ancient Cosmology and the Origins Debate* (Downers Grove, IL: IVP Academic, 2009); and J. Daniel Hays, *The Temple and the Tabernacle: A Study of God's Dwelling Places from Genesis to Revelation* (Grand Rapids: Baker Books, 2016), chap. 2; cf. also Frank D. Macchia, *Justified in the Spirit: Creation, Redemption, and the Triune God* (Grand Rapids: Eerdmans, 2010), esp. part 3.

second pentateuchal book, the swirling wind drowned the Egyptian army. The divine breath is life-giving on the one hand but life-denying on the other, precipitating the flood (§1.1) and prophesying judgment on even the people of God (§1.5). Both Israel and others are judged and saved in these early books of the Bible.[5] The *missio spiritus* is therefore neither neat and tidy nor one-dimensional. Instead, as the ruahic references in the Torah suggest, the divine breath is creative and redemptive, with the latter occurring in and through, rather than having nothing to do with, devastation and ruin. As we shall see, Israel "as the priestly enclave in a single world empire"[6] thereby carries out its mission and witness to others in part through being ruled over and oppressed by them, both aspects of the divine wind's activities.

Note, though, that here at the beginning of the canon we are establishing our ruahological and missiological foundations. Although Christians have read the Bible historically as a medium of progressive revelation, culminating in Christ and the New Testament, we will want to observe here what our bifocal lens spotlights. Especially in this first chapter, our approach will be thematic, guided bifocally and literarily, attentive first and foremost to the final form of the text, rather than engaged primarily with historical or critical matters (which are as intensely disputed as they are widely disparate). The ground will be laid, perhaps not in terms of explicit ruahological and missiological content—although even here, we can and will be surprised— but in terms of method and hermeneutic. *How* to read ruahologically and missiologically—theologically, in other words—is just as important at this point; so practicing such readings is part and parcel of the journey on which this first chapter invites us to go.

1.1 Genesis, Part 1—The Life-Giving Spirit: Creation and Fall

The scriptural canon of course begins with these well-known words: "In the beginning when God created the heavens and the earth, the earth was a formless void and darkness covered the face of the deep, while a wind from God swept over the face of the waters. Then God said, 'Let there be light'; and there was light" (Gen. 1:1–3). Although the Christian New Testament clearly stipulates that all things were created through the Son, the Word or Logos of

5. An overview of *ruah* in the Torah is provided by Walter C. Kaiser Jr., "The Pentateuch," in *A Biblical Theology of the Holy Spirit*, ed. Trevor J. Burke and Keith Warrington (Eugene, OR: Cascade, 2014), 1–11; ours, of course, is not only a ruahological but also a missiological consideration.

6. Norman K. Gottwald, *All the Kingdoms of the Earth: Israelite Prophecy and International Relations in the Ancient Near East* (New York: Harper & Row, 1964), 387.

God (John 1:3; Heb. 1:2), these opening words of the Bible indicate that the creative word of God was carried and even spoken through the divine wind or breath (*ruah Elohim*). If the wind or breath of God is understood also as the spirit of God, then in these ancient words we have a triune—indeed, the broader Christian theological tradition has said: proto-trinitarian—image of the primordial creation: that God fashioned the world through his word and spirit.[7] Even if things are not so simple, if we wanted to avoid imposing later understandings on this passage, such conclusions are appropriate certainly from a canonical perspective long before we adopt any later historical vantage point.

What is intimated is that we are invited from such a stance to consider the rest of the biblical drama, the entirety of creation's fortunes, as it were, from such a ruah-initiated perspective. The intimate presence of the divine breath or spirit in effect concurs with what kick-starts the cosmos. Certainly the movement of God's spirit either catalyzes or participates in—or both—the formation of creation that fills in or overcomes the void and that carries the divine light that counters or disperses the darkness of the deep. In this sense, then, the creative work of God over six days can also be understood ruahically, as precipitated by the divine spirit's sweeping over the primeval waters. By extension, it is the spirit's elemental stirrings that in this respect induce the world's coming into being and its subsequent history, and this also invites us to consider in ruahological terms not only the divine creation and in its various orders delineated in the first chapter of Genesis but also the divine sustenance of the world, in all its ever-developing complexity.[8]

But this narrative additionally announces, even if less explicitly, that the divine spirit's mission is not only creative but also redemptive.[9] On the one hand, the spirit of creation hovers over the forming of the unformed, the delimiting of the unlimited, the filling of the unfilled, and the separating out from what was previously indistinct.[10] On the other hand, one might understand divine creation to be redemptive either in its opposing the formlessness of the void or in resisting the darkness of the deep. We cannot here resolve the

---

7. For discussion of God as creator through word and spirit, see Yong, *Spirit-Word-Community: Theological Hermeneutics in Trinitarian Perspective*, New Critical Thinking in Religion, Theology, and Biblical Studies (Burlington, VT: Ashgate, 2002), §2.1.

8. This is what I argued in *The Spirit of Creation: Modern Science and Divine Action in the Pentecostal-Charismatic Imagination*, Pentecostal Manifestos 4 (Grand Rapids: Eerdmans, 2011), chap. 5.

9. This is to put in pneumatological/ruahological perspective the claim that Genesis 1 provides "a blueprint for mission." James Chukwuma Okoye, *Israel and the Nations: A Mission Theology of the Old Testament* (Maryknoll, NY: Orbis, 2006), 24.

10. See Rick Wadholm Jr., "What Is in a Day? The Theological Significance of Yôm in Genesis 1," *Didaskalia* 24 (2015): 75–98.

recurrent questions of whether this text teaches an unprecedented creation out of nothing or a creation out of chaos (the "formless void"),[11] but it is clear that the spirit's brooding converges with the creative transformation of primordial waters into cosmos, and from that perspective has an interlaced creative-redemptive dimension.[12] From this viewpoint, the formless void may still intimate that which perennially threatens the creation.[13] In the face of this persistent menace, the opening lines of Genesis announce the all-encompassing blowing of the divine spirit.[14]

Yet the hazard of this cosmic "formless void" should never be minimized. The initial lines of Genesis open up to a creation story that tells of a flourishing world God repeatedly sees as good. But hardly has God or his creatures had the opportunity to rest on the seventh day when the creation is plunged back into disorder with the disobedience of the prehistoric couple, the primal murder, and the banishment of humanity not only from the idyllic garden but also from the company of God. Human beings defiled by sin will have to constantly strive amid a cursed environment (Gen. 3:17; 4:11) and do so as fugitives and wanderers (Gen. 4:15) seeking the divine rest and shalom.

The next time the divine wind appears is when Yahweh says, "My spirit [*ruah*] shall not abide in mortals forever, for they are flesh; their days shall be one hundred and twenty years" (Gen. 6:3). This is a difficult passage for many reasons, not the least of which is that we know little about the "sons of God" and the "Nephilim" referred to in the verses before and following, and therefore do not understand what it means that the latter were said to be "heroes that were of old, warriors of renown" (Gen. 6:4). It would seem as if the Nephilim found a way to survive the Noahic flood, since they are found in Canaan later on during the time of Moses and Caleb (Num. 13:33), although the biblical traditions are silent about whether and how this might be the case.[15]

11. Walter Brueggemann suggests that the text allows for both possibilities; see *Genesis* (Louisville: Westminster John Knox, 1982), 29–30.

12. I put it this way in part following the arguments of David Tsumura, whose *Creation and Destruction: A Reappraisal of the Chaoskampf Theory in the Old Testament* (Winona Lake, IN: Eisenbrauns, 2005) suggests that here the earth emerges from out of the recession of the primordial waters, which is different from the way in which other biblical texts deployed or alluded to ancient Near Eastern myths regarding the watery chaos.

13. Here connecting with Susan Niditch, whose work encompasses the broader witness of the Jewish sacred scriptures; see *Chaos to Cosmos: Studies in Biblical Patterns of Creation* (Chico, CA: Scholars Press, 1985).

14. This is my pneumatological gloss on a similar point made about Gen. 1:1–2 by John C. L. Gibson, *Genesis* (Philadelphia: Westminster, 1981), 1:37–38.

15. For a fascinating discussion of the various possibilities as preserved especially in intertestamental literature, see Loren T. Stuckenbruck, "The 'Angels' and 'Giants' of Genesis 6:1–4

Although any attempts to adjudicate these otherwise remarkable allusions would take us too far afield, the ruahological connections are particularly noteworthy. If in the first few verses of this book the movement of the divine wind at least hints at the surgings of a subterranean turmoil, here the divine breath is expected to depart from, even disengage with, human mortals. This is surely Yahweh's counterthreat, imminently carried out, in response to the "wickedness of humankind [that] was great in the earth" (Gen. 6:5). So, on the one side, the creatures of the world are given life through the divine breath (Gen. 1:30), including human beings: "The Lᴏʀᴅ God formed man from the dust of the ground, and breathed [*neshamah*, which is distinct from but syntactically related to *ruah*] into his nostrils the breath of life" (Gen. 2:7).[16] On the other side, the evil and iniquity of humanity now leads the creator to cease animating their flesh, thus effectively ensuring their demise (through the flood; cf. Gen. 6:17; 7:15, 22).[17] Although there may be some justification for understanding the reference to 120 years as denoting the divinely sanctioned upper limits for human life, there are arguably better reasons for thinking it either "imposes limits on human life in order to keep human beings from an eternal existence in the state of sin,"[18] or specifies "the period of grace during which the judgment of God upon that generation would be postponed,"[19] until the six hundredth year of Noah, as it were (see Gen. 7:6).

The conclusion of the flood narrative, however, is consistent with the creational accounts in that, despite a fall from grace, God's calling the world and human creatures into being intends their flourishing (Gen. 9:1–17). In fact, the narrator specifically says that the flood abates because of a divine *ruah*: "God

---

in Second and Third Century BCE Jewish Interpretation: Reflections on the Posture of Early Apocalyptic Traditions," *Dead Sea Discoveries* 7:3 (2000): 354–77.

16. The Hebrew here suggests *Yahweh's* breathing as much as it does the breath of life being Yahweh's, which is to say not that the latter is impossible but that it is not specified; for the distinction, see Annette Weissenrieder, "The Infusion of the Spirit: The Meaning of ἐμφυσάω in John 20:22–23," in *The Holy Spirit, Inspiration, and the Cultures of Antiquity: Multidisciplinary Perspectives*, ed. Jörg Frey and John R. Levison, Ekstasis: Religious Experience from Antiquity to the Middle Ages 5 (Berlin: de Gruyter, 2014), 119–51, esp. 138–42 on Gen. 2:7, particularly in the Septuagint translation of the Hebrew.

17. The deluge almost wipes humankind off the face of the earth, as if effectively undermining the creator's intention that human beings should "be fruitful and multiply, and fill the earth and subdue it" (Gen. 1:28), so much so that the intentions of the deity struggle for realization and have to wait until the Exodus narrative to begin recovery; see Carol M. Kaminski, *From Noah to Israel: Realization of the Primaeval Blessing after the Flood*, JSOTSup 413 (New York: T&T Clark, 2004).

18. Wilf Hildebrandt, *An Old Testament Theology of the Spirit of God* (Peabody, MA: Hendrickson, 1995), 84.

19. G. Ch. Aalders, *Genesis*, trans. William Heynen (Grand Rapids: Zondervan, 1981), 1:155.

The Genesis of Divine Breath
Long before Pentecost!

Paulson Pulikottil, professor of biblical studies, Union Biblical Seminary, Pune, India

I still remember the conversation that I had with a famous itinerant evangelist over lunch. His community considers him an expert Bible scholar. Naturally, our conversation strayed into the topic of the holy spirit. He thinks that the holy spirit descended to the earth from heaven on the day of Pentecost. I tried hard to convince him that though the holy spirit descended *on the disciples* on that day of Pentecost, he was already there on earth. He looked at me with disbelief when I told him that the spirit of God was at work from creation. The spirit of God has always been there, empowering people to serve God's creative and redemptive purposes on earth. A thorough survey of the presence and work of the spirit of God through the Torah tradition is thus an eye-opener for those who think that the work and mission of the spirit commences with the New Testament.

made a wind blow over the earth, and the waters subsided" (Gen. 8:1).[20] The blowing of the divine wind oftentimes portends destruction and judgment, but with this divine breathing the deluge dries up and the world is renewed, as if there is thus "a second beginning of the earth."[21] Noteworthy, then, is that these opening chapters of the biblical canon associate the presence and activity of the divine breath with creation and life on the one hand and the absence and departure of the same with judgment and death on the other hand, even if the former's reiteration signals the deity's character as creator. Such connections situate the biblical drama of creation, fall, and redemption within an overarching ruahological framework. Similarly, the mission of God in creation and redemption can be understood also as the mission of the divine *ruah*, even as the twists and turns of human history now, and the eschaton also as proleptically experienced, resound with, against, and according to the comings and goings of God's wind.

20. Not quite *the* divine *ruah*—see Claus Westermann, *Genesis 1–11: A Commentary*, trans. John J. Scullion, SJ (Minneapolis: Augsburg, 1984), 441—but acting with similar effectiveness, at least phenomenologically (cf. Exod. 14:21 and 15:8–10; see also §1.3 below).

21. See Kenneth A. Matthews, *Genesis 1–11:26*, New American Commentary 1A (Nashville: Holman, 1996), 384.

1.2 Genesis, Part 2—Joseph and the Spirit: The Mission of God through the Patriarchs

The only other appearance of the divine spirit in the book of Genesis comes from a question that the pharaoh of Egypt poses to his servants about Joseph: "Can we find anyone else like this—one in whom is the spirit of God?" (Gen. 41:38). Pharaoh himself clarifies in what follows that one in whom the divine spirit resides is "discerning and wise" and is thus deserving to "be over my house, and all my people" (41:39–40 ESV). Hence Pharaoh proclaims to Joseph, "Without your consent no one shall lift up hand or foot in all the land of Egypt," and gives him "authority over the land of Egypt" (41:44–45). Clearly, the inhabitation of God's spirit was remarkable, even to an unbeliever like Pharaoh, and Joseph was essentially elevated to the position of vizier (prime minister) of the land.[22]

The main lines of the Joseph story up to now can be quickly recalled. He was the favorite of his father, Jacob, susceptible to dreams (and their interpretations) that exacerbated the jealousy of his eleven brothers, and as a result got sold off by them to traders who in turn peddled him in Egypt to Potiphar, "an officer of Pharaoh, the captain of the guard" (Gen. 37:36 ESV). Because he did not give in to the seductions of Potiphar's wife, he was thrown in prison. But while there, he correctly interpreted the dreams of two coprisoners, the king's cupbearer and baker, and the former later recalled Joseph's abilities when Pharaoh himself had dreams that troubled him and no viable interpretations were forthcoming from his court. Joseph not only interpreted Pharaoh's dreams but also commended to him an administrative plan for responding to the famines portended by the dreams. A foreigner sold across borders into servitude by his kinsmen arose to imperial prominence![23]

Note that Pharaoh identifies Joseph as one who has the divine spirit not merely because he has dream-interpretive capacities but because he is sagacious with regard to what ought to be done in anticipation of what the dreams say will come to pass. The narrative is silent about how Joseph might have cultivated such astuteness and prudence, but the witness to the presence of the spirit of God in his life suggests that the gaining of such wisdom emerged at least in part through the difficult life circumstances that he had experienced.[24]

22. For more on Egyptian viziership, see Gordon J. Wenham, *Genesis 16–50*, WBC 2 (Dallas: Word, 1994), 394–97.

23. See also Francisco García-Treto, "Hyphenating Joseph: A View of Genesis 39–41 from the Cuban Diaspora," in *Interpreting across Borders*, ed. Fernando F. Segovia, The Bible and Postcolonialism 3 (Sheffield: Sheffield Academic, 2000), 134–45.

24. See John R. Levison, *Inspired: The Holy Spirit and the Mind of Faith* (Grand Rapids: Eerdmans, 2013), 25–27.

We don't know to what degree or if at all Joseph himself might have sought specifically after God's spirit, but Pharaoh concludes, according to the conventions of his place and time, that the insight and knowledge Joseph manifested could be explicable only given the presence of deity.

To be sure, Pharaoh's claim asserts nothing more than the recognition that divinity in general—*ruah Elohim*, to be exact—resided within Joseph. This tells us little beyond the fact that Pharaoh and the Egyptian religious culture of his time—at least as understood by the author(s) or editor(s) of this segment of the Genesis narrative—acknowledged that Elohim might be involved with human endeavors and that, in this case, Elohim had sent warnings via the dreams and provided interpretation of such for the sake of the people. Egyptian ruahology, from this point of view, is equivalent to Egyptian theology.

Yet a biblically framed ruahology of mission would note also that so-called pagans—in this case the political oppressors of the elect people of God—have a basic ability for spiritual discernment.[25] Such might be no more than the premonition of divinity based on a clear display of the cross-culturally agreed upon virtues, although even in these cases, such associations would only ensue given preexisting religious or spiritual dispositions. From a missiological perspective, Pharaoh-like discernments amid political-religious exile are bridges for exploring the whences and whithers of the divine wind that are otherwise difficult to track.

The presence of God's spirit with Joseph in the land of Egypt is also missiologically pertinent against the wider backdrop of his being the son of Jacob, or Israel, and thus within the lineage of Abraham. If the election of Abraham is understood as initiating a redemptive sequence of events in a postdiluvian world, the ethnic particularity of this choice is immediately shown as intertwined with God's intention to bless the world.[26] Thus the promise was not only to make of Abraham a great nation (Gen. 12:2; cf. 17:4–6) but also that "in you all the families of the earth shall be blessed" (12:3 ESV).[27] The guarantee of blessing

25. John R. Levison provides the framework for relating pneumatology and anthropology through the divine life-spirit given to each at birth; see *Filled with the Spirit* (Grand Rapids: Eerdmans, 2009). It is from this perspective that any pneumatology of mission also can and even ought to proceed.

26. God's design to save the world through the specificity of Abrahamic ethnicity is unfolded in Mark R. Kreitzer, *The Concept of Ethnicity in the Bible: A Theological Analysis* (Lewiston, NY: Edwin Mellen, 2008), esp. chap. 5. I think this overarching argument is defensible apart from Kreitzer's covenantal Reformed theological underpinnings, even as this book provides one of the most missiologically informed analyses of an otherwise challenging biblical idea.

27. Thus has the Abrahamic covenant also been called "the universal covenant"; see Richard R. de Ridder, *Discipling the Nations* (Grand Rapids: Baker, 1975), 22–30. For discussion of Gen. 17 as ratifying the international dimensions of the Abrahamic covenant, see Paul R. Williamson,

for the entire world is multiply repeated to Abraham and his descendants in the patriarchal account (Gen. 18:18 to Abraham; 26:4 to Isaac; 28:18 to Jacob),[28] even if such assurance is also somehow contingent on Abraham's obedience (Gen. 22:18).[29] Note also, however, that the nations are cursed, but only if they reject the Lord's chosen people; otherwise, these others are also recipients of blessing *in* Abraham, as an outflow of God's assurances to his descendants.[30]

Might we then consider the presence and activity of the divine spirit in and with Joseph to be a sign that God is continuing to bring about his promise of blessing to the world even if through the exile of his chosen people? This stay in Egypt turns into the first of many exiles for Israel—indeed, prolonged existence under the rule of others becomes the norm for the people of God. And although Jewish commentators have been vexed about the rationale for this exile, foretold actually by God (Gen. 15:13), it is difficult to avoid the conclusion that the preservation of Israel in and through their Egyptian sojourn emanates "a shining example of light and hope to the whole world."[31] To be sure, Israel here is not called to go out to the world as the apostles are sent in the New Testament; simultaneously, God sends Israel into the world, in this case drives them into the land of Egypt, and yet remains with them by his breath so that they may indeed be a blessing to the world. The wisdom of the divine spirit here surely saves not only the families of Israel (Gen. 42–46) but also the Egyptians during the famine that ravaged the land. Indeed, "*all the world* came to Joseph in Egypt to buy grain, because the famine became severe throughout the world" (Gen. 41:57; emphasis added), so that the mission of God here finds "universal" fulfillment, at least according to the understanding of that time.[32]

Much more can and ought to be said about the mission of God inaugurated in both the creation and the patriarchal narratives of Genesis. From

---

Abraham, Israel and the Nations: The Patriarchal Promise and Its Covenantal Development in Genesis, JSOTSup 315 (Sheffield: Sheffield Academic, 2001), 207–13.

28. And if Abraham, Isaac, and Jacob are the line of the elect, then Lot, Ishmael, and Esau are not. See, e.g., R. Christopher Heard, who suggests how the patriarchal narratives function to distinguish the faithful Jewish remnant from Persia from the indigenous inhabitants of the land and their neighbors. *Dynamics of Diselection: Ambiguity in Genesis 12–36 and Ethnic Boundaries in Post-exilic Judah*, Semeia Studies 39 (Atlanta: Society of Biblical Literature, 2001).

29. See the discussion of Gen. 22:18 in James A. Meek, *The Gentile Mission in Old Testament Citations in Acts: Text, Hermeneutic, and Purpose* (New York: T&T Clark, 2008), 114–30.

30. Keith N. Grüneberg, *Abraham, Blessing and the Nations: A Philological and Exegetical Study of Genesis 12:3 in Its Narrative Context*, BZAW 332 (Berlin: de Gruyter, 2003), 242–45.

31. Theodore Steinberg, "End of Exile?," *JBQ* 34:2 (2006): 131–32, here 132.

32. Thus, we can, with Shawn B. Redford, "consider Joseph's life to be a genre that is a 'living image' of promise in that his real life reflects a larger missional fulfillment and acts as a reminder of God's plan," at least as unfolded through the book of Genesis. *Missiological Hermeneutics: Biblical Interpretation for a Global Church* (Eugene, OR: Pickwick, 2012), 10–46, here 40.

a ruahological perspective, however, the creator spirit is also the redeeming spirit, present and active to Israel and others with whom they are related even in and through the most trying times when the hand of God is otherwise only opaquely discernible. And this redemptive spirit works not only on behalf of God's people but also in and through others.

1.3 Exodus, Part 1—The Wind and Breath of Yahweh: Liberation and Mission

There are at least three trajectories of missiological readings of the book of Exodus. In the next section, we will look at that which links the Sinaitic covenant with Israel's witness to the nations. The other two are intertwined, involving Israel's liberation from Egypt and Israel's "mission" in or to Egypt. Most readings, especially in our modern and late modern context, of Israel and Egypt are binary, with the former symbolizing chosenness and the latter damnation.[33] Our ruahological perspective, however, suggests a much less starkly contrasting relationship between Israel and these otherwise othered nations.

That the missiological theme of Israel's deliverance from Egypt has been championed in the last generation not least by liberation theologians should not thereby be dismissed by those who approach the Bible from other theological commitments.[34] Liberation readings of the scriptures have drawn deeply from the Exodus narrative to explicate how God delivers his people, whether spiritually or historically, from the many ways in which human beings live under subjugation, and these emphases are embedded across the scriptural traditions themselves.[35] Without minimizing these scriptural accents—to which we will have occasion to return throughout the remainder of this book—for the moment it is important to highlight more recent postcolonial interpretations that have called attention both to how the people of God ought not to

33. Anthony D. Smith explicates aspects of the reception history of the Torah, in particular the early Exodus account, that has both shaped the emergence of the modern nation-state, inevitably set off against other nation-states in this binarily constructed manner, and been understood from that same dualistic (effectively zero-sum) perspective. "Biblical Beliefs in the Shaping of Modern Nations," *Nations and Nationalism: Journal of the Association for the Study of Ethnicity and Nationalism* 21:3 (2015): 403–22, esp. 406–9.

34. George V. Pixley, *On Exodus: A Liberation Perspective*, trans. Robert R. Barr (Maryknoll, NY: Orbis, 1987), and, a bit earlier, J. Severino Croatto, *Exodus: A Hermeneutics of Freedom*, trans. Salvator Attanasio (Maryknoll, NY: Orbis, 1981).

35. So much so that liberationist approaches are not needed to foreground the movement across the Exodus narrative as one from "tyranny to freedom"; see J. G. McConville, *God and Earthly Power: An Old Testament Political Theology, Genesis–Kings*, LHBOTS 454 (New York: T&T Clark, 2006), chap. 4.

identify only with the Israelites or Hebrews over against their Egyptian oppressors, and to the fact that identity in the narratives of ancient Israel generally, but also specifically here in the book of Exodus, is much more fluid than the oppressed-oppressor binary prevalent in liberation readings.[36] Instead, in the contemporary Western world, more often than not, affluent Christians have more in common with Egyptians masters than with the Hebrew slaves, and liberation hence involves experiencing salvation at least as much from *within*, rather than escaping *from*, the prevailing system of domination.[37]

In fact, the second, more minority report picks up on this theme of God's liberative mission *in* and *to* Egypt.[38] From this perspective, the entire sequence of events related to Israel's sojourn in Egypt (see §1.2) and then God's rescuing them from the hands of the pharaoh through a series of plagues happens so that, apart from the reasons related to Israel's restoration, all of "the Egyptians shall know that I am the Lord" (Exod. 7:5 ESV). At one level, the Egyptians come to experience Yahweh's lordship through his judgment, and Israel's perennial celebration of Yahweh's deliverance witnesses to his rule not just to later generations of Egyptians but to the nations far and wide (cf. Exod. 9:16). At another level, there also appears to have been an open invitation for Egyptians, not to mention other aliens and foreigners to the Abrahamic descendants, to leave with the Hebrews and even some indication that at least a few if not many did so (Exod. 12:38; cf. Lev. 24:10).[39] Perhaps this explains the need for guidelines for non-Hebrew participation in the Passover celebration (Exod. 12:43–49),[40] which itself is representative of the incorporation of these sojourners, aliens, and foreigners into the covenant between Yahweh and Israel.[41] In fact, the Israelite law forged during the monarchic

---

36. See Federico Alfredo Roth, *Hyphenating Moses: A Postcolonial Exegesis of Identity in Exodus 1:1–3:15*, BibInt 154 (Leiden: Brill, 2017), esp. chap. 2.

37. E.g., Laurel A. Dykstra, *Set Them Free: The Other Side of Exodus* (Maryknoll, NY: Orbis, 2002).

38. Bradley P. Roderick, "God's Mission to Egypt in the Exodus," *Theological Educator* 52 (1995): 21–26.

39. Rikk E. Watts writes, "The social group described as aliens and sojourners [are] mentioned in some sixty places throughout Leviticus, Numbers, and Deuteronomy," thus indicating that this embrace of non-Israelite others, while a minor theme in the secondary literature, was a substantive and major phenomenon in Israel's early life and history. "Echoes from the Past: Israel's Ancient Traditions and the Destiny of the Nations in Isaiah 40–55," *JSOT* 28:4 (2004): 481–508, here 496.

40. As Christiana van Houten clarifies, aliens were welcomed during the historical periods in which the Pentateuch and books on Israel's early history were formulated, but were perceived more as a threat in the postexilic period; see *The Alien in Israelite Law*, JSOTSup 107 (Sheffield: JSOT Press, 1991), 164–65. See also the discussion of Nehemiah in §3.2 below.

41. See J. Daniel Hays, *From Every People and Nation: A Biblical Theology of Race*, NSBT 14 (Downers Grove, IL: InterVarsity, 2003), 69–70.

period codified embrace of non-Israelites on the basis of memory of this ruahic deliverance: "The alien who resides with you shall be to you as the citizen among you; you shall love the alien as yourself, for you were aliens in the land of Egypt: I am the LORD your God" (Lev. 19:34).[42] In any case, the exodus thereby includes not only Hebrews but also others within the Egyptian regime, and it anticipates the eschatological redemption of Egypt (cf. Isa. 11:11, 16; 19:19–25; 27:13) and the inclusion of this ancient oppressor among other nations in Israel's final salvation.

It is against this backdrop that two oblique references to the breath of Yahweh provide some ruahological perspective on the exodus. These appear in the so-called Song of the Sea (Exod. 15:1–19; vv. 20–21 record a version of this song as sung by Miriam and the women and may actually have been the earliest version of the song), which not only commemorates but also summarizes, within a worship or cultic context, Yahweh's deliverance. In the middle of the victorious celebration, these words are sung:

> At the blast of your nostrils [*ruah appeka*] the waters piled up,
>   the floods stood up in a heap;
>   the deeps congealed in the heart of the sea. . . .
> You blew with your wind [*nashapta beruhaka*], the sea covered them;
>   they sank like lead in the mighty waters. (Exod. 15:8, 10)

If this song belongs to an earlier rather than later (postmonarchic or even postexilic) strata of Israel's history, then there are good reasons to stay with the more figurative understandings that equate Yahweh's breath and wind with the natural elements that both made a way for the Hebrews' escape (through the Red Sea; Exod. 14:21–22) and destroyed their Egyptian pursuers (14:23–31). On the other hand, it is also specifically as a reference to Yahweh's power that the divine breath and wind achieved release for the people of God—uncannily like and unlike the wind that caused the subsiding of the flood waters (Gen. 8:1) discussed earlier in this chapter (§1.1)—and it is this power that becomes central to later biblical ruahology.[43]

---

42. The Torah's provisions for outsiders suggests that the presence of foreigners within ancient Israel was more rather than less prevalent (e.g., Exod. 22:21–31; 23:9, 12; Lev. 16:29; 19:10; 23:22; 25:23, 35, 47; Num. 9:14; Deut. 5:14; 10:18–19; 14:21, 29; 16:11, 14; 23:7; 24:14, 17–22; 26:11–13; 27:19). See for further discussion Walther Zimmerli, *The Old Testament and the World*, trans. John J. Scullion (Atlanta: John Knox, 1976), chap. 8.

43. This is how Lloyd R. Neve handles this passage in *The Spirit of God in the Old Testament* (Cleveland, TN: CPT, 2011), 7–11. It was Neve's discussion that prompted my own treatment of this text since I might have otherwise overlooked the ruahic underpinnings of the deliverance from Egypt.

A number of considerations emerge when such ruahological cues are foregrounded. To be sure, the breath of Yahweh is not only creative and liberative (or redemptive)[44] but also associated with the divine destruction and judgment, themes that we have already identified in the first book of the Torah (§1.1). Yet if in the primeval history withdrawal of the divine breath precipitates the flood and its judgment of inundation, here it is the fury of the divine wind that activates the waters of the sea and executes the judgment that overcomes, overpowers, even destroys. How then might we understand the mission of God's spirit if such a liberative ruahology is also destructive, even of the human life that God desires not to perish? At least three lines of reflection present themselves.

First, the breath of God that liberates through wind and water does so in order that the people of God can be redeemed from slavery to experience God's salvation. The Song of Moses—another title for the Song of the Sea—uses metaphors that communicate Yahweh is not only warrior (Exod. 15:3) but also lover, protector, shepherd, and tender of plantations (15:17).[45] The song also anticipates the later conquest of Canaan (15:14–15),[46] the land promised to Israel's ancestors. In other words, the divine wind that saves is also the divine breath that sanctifies, and redemption involves not only deliverance *from* but also transformation *to* being God's special possession. That the Song of Moses associates Yahweh's liberative acts with the divine wind and breath indicates that salvation as encountered in human history is indeed accomplishable only by God, indeed the very being, even spirit, of the living God. Neither Israel nor the Egyptians that experienced liberation were able to orchestrate emancipation through the wind and water. Only Yahweh as God saves through his own strength and might, and therefore only Yahweh is to be praised and exalted (15:2).

44. Brian D. Russell suggests that this song not only is the pivot around which the book turns (in summarizing the deliverance from Egypt through the first fourteen chapters and also introducing themes from the second half of Exodus) but also surely in this regard tells of the deliverance of the Hebrews and of the creation, or founding or establishing, of Israel under the Mosaic or Sinaitic covenant; in Russell's sense, then, the song lifts up Yahweh as deliverer *and* new creator of covenant Israel. See Russell, *The Song of the Sea: The Date of Composition and Influence of Exodus 15:1–21*, StBibLit 101 (New York: Peter Lang, 2007), 55 and 149.

45. For explication, see Dennis T. Olson, "God for Us, God against Us: Singing the Pentateuch's Songs of Praise in Exodus 15 and Deuteronomy 32," *Theology Today* 70:1 (2013): 54–61.

46. Although modern scholarship in general presumes that the references to the conquest of Canaan are later insertions into what is otherwise an ancient song, good arguments can be made from the imperfect tenses employed that these belong just as naturally in the aftermath of the exodus *Sitz im Leben*; see David Noel Freedman, "Moses and Miriam: The Song of the Sea (Exodus 15:1–18, 21)," in *Realia Dei: Essays in Archeology and Biblical Interpretation in Honor of Edward F. Campbell, Jr., at His Retirement*, ed. Prescott H. Williams Jr. and Theodore Hiebert (Chico, CA: Scholars Press, 1999), 67–77.

Second, and relatedly, salvation can come only from the depths of destruction, and so in that case, mission emerges from the darkest moments of human tragedy and lostness. Thus, it is declared: "And the Egyptians shall know that I am the LORD, when I have gotten glory over Pharaoh, his chariots, and his horsemen" (Exod. 14:18 ESV). It is in a sense only through realization of their own doom that the Egyptians come to recognize Yahweh as even their own deliverer. What is condemned and judged, however, are not Egyptians as Egyptians, but Egyptians as representative of a posture opposed to Yahweh's willful call of Israel to worship in the desert (15:9).[47] In this sense, the exodus provides a message not only for Egyptians but also for Moses and Israel—and indeed for the nations—so that the people of God come to fathom that Yahweh's deliverance and salvation are the flip side of Yahweh's judgment.[48] But the point I wish to press here is that the wind of Yahweh not only liberates human subjects but does so using the sea, the very means of entombment and judgment. In effect, the "subterranean waters," which according to ancient Near Eastern myth represented the tumultuous deity of the sea,[49] are hereby the conduit of Israel's liberation. The paradox, then, is that the wind of God accomplishes judgment even as it redemptively breathes life from death.

Third, this leads for our purposes to the ruahological theme that connects the divine wind both to the waters that destroy and purify and to the breaths that resound in celebrative praise as a witness to the nations. On the one hand, the voices rejoicing over the victory wrought by Yahweh over the Egyptians acknowledge that it is his powerful breath that has delivered them through the sea. On the other hand, these same voices extol, within a worshiping environment, the majesty, holiness, awesomeness, splendor, and wondrousness of Yahweh as savior and deliverer, declaring, "Who is like you, O LORD, among the gods?" (Exod. 15:11 ESV), not only to the Egyptians in their midst and surrounding them, but also to Edomites, Moabites, and Canaanites, among other people to whom Israel is called to witness (15:15). Thus, the waters of destruction are also thereby understood as nothing less than the vaporous winds of Yahweh's redemptive acts, even as the latter are also the life-giving breath that enables human praise to ascend so that the nations might know and that God may be enthroned in his cosmic sanctuary and "reign forever and ever" (15:18 ESV).[50]

47. For this point that the multiple *I wills* of the Egyptians (Exod. 15:9) are answered by the blowing of Yahweh's wind, see John I. Durham, *Exodus*, WBC 3 (Waco: Word, 1987), 207.

48. William A. Ford, *God, Pharaoh and Moses: Explaining the Lord's Actions in the Exodus Plague Narrative* (Milton Keynes, UK: Paternoster, 2006), esp. 215–16.

49. J. Philip Hyatt, *Exodus*, NCBC (Grand Rapids: Eerdmans, 1971), 164.

50. This point about praise as missiological, along with much of this final paragraph, is inspired from the discussion of the Song of the Sea by Terence E. Fretheim, *Exodus*, IBC

1.4   Exodus, Part 2—The Crafts of the Spirit: A Missional Vocation

If the first half of the book of Exodus preserves the all-important account of Israel's historic deliverance from Egypt and culminates with the Song of the Sea, then the rest of this second book of Torah tells about the covenant between Yahweh and Israel at Sinai and delineates details of how Yahweh's presence is intended to be manifest in the midst of the people. Within this latter half of Exodus, arguably the most important missiological theme in this book, at least as found in more classically articulated theologies of mission, is located at the heart of the Sinaitic covenant. There, so the traditional missiological reading proceeds, Yahweh speaks to Moses as leader and representative of the people and in effect commissions Israel as a holy priesthood to the nations: "If you obey my voice and keep my covenant, you shall be my treasured possession out of all the peoples. Indeed, the whole earth is mine, but you shall be for me a priestly kingdom and a holy nation" (Exod. 19:5–6).[51] It is particularly noteworthy here that Yahweh's election of Israel is for the purposes of representing the nations, in effect to serve as mediator between God and the world, so that such calling and vocation, rather than being meritorious (which the biblical traditions themselves clearly dismiss: e.g., Deut. 7:7; 9:4–6), are first and foremost missiological. If that is the case, then Israel's failure to live into the covenant can also be understood as a failure to fulfill its missionary calling, and hence Israel's not experiencing the covenantal promises but instead incurring the judgments (in exile later) can also be viewed as an indictment for neglecting its missionary vocation.[52]

It is within this framework that we must understand the extensive Sinaitic instructions to build the tabernacle for Yahweh's presence, as well as the details pertinent to its furnishings (the ark, table, lampstand, altar), the priestly vestments, and the rites of worship (including the worship paraphernalia like lavers, anointing oils, and oils of incense). What appears to be a tedious repetitiveness of commissioning (Exod. 25–31) and then implementing (Exod. 35–40) Israel's worship instead denotes establishment of the means through which Israel, as a priestly nation, is supposed to represent "all the peoples," indeed "the whole earth" (Exod. 19:5), before and

---

(Louisville: John Knox, 1991), 161–70, a section that Fretheim titles, aptly for our purposes also, "A Cosmic Victory."

51. A solid discussion of the mission-to-the-nations theme in Exodus as emergent from this text is found in Michael W. Goheen, *A Light to the Nations: The Missional Church and the Biblical Story* (Grand Rapids: Baker Academic, 2011), 32–48.

52. Heinz Kruse, "Exodus 19:5 and the Mission of Israel," *Northeast Asia Journal of Theology* 24–25 (1980): 129–35.

The Divine Wind Blowing on the Underside of History
From Ancient Egypt to Contemporary Latin America and Beyond

Federico Roth, associate professor of biblical studies, Azusa Pacific University, Azusa, California, USA

Latin American engagements with the Bible have tended to foreground the story of Exodus to good, but perhaps limited, results. The *missio spiritus* hermeneutic articulated here allows for the sourcing of new liberative narratives and theological trajectories that serve to nuance and renew under-exegeted biblical texts for our postmodern contexts. Here the Joseph tale is illuminated for the ways it not only anticipates Moses but resonates with the sociopolitical realities of our own present times as Latin Americans. Refracted through a *ruahological* prism, the Joseph narrative reveals the work of the divine breath as residing with and within the most reviled and forgotten—the displaced, unauthorized, and underdocumented—and so at work in the lives of liminal figures who find themselves at/on borders, themselves crossed and crisscrossed by multiple identities and positionalities far beyond simplistic oppressor/oppressed modalities. Moreover, the spirit in Joseph partners to effect the survival of those caught in the web of colonial power by eroding its artificial binaries (e.g., white/brown, conservative/liberal, us/them) now resurgent in popular political and social discourse and regularly deployed to vilify black and brown people. For the breath of God serves as the linking agent between powerful (Pharaoh) and powerless (Joseph), dissolving the distance of privilege, and so works toward the full redemption of *all* (Egyptian, Hebrew, Latinx, Euro-American) who suffered and suffer from the myriad dehumanizing effects of colonialism.

to God. Going further, it would also be appropriate to say that in Israel's worship, the nations and humanity as well come doxologically before the God of the earth.

Set against this background, the practically singular references to the *ruah Elohim* in this book stand out starkly. We are told first, by Yahweh himself as it were, about a certain Bezalel: "I have filled him with divine spirit, with ability, intelligence, and knowledge in every kind of craft, to devise artistic designs, to work in gold, silver, and bronze, in cutting stones for setting, and in carving wood, in every kind of craft" (Exod. 31:3–5). This is confirmed, almost verbatim by Moses, after the quelling of the rebellion related to the golden calf: "See, the LORD has called by name Bezalel son of Uri son of Hur, of the tribe of Judah; he has filled him with divine spirit, with skill, intelligence, and knowledge in every kind of craft, to devise artistic designs, to work in gold, silver, and bronze, in cutting stones for setting, and in carving wood, in every kind of craft" (35:30–33). It is implied that Bezalel's colleague Oholiab, of the tribe of Dan, is similarly anointed for these same purposes (31:6; 35:34), although the explicit reference to the divine breath is made only in connection to the former. It is certainly the case here that the gift of the divine *ruah* enables the creativity, skill, and expertise needed for the construction of the dwelling place of Yahweh.[53] Our question is how these accounts further illuminate the mission of God in ruahological perspective. Three lines of reflection follow.

First, and most obviously, if the enabling of the divine spirit is essential for forming Israel as a priestly and missionary people for the nations of the world, it might be expected that the *ruah Elohim* be given to those overseeing the construction of the earthly sanctuary that would facilitate, both literally and figuratively, such priestly (and mediatorial and missionary) functions. More specifically, Yahweh "has inspired him [Bezalel] *to teach*, both him and Oholiab" (Exod. 35:34 ESV; emphasis added), so that "all who have ability, whom I [Yahweh] have endowed with skill"—in fact, "every skillful one to whom the LORD has given skill and understanding to know how to do any work in the construction of the sanctuary"—"shall work in accordance with all that the LORD has commanded" (28:3; 36:1).[54] Bezalel and Oholiab, then, are not merely practitioner craftsmen, insofar as they are also teachers, but they are simultaneously no mere theoreticians but mentors and apprentices, imparting to the people the knowledge *and* skills needed for the task at hand.[55] The missiological point is that the gift of the divine spirit enables the building of Yahweh's abode and facilitates Yahweh's habitation in the presence of his people, surely so that Israel may serve the nations and that all the world may come to know the Lord and be blessed through the promises given to Abraham.

But second, although it is possible to reason from the fact that only Bezalel is said to be given the *ruah Elohim* to the conclusion that the gift of the spirit

---

53. Richard S. Hess, "Bezalel and Oholiab: Spirit and Creativity," in *Presence, Power, and Promise: The Role of the Spirit of God in the Old Testament*, ed. David G. Firth and Paul D. Wegner (Downers Grove, IL: IVP Academic, 2011), 161–72.

54. Levison (*Filled with the Spirit*, 52–58) emphasizes how Bezalel and Oholiab work not on their own but as leaders of a group of people, both skilled and wise, that were assembled for this undertaking.

55. I owe this insight to Durham, *Exodus*, 410.

enables and empowers his work, literary, contextual, and narrative cues suggest it is just as likely, if not more appropriate, that "God calls them [Bezalel and others] to work because they are *filled* with spirit of wisdom so that they can *ful-fill* the extraordinary task ahead of them."[56] In other words, here the lines are blurred between understanding the divine spirit as transcendent over or above human spirits and viewing the divine and human breaths as collaborative, if not convergent. Thus, the spirit of creation can be seen to harness the energies of those with the breath of life for divinely redemptive purposes, not as if descending from above or arriving from without, but as heightening and intensifying creaturely endowments from within, as it were. From a missiological perspective, this invites consideration of how the people of God can meet those outside the community of faith in the spirit of the *ruah Elohim*, perhaps recognizing in the creativity, wisdom, skill, and capacity of those among the nations of the world the presence of the divine breath that provides a bridge, a point of contact even, for common cause, if not for bearing witness to the mission of God.

Last but not least, for our purposes, I want to extrapolate canonically from the Exodus narrative to observe that the earthly tabernacle constructed under the oversight of Bezalel both looks back to the creation itself as the temple of God in Genesis 1 and anticipates the redeemed cosmos as the habitation of the triune God in the Apocalypse.[57] If that is the case, then the *ruah Elohim* who enables Bezalel and others in erecting the physical sanctuary is the same wind of God that brought forth the primordial world and the same spirit that, with the bride, welcomes all who are thirsty to "take the water of life as a gift" (Rev. 22:17) in the eschatological presence of the divine that pervades the new heavens and new earth. In that case, the spirit of creation and redemption can be understood as being continuously at work, not only here in the history of ancient Israel, but also in any present historical moment, in taking the creational elements, whether metals, stones, or trees, as well as consecrating creative activities, all for the sake of finally accomplishing the cosmic mission of a saving God.

1.5 Numbers, Part 1—The Spirit's Dangerous Answer to Prayer: Intercessory Mission

Much has been made by modern Pentecostal interpreters of the spirit's filling of the seventy elders in Numbers 11 as an Old Testament prototype of the

56. Levison, *Filled with the Spirit*, 58 (emphasis original).
57. Fretheim, *Exodus*, parts 7 and 9, esp. 269 and 315; see also G. K. Beale, *The Temple and the Church's Mission: A Biblical Theology of the Dwelling Place of God* (Downers Grove, IL: IVP Academic, 2004).

Pentecost event in Acts 2.[58] There are certainly many observable parallels, for instance, of Moses as spirit-filled leader of the people of God being a type of Jesus, the spirit-anointed Messiah; of the seventy elders and the one hundred twenty Messianists (see Acts 1:15) as representative leadership under the two (Mosaic and Pentecostal) covenants; of the prophesying of the seventy elders and the glossolalia of the one hundred twenty disciples, among other aspects. Without denying the correspondences, our focus here will be on understanding the connections between the sendings of the spirit of Yahweh not only on the seventy elders but also "from the sea" (Num. 11:31 ESV). Any ruahological reading of Numbers 11 will need to be expansive enough to account for both manifestations of the divine *ruah*.

The steep contrast between what the two blowings of the wind of Yahweh (Num. 11:17, 31) achieve have to be explicated in light of the wider context. The passage concerns, first and foremost, the dissatisfaction of the Israelites with their daily provision of manna: "Oh that we had meat to eat!" (Num. 11:4 ESV). Whereas on prior occasions Moses had defended the grumbling Israelites and even interceded for their very existence in the face of an angered Yahweh who was ready to destroy them and transfer his covenant to Moses and his descendants instead (e.g., Exod. 32:9–14), this time Moses begged for relief, even of the most ultimate kind: "If you [Yahweh] will treat me like this, kill me at once, if I find favor in your sight, that I may not see my wretchedness" (Num. 11:15 ESV).

The divine *ruah* appears in response to both complaints. To address Moses's plight, Yahweh commissions seventy Israelite elders: "I will take some of the spirit that is on you and put it on them; and they shall bear the burden of the people along with you so that you will not bear it all by yourself" (Num. 11:17). On this occasion, "when the spirit rested upon them, they prophesied. But they did not do so again" (11:25).[59] Interestingly, there is also special mention of Eldad and Medad; perhaps they were part of the seventy elders, perhaps not,[60] even as it is unclear whether the seventy were part of a

58. E.g., Roger D. Cotton, "The Pentecostal Significance of Numbers 11," *JPT* 10:1 (2001): 3–10; and David Hymes, "Numbers 11: A Pentecostal Perspective," *AJPS* 13:2 (2010): 257–81.

59. The King James Version ends 11:25 this way: "when the spirit rested upon them, they prophesied, and did not cease." This follows an alternative vocalization of the Hebrew text that is accepted in the Targum and the Vulgate. See A. Noordtzij, *Numbers*, trans. Ed van der Maas, Bible Student's Commentary (Grand Rapids: Zondervan, 1983), 103; and Martin Noth, *Numbers: A Commentary*, trans. James D. Martin, OTL (Philadelphia: Westminster, 1968), 89. If this rendition is adopted, it could be read as providing a transition to the prophesying of Eldad and Medad in the next verses.

60. Dennis T. Olson suggests that Eldad and Medad were "among those outside the institutional leadership of God's people," and this would be consistent with the ongoing democrati-

larger number of elders (cf. Exod. 18:25–26; 24:1). Eldad and Medad received the *ruah* of Yahweh and also prophesied, albeit outside the tent of meeting (Num. 11:26–27). Ruahologically, we might say that here Yahweh's response to Moses's prayer is to empower others to bear the burden with him of leading Israel's return to Canaan.

But Yahweh also sends his wind in response to the murmurings of the Israelites: "Then a wind from the LORD sprang up, and it brought quail from the sea and let them fall beside the camp, about a day's journey on this side and a day's journey on the other side, around the camp, and about two cubits above the ground" (Num. 11:31 ESV). Beyond the massive torrent of quail deposited, it is what happened next that is noteworthy: "While the meat was yet between their teeth, before it was consumed, the anger of the LORD was kindled against the people, and the LORD struck down the people with a very great plague. Therefore the name of that place was called Kibroth-hattaavah, because there they buried the people who had the craving" (11:33–34 ESV). In effect, the cravings of the people for meat were only partially satisfied; their very lives were cut short, not to mention that they did not even get to enjoy and complete their meal. Ruahologically, the divine wind precedes, and sometimes is a constitutive expression of, Yahweh's anger; if previously the "blast" of Yahweh's nostrils sent the waters to destroy the Egyptians (Exod. 15:8; see §1.3 above), here the strong winds of God send the quail that afflict and doom the Israelites.

To be sure, divine judgments in the book of Numbers are not always ruahologically mediated. There is plenty of "bad news," we might say, related to Israelite disobedience, whether of the divine consumption by fire at Taberah (Num. 11:1–3), of an unspecified plague on the spies who discouraged Israelite annexation of Canaan (14:36–37), of a destructive earthquake that swallowed up Korah and his family and followers and the related fire that devoured those with him (16:31–35), of venomous snakes in the desert of Edom (21:6), and of another plague that took the lives of 24,000-plus in the plains of Moab (25:1–9), just to name the most obvious. What is unique about ruahological judgment in the case of Numbers 11 is that the wind of Yahweh also brings relief, or at least is intended to do so, whether or not the seventy elders do actually, in the long run, assist Moses in shouldering the burden of leading the people of Israel.

Also noteworthy, a point not mentioned above, is that after Yahweh tells Moses how his leadership challenges will be dealt with (through the dispensing

---

zation of power more clearly manifest in the New Testament. See Olson, *Numbers*, IBC (Louisville: John Knox, 1996), 68.

of Moses's spirit to the seventy elders), the problem of the people's griev-
ances is addressed through Yahweh's instruction through Moses: "Say to the
people: Consecrate yourselves for tomorrow, and you shall eat meat" (Num.
11:18 ESV). The call here is, clearly, also a ruahic trope: the people are to
"consecrate yourselves."[61] There is no indication in this call for consecration
and sanctification that judgment is impending, only the admonition that
Yahweh's answer to the people's cries for meat will result in their loathing it
(11:19–20). Yet it is also unmistakable that the path of sanctification involves
that of purification, which in this case includes the elimination of those whose
attitudes and passions inhibit their experiencing the blessings of Yahweh.

These early references to the wind or breath of God in the Torah are
indicative not only of the creative power of the divine spirit but also of its
refining character, even to the point of death and destruction. The spirit of
creation works as the spirit of redemption amid a fallen creation and through
fallen human creatures. The mission of the spirit thus judges and purifies in
anticipation of the redemption to come. Even in Numbers this is heralded
in the last few chapters, with developments unfolded in chapters 26–36 as
representative of the experiences of the generation that enters into the land
of Canaan. We will pick up on this theme in our reflections on the book
of Deuteronomy. Meanwhile, we must look at the *ruah* of Yahweh on the
mountains and plains of Moab.

1.6 Numbers, Part 2—Spirit outside the Camp: Mission and Divination outside the Covenant

"Now Balaam saw that it pleased the LORD to bless Israel, so he did not go,
as at other times, to look for omens, but set his face toward the wilderness.
Balaam looked up and saw Israel camping tribe by tribe. Then the spirit of
God [*ruah Elohim*] came upon him, and he uttered his oracle" (Num. 24:1–3)
and proceeded to bless Israel (24:3–10). What is unexpected about the divine
spirit's alighting on Balaam is that he is not an Israelite (22:4–5).[62] Further,
he is not only an unbeliever outside the covenant with Israel but a diviner
(22:7), one who had been hired by Balak, a Moabite king, to curse Israel in

61. "Here and elsewhere, this formula functions in a situation of confrontation between
Yahweh and the people as the time frame for a coming, decisive act of God. The people are,
literally, 'to make themselves holy' today because *tomorrow* . . . Yahweh will act." Timothy R.
Ashley, *The Book of Numbers* (Grand Rapids: Eerdmans, 1993), 212 (emphasis original).

62. Balaam may have been a Midianite, given his association with them in Num. 25, or even
an Ammonite—see Michael L. Barré, "The Portrait of Balaam in Numbers 22–24," *Int* 51:3
(1997): 254–66, here 255—but in any case, he was not of Israel.

anticipation of its invasion of his country. As recorded in Numbers 22–24, Balaam eventually pronounced four oracles that amounted to four blessings on Israel, all despite Balak's provision of multiple occasions for Balaam to thwart, through his sorcery, the perceived Israelite menace.

This Balaam episode in Israel's history is extremely complicated, but our questions concern the missiological implications of this work of the divine spirit. One set of implications perpetuated by the biblical traditions is that it is only through Elohim's intervention that the curses intended for Israel were turned into blessing. Balaam's legacy has been associated more so with one clause in Numbers 31:16 (cf. Rev. 2:14)—indicating he advised Moabite and Midianite women to seduce Israelite men,[63] which resulted in a massive plague that claimed twenty-four thousand Israelite lives (Num. 25)[64]—than with the three chapters recounting his blessing Israel. In fact, of the oracles of blessing spoken by Balaam, it is said elsewhere in the Old Testament that "the Lord your God would not listen to Balaam; instead the Lord your God turned the curse into a blessing for you" (Deut. 23:5 ESV; cf. Josh. 24:10; Neh. 13:2). What might be understood here is not only that the latter oracles were explicitly mentioned as brought about by the spirit of Yahweh, but also that all the blessings were given by Yahweh through Balaam (Num. 23:5, 16). So God brought about good from all that Balaam meant for evil, and for the latter, the Israelites eventually "put to the sword Balaam son of Beor, who practiced divination" (Josh. 13:22; cf. Num. 31:8).[65] Applied more

63. Part of the challenge of understanding the Balaam story relates to these complications regarding the Midianite threat. Within the larger scheme of the wilderness journey, it might be said that although the Midianites were originally a resource for Moses through Jethro and Zipporah, in the end their cult was deemed incompatible with that devoted to Yahweh, and hence the ending of Numbers insists on nothing less than their extermination. (From a missiological perspective, I note that the eschatological redemption of Midian is intimated, in a vague manner through Israel, in Isa. 60:6, but space constraints do not allow development of this notion.) For discussion of Midian within the book of Numbers, see Thomas B. Dozeman, "The Midianites in the Formation of the Book of Numbers," in *Studies in Leviticus and Numbers*, ed. Thomas Römer (Leuven: Leuven University Press, 2008), 261–84; and Adriane Leveen, "Inside Out: Jethro, the Midianites and a Biblical Construction of the Outsider," *JSOT* 34:4 (2010): 395–417.

64. For a reading of the Balaam story that includes rather than neglects Num. 25, see Nili Sacher Fox, "בלק Balak: Numbers 22:2–25:9—Dangerous Foreigners," in *The Torah: A Women's Commentary*, ed. Tamara Cohn Eskenazi and Andrea L. Weiss (New York: Union for Reformed Judaism, 2007), 937–53, esp. 951–53.

65. From these references to Balaam outside Num. 22–24, the rabbinic tradition, as well as patristic Christian writers after this, has understood that he represents the villainous gentile world that opposes Israel as the elect of God. It is also possible to read these various scriptural and even extrascriptural Balaam traditions as reflecting ancient Israelites' wrestling with notions of divination prevalent in the surrounding ancient Near Eastern cultures and, in effect, rejecting these practices in favor of monotheistic commitments. For explications of these two approaches to the Balaam materials, see, respectively, Judith R. Baskin, *Pharaoh's Counsellors:*

broadly missiologically in this way, then, the redemption of the nations can only happen through Yahweh's direct and protective intervention. Human activity, no matter how well intentioned, cannot achieve such. Instead, even the goodwill of pious outsiders to the covenant ultimately leads only to sin and destruction. If there is a general sense in which such a perspective is true, this ignores how the text of Numbers 22–24 actually describes Balaam's actions and attitudes.

Attentiveness to the Balak and Balaam narrative suggests instead that the divine spirit is surely capable of working together with those outside the community of faith, even with putatively pagan sorcerers. Balaam's response to Balak and his elders from the beginning was to defer to Yahweh (Num. 22:8, 12, 13), whom Balaam referred to as "the LORD my God" (22:18 ESV). Although Yahweh initially prohibited Balaam from responding to Balak's offer (22:12), he was later advised, "Go with them; but only do what I tell you" (22:20 ESV; cf. 22:35). From all appearances, Balaam heeded Yahweh's admonition, telling Balak no less than four times, "The word that God puts in my mouth, that must I speak" (22:38 ESV; cf. 23:3, 26; 24:13). So, whatever Balak devised or desired, Balaam responded contrarily (cf. Mic. 6:5). From this perspective, the spirit of Yahweh comes upon a vessel who not only had shown the desire to cooperate with but was fully intending to please Israel's God. This point should not be lost even if such vessels of Yahweh are no less immune to also working against divine purposes in the big scheme of things.

It is ironic, then, that the non-Israelite conduit through whom Yahweh's breath recalled the Abrahamic promise that blessings follow those who cast these blessings on Israel (Num. 24:9; cf. Gen. 12:3) would himself be part of a reception history of being cursed![66] Although the author of 2 Peter speaks of Balaam's "madness"[67] and identifies him as one "who loved the wages of

---

Job, Jethro, and Balaam in Rabbinic and Patristic Tradition (Chico, CA: Scholars Press, 1983); and Michael S. Moore, The Balaam Traditions: Their Character and Development, SBLDS 113 (Atlanta: Scholars Press, 1990).

66. Grüneberg (Abraham, Blessing and the Nations, 22–33) discusses Num. 24:9 vis-à-vis Gen. 12:3 as indicative of the divine reassurance to Israel rather than as prioritizing blessings to the nations.

67. This pejorative description is surely an extension of the tradition that associated Balaam's falling down under the impact of the divine spirit (Num. 24:4, 16) with his entering into some sort of ecstatic trance that generated the oracle of blessing. Cf. Gordon J. Wenham, who presents reasons for this view, with John N. Oswalt, who counter-argues that, parallel to what is described of David in 2 Sam. 23:1, Balaam prophesies under the spirit's unction but yet retains full control of his faculties; see Wenham, Numbers: An Introduction and Commentary (Downers Grove, IL: InterVarsity, 1981), 176–77; and Oswalt, "Is Balaam's Donkey the Real Prophet (Numbers 24:1–4)?," in Firth and Wegner, Presence, Power, and Promise, 208–19.

doing wrong" (2 Pet. 2:15–16; cf. Jude 11), there are further ruahological—
and by extension missiological—connections that are worth exploring from
this text.[68] Not only does the second Petrine letter earlier insist that "no
prophecy ever came by human will, but men and women moved by the
Holy Spirit spoke from God" (1:21; see §7.4 below), but it also records
that God's prophetic messages are designed to accomplish divine purposes
in anticipation of and "until the day dawns and the morning star rises in
your hearts" (1:19 ESV). By extension, then, despite "the prophet's madness" (2:16), the presence of the divine breath guaranteed the achievement
of God's resolutions. Indeed, under the inspiration of the *ruah Elohim*,
Balaam foretold that "a star shall come out of Jacob" (Num. 24:17 ESV),
thus initiating the "morning star" notion found variously in the biblical
tradition, including that in the Petrine castigating of Balaam.[69] In short,
whatever might have been Balaam's motivations and however his heritage
might be interpreted, there is still no minimizing his prophesying under
the oversight of the spirit of Yahweh. Extended missiologically, such an
emphasis is consistent with the search for signs of the divine spirit's presence and activity even in cultures outside Israel, even cursed (!) ones, that
might find final fulfillment in the person and work of Christ, the spirit-
anointed one.

It is important to emphasize how impossible it is "to know precisely the
nature of the experience expressed by the words *the spirit of God came
upon him.*"[70] Yet this much is clear: the divine spirit appears in this text at a
liminal space and time in Israel's historical self-understanding, at the preci-
pice of their entry into the promised land of Canaan, but yet without any
guarantees that they would so complete their sojourn. And it is just amid this
precarious betwixt-and-betweenness that they find themselves assailed not
only from without (in the immediate scenario by the Moabites under Balak's
leadership) but also from within (through the seductions of the Midianite

68. For discussion of Balaam reception and reinterpretation among Jews during the time
of the first Christian writings, see John R. Levison, *The Spirit in First Century Judaism*, Arbeiten zur Geschichte des antiken Judentums und des Urchristentums 29 (Leiden: Brill, 1997),
part 1. John T. Greene shows that the central question motivating the extensive development
of Balaam traditions is, "Who is the *legitimate* spokesperson for deity (or deities)?" Greene,
Balaam and His Interpreters: A Hermeneutical History of the Balaam Traditions, Brown
Judaic Studies 244 (Atlanta: Scholars Press, 1992), 165 (emphasis original). In light of the
complex and complicated history of Balaam reception and interpretation, Greene's book
cautions anyone, therefore, against making too much of this ruahological question regarding
prophecy; but even at the risk of saying too much, I take it up again for missiological purposes.
69. See Thomas Scott Caulley, "ΒΑΛΑΑΚ in the 𝔓72 Text of Jude 11: A Proposal," *NTS* 55
(2009): 73–82.
70. Ashley, *Book of Numbers*, 487 (emphasis original).

women). If Israel is here thereby vulnerable on every side and even unsure of its survival, much less its mission, then what we are given here is, in effect, a spirit-prompted view of Israel from the perspective of the nations that Israel is attempting to overcome on the one hand but yet having to bear witness to on the other hand. Balak's fears provoked strategic counter-resistance, but Balaam's prophecies, inspired by the divine breath, enable Israel to understand itself and its mission through an outside mirror.[71]

Missiologically, then, the Balaam narrative invites consideration of how the mission of God might be illuminated from the perspective of the nations, including nations dominated by traditions and realities considered hostile to the biblical witness of the people of God. Those who would bear witness to the God of Israel might even find their testimonies refracted through the witness of others. This may not happen as often as we might like, but if the divine breath can speak both through an animal and its non-Israelite owner (Num. 22:22–30),[72] then we ought never to presume that the nations or groups of others to whom we are called and even to whom we might feel opposed could not also speak back to us the voice of God.

1.7 Numbers and Deuteronomy—Leadership in the Spirit? From Conquest to the Renewal of Mission

Only one reference to the divine wind appears in Deuteronomy: "Joshua the son of Nun was full of the spirit of wisdom, for Moses had laid his hands on him. So the people of Israel obeyed him and did as the LORD had commanded Moses" (34:9 ESV). In what follows, I quickly assess the missiological relevance of this text at three levels: that of the text itself, including its relationship to references in the book of Numbers; that with regard to the role of this text within the wider so-called Deuteronomistic history (especially the book of Joshua and its narrative of Canaanite conquest);[73] and that related to a broader understanding for contemporary theology of mission.

71. Ulrike Sals, "The Hybrid Story of Balaam (Numbers 22–24): Theology for the Diaspora in the Torah," *BibInt* 16:4 (2008): 315–35, esp. 317.

72. See Joel N. Lohr, *Chosen and Unchosen: Conceptions of Election in the Pentateuch and Jewish-Christian Interpretation*, Siphrut: Literature and Theology of the Hebrew Scriptures 2 (Winona Lake, IN: Eisenbrauns, 2009), 138.

73. Deut. 34 and its preceding chapters together constitute one of the reasons that this book has been read in critical scholarship as much with Joshua and the historical books of Samuel–Kings as with Genesis through Numbers. For an argument for this passage being of later provenance, with the historical writings, see Felix García López, "La Muerte de Moisés, la Sucesión de Josué y la Escritura de la Tôrah," in *The Future of the Deuteronomistic History*, ed. Thomas C. Römer, BETL 147 (Leuven: Leuven University Press and Uitgeverij Peeters,

At the textual level, the Hebrew grammar could be interpreted in a way that minimizes the import of the ruahological reference so that rather than positing a direct causal relationship between the divine wind and Joshua's leadership (as if it were because of the laying on of hands that he is filled with the breath of God), the former could stand more or less on its own, apart from the latter, and thus the second part of the verse would be read as making a separate point: "When (or Since) Moses had laid his hands upon him, the people of Israel obeyed him."[74] Yet even if this rendition is adopted, it might suggest that it was because Joshua was full of the "spirit of wisdom" that Moses laid his hands on him and, more importantly, that he was obeyed by the Israelites. This reading is actually consistent with the parallel passage in Numbers, where "the LORD said to Moses, 'Take Joshua son of Nun, a man in whom is the spirit, and lay your hand upon him'" (27:18).[75] In either case, it ought not to be overlooked that even if the divine wind is not given *through* Moses's laying on of hands,[76] Moses's investiture, uniquely recorded in the Torah, can be understood as completing the enabling of Joshua for the task set before him: to lead Israel into the promised land.[77] In this case, the "spirit of wisdom" has less to do with what is known as the Wisdom section of the Ketuvim (the third section of the Tanakh) and more to do with Joshua as a prophet-leader like Moses (Deut. 34:10–12; cf. 3:21; 31:7, 23).[78] From a missiological perspective, Joshua needs the full presence of the divine breath for the task ahead (the conquest of Canaan), just as Moses also needed divine inspiration (for the exodus from Egypt and the wilderness sojourn). Arguably if Israel is to be a witness and even a blessing to the nations,[79]

2000), 85–100. Our own ruahic consideration, however, goes both "backward" to Numbers and "forward" to Joshua.

74. Walter Vogels, "The Spirit in Joshua and the Laying on of Hands by Moses," *Laval théologique et philosophique* 38:1 (1982): 3–7, here 7.

75. As mentioned, the relationship between Numbers and Deuteronomy is a complicated one, depending on the direction from which the question is approached. For a sampling of the possibilities, see Konrad Schmid and Raymond F. Person Jr., eds., *Deuteronomy in the Pentateuch, Hexateuch, and the Deuteronomistic History*, FAT 2/56 (Tübingen: Mohr Siebeck, 2012).

76. Note, though, that the laying on of hands in Num. 27:23 is connected less to Joshua as inspirited leader than to the word of Yahweh in relation to the people. For more on this, see Keith Mattingly, "The Significance of Joshua's Reception of the Laying on of Hands in Numbers 27:12–23," *AUSS* 39:2 (2001): 191–208, here 207.

77. Thus, this commissioning is an "act of completion," Mattingly suggests in a follow-up study; see Keith Mattingly, "Joshua's Reception of the Laying on of Hands, Part 2: Deuteronomy 34:7 and Conclusion," *AUSS* 40:1 (2002): 89–103, here 94.

78. Moses is an "enduring model" in so many ways, proceeding from this inauguration of ruahic authority on Joshua. See Deanna A. Thompson, *Deuteronomy*, Belief: A Theological Commentary on the Bible (Louisville: Westminster John Knox, 2014), 244.

79. For more on the theology of blessing for the nations across the books associated with the "Deuteronomist," see J. Gary Millar, *Now Choose Life: Theology and Ethics in Deuteronomy*

as urged by the Abrahamic and Sinaitic covenants and as reiterated variously in Deuteronomy—the Lord will set Israel "in praise and in fame and in honor high above all nations that he has made" (26:19 ESV)—then its people need a leader full of divine wisdom.[80]

At this wider canonical level, however, we encounter multiple interpretive and theological and related missiological considerations, all of which are interrelated. Exegetically, the questions are legion and concern contested scholarly understandings of the relationship between chapter 34 and in particular the book of Deuteronomy and in general the Torah and subsequent historical material from Joshua and Judges onward. Theologically, the problem is most acute when we consider Joshua's leadership as involving the conquest of Canaan and the authorized genocide, if not actually carried out, under the dictates of Yahweh himself. Without minimizing the severity of the deity's instruction to the people to "utterly destroy" the existing inhabitants of the land (Deut. 7:2) as well as hardening their hearts in the process (see 2:30–31; cf. Josh. 11:20), the associations between chosen and elect versus unchosen and damned that seem obvious on the rhetorical surface of the text are much less binary from other perspectives. First, it is unlikely that such genocide occurred historically (and likely instead that occupants of the land of Canaan had opportunities to embrace the God of Israel as did Rahab and the Gibeonites in Joshua 2 and 9, respectively). Second, perhaps the later generations responsible for the canonical formation of the Pentateuch and historical books were desirous of emphasizing that Israel failed to live faithfully before Yahweh and did not fear that naming the seductive nations (e.g., Deut. 7:1) in such stark anti-elect terms risked xenophobic reaction since these "nations" no longer existed in the land.[81] To be sure, these lines of response are simplistic in the face of one of the deepest theological problems and questions in the Bible,[82] but enough has been said to discern at least a possible missiological application.

(Grand Rapids: Eerdmans, 1998), 151–55. Unfortunately, Millar leaves this material on blessing unresolved vis-à-vis the material regarding the Canaanite genocide (see below).

80. See discussion on "The Privilege of Calling: The Mosaic Paradigm for Missions (Deut 26:16–19)," which is chap. 7 of Daniel I. Block, *How I Love Your Torah, O Lord! Studies in the Book of Deuteronomy* (Eugene, OR: Cascade, 2011).

81. See Lohr, *Chosen and Unchosen*, chap. 6, esp. 161–67. Note that despite Lohr's title, his argument is that unchosen/chosen is not a binary construct and that, particularly in the Pentateuch, the unchosen are not objects of mission and not outside the scope of divine love but are also invited to respond to God. See also Charlie Trimm, "Did YHWH Condemn the Nations When He Elected Israel? YHWH's Disposition toward Non-Israelites in the Torah," *JETS* 55:3 (2012): 521–36.

82. To say just a bit more, I am dissatisfied with at least the predominant evangelical proposals intended to alleviate the problem of the genocidal character of the conquest narratives, taken on their own. For instance, in Stanley N. Gundry, ed., *Show Them No Mercy: Four Views on God*

I suggest that no matter the provenance of Deuteronomy 34,[83] a canonical reading of this passage understands it as symbolic of the transition of leadership from Moses to Joshua. Understood in this sense, this thirty-fourth chapter communicates at least this important missiological point: the renewal of the covenant (looking backward through the book of Deuteronomy) is important not only for Israel's ongoing life (looking ahead to Joshua and the conquest)[84] but also for how the people of God can yet bear adequate witness to Yahweh amid and among their complicated and conflicted relationship with the nations.[85] More to the point, Israel is to bear witness to its God by being distinguished from the nations: worshiping Yahweh rather than their gods; having a king who is attentive to the divine law rather than one that acts as do other kings that lord it over their peoples (Deut. 17:14–20); and being led not by the practice of sorcery and divination but by Yahweh's appointed prophets (18:9–22), among other distinctions.[86] Moses becomes the

---

and Canaanite Genocide (Grand Rapids: Zondervan, 2003), Wesleyan and dispensationalist discontinuationists privilege christological or gospel (good news) hermeneutical approaches but seem to undermine the authority of these sections of the Old Testament, while Lutheran and Reformed continuationists emphasize eschatological or spiritual-typological interpretive strategies but minimize, ignore, or appear to explain away the plain sense if not historicity of these texts. Better—and consistent with what is said in the preceding note—is Paul Copan, *Is God a Moral Monster? Making Sense of the Old Testament Data* (Grand Rapids: Baker Books, 2011), esp. chaps. 15–17, which highlights the hyperbolic character of ancient Near Eastern literary construals that in turn allow us to understand how other strands of the Jewish scriptures can testify to the eventual salvation and redemption of at least the Philistine inhabitants of Canaan (e.g., Zech. 9:7; Ps. 87:4–6). Building on platforms such as this, my own pentecostal and pneumatological approach also insists on the need for the plurality of these perspectives as checking, balancing, interrogating, and stretching each other, all the while being attentive to historical realities that include how these texts have been appropriated for postbiblical and colonial purposes, especially including the conquest of Native America (which interestingly receives scant reference from the contributors to Gundry's book). See also Amos Yong and Barbara Brown Zikmund, eds., *Remembering Jamestown: Hard Questions about Christian Mission* (Eugene, OR: Pickwick, 2010). More on this important issue in the next chapter.

83. Randall Heskett provides as coherent an account as any of the historical-critical matters while respecting the canonical shape of the final text and the need for faithful reception and reading of such as scripture. "Deuteronomy 29–34 and the Formation of the Torah," in *The Bible as a Human Witness to Divine Revelation: Hearing the Word of God through Historically Dissimilar Traditions*, ed. Randall Heskett and Brian Irwin (New York: T&T Clark, 2012), 32–50.

84. See E. Theodore Mullen Jr., *Narrative History and Ethnic Boundaries: The Deuteronomistic Historian and the Creation of Israelite National Identity* (Atlanta: Scholars Press, 1993), chap. 3, which explicates covenant renewal in relationship to ethnic formation in ancient Israel, especially during and after the exile.

85. On covenant renewal as not only a central theme but also a leading missiological motif in Deuteronomy, see Petros Vassiliadis, "God's Will for His People: Deuteronomy 6:20–25," *IRM* 77:306 (1988): 179–84.

86. See discussion in Mark O'Brien, "Deuteronomy 16.18–18.22: Meeting the Challenge of Towns and Nations," *JSOT* 33:2 (2008): 155–72.

prototypical prophet (18:15, 17) and even paradigmatic prophet-missioner or missionary that leads Israel's exemplary witness to others (26:16–19),[87] and it is in his footsteps and "spirit" that Joshua is now appointed as prophetic leader of Israel anticipating settling in the land provided to them by Yahweh.

Joshua's track record as unfolded through the conquest narratives may not be exemplary when considered in postcolonial perspective. His just treatment of Rahab (Josh. 2) and the Gibeonites (Josh. 9) do not justify the violence wreaked on the indigenous women and children land-dwellers explicit elsewhere in the book of Joshua. Yet there is no downplaying Joshua's attempt to remain faithful to Yahweh throughout his life. This is evident in his encouragement of Israel's continued faithfulness in following his example: "As for me and my house, we will serve the LORD" (24:15 ESV). In that sense, Joshua is the worthy divinely enabled and inspired successor to Moses. Hence, recognizing Joshua as one "full of the spirit of wisdom" is not to assert a flawless character but to acknowledge that he leads in the authority and spirit of Moses (cf. Num. 27:20). Such leadership emerges from encounter with the living God, and it is only through such dynamic relationship that the covenant is to be both renewed and abided by.[88] If Joshua lives into his vocation not out of his natural charismatic abilities but in and through the divine breath, then the witness of Israel to the nations also succeeds only by the *ruah* of Yahweh.

This indispensability of the divine wind must be further noted when considering the implications of this text for contemporary theology of mission. Recall that Joshua's ruahic installation as the next leader of Israel under the hand of Moses occurs because the latter specifically asks Yahweh to be mindful of his people: "Let the LORD, the God of the spirits of all flesh, appoint someone over the congregation who shall go out before them and come in before them, who shall lead them out and bring them in, so that the congregation of the LORD may not be like sheep without a shepherd" (Num. 27:16–17). Interestingly, in this passage "the God of the spirits of all flesh" identifies the God *of Israel*. The only other time this phrase appears is when the destruction of Israel is threatened by the sins of Korah, Dathan, and Abiram (Num. 16). There Moses pleads on behalf of Israel by naming

---

87. Daniel I. Block, "The Privilege of Calling: The Mosaic Paradigm for Missions (Deut. 26:16–19)," *BSac* 162 (2005): 387–405.

88. Thus, pentecostal biblical scholar Rickie D. Moore argues that the written law of Sinai is mediated to the covenantal community at the threshold of the promised land (at Mount Horeb) through the living voice of Yahweh, thus bringing forward to the people of God a dynamic word for their present; see *The Spirit of the Old Testament*, JPTSup 35 (Blandford Forum, UK: Deo, 2011), chaps. 2–3, titled "Canon and Charisma in the Book of Deuteronomy" and "Deuteronomy and the Fire of God: A Critical Charismatic Interpretation."

Yahweh as "the God of the spirits of all flesh" (16:22 ESV), in effect addressing Yahweh as the creator *of all life*,[89] and thus with a special obligation to sustain rather than eradicate such life, even when these living beings are the enemies of God. Within this context, Israel not only lives among and is called to bear witness to the nations, but Yahweh is also "Most High" over all the nations (Deut. 32:8).[90] Human participation in the mission of God thus unfolds under ambiguous circumstances, and this necessitates that those who might emerge amid the *missio Dei* are inspirited by the wind of Yahweh to stand in the gap on behalf of all others that exist merely via the breath of life.

Discussion Questions

1. We commonly associate the divine spirit with the breath of life, and we see that in the creation narratives of the Bible; but we less often connect the divine wind with destruction and judgment. What role, if any, does the theme of judgment play in contemporary Christian mission and witness?

2. The Torah gives us at least two instances—Pharaoh and Balaam—of pagans recognizing the presence and activity of the divine spirit (and more examples will be seen later in the Old Testament, e.g., Babylonian regents). How might it affect our understanding of Christian witness among unbelievers if it is possible they would also have such discerning capacities?

3. Israel was called to represent the other nations and peoples of the world before God. What might it mean for the church to embrace a similar missional or missiological vocation?

---

89. Martin Noth comments on this phrase here in Numbers 16: "*rūah*, in the plural here, is to be understood in this [universal] sense" (*Numbers*, 127). That this phrase is also well attested in postbiblical literature (e.g., Jubilees 10:3; 2 Maccabees 3:24; 14:46; cf. Philip J. Budd, *Numbers*, WBC 5 [Waco: Word, 1984], 188) is suggestive not only of a later exilic or postexilic date for this material in Numbers but also that its considerations are being forged against a wider transnational horizon including the nations.

90. Whether directly over the nations or indirectly if Yahweh reserves Israel particularly for his chosen and special possession; see N. Wyatt, "The Seventy Sons of Athirat, the Nations of the World, Deuteronomy 32.6b, 8–9, and the Myth of Divine Election," in *Reflection and Refraction: Studies in Biblical Historiography in Honour of A. Graeme Auld*, ed. Robert Rezetko, Timothy H. Lim, and W. Brian Aucker, Supplements to Vetus Testamentum 113 (Leiden: Brill, 2007), 547–56.

2

The Spirits of Ancient Israel

Ambiguity in Mission

Introduction

This chapter focuses on what in the Tanakh is usually known as the Former Prophets (*Nevi'im Rishonim*): Joshua through 2 Kings (Ruth excepted). But we begin with Judges because the divine wind does not appear in the first book in this section. Within the guild of biblical studies, some hypothesize that this collection of biblical books, plus Deuteronomy (which from the canonical perspective is usually included with the first four books and together called the Pentateuch), is the result of the work of an editor or a group of editors from the seventh to the fifth century BCE identified as the *Deuteronomist* historian or school.[1] While variously accepted and contested in scholarship on the Old Testament, much of this reconstruction is speculative.[2] In this

---

1. This is a theory with a long history stretching back to the mid-nineteenth century. The argument for a single editor came into prominence with Martin Noth's *Überlieferungsgeschichtliche Studien*, 2nd ed. (Halle: M. Niemeyer, 1943); *The Deuteronomistic History*, trans. David J. A. Clines et al., JSOTSup 15 (Sheffield: University of Sheffield, 1981).

2. Hans Ausloos, *The Deuteronomist's History: The Role of the Deuteronomist in Historical-Critical Research into Genesis-Numbers*, Oudtestamentische Studiën 67 (Leiden: Brill, 2015), 259, summarizes the available positions—e.g., "pre-Deuteronomic, proto-Deuteronomic, Deuteronomic, Deuteronomistic, late-Deuteronomistic, post-Deuteronomistic and anti-Deuteronom(ist)ic," with the former *Deuteronomic* related to theories concerning the canonical book of Deuteronomy and the latter *Deuteronomistic* concerning schemes regarding the historical material especially from Deuteronomy through 2 Kings—which is indicative of the contestedness of the field. There has even emerged what some have called a *pan-Deuteronomistic* theory that effectively sees the legacy of the Deuteronomist historian (or historians) as influencing not just this collection of

chapter, I will periodically refer to the Deuteronomist not because I am convinced of its definitiveness but since it is presumed in some of the scholarly
literature that we will be engaging and it serves as a convenient shorthand for
discussing this group of historical books. What is not under dispute is that
what is recorded in these texts emerged into prominence during the centuries
leading up to the exile to Babylon and they recount a retributive theology and
provide at least one explanation for why the covenant people, recipients of
the promises made to Moses first and David later, have been taken into exile
(because of their unfaithfulness).

What is important to note is that if Torah is about the calling and liberation of a nation out of all nations, then the history of ancient Israel is about
this chosen people's—and its kings'—(oppositional) relationship vis-à-vis
these other nations. On the one hand, as it is political states that make and
write history,[3] it ought not to be surprising that in the re-narration of this
account, Israel is understood normatively and the others subordinately. After
all, nation building involves securing borders and developing a core identity
capable of negotiating alliances, so we would not expect anything less (manifest in §§2.4, 2.6),[4] and this is rather urgent leading up to and during the
exile when these texts were collected and preserved precisely because they
nurtured such an identity under the felt threat of extinction. On the other
hand, for our missiological purposes and from the perspective of the election
of Israel to be a priestly representative of Yahweh to the nations, this historical reconstruction (whether of the Deuteronomist or otherwise) of Israel
over against its neighbors is a bit more problematic. What is undeniable is
that the same tension of the divine wind as both life-giving and life-denying
evident in the Pentateuch is also evident across the ruahic dynamics in these
historical books, whether in terms of the spiral of violence enwrapping the
judges, the intramural intrigue between the Saulide and Davidic monarchies
and their crises,[5] or the international wars described across these pages.

---

books but practically the entire Jewish canon. For these and related ongoing debates, see Linda S.
Schearing and Steven L. McKenzie, eds., *Those Elusive Deuteronomists: The Phenomenon of
Pan-Deuteronomism*, JSOTSup 268 (Sheffield: Sheffield Academic, 1999); and Thomas C. Römer,
ed., *The Future of the Deuteronomistic History*, BETL 147 (Leuven: Leuven University Press
and Uitgeverij Peeters, 2000).

3. We are reminded about this by Ben C. Ollenburger, "Gerhard von Rad's Theory of Holy
War," in *Holy War in Ancient Israel*, trans. Marva J. Dawn (Grand Rapids: Eerdmans, 1991),
1–33, here 16.

4. F. F. Bruce, *Israel and the Nations: From the Exodus to the Fall of the Second Temple*
(Grand Rapids: Eerdmans, 1985).

5. A. D. H. Mayes, "The Rise of the Israelite Monarchy," *ZAW* 90 (1978): 1–19; Dennis J.
McCarthy, "The Inauguration of Monarchy in Israel: A Form-Critical Study of I Samuel 8–12,"
Int 27 (1993): 401–12.

The abiding question from these texts for contemporary missiology in a postcolonial and postmodern time is whether and how Christian witness can persist apart from nationalistic sentiments and tribalistic commitments. Indeed, can these texts that are (centripetally) absorbed with Israel's self-establishment, discovery, and preservation serve as any kind of springboard for thinking (centrifugally) about mission outward to the nations as in the classical paradigm?

Yet the *other* in this chapter involves not only the non-Israelite nations but also the religious traditions and practices of the residents of the land of Canaan that were perceived as hazards to Israel's holiness perhaps paradoxically from both within and without. The former relates to the fact that in the conquest of Canaan there is as much mixing going on between the tribes and their existing inhabitants—seen in terms also of how the "fight" against Baal (see §2.5) is a local affair around Mount Carmel—while the latter relates to the intermarriages between Israel and those in other nations, as in the Solomonic alliances. The overarching Israelite trajectory here is from the original cultic origins of Yahweh as warrior that are tempered during monarchy,[6] through a course of adjustment especially via prophetic criticisms in and around royal courts, to a much greater sense of national awareness of being related to other surrounding peoples (outside cultic contexts).[7] In terms of the interreligious dynamics of ancient Israel, however, the same tension exists. On the one hand, the ongoing development of monotheistic tendencies prompts an intensifyingly vehement exclusivistic and competitive attitude toward other religious neighbors and their practices.[8] On the other hand, there existed a more relativistic and pluralistic posture that allowed others to worship their own deities so long as these were not attractive to the covenant people.[9] Missiological questions remain for us from these ancient Israelite times. How do we engage people of other faiths in a post-Christian and certainly post-Christendom time, not only in historically so-called Christian national environments but also where

6. Walther Zimmerli, *The Old Testament and the World*, trans. John J. Scullion (Atlanta: John Knox, 1976), chap. 5.

7. Gerhard von Rad, *Holy War in Ancient Israel*, trans. Marva J. Dawn (Grand Rapids: Eerdmans, 1991).

8. These religious developments are described in Morton Smith, *Palestinian Parties and Politics That Shaped the Old Testament*, 2nd ed. (London: SCM, 1987), chap. 2. Instructively for us, Smith comments, "In the ancient world foreign policy was expressed in religious ceremonies" (29), including cultic sites and marriages, and that the prophets were constantly rebuking and warning against these indicates their widespread pervasiveness.

9. See Robert Goldenberg, *The Nations That Know Thee Not: Ancient Jewish Attitudes toward Other Religions* (Washington Square: New York University Press, 1998). Some of the more relaxed attitudes include those seen in Deut. 4:19; 29:25–26; Judg. 11:23–24; Ruth 1:15–16; 2 Kings 5:18; Dan. 10; Jon. 1:5–6; and Mic. 4:5.

Christians are minority or marginal groups in other (non-Christian) political states and regions?

If, as this chapter shows, tribalistic- and monarchic-funded aggression against outsiders undermines rather than fuels Israel's vocation, which is to be a light and witness to the nations, then how can we receive the testimonies of early Israel for our missiological reconstruction today? We have seen in the first chapter that the divine wind liberates the people of God from Egypt, so now we will observe how the *ruah* can be understood, broadly speaking, to be "building up the household of faith."[10] The missiological question is what this means for the *others*—political, transnational, and religious—that are supposed to be the recipients of the people of God's (priestly) witness.

2.1   Judges, Part 1—The Wind of Yahweh: Defensive Mission?

The canonical book of Judges, with its bloodshed and gruesome violence, is a challenge for any biblical theology of mission. At their best, missiological readings of Judges point out that the judges are deliverers, effectively those sent by God to save Israel, or that the book epitomizes the cosmic battle between goodness and evil, between God and the powers of sin and rebelliousness.[11] As is well known, the stories of the judges involve the cyclical movement of the tribes of Israel being seduced by the idolatry of their neighbors, being subjugated under foreign kings and their armies, calling to God from out of their pain and suffering, and then experiencing liberation through the divine empowerment of a judge who leads them to overthrow the yoke of oppression. But the missiological problem is at least twofold. First, those to whom Israel is supposed to be "a priestly nation" (Exod. 19:6; see §1.4 above) lead Israel astray. Thus, Yahweh warned, "They shall become adversaries to you, and their gods shall be a snare to you" (Judg. 2:3). Second, and relatedly, these same names are targeted, by divine authorization no less, for obliteration and extermination: "But as for the towns of these peoples that the LORD your God is giving you as an inheritance, you must not let anything that breathes remain alive. You shall annihilate them—the Hittites and the Amorites, the Canaanites

---

10. Morris A. Inch, *The Saga of the Spirit: A Biblical, Systematic, and Historical Theology of the Holy Spirit* (Grand Rapids: Baker, 1985), 51.

11. The former emphasis is part of one paragraph on Judges in Christopher J. H. Wright, *The Mission of God's People: A Biblical Theology of the Church's Mission* (Grand Rapids: Zondervan, 2010), 205, while the latter derives from a whole subsection (of just over one page in length) in Arthur F. Glasser, with Charles E. Van Engen, Dean S. Gilliland, and Shawn B. Redford, *Announcing God's Kingdom: The Story of God's Mission in the Bible* (Grand Rapids: Baker Academic, 2003), 99–100.

and the Perizzites, the Hivites and the Jebusites—just as the LORD your God has commanded, so that they may not teach you to do all the abhorrent things that they do for their gods, and you thus sin against the LORD your God" (Deut. 20:16–18; cf. Lev. 20:22–23 and Judg. 3:1–6). If from a missiological perspective the people of God are to participate in the *missio Dei* to save the world, it is no wonder that the narratives of the judges are often marginalized if not altogether absent in mission theology. The nations in Judges are not the objects of Israel's witness as much as, initially, subjects of God's testing of the Israelites' devotion and commitment (Judg. 2:22; 3:1, 4) and, subsequently, targets of the deity's holy and destructive will.

As already indicated (§1.7), the difficulties related to commands to decimate the indigenous inhabitants of the land might be alleviated at least in part when we see these native dwellers less as contemporary people groups at the time of writing and canonization than as symbolic of the kinds of practices perceived as threatening the monotheistic devotion of postexilic Israel.[12] As these named groups (e.g., the seven nations in Deut. 7:1 and the six in Judg. 3:5) are primordial rather than historical references, designated in hindsight, as it were, from the standpoint of the Deuteronomistic historian (as reconstructed by scholars) or of editors or redactors during or following the Babylonian exile when these texts were finalized,[13] it is easier to call for the extermination of those from a time in the past than of current and actual neighbors.[14] Yet this does not minimize the fact that the rationales given for their not being able to coexist with Israel had to do with their worshiping of other deities and their immorality (e.g., Deut. 7:5; 9:4). Intriguingly, there is continuous evidence that the natives of Canaan were never thoroughly eradicated, and were even assimilated, to some degree, into the life of Israel, whether because some of them, as destitute foreigners and supportive aliens, were initially welcomed into the Yahwistic community or whether they were later forcibly subordinated by judges and monarchs in the service of the Israelite state (cf. Exod. 12:48–49; 20:20; Deut. 5:14, with 1 Kings 9:20–21). Part of my point is that the fortunes of the nations had been inextricably intertwined with

12. Edwin C. Hostetter highlights the relationship of these aboriginal peoples to their promised land as being one of the major impulses underneath the biblical authors' categorizations; see *Nations Mightier and More Numerous: The Biblical View of Palestine's Pre-Israelite Peoples*, BIBAL Dissertation Series 3 (Berkeley: BIBAL, 1995), 142–43.

13. See, e.g., Kristin A. Swanson, "Judges as a Parody of Leadership in the Persian Period," in *Focusing Biblical Studies: The Crucial Nature of the Persian and Hellenistic Periods—Essays in Honor of Douglas A. Knight*, ed. Jon L. Berquist and Alice Hunt (New York: T&T Clark, 2012), 94–106.

14. See also Lawrence M. Wills, *Not God's People: Insiders and Outsiders in the Biblical World* (Lanham, MD: Rowman & Littlefield, 2008), 31–34.

that of Israel from the beginning, regardless of the strong "us-them" rhetoric prevalent through the Hebrew writings.

We will consider these issues throughout the remainder of this chapter, but for the moment, what if we were to reconsider the book of Judges from a ruahological perspective? There are here seven references to the presence and activity of the *ruah* of Yahweh: on Othniel (Judg. 3:10), Gideon (6:34), Jephthah (11:29), and Samson (four references in chaps. 13–15, to be discussed in §2.2). The divine wind enables Othniel to prevail over King Cushan-rishathaim of Aram, while the spirit leads Gideon to mobilize the Abiezrites, "the weakest in Manasseh" (6:15 ESV), and those from other tribes to resist, and eventually repel, the invading Midianites. The case of Jephthah is a bit different, as it says only that upon the arrival of the divine breath, he "passed through Gilead and Manasseh and passed on to Mizpah of Gilead, and from Mizpah of Gilead he passed on to the Ammonites" (11:29 ESV), defeating eventually the latter antagonists through the enablement of the wind of Yahweh. In between, however, he makes his fateful vow, an apparent attempt to secure Yahweh's favor by promising a sacrificial offering in return (as if not fully trusting the divinity, the text suggests), which turns out to be his only daughter (11:30–34).[15]

As there are many more judges in the book than these four, the question arises as to why the divine *ruah* is mentioned only in these cases.[16] With regard to Othniel's exploits, this account established "the five-element pattern for the subsequent [judge] narratives in Judges: sin, punishment, crying out, salvation, and quiet,"[17] so that the intervention of the divine breath can also

---

15. As suggested by Barbara Miller, *Tell It on the Mountain: The Daughter of Jephthah in Judges 11* (Collegeville, MN: Liturgical Press, 2005), 6. Similarly, in Gideon's case, "the divine spirit is sufficient to counteract fear . . . but not skepticism," as reflected in the fact that this deliverer of Israel still had to put out fleeces before Yahweh after receiving the spirit; see Lillian R. Klein, *The Triumph of Irony in the Book of Judges*, Bible and Literature Series 14 (Sheffield: Sheffield Academic, 1988), 55.

16. The suggestion that Deborah also acts as one under the spirit because she is identified explicitly as a prophetess (Judg. 4:4)—made by George T. Montague, *The Holy Spirit: Growth of a Biblical Tradition* (Peabody, MA: Hendrickson, 1994), 18—is unconvincing, if not irrefutable as an "argument" from silence.

17. Rodney Steven Sadler Jr., *Can a Cushite Change His Skin? An Examination of Race, Ethnicity, and Othering in the Hebrew Canon*, LHBOTS 425 (New York: T&T Clark, 2005), 108. Note that Sadler's analysis of the Othniel passage is focused on the Aramite king Cushan-rishathaim (Judg. 3:7–11), observing that, even if the Cushan connections or identity of this figure are ambiguous, this text is "the only instance where a Cush-related ethnic term is used to mock or deride a foe in the Hebrew canon" (112), understandable with regard to the function of such derision in this Judges context, albeit not representative of a broad spectrum of references to Cush across the Old Testament, including numerous indications of their final submission to and salvation by God (see Ps. 68:31; 87:3–4; Isa. 18:1–7; Zeph. 3:10; cf. Jer. 39:15–18).

be presumed to be part of Yahweh's deliverance in the subsequent episodes. Beyond this consideration, it can also be observed that each of those is specifically indicated to be enabled by the spirit to fend off military incursions from geographical areas beyond the land of Canaan. Othniel defends in the south (against the Mesopotamians), Gideon in the north (against the Midianites), Jephthah in the east (against the Ammonites), and Samson contests in the west (against the Philistines). An argument could be made that these ruahic references are representative of Yahweh's intention to completely deliver Israel and secure its peaceful habitation of the land promised to Abraham and his descendants.[18] What is undeniable within the scope of the Judges narrative is that despite Israel's repeated unfaithfulness, Yahweh is not uncompassionate when Israel "cried out" to the Lord under enemy subjugation (e.g., Judg. 3:9; 6:6–7; cf. 2:18), and the sending of his spirit to raise up liberators is a direct response to their cry.[19] Yet even from this perspective, God is also understood as empowering Israel to dispossess the surrounding nations (11:24), at least of their lands, if not also of their lives, and hence the wind of God exacerbates missiology as a problem rather than inspires witness to Yahweh.

I would like, however, to suggest another perspective on the breath of Yahweh, one that follows the structure provided by Yahweh's three speeches in the book: that of setting up the story's main tension regarding whether or not Israel will be faithful to the covenant (Judg. 2:1–5); that in which there is a midpoint assessment regarding Israel's persisting infidelity, which intensifies the tension (6:7–10); and that which denounces Israel for its disloyalty despite Yahweh's continuing salvation (10:11–16), thereby collapsing the tension and opening up to the disintegration in the last half of the book.[20]

18. This theory is briefly articulated by John Ragsdale, "Why Some and Not Others: A Proposal Concerning the Deuteronomistic Historian's Association of the Divine Spirit with Othniel, Gideon, Jephthah and Samson" (paper presented to the 38th annual meeting of the Society for Pentecostal Studies, Eugene Bible College, Eugene, Oregon, March 2009). Ragsdale further suggests that such a geographical consideration of the ruahology of Judges is consistent with, if not anticipates, that in the book of Acts when the outpouring of the spirit empowers the witness of Jesus "to the ends of the earth" (Acts 1:8). I would further note, from personal correspondence with Rick Wadholm, that the ruahic fight in Judges is more explicit against intruders from outside Canaan than against the (seven or six) nations under the Deuteronomic ban.

19. As compellingly argued by Michael Welker, *God the Spirit*, trans. John F. Hoffmeyer (Minneapolis: Fortress, 1994), 52–65.

20. For this threefold scheme demarcated by Yahweh's speeches, see Lee Roy Martin, *The Unheard Voice of God: A Pentecostal Hearing of the Book of Judges*, JPTSup 32 (Blandford Forum, UK: Deo, 2008), esp. chap. 4. While both J. Paul Tanner, "The Gideon Narrative as the Focal Point of Judges," *BSac* 149:594 (1992): 146–61; and L. Juliana M. Claassens, "The Character of God in Judges 6–8: The Gideon Narrative as Theological and Moral Resource," *Horizons in Biblical Theology* 23:1 (2001): 51–71, consider the Gideon story as the fulcrum upon which Judges turns, this is consistent with Martin's view that what happens with Gideon

Within this framework, then, the first three references to the divine breath can be correlated with these divine speeches. The wind's blowing on Othniel makes good on Yahweh's promise to be with Israel even in its time of trouble. Next, the breath's presence with Gideon—literally being clothed with Gideon, as if residing within him[21]—testifies to Yahweh's resolve amid, even within the depths of, Israel's increasing instability, volatility, and unreliability, particularly when viewed through Gideon's own post-ruahic leadership of the people into idolatry (8:22–28). And despite this failure, God's wind still brings about victory through Jephthah but also, surely because of Israel's stubborn waywardness, precipitates its dissolution into chaos and anarchy as symbolized by the ruin of Jephthah and the destruction of his innocent daughter (with things getting even worse with Samson and the rest of the book, as we shall see next). From this perspective, the charismatic endowments of the spirit are for the salvation of Israel, reflecting Yahweh's passion to keep covenant with Israel (neither provoking nor preventing the judges' failings in the process),[22] in effect sustaining hope against hope despite and amid Israel's inexorable ruin as those given the breath of life who continue in their insubordination.[23]

What then is the missiological lesson for us at this midpoint of the Judges narrative? To be sure, our commissioning for the *missio spiritus* can enable our participation in the redemptive work of God even as it can devolve into our own agendas, replete with cultural ethnocentrism, economic imperialism, political colonialism, and religious fanaticism. If we think ourselves immune from such seductions, we need only to consider the judges and the spiral of violence unleashed in a history where the spirit was still visibly present. Attempting to discern the *missio spiritus* in Judges thus invites us to think about

intensifies the plot, which presses the question about Israel's faithfulness, with the resulting persistence of disobedience leading then to the denouement—the beginning of the end, as it were—featured in the Jephthah account.

21. Tetsuo Sasaki writes, "These three examples [Judg. 6:34; 1 Chron. 12:19; 2 Chron. 24:20] can be translated as 'the Spirit puts on a person'; that is, the Spirit (the subject), is located on the inside, and the person (the object), is located on the outside"; part of his point, rightfully made, is that in the end Israel's wars are won not by their armies but by the power of Israel's God. Sasaki, *The Concept of War in the Book of Judges: A Strategical Evaluation of the Wars of Gideon, Deborah, Samson, and Abimelech* (Tokyo: Gakujutsu Tosho Shuppan-Sha, 2001), 92.

22. See Lee Roy Martin, "Power to Save!? The Role of the Spirit of the Lord in the Book of Judges," *JPT* 16:2 (2008): 21–50, here 41. I prefer Martin's way of putting it than to say that the charismatic empowerment of the *ruah Yahweh* in this book leads to violence also, as suggested by Mieke Bal, *Death and Dissymmetry: The Politics of Coherence in the Book of Judges* (Chicago: University of Chicago Press, 1988), 132–33.

23. Thus, the spirit "works redemptively with the sometimes grim realities of a prodigal people of God, sometimes to chastise, on other occasions to console, and to deliver when the time was ripe" (Inch, *Saga of the Spirit*, 38).

Mission Begins "at Home" among the People of God

William Lacy Lane, professor of biblical studies, Faculdade
Teológica Sul Americana,Londrina, Brazil

If the historical books of the Old Testament and Israel's aggression against
the nations were ever excuses for a missionary imperialistic enterprise, a
missio spiritus theology will clarify that the primary aim of the divine *ruah's*
restoring action in these books is God's own people. Not the nations, but
Israel itself had to come to terms with God's covenantal bindings in order to
be a witness to God's saving justice. As it remained faithful to the covenant,
Israel became a community of justice and compassion. Postcolonial and
postmodern readers of mission theology must approach these stories in a
humble and confessing attitude and be willing to discern the winds of new
possibilities in mission thinking and practice. Furthermore, a *missio spiritus* will
guide us away from replicating the ideological, social, economic, and cultural
domineering structures of secular society into our own missionary activity.

---

how the spirit of God might check our imprudent zealousness (here the spirit
decommissions us and our misguided agendas, even as we ought to detangle
our own aspirations from divine commissions). More importantly, it suggests
that the mission of the spirit, while always replete with implications for our
relations and engagement with others, is no less concerned with us, with
how we are to live in faithfulness into the covenant story of God. Without
the latter, the *missio Dei* will unravel, perhaps even brutally.

2.2   Judges, Part 2—Spirit and Strength: Diffusing "Mission"?

If the Jephthah narrative signals the beginning of the end of Israel's generations under judges and foreign rule, then we can understand why his judgeship
lasts only six years, a relatively short span compared to the eighty years with
Ehud and the forty with Othniel, Deborah, and Gideon (cf. Judg. 3:11, 30;
5:31; 8:28; 12:7), and that it was all downhill after that, as the saying goes.
After Jephthah, as if the ending to that story wasn't bad enough, the account
turns to the tragedy of Samson (Judg. 13–16) and, worse, the idolatry of
Micah and the Danites (chaps. 17–18), the ghastly rape and murder of the
Levite's concubine by the Benjamites (chaps. 19–20), and the decimation,

almost extinction, of this tribe (chap. 21). If the first half of Judges recounts
Yahweh's repeated deliverance of Israel from their suffering, even through the
hands of those unqualified and perhaps even uninterested in being liberators,[24]
the second half is dominated not by Yahweh's intervention (although that
is not wholly absent) but by Israel's descent, headlong after Jephthah, as it
were, into catastrophic national mayhem and disaster.

It is within this context that we find the Samson saga.[25] His exploits are well
known, legendary even, leading modern scholars to question his historicity.
Even for those who are disinclined to dismiss the historical authenticity of
this narrative, questions persist about its lengthiness (no other judge is given
as much time or space as Samson) and its role in the book. Perhaps the final
redactor of Judges was either acquainted with Samson or a close contemporary.[26] Although we do not need to resolve these issues, from our vantage
point this longest of stories about a single judge also includes four references
to the wind of Yahweh.

The first occasion sets the stage for understanding Samson's as what might
be called a spirit-empowered life, since we are told, "The woman [the wife
of Manoah, father of Samson] bore a son, and named him Samson. The boy
grew, and the LORD blessed him. The spirit of the LORD began to stir him in
Mahaneh-dan, between Zorah and Eshtaol" (Judg. 13:24–25).[27] We are told
next, in the context of Yahweh's "seeking a pretext to act against the Philistines" (14:4) and Samson's journeying to court to marry a Philistine woman
from their town, Timnah, "suddenly a young lion roared at him. The spirit
of the LORD rushed on him, and he tore the lion apart with his bare hands
as one might tear apart a kid" (14:5–6). Then, when the Philistines extracted
information from his wife in order to answer a riddle Samson posed to stump
them—the resolution of which left him indebted to them rather than vice
versa—he was livid: "Then the spirit of the LORD rushed on him, and he went
down to Ashkelon [another important Philistine center]. He killed thirty men

24. Daniel I. Block, "Empowered by the Spirit of God: The Holy Spirit in the Historiographic
Writings of the Old Testament," *Southern Baptist Journal of Theology* 1:1 (1997): 42–61, here 45.
25. An excellent scholarly study is Pnina Galpaz-Feller, *Samson: The Hero and the Man—
The Story of Samson (Judges 13–16)*, Bible in History 7 (Bern: Peter Lang, 2006).
26. The orderly and well-constructed Samson narrative suggests the unit's formulation did
not depend on having to sort through underlying documents or traditions; see C. J. Goslinga,
Joshua, Judges, Ruth, trans. Ray Togtman (Grand Rapids: Regency Reference Library, 1986),
209–10 and 402–10, for more on this authorial hypothesis and a more conservative approach
defending the coherence of the Samson literary unit.
27. The Hebrew verb translated "to stir" is "used only four times elsewhere in the Old Testament, always with the meaning of 'to trouble' (Gen. 41.8; Ps. 77.5; Dan. 2.1, 3)." Lloyd R. Neve,
The Spirit of God in the Old Testament (Cleveland, TN: CPT, 2011), 19.

of the town, took their spoil, and gave the festal garments to those who had explained the riddle. In hot anger, he went back to his father's house" (14:19). Interestingly, after the Ashkelon carnage, there is another event wherein Samson inflicts a "great slaughter" on the Philistines (15:8) about which no mention of the *ruah* is made. Yet shortly thereafter, he gives three thousand Judeans (15:11) permission to broker an exchange with the Philistines—himself to the latter (Philistines) for some relief for the former (Judeans)—and is bound and handed to them. Then the final mention of the *ruah* unfolds: "When . . . the Philistines came shouting to meet him; and the spirit of the LORD rushed on him, and the ropes that were on his arms became like flax that has caught fire, and his bonds melted off his hands. Then he found a fresh jawbone of a donkey, reached down and took it, and with it he killed a thousand men" (15:14–15). In each of these last three cases, the wind of Yahweh "rushed on him," as if violently, resulting in his own increasingly vicious response, each time taking a greater toll on other lives than before.[28]

One way to appreciate the ruahology of the life of Samson is to understand that he, and Israel with him, is saved on numerous occasions from the threatening Philistines by the *ruah* Yahweh. On the other hand, similar to the manifestations of the wind of Yahweh in the first half of Judges, the salvific presence and activity of divine spirit neither condones nor inhibits his deadly deeds. At the same time, even if few of the commentaries I consulted make any effort to explain the larger number of references to the breath of Yahweh in the Samson narrative compared to the first half of the book,[29] perhaps there is also a parallel here to the spirit's movements as structured by the previously discussed speeches of Yahweh. After the narrator introduces Samson's public ministry as one stirred by the divine wind, this tripartite frame can be discerned. The saving of Samson from the lion may from this perspective be understood as confirming his appearance as deliverer, here setting up the tension of confrontation with the Philistines comparable to the Othniel account. The next manifestation of the spirit's power marks a turning point, like that in the Gideon story, as, amid the wide range of possibilities opened up before him for responding to the Philistines' solving his riddle, Samson responds violently instead, killing thirty Ashkelonites. From this moment on, it would

28. Eugene H. Merrill highlights these occasions as "forcible interventions of the Spirit." "The Samson Saga and Spiritual Leadership," in *Presence, Power, and Promise: The Role of the Spirit of God in the Old Testament*, ed. David G. Firth and Paul D. Wegner (Downers Grove, IL: IVP Academic, 2011), 281–93, here 289.

29. For instance, A. Graeme Auld, in the usually reliable Daily Study Bible Commentary on the Old Testament, mentions the spirit in passing on two of the four occasions in chaps. 13–16, but without any discussion. *Joshua, Judges, and Ruth* (Philadelphia: Westminster, 1984).

appear only a miracle can avert any final conflagration between him and the Israelite oppressors. Sure enough, even as the spirit's visitation of Jephthah signaled the beginning of the end for the period of the judges, so also does the final episode of the *ruah*'s work in Samson seal his, Israel's, and the Philistines' fate: he kills a thousand of them, setting in motion the plot that traps him, the results of which include the gouging out of his eyes and his death.[30]

We will turn (in the next section) to reconsider the Philistines not as Israel's enemy but from a broader mission-theological point of view. For now, however, we note that here was a man of faith—remember Samson calls out to God (Judg. 15:18; 16:30; cf. Heb. 11:32)—that the *ruah* Yahweh raised up (Judg. 14:19) and used as Israel's judge for twenty years (15:20; 16:31). At the same time, power, even divinely derived power, can always be abused by human creatures.[31] Amid the opportunities he had to bless Israel, and perhaps even Israel's neighbors, power corrupted this judge. The detailed unfolding of Samson's life was not to endorse his violence but to show that even with the favor of God, the will of God could be thwarted not only at the level of individual lives but also for the people of God and even for nations.[32] Then, as the redactor summarizes coming out of the Samson episode, "In those days there was no king in Israel; all the people did what was right in their own eyes" (17:6; cf. 18:1; 19:1; 21:25), we can see how the Samson saga opens up to another story. Here it is worthwhile to mention that the narrator of Judges introduces Samson thus: "It is he *who shall begin to deliver* Israel from the hand of the Philistines" (13:5; emphasis added). In effect, then, the account is designed to enable readers of the history of ancient Israel to anticipate God's more definitive answer to the plight of his people (to be given by King David later in the books of Samuel).[33]

---

30. Recall in the previous section that the Jephthah story intensifies the downward spiral of the second half of Judges. If this is right, then the Samson narrative is the central node between the sacrifice of Jephthah's daughter and the dismemberment of the Levite's concubine. Barry G. Webb confirms in these words: Samson "arises at a moment when the downward spiral in Israel's fortunes which can be traced through the whole central section of the book has reached its lowest point. . . . Israel no longer even cries out for deliverance, and even Judah, the tribe designated leader in chapter 1, now accepts Philistine rule as an established fact (15:11)." "A Serious Reading of the Samson Story (Judges 13–16)," *RTR* 43:3 (1995): 110–20, here 112.

31. See Wonsuk Ma, "Tragedy of Spirit-Empowered Heroes: A Close Look at Samson and Saul," *Spiritus: ORU Journal of Theology* 2 (2017): 23–38, available at https://digitalshowcase .oru.edu/spiritus/vol2/iss2.

32. See also Richard G. Bowman and Richard W. Swanson, "Samson and the Son of God or Dead Heroes and Dead Goats: Ethical Readings of Narrative Violence in Judges and Matthew," *Semeia* 77 (1997): 59–73.

33. In fact, within the broader narrative of Israel's "history"—as told, for instance, by E. Theodore Mullen Jr., *Narrative History and Ethnic Boundaries: The Deuteronomistic Historian and the Creation of Israelite National Identity* (Atlanta: Scholars Press, 1993), chap. 5—Judges

From the present missiological perspective, we can learn that however pure our motives might begin, we can be caught up by the adrenalin of mission and deceitfully justify our own use and even abuse of power as given by the spirit. In these cases, the *missio Dei* devolves and disintegrates amid our own destructive agendas, and these must be diffused rather than presumed to be divinely sanctioned. What the spirit meant for good can easily be co-opted by our own thirst for power or, more surreptitiously, by our self-reliance in carrying out what we believe to be God's mission. Others, to whom we are called to bear witness, then suffer at our hands. Is there then no guarantee that God can, even through his breath on and in us, accomplish his will and mission? Or maybe sometimes God allows some of our (misguided) mission efforts to fail in order that we might be forced to turn back to God for direction and help, just as Israel was turned back to God by the prophet Samuel.[34]

2.3   1 Samuel—Saul among the Prophetic Spirits? Decentering "Our" Mission

If Samuel was the last judge and David the king with whom Yahweh elected to enter into an everlasting covenant, then Saul becomes a transitionary figure, heroic in many respects, but also fundamentally tragic, haunted by the presence (and absence) of both Samuel and David, albeit for very different reasons.[35] Here was the one who in effect began both to unite the tribes of Israel into a federacy and to solidify their sole allegiance to Yahweh, but alas, he is king because of Israel's desires to be like other nations (1 Sam. 8:19–22) and therefore not only not the divine choice but also representative of Israel's rejection of their God (8:7; 10:18–19).[36] Whereas David, despite his obvious flaws, could do no wrong in Yahweh's eyes, irrespective of his best efforts, Saul could do no right.[37]

---

might be understood as exemplifying what happens when the people of God live according to their own dictates, improperly mixing with "the world" and embracing their neighbors' values and lives (not to mention wives!) indiscriminately; in that case, the response is that ancient Israel's witness to the nations involves some, but not any kind of, interaction and interrelationship.

34. Thanks to Lee Roy Martin for his helpful comments on these Judges sections.

35. See Gregory Mobley, "Glimpses of the Heroic Saul," in *Saul in Story and Tradition*, ed. Carl S. Ehrlich with Marsha C. White, FAT 47 (Tübingen: Mohr Siebeck, 2006), 80–87.

36. As Eben Scheffler writes, "It is a bitter irony that Saul was by his later historiographers [e.g., 1 Chron. 10:13–14] said to be deterred and rejected by the very same God who he [Saul] himself had initially introduced to his people." "Saving Saul from the Deuteronomist," in *Past, Present, Future: The Deuteronomistic History and the Prophets*, ed. Johannes C. de Moor and Harry F. van Rooy, Oudtestamentische Studiën 44 (Leiden: Brill, 2000), 263–71, here 271.

37. "For David, Yahweh is 'Providence'; for Saul, Yahweh is 'Fate,'" as insightfully summarized by David M. Gunn, *The Fate of King Saul: An Interpretation of a Biblical Story*, JSOTSup 14 (Sheffield: JSOT Press, 1980), 116.

Intriguingly, there is not only as much charismatic activity associated with Saul as Samson, but the references are doubled if we include the former being assailed by an "evil spirit" from God.[38] I propose Saul's encounters with the divine breath are also comprehensible according to the Judges pattern of introduction/call, intensification of tension, and denouement, although Saul's last "stage" also unfolds according to this threefold configuration, but in relation to the "evil spirit."[39] A schematization of these would be as follows:

A. Introduction of Saul and confirmation of his leadership over the transitional "kingdom": the spirit of God enables Saul's prophesying (1 Sam. 10:5–11), leading to the proverb regarding him being among the prophets (10:12).

B. Intensification of the stakes involved in Saul's leadership: the *ruah Elohim* enables Saul's rescue of Israel from the Ammonite threat and initiates him into the political sequence of events that leads to his undoing (11:6).

C. Transition of leadership from Saul to David: the *ruah* Yahweh comes on David but departs from Saul (16:13–14),[40] and the spirit's alighting on Saul leads to disgraceful behavior (19:23–24): "He too stripped off his clothes, and he too fell into a frenzy before Samuel. He lay naked all that day and all that night" (19:24)

C[1]. The "beginning" of Saul's "end": the *ruah* Yahweh departs and "an evil spirit from the LORD tormented him" (16:14).[41]

---

38. The dominant explanation for this relative effusion of the *ruah Yahweh* and *ruah Elohim* has to do with later reception of the earlier materials by those associated with various prophetic circles. An alternative theory is related to postexilic concerns for discerning charismatic prophecy. I am intrigued but not completely convinced by the latter, given the hypothetical character of relating the so-called Deuteronomistic historian to the postexilic redactor/redactors, but our discussion here does not depend on adjudicating this matter. See Christophe Nihan, "Saul among the Prophets (1 Sam 10:10–12 and 19:18–24): The Reworking of Saul's Figure in the Context of the Debate on 'Charismatic Prophecy' in the Persian Era," in Ehrlich with White, *Saul in Story and Tradition*, 88–118.

39. That evil spirits might in some cases come from God is seen not only here in 1 Samuel but also in Judg. 9:23 and 1 Kings 22:21–24. I return momentarily to further comment on the latter text, but for now, it suffices to say that these books associated by scholars with the Deuteronomist seem to straddle the earlier henotheistic views of Yahweh as ruling over a heavenly council and later perspectives influenced by more dualistic cosmologies that divided the world between a benevolent God and malevolent spiritual beings; at least this is how most evangelical commentators handle these references—e.g., Leon J. Wood, *The Holy Spirit in the Old Testament* (Grand Rapids: Zondervan, 1976), 126–38; and Robin Routledge, "'An Evil Spirit from the Lord': Demonic Influence or Divine Instrument?," *EvQ* 70:1 (1998): 3–22.

40. Thus does David M. Howard Jr. interpret these references to the evil spirit from the Lord; see "The Transfer of Power from Saul to David in 1 Sam 16:13–14," *JETS* 32 (1989): 473–83.

41. Here and in the other references to Saul, "evil" can be understood as "bad" (as opposed to "wicked"), particularly in relationship to the bad or negative effects of Saul's experience; see

C². Intensification of Saul's tormented state: the evil spirit prompts his attempts to murder David (18:10–11).

C³. The "end" of Saul's tenure heralded, at least spiritually: the evil spirit persists in attempting to destroy David, but Saul's frantic efforts toward this end press the rhetorical question, "Is Saul also among the prophets?" (19:8–24), which is not commendatory as in the original instance of the proverb but invites as response (from the Davidic perspective) a resounding, "No! He is mad and insane."[42]

Here in this transitional judge-king, the ruahology of Judges is doubled (in terms of the number of references), indicative not only of the permissive effects of the divine breath (in giving Israel its king)—including the effectively destructive ends unfolded in Saul's kingship[43]—but also of the ultimate ends of the winds of God (in installing the eternal Davidic covenant).

Yet our purposes here are not only ruahological but also missiological. Given that the whole Samuel narrative, not just 1 Samuel, is focused on the rise and fortunes of David's kingship, little has been written from a missiological perspective.[44] I am intrigued, however, by the fact that more than one-half of the references to the Philistines in the Old Testament occur in 1 Samuel, and more than two-thirds when considering only the presumed Deuteronomistic books.[45] Although it would be worthwhile in light of this concentration to inquire about a missiology to the Philistines or about a contextual or intercultural theology in Philistine perspective, our goals here are more constrained: How might the preceding ruahological reading of the

---

John Goldingay, *1 and 2 Samuel for Everyone* (Louisville: Westminster John Knox, 2011), 80; and David Toshio Tsumura, *The First Book of Samuel* (Grand Rapids: Eerdmans, 2007), 426.

42. My paraphrase of the argument in John Sturdy, "The Original Meaning of 'Is Saul also among the Prophets?' (1 Samuel X 11, 12, XIX 24)," *VT* 20:2 (1970): 206–13; see also Victor Eppstein, "Was Saul Also among the Prophets?," *ZAW* 81:3 (1969): 287–304; and David G. Firth, "Is Saul Also among the Prophets? Saul's Prophecy in 1 Samuel 19:23," in Firth and Wegner, *Presence, Power, and Promise*, 294–305.

43. Thus, another way to understand these evil spirits from the deity is that the "Spirit is 'bad' because the effects of his possession are negative and destructive for the object" (Block, "Empowered by the Spirit of God," 47–52, here 47).

44. One brief article I found is more homiletic and hortatory: Gary Corwin, "Implications for Missions from 1 Samuel 13 & 14," *Evangelical Missions Quarterly* 48:4 (2102): 392–93.

45. David Jobling notes, "The Philistine presence is more pervasive in 1 Samuel than in any other book of the Bible." Jobling, *1 Samuel*, Berit Olam: Studies in Hebrew Narrative and Poetry (Collegeville, MN: Liturgical Press, 1998), 212. Jobling's poststructuralist approach predicated on gender, class, and race analyses led him to focus on the Philistines as a class or category of racialized others in ancient Israel, and this has in turn prompted the following considerations.

Saulide narrative in particular illuminate missiological issues when refracted through the pervasiveness of the Philistines in the text?[46]

Some historical assessment, however, complicates an already difficult question. The historical narrative portrays the Philistines as being Israel's perennial enemy, at least through the five major battles in 1 Samuel alone (4:1–10; 7:3–14; and chaps. 14, 17, and 31), so that is unambiguous. But the origins of the Philistines are difficult to determine because of conflicting etymological and other data.[47] Archeological discoveries unveil a developed Philistine historical self-understanding, a robust economic life, and a developed material culture, all of which no doubt combined to pose them as a formidable foe for an Israelite group of tribes struggling to establish their own national self-identity.[48] From this perspective, however, reading between the lines of 1 Samuel, their relationship with Israel was not always antagonistic, perhaps a legacy of the covenants with the Philistines recorded earlier in Israel's history (e.g., Gen. 21:22–34 and 26:26–31).[49] Their political economies were intertwined at various times (one window of which is given in the Israelite reliance on the Philistine metallurgical guild in 1 Sam. 13:19–21),[50] even as David himself "enlisted Philistine mercenaries" and lived among the Philistines for sixteen months apparently as a vassal of their king (1 Sam. 27).[51] Against

46. Attempting to engage these matters from such a perspective raises many questions about Philistine sources and the extensive secondary literature on this one of Israel's neighbors/enemies. The following cannot hope to seriously pursue this task (that would take another book), but it at least cautions us about missiological approaches and assumptions that ignore completely the issue of how the nations surrounding ancient Israel might have understood their relationships (or lack thereof). For a window into the complex interfaces, interactions, and interdependent political, economic, and social forces that shaped Israel's history and no doubt informed its own self-understanding as reflected in the Jewish sacred writings, see Bustenay Oded, "Israel's Neighbors," in *The Biblical World*, ed. John Barton (New York: Routledge, 2002), 1:492–525, which includes an overview of the Philistines as well (492–99).

47. For more on the Philistines particularly in the Samuel literature, see Israel Finkelstein, "The Philistines in the Bible: A Late-Monarchic Perspective," *JSOT* 27:2 (2002): 131–67.

48. Trude Dothan and Robert L. Cohn, "The Philistine as Other: Biblical Rhetoric and Archaeological Reality," in *The Other in Jewish Thought and History: Constructions of Jewish Culture and Identity*, ed. Laurence J. Silberstein and Robert L. Cohn, New Perspectives on Jewish Studies (New York: New York University Press, 1994), 61–73.

49. See Siegfried Kreuzer, "Saul—Not Always—at War: A New Perspective on the Rise of Kingship in Israel," in Ehrlich with White, *Saul in Story and Tradition*, 39–58.

50. Erik Eynikel, "'Now There Was No Smith to Be Found throughout All the Land of Israel' (1 Sam 13:19): A Philistine Monopoly on Metallurgy in Iron Age I?," in *"My Spirit at Rest in the North Country" (Zechariah 6.8): Collected Communications to the XXth Congress of the International Organization for the Study of the Old Testament, Helsinki 2010*, ed. Hermann Michael Niemann (Frankfurt am Main: Peter Lang, 2011), 41–50.

51. Wills, *Not God's People*, 37; cf. Ernst Axel Knauf, "Saul, David, and the Philistines: From Geography to History," *Biblische Notizen* 109 (2001): 15–18, here 17; Bruce (*Israel and*

this horizon, while there is no denying the historical antagonism between Israel and the Philistines, there are also obvious ties and relationships between these neighbors in the Samuel narrative.

Stepping back from but not leaving behind the details of the ruahological and Philistine-related references in 1 Samuel, I present the following programmatic missiological considerations. First, although the political can be a site of divine presence, as clearly manifested in the blowing of the divine breath in some of the Saulide episodes, that Saul's "reign" was first and foremost the result of the people's ambitions undermined the Israelite capacity to live as light and priest to their neighbors, the Philistines included. Creaturely participation in the mission of God depends as much if not supremely on working according to the passageways of the divine breath rather than the structures of human erection.

Second, and relatedly, the self-orientation of the Israelites compromised their missional call. The desire to be just like the nations is counterproductive to bearing witness to others about what it meant to live as the people of Yahweh.[52] How might mission flow forth more effectively out of our being distinct from those around us? No doubt Israel's perennial problem of wanting to be like its neighbors extended also in the direction of worshiping their deities. Although the Philistines are never directly indicated as tempting the Israelites to idolatry, that was always an issue with many of the other peoples around them. Therefore, rather than lifting up Yahweh's name, opportunities were missed over time to influence the surrounding inhabitants and nations. Hence, if God is going to redeem even the Philistines (see, e.g., Zech. 9:6–7), God will have to do so despite Israel's lost witness over the centuries,[53] and specifically during these Saulide years.

Last but not least, discernment of the divine and the demonic in the missiological context is no less unambiguous than in the so-thought safe havens of our own situation, as evidenced by the conflicting ruahic currents raging through Saul's plight. We would prefer that we always be filled with the divine spirit and that it is only others—religious, cultural, and political others—who

---

the Nations, 22) reminds us that even back as far as the time of Samson, some of the tribes of Israel were quite content to live under Philistine rule.

52. Ironically, the Deuteronomist portrayal of the Philistines others them as a foe rather than engages with them mutually as those who may even have prior claims to the contested land; see here David Jobling and Catherine Rose, "Reading as a Philistine: The Ancient and Modern History of a Cultural Slur," in *Ethnicity and the Bible*, ed. Mark G. Brett, BibInt 19 (Leiden: Brill, 1996), 381–417, esp. 402–6.

53. I am indebted here to the discussion of Norman K. Gottwald, *All the Kingdoms of the Earth: Israelite Prophecy and International Relations in the Ancient Near East* (New York: Harper & Row, 1964), 216–17.

are inspirated by less noble entities, but things are never always that simple. Perhaps Saul was an anomaly whose experiences none of us are ever subjected to. After all, isn't his successor David our exemplar?

2.4   1–2 Samuel—David's Messianic Anointing: Denationalizing Mission?

The David story, at least as told in the books of Samuel, is sandwiched by references to the *ruah* Yahweh coming upon and working through him. At the beginning, "Samuel took the horn of oil, and anointed him in the presence of his brothers; and the spirit of the LORD came mightily upon David *from that day forward*" (1 Sam. 16:13; emphasis added). At the end, when reflecting retrospectively, David introduces his last words thus: "The spirit of the LORD speaks through me, his word is upon my tongue" (2 Sam 23:2). Thus does the Samuel narrative portray David's life and achievements as inspired by the divine breath.[54] The latter notion of David as prophet and poet of the divine *ruah* is consistent with our reading of the Psalms as David's book, so to speak, to which we will return in the next chapter (and which also features in New Testament understandings of David, as we shall observe in part 2 of this volume). For now, it is important only to note that the monarchic historian's account of David's life can be read within this ruahic frame: David's subduing the threats to his rule, both inside and outside his family (e.g., whether of his son Absalom, or Saul's son Ishbosheth, or Sheba a Benjamite, not to mention Adonijah, the fourth son of David, in 1 Kings 1), and his overcoming political intrigue (e.g., in the Abner-Joab rivalry, the betrayal of his counselor Ahithophel, and the tormenting of Shimei) can all be understood as reflective of his acting as one carried by the breath of God.[55] Unfortunately, David acts as much out of his own flesh and carnality as under the unction of the divine *ruah*, as when, for instance, he not only commits adultery with Bathsheba but then also murders her husband. When other "sex-capades" in 2 Samuel are added into the mix—Amnon and Tamar (2 Sam. 13), and Absalom and David's concubines (16:20–23), most palpably—we can see why the story

---

54. As Block ("Empowered by the Spirit of God," 52) emphasizes, the spirit's descent upon David "was never retracted."

55. Walter Harrelson reads the divine *ruah* in 23:2 as enabling prophetic and poetic capacity, particularly forms of the latter such as retained in the rest of 2 Sam. 23; without denying Harrelson's point, ours of course is a more expansive ruahological theology of the Davidic life and mission. See Harrelson, "Creative Spirit in the Old Testament: A Study of the Last Words of David (2 Sam 23:1–7)," in *Sin, Salvation, and the Spirit: Commemorating the Fiftieth Year of the Liturgical Press*, ed. Daniel Durken (Collegeville, MN: Liturgical Press, 1979), 127–33.

of David is a religious one that perennially has been provocative at so many levels.[56] Yet that David himself recognizes the *ruah* Yahweh as inspiring just rule "in the fear of God" (23:3) means that the divine breath enables critical perspective on his own life, and that in turn underwrites our evaluation.[57]

But how does David the king being impelled by the wind of Yahweh add to our understanding of the mission of God? If Israel is called to be a priestly kingdom among the nations (Exod. 19:5–6), then does the rise of the Davidic monarchy, under the impulses of the *ruah Elohim*, elevate Israel toward that priestly mission?[58] There is some suggestion, implicit though such is, that this could have been the case. When David had subdued the enemies of Israel (2 Sam. 8:1–14), we not only are told that he "administered justice and equity to all his people" (8:15 ESV) but also are given the names of the nation's priests (8:17). The broader context of this summation suggests that "his people" is all-inclusive, not just of Israel but of its vassal states (the Philistines, Moabites, Arameans, and Edomites in 8:1–14),[59] and this is consistent with the final spirit-inspired oracle that extols David's "ruling in the fear of God, . . . like the light of morning, like the sun rising on a cloudless morning, gleaming from the rain on the grassy land" (23:3–4), which compares his suzerainty over his subjects to be as nondiscriminative as nature's effects. If this is so, then justice extended in the Davidic reign could surely have included the priestly witness toward which Israel had been called, so that even "David's sons were priests" (8:18 ESV), extending his kingship in service to Israel and the surrounding peoples.[60]

---

56. In the words of Robert Alter, "The story of David is probably the greatest single narrative representation in antiquity of a human life evolving by slow stages through time, shaped and altered by the pressures of political life, public institutions, family, the impulses of body and spirit, the eventual sad decay of the flesh. . . . And nowhere is the Bible's astringent narrative economy, its ability to define characters and etch revelatory dialogue in a few telling strokes, more brilliantly deployed." *The David Story: A Translation with Commentary of 1 and 2 Samuel* (New York: Norton, 1999), x.

57. 2 Sam. 23:2–3 thus provides a critical "hermeneutic of the Spirit" for reassessing David's legacy; see Rickie D. Moore and Brian Neil Peterson, *Voice, Word, and Spirit: A Pentecostal Old Testament Survey* (Nashville: Abingdon, 2017), 103.

58. Thus does Michael W. Goheen suggest understanding the Davidic monarchy as "a priestly kingdom 'in the center of the nations.'" *A Light to the Nations: The Missional Church and the Biblical Story* (Grand Rapids: Baker Academic, 2011), 54.

59. We have already discussed the Philistines (§2.2). For more on David's "rule" over Edom, see John R. Bartlett, *Edom and the Edomites*, JSOTSup 77 (Sheffield: Sheffield Academic, 1989), chap. 5, and also the discussion in §4.1. See the last section of this chapter (§2.6) for more on the Arameans.

60. Gnana Robinson indicates that this reference to David's sons serving in this specific role reflects a tradition "which saw kingship in Jerusalem as a priestly kingship after the order of Melchizedek, and as such recognized the Davidic kingship also as a priestly kingship." *Let*

Perhaps most importantly, David recognizes that the revelation of the eternal covenant ought itself to serve as *torat ha'adam* (2 Sam. 7:19). The NRSV translation, "be instruction for the people" (7:19), does not quite emphasize how the covenant serves as an instructive charter for *all humanity*.[61] This reflects David's own awareness—and perhaps the Deuteronomist's— that the blessings of the covenant were designed not only for Israel but for the world.

But does Israel arise to her calling to bear priestly mission and witness to her neighbors? The Samuel narrative suggests that even if that somehow happened, emphases were placed elsewhere. Whether against the Philistines on the coastal plains (2 Sam. 5:17–25; 21:15–22), the Arameans (Syrians) in the north (8:5–6; 10:6–19), the Moabites in the east (8:2), the Ammonites in the south (2 Sam. 10; 12:26–31), or among other peoples, David conquered Israel's enemies on every side and "made a name for himself" (8:13 ESV).[62] If Saul could never overcome the Philistine threat (remember that he dies in a final conflagration with the Philistines, from which they emerged victorious; 1 Sam. 31), "the LORD gave victory to David wherever he went" (2 Sam. 8:14 ESV). Not only did they pay tribute to David and his kingdom—expected of those conquered by others in those times—but they also became servants in David's emerging empire (8:2, 6, 14). In some cases, David "set them to labor with saws and iron picks and iron axes and made them toil at the brick kilns" (12:31 ESV).[63]

Early on in the Samuel narrative, Yahweh had warned the people through the prophet about what kingship entailed:

Us Be Like the Nations: A Commentary on the Books of 1 and 2 Samuel, ITC (Grand Rapids: Eerdmans, 1993), 198.

61. See Walter C. Kaiser Jr., *Mission in the Old Testament*, 2nd ed. (Grand Rapids: Baker Academic, 2012), 23–25; Kaiser further highlights that the covenantal promises of 2 Sam. 7, repeated in 1 Chron. 17 and commented on in Ps. 89, "will stand forever as one of the grand high points of God's revelation to humankind" (22).

62. David thus vindicates not only his name but those of his people and, perhaps most importantly, his deity; see Philip F. Esler, "2 Samuel—David and the Ammonite War: A Narrative and Social-Scientific Interpretation of 2 Samuel 10–12," in *Ancient Israel: The Old Testament in Its Social Context*, ed. Philip F. Esler (Minneapolis: Fortress, 2006), 191–207.

63. The Hebrew here is convoluted enough, but the more literal rendition is "he brought forth the people that were therein, and put them under saws, and under harrows of iron, and under axes of iron, and made them pass through the brick-kiln" (KJV). Whatever the truth of what happened with the Ammonites (the subject of this passage), the view in these books on ancient Israel's history was consistent with the instructions given regarding warfare against resistant enemies (Deut. 20:10–18). See John F. A. Sawyer, "King David's Treatment of the Ammonites (2 Samuel 12:31)," in *Law, Morality, and Religion: Global Perspectives*, ed. Alan Watson, Studies in Comparative Legal History (Berkeley: Robbins Collection Publication, UC Berkeley School of Law, 1996), 165–78.

These will be the ways of the king who will reign over you: he will take your sons and appoint them to his chariots and to be his horsemen, and to run before his chariots; and he will appoint for himself commanders of thousands and commanders of fifties, and some to plough his ground and to reap his harvest, and to make his implements of war and the equipment of his chariots. . . . He will take your male and female slaves, and the best of your cattle and donkeys, and put them to his work. He will take one-tenth of your flocks, and you shall be his slaves. (1 Sam. 8:11–12, 16–17)[64]

From a missiological perspective, however, the costs would be exacted not only on Israel's sons and daughters but also on those of its subjugated neighbors. Israel's rise to international prominence came, then, at the expense of its living fully into its calling as a priestly nation to others.[65] The height of David's spirit-propelled rule and reign in this regard also opened up to, ironically, the basest depths under which Israel's witness to others would be downtrodden.

It is one thing to wage spiritual warfare against the idolatry of others, but it is difficult not to confuse our nationalistic aspirations with our missional calling to the detriment of the latter. If at one level it might be understandable that Israel needed to drive out the nations from the land given to them by Yahweh in order to avoid corruption by other gods (see 2 Sam. 7:23), at another level national military power is intoxicating to the degree that, once activated, it motivates the suppression of the other not only spiritually but also politically, rather than enables missional service to them. How else, one wonders, will God restore the nations, including the Moabites and Ammonites that David himself had subdued?[66] And this happens even to those of us most spiritually attuned to the winds of Yahweh, as David is said to have been. If so, how then will it be possible for the Davidic covenant to be redeemed so that Israel can live more fully into its elected purposes?[67]

64. Note that here the actions predicted of Israel's desired king are antithetical to those urged by Yahweh as recorded earlier by the author of Deuteronomy: "Even so, he must not acquire many horses for himself, or return the people to Egypt in order to acquire more horses, since the LORD has said to you, 'You must never return that way again.' And he must not acquire many wives for himself, or else his heart will turn away; also silver and gold he must not acquire in great quantity for himself" (Deut. 17:16–17). This is why Israel's king is rightly labeled "a king unlike all the nations," as described by Mark O'Brien, "Deuteronomy 16.18–18.22: Meeting the Challenge of Towns and Nations," *JSOT* 33:2 (2008): 155–72, here 165.

65. Robinson (*Let Us Be Like the Nations*, 216–17) makes the additional point that the forced labor system of Israel's foreign slaves proceeded through forgetting exactly what they had been urged to remember: that they themselves were once the servants of others (Exod. 22:21; 23:9).

66. See Jer. 48:47 and 49:6; cf. Ida Glasser, *The Bible and Other Faiths: What Does the Lord Require of Us?* (Carlisle, UK: Langham Global Library, 2005), 107.

67. As David Burnett writes, "The surprising paradox of this whole story is that although the monarchy was of human origin, God took it up and wove into it his redemptive purposes."

2.5   1–2 Kings—Not Knowing Where the Wind Blows, Except against Baal: Recalibrating Mission

Interestingly, the two references to the spirit of Yahweh in relation to the prophet Elijah the Tishbite concern his mysterious mobility. Initially, Obadiah, the one "who was in charge of the palace" (1 Kings 18:3) of Ahab, king of Israel and Elijah's nemesis, was told by the prophet to convey to the king that Elijah had been found. The servant expressed his worry that "as soon as I have gone from you, the spirit of the LORD will carry you I know not where; so, when I come and tell Ahab and he cannot find you, he will kill me, although I your servant have revered the LORD from my youth" (18:12). Then, at the end of Elijah's ministry, a group of prophets wondered with Elisha, the protégé of Elijah: "See now, we have fifty strong men among your servants; please let them go and seek your master; it may be that the spirit of the LORD has caught him up and thrown him down on some mountain or into some valley" (2 Kings. 2:16).[68] Clearly by the time traditions of Elijah's legacy had begun to circulate, surely by when the Kings narrative came into its final form during the exilic period, his capacity to be transposed from one to another locality had become legendary.[69] Doubtless, Elisha's testimony that Elijah's earthly departure was via ascension "by a whirlwind into heaven" (2:11 ESV) contributed to the belief persisting over the centuries that he would return "before the great and terrible day of the LORD comes" (Mal. 4:5; cf. Mark 8:28 and parallels). Perhaps unsurprisingly, Jesus's followers later "see" him (Mark 9:2–14 and parallels),[70] along with Moses, whose death and burial are also shrouded in mystery (Deut. 34:5–6), even as many anticipate Elijah will return yet again in the eschatological city as one of the two

---

God's Mission: Healing the Nations (London: Marc Europe / Evangelical Missionary Alliance / Send the Light, 1986), 76. Ours is a much more qualified affirmation of this assessment, to which theme we shall return repeatedly in the rest of part 1.

68. This narrative has generated an extensive secondary literature. Helpful for historical and canonical analysis is Elliot B. Gertel, "Moses, Elisha and Transferred Spirit: The Height of Biblical Prophecy? Part 2," *JBQ* 30:2 (2002): 171–77. A more phenomenological discussion is Robert B. Chisholm Jr., "The 'Spirit of the Lord' in 2 Kings 2:16," in Firth and Wegner, *Presence, Power, and Promise*, 306–17.

69. Some commentators observe that "Elijah had so frequently successfully eluded Ahab's officers that he gained a reputation as the possessor of supernatural powers"; see Mordecai Cogan, *1 Kings: A New Translation with Introduction and Commentary*, AB 10 (New York: Doubleday, 2001), 438, and the literature cited there. That the breath and wind of the God of Israel moved people is seen further in Ezekiel (see §4.4 below).

70. Some scholars believe that the secrecy motif in the Gospel of Mark, for instance, refers to the anti-imperial rule and reign of God in Jerusalem and Samaria modeled on the prophetic ministry of Elijah and Elisha that opposed the idolatrous rule of Ahab and his posterity; see, e.g., Wolfgang M. W. Roth, "The Secret of the Kingdom," *Christian Century* 100:6 (1983): 179–82.

The Witness of Israel, by the Power of the Spirit

Athena E. Gorospe, associate professor for Old Testament exegesis, Asian Theological Seminary, Quezon City, The Philippines

If we see missions in terms of how Israel's life witnesses to the nations about the one true God, we see that the work of the spirit in Joshua–Kings is broader than conversion. In Judges, the nations come to know the God who liberates Israel and who judges oppressive nations through the empowering work of the spirit in raising up individual deliverers. In Samuel–Kings, the spirit's work is manifested in prophetic activity that proclaims who Yahweh is, in contrast to the idolatry of the false prophets, and in the anointing and enabling of Israel's kings, whose task is to represent Yahweh and Israel to the nations by being faithful covenant administrators—a task which they often failed to do. If, as biblical mission theologians like Christopher Wright have indicated, the task of biblical mission is to lead people to acknowledge the only true and living God,* these Old Testament books show this work happens through the enabling power of the spirit.

* Christopher J. H. Wright, *The Mission of God: Unlocking the Bible's Grand Narrative* (Downers Grove, IL: IVP Academic, 2006), 171.

witnesses and even then will once more depart "up to heaven in a cloud" (Rev. 11:12 ESV).

Equally interesting, Elijah's departure narrative involves bestowal of a "double share" of his spirit on Elisha (2 Kings 2:9), similar to an Israelite firstborn son getting a "double portion" of the father's inheritance (Deut. 21:17).[71] Although Jewish tradition has then perpetuated that Elisha accomplished twice as many miracles as Elijah (not demonstrable as such from the Kings narrative), I note that the biblical text only inferentially—through *Elijah's spirit*—but never explicitly connects the younger prophet directly to the divine *ruah*.[72] Simultaneously, the Elisha narrative has generated at least some

71. For more on Elijah as mentor to Elisha, see Rickie D. Moore, *The Spirit of the Old Testament*, JPTSup 35 (Blandford Forum, UK: Deo, 2011), 74–77.

72. So, although Richard I. McNeely calls Elisha "the man of the Spirit" (*First and Second Kings* [Chicago: Moody, 1978], chap. 5), one scholar notes that "there is a strange silence in that we *never* find reported *direct speech* of God to Elisha" (Nachman Levine, "Twice as Much of Your Spirit: Pattern, Parallel and Paronomasia in the Miracles of Elijah and Elisha," *JSOT* 85

missiological commentary (less prevalent than that from the Elijah stories),[73] and there may yet be a case to be made for him as doubly spirit-empowered vis-à-vis Elijah for the work of God.[74] Still, as indicated, the role of the divine wind in these texts is ambiguous and obscure, without any apparent missiological link.

I want now to step back from the details of what the *ruah* Yahweh is said specifically to do in (or with) Elijah, and to ask about his prophetic ministry amid Israel's relationship with the nations at that time. What is of dominant concern, at least as unfolded in the Kings narrative, is that Elijah's antagonist, Ahab, is no less complicated and complex, if not also conflicted.[75] On the one hand, Ahab is interested in hearing the truth from the Lord and his prophets (see 1 Kings 22:16, to which I will return later), but on the other hand, he is seemingly dominated by his wife, Jezebel, daughter of the king of Sidon (1 Kings 16:31), who appears to have led him and the nation into idolatry. Ahab, we are told, "erected an altar for Baal in the house of Baal, which he built in Samaria. Ahab also made a sacred pole [Hebrew *asherah*]" (16:32–33).[76]

Here we note how the biblical text clearly indicates that Elijah understood his own mission as one of resistance against the religion of Baal, a Canaanite fertility deity, and Asherah, a goddess and consort of Baal, so much so that he called their 850 prophets (1 Kings 18:19) to a showdown on Mount Carmel. If these local deities were expected to prosper the land and its inhabitants by enabling the conditions for plentiful harvest, Elijah's confrontation with their prophets resoundingly communicated that it is ultimately Yahweh who is sovereign over water and fire (18:22–39), the very natural elements over which

---

[1999]: 25–46, here 44–45; emphasis original). But then, on a similar point, for all the activity of the wind of Yahweh in moving Elijah around and about, the divine spirit is also never said to have descended on the elder prophet; on this matter see Ze'ev Weisman, "The Personal Spirit as Imparting Authority," *ZAW* 93:2 (1981): 225–34.

73. Note that the missiological readings are more practical than theological or exegetical; see, for instance, Walter A. Meier III, "The Healing of Naaman in Missiological Perspective," *Concordia Theological Quarterly* 61:3 (1997): 177–96; and Allan L. Effa, "Prophet, Kings, Servants, and Lepers: A Missiological Reading of an Ancient Drama," *Missiology* 32:4 (2004): 465–73. But then again, as Gottwald (*All the Kingdoms of the Earth*, 70–83) notes, the Elisha stories are unfolded more prominently vis-à-vis the nations than those of Elijah, the latter being more a rural prophet than the former.

74. See Walter Brueggemann, "Elisha as the Original Pentecost Guy: Ten Theses," *Journal for Preachers* 32:4 (2009): 41–47.

75. As described by Gina Hens-Piazza, *1–2 Kings*, Abingdon Old Testament Commentaries (Nashville: Abingdon, 2006), 221–23.

76. Thus Gene Rice notes, "Under the leadership of Ahab and Jezebel, it was state policy to worship Canaanite gods along with the Lord." "Elijah's Requirement for Prophetic Leadership (2 Kings 2:1–18)," *Journal of Religious Thought* 59–60:1 (2006–2007): 1–12, here 2.

fertility gods were supposed to have had authority.[77] Clearly this demonstration did not lead to the eradication of Baal worship across Ahab's twenty-two-year reign (16:29), so that his own renown in the end was that he "did more to provoke the LORD, the God of Israel, to anger than all the kings of Israel who were before him" (16:33 ESV).[78] Nevertheless, it is certainly appropriate to understand that however the winds of Yahweh may have blown during Elijah's ministry, they not only protected and sustained at least this of the Lord's prophets (19:9) but also enabled his witness to the true and living God in opposition to, even if also incorporating and assimilating the potencies of, the Baals and Asherahs.[79] That same *ruah*, however, also empowered prophetic witness that confronted the injustices of kings against their subjects.[80]

The missiological point at this juncture is not first and foremost that sometimes power encounters are needed in the missionary endeavor but that the false idols of our mission contexts need to be unmasked and illumined. Although there are times and places when authentic power encounters are needed, in this case the Kings narrative exposes the Baalite power as illusory and impotent, even though it had been woven into the fabric of Israel as a nation by its leading couple. Israel is in no place to be a light to the nations when it is instead adhering to their "witness," and it is the latter that needs to be countered.

From a ruahological perspective, I note two things: (1) the same wind that supra-naturally transports the prophet quite apart from conventional means also works "naturally" to enable his movement (1 Kings 18:45–46) and (2) the winds that swirled around the prophet were also not always carriers

77. Here I glean from Leah Bronner, whose thesis is that these prophets' miracles were used "to expose the incompetence of Baal, and the numerous functions that the myths ascribed to him," and to show "through the agency of concrete examples and incidents that all the powers ascribed by Ugaritic mythology to Baal [fire, rain, oil, corn, child giving, healing, resurrection, ascent, river, and so on] are really the attributes only of the God, the Lord of Israel." *The Stories of Elijah and Elisha as Polemics against Baal Worship*, Pretoria Oriental Series 6 (Leiden: Brill, 1968), x, 54.

78. For perspective on how a mixed legacy of achievements eventuates in this fundamentally negative Deuteronomistic assessment, see Jerome T. Walsh, *Ahab: The Construction of a King* (Collegeville, MN: Liturgical Press, 2006).

79. See Mark S. Smith, *The Early History of God: Yahweh and the Other Deities in Ancient Israel*, 2nd ed. (Grand Rapids: Eerdmans, 2002), esp. 184–85.

80. For the arguments that Elijah symbolized opposition to anything less than the monotheism that was itself imperiled for the exilic community that in all probability was the original audience of the putative Deuteronomistic history in general and the Samuel–Kings narratives in particular, and that Elijah's message also exposed as unjust Ahab's greed as exemplified in the Naboth narrative (1 Kings 21), see Hillel I. Millgram, *The Elijah Enigma: The Prophet, King Ahab and the Rebirth of Monotheism in the Book of Kings* (Jefferson, NC: McFarland, 2014), esp. chap. 19.

of Yahweh's presence (19:11). Hence what is consistent about the divine *ruah* in the mission of Elijah is its unpredictability and volatility. If "God's whirlwind blows away every love, every security, every safety,"[81] this is no less true for Elijah's experience of Yahweh than it is for Ahab's. The latter sought to stabilize his kingdom through alliance with foreign kings and their daughters, and then through embrace of alien deities and prophetic entourages. Yet such efforts to procure security, both personal and national, are fleeting. The perennial missional lesson, then, refracted ruahically, is to trust not human programs, strategies, or ingenuity but the uncontrollable wind of God that makes all things new.

2.6 1 Kings 22:24—Which Way Did the Spirit Go? Depoliticizing the Prophetic, Demilitarizing Mission

King Ahab's life and achievements (1 Kings 16:29–22:40) provide context not only for the prophetic ministry of Elijah but also for the only other reference to the "spirit of the LORD" in Kings (1 Kings 22:24). To appreciate the ruahic-missiological connections of this passage, some perspective on the wider message of Ahab and his fellow kings will be helpful. Given that the division of Kings into two books is a later convention and that the story concludes with the fall of Jerusalem to the Babylonians in the early sixth century BCE (2 Kings 25), it is clear that this is no mere dispassionate history according to modern understandings of the notion, but a theological explanation of the nation's unfaithfulness to Yahweh that brought about oppression by its enemies across the centuries, culminating in this final catastrophe.[82] So if within the reputed Deuteronomistic history the rebellions of the regal heads of (northern) Israel and (southern) Judah were but the latest replications of covenant infidelity manifest in earlier cycles of judges, the Kings narrative charts the devolution from Solomonic blessing into Babylonian exile specifically due to the continual idolatry of the people and their leaders.[83] An important subplot here is that from the beginning the people were warned about having kings like other nations—not only as if to anticipate that they would lead Israel astray but also to highlight how Yahweh had to continuously

81. Richard D. Nelson, *First and Second Kings*, IBC (Atlanta: John Knox, 1987), 163.

82. Nelson, *First and Second Kings*, 2; thus also do Moore and Peterson (*Voice, Word, and Spirit*, 119) call Kings "a tragic story—a *story of kings* that, from beginning to end, fulfills the *words of prophets*" (emphasis original).

83. As Hens-Piazza (*1–2 Kings*, 7) puts it, one way to understand the purpose of the Kings narrative is as being "designed to change [the people's] inner orientation to God, who (it claims) had turned against the people and undone the exodus by sending them back into exile."

intervene, whether through judges (earlier) or prophets (later in the books of Samuel and Kings), to save the nation from its oppressors. But this meant that the stage was set for ongoing tension, if not outright conflict, between Yahweh's prophets and the kings, from Samuel and Saul onward into the Elijah and Elisha stories and beyond.[84]

The immediate context for our passage is introduced as follows: "For three years Aram and Israel continued without war" (1 Kings 22:1). Although there are indications of ongoing peaceful, or at least cordial, relations between Israel and Aram (e.g., 2 Kings 5:1, 23; 8:7–8),[85] by and large the story is one of ongoing conflict between the two groups of people. Ahab had inherited hostilities led by David, Solomon, and Baasha at least (2 Sam. 8:5–6; 10:6–19; 1 Kings 11:25; 15:16), and himself had already fought some major battles against the Arameans (1 Kings 20:1–35).[86] Yet the narrative is clear that circumstances were conducive toward reparative gestures toward the Arameans (e.g., 20:30–34) that resulted in a period of calm, so there were no instigating factors, certainly no external precipitating causes, except Ahab's own initiative, even greed (22:2–4), to rekindle hostilities.[87] Might this have been a missed opportunity for Israel to be a light to Aram rather than provoke them, unjustifiably, back to war? How might the fortunes of Israel, at least vis-à-vis Aram if not also with regard to other surrounding nations, have been different if, rather than deploying military resources for defensive or other reasons, dialogue, mutuality, and collaboration had been sought instead?

It is at this juncture that Ahab and his collaborator, Jehoshaphat of Judah, inquire from the prophets about what we might call their "Operation

---

84. The latter prophetic ministries are analyzed thus by Walter Brueggemann and Davis Hankins, "The Affirmation of Prophetic Power and Deconstruction of Royal Authority in the Elisha Narratives," *CBQ* 76 (2014): 58–76.

85. Aram's progenitor, by the way, was identified as Abraham's grandnephew (Gen. 22:21), and David "married an Aramean, the mother of Absalom" (cf. 2 Sam. 3:3). Further, the alliances between Israel and her surrounding neighbors is much more complicated than read off the surface of the biblical texts since, for other instances, there are "positive relations" with Moab (Deut. 2:9; 1 Sam. 22:3–4; Ruth), Solomon marries an Ammonite (1 Kings 14:21), and David's court includes Zelek the Ammonite (2 Sam. 23:37). See Wills, *Not God's People*, 35–36.

86. For a summary of Ahab's relationship with the Arameans, see Merrill F. Unger, *Israel and the Arameans of Damascus: A Study in Archaeological Illumination of Bible History* (Grand Rapids: Zondervan, 1957), 64–69.

87. I follow here the astute analysis of Hemehand Gossai, "Challenging the Empire: The Conscience of the Prophet and the Prophetic Dissent from a Postcolonial Perspective," in *Postcolonial Interventions: Essays in Honor of R. S. Sugirtharajah*, ed. Tat-siong Benny Liew (Sheffield: Sheffield Phoenix, 2009), 98–108; but note also that Ahab may have been provoked by Aramean king Ben-hadad's failure to return Ramoth-gilead to Israel, according to the treaty that was crafted between these two when the latter was defeated by the former (see 1 Kings 20:34; 22:3; and Millgram, *Elijah Enigma*, 326).

Ramoth-gilead," the city whose control they wanted to wrest from the Arameans.[88] As we know, Ahab was no stranger to prophets, having dealt not only with Elijah (see §2.5 immediately above) but also with other unnamed mouthpieces of Yahweh (1 Kings 20:35–43). The four hundred prophets consulted unanimously urged the aggression, but Jehoshaphat wanted to hear specifically from a "prophet of the LORD" (22:7 ESV), to which Ahab identifies "Micaiah the son of Imlah, but I hate him, for he never prophesies good concerning me, but evil" (22:8 ESV). Still, at Jehoshaphat's persistence, Ahab's messengers approach Micaiah about meeting the king, and he responds, "As the LORD lives, what the LORD says to me, that I will speak" (22:14 ESV). Then when he initially confirms the four hundred prophets, Ahab suspects otherwise and insists he "speak to me nothing but the truth in the name of the LORD" (22:16 ESV). Then Micaiah speaks contrarily, foretelling destruction, and explains to Ahab that in a meeting of the heavenly court a volunteer came forward to "be a lying spirit in the mouth of all [Ahab's] prophets" (22:22 ESV), and Yahweh agreed to "put a lying spirit" therein (22:23 ESV). It is then that Zedekiah, son of Chenaanah, one of Ahab's prophets who had led the enthusiastic support of the campaign (22:11), retorts to Micaiah, "Which way did the spirit of the LORD pass from me to speak to you?" (22:24). Micaiah's rejoinder is that events will reveal who is telling the truth, and the following narrative confirms Micaiah's prophecy over that of Zedekiah. The story ends in Ahab's demise and an (apparent) Aramean victory over Israel (22:29–38).

But the point is that, as in the preceding discussion of Elijah, reference to the *ruah* Yahweh in the Kings narrative comes not from one of Yahweh's appointed spokespersons but from another marginal figure, in this case, more accurately, a false prophet, Zedekiah. Understandably, this passage has attracted extensive commentary because of the theological implications of Yahweh's authorization of a lying spirit. Textually or literarily, some observe that at best Yahweh only allows a lying spirit, from another source, to be put in the prophets' mouths (and even then this is a *temporary* lying spirit), or see the narrator distancing himself from each of the major characters in the story,[89]

---

88. Although the actual historical events are only dimly discernible between the lines of this text (see Walsh, *Ahab*, 104–10), these do not need resolution within the frame of our canonical approach.

89. P. J. Williams provides an evangelical textual assessment that has an apologetic edge ("Lying Spirits Sent by God? The Case of Micaiah's Prophecy," in *The Trustworthiness of God: Perspectives on the Nature of Scripture*, ed. Paul Helm and Carl R. Trueman [Grand Rapids: Eerdmans, 2002], 58–66), while Terence E. Fretheim makes the suggestion that the lying spirit is temporary (*First and Second Kings*, Westminster Bible Companion [Louisville: Westminster John Knox, 1999], 124). David Robertson presents a literary approach that intriguingly observes how the narrator presents complex characterizations—e.g., that Ahab wants the truth but does not

while historical approaches range from reconstructionist theories about the development of the narrative to arguments that this story of divine deception reflects an earlier moment in the movement of salvation history toward purer and higher ideals of divinity.[90]

Stepping back from the details of this encounter, here midway through the Kings narrative Ahab is reminded through the prophet Micaiah that the fortunes of Israel, for good or ill, are dependent not on the military prowess of its kings nor on the nation's resources, but on the covenantal governance of Yahweh.[91] Both northern and southern kingdoms were out of joint because of the rejection of Yahweh's rule and the desire to be regally run like the other nations, which inevitably wrought aggression, exploitation, and violence. The Micaiah narrative exposes the cracks and fissures of this arrangement—of prophet against prophet, prophet against king and vice versa, and kings against Yahweh—that implodes by the end of the Kings narrative, resulting in the Babylonian exile.[92] To be sure, in this specific instance Ahab was given yet another opportunity to heed the word of Yahweh, retreat from Ramoth-gilead, and perhaps extend his life, but his primary loyalties to other deities prevented the needed discernment.[93] If Yahweh's purposes can be inexorably accomplished through the will to power, deceit, and violence of earthly wars, then lying spirits would seem to be part of such dynamics.

heed it, Jehoshaphat want a true prophet but also is not admonished, Micaiah says he will tell the truth but does not initially, and Yahweh seems collusive in deception, even if for the purposes of destroying an idolatrous king and rule—that find resolution only at the end of the story, and even then do not necessarily adjudicate on behalf of one over another character in the plot; see "Micaiah ben Imlah: A Literary View," in *The Biblical Mosaic: Changing Perspectives*, ed. Robert Polzin and Eugene Rothman (Chico, CA: Scholars Press, 1982), 139–46, esp. 143–46,

90. Wolfgang Roth provides an excellent overview of historical-critical readings in "The Story of the Prophet Micaiah (1 Kings 22) in Historical-Critical Interpretation, 1876–1976," in Polzin and Rothman, *Biblical Mosaic*, 105–37.

91. Thus does the (so-called) Deuteronomistic Yahweh continue his rule over Israel primarily by prophet rather than by king; see Millard C. Lind, *Yahweh Is a Warrior: The Theology of Warfare in Ancient Israel* (Scottdale, PA: Herald, 1980), chap. 8.

92. Simon J. De Vries, *Prophet against Prophet: The Role of the Micaiah Narrative (I Kings 22) in the Development of Early Prophetic Tradition* (Grand Rapids: Eerdmans, 1978), viii. De Vries further comments on "the constant, overriding concern of the entire prophetic movement in its early phases to counteract the threat of political power, ever used to undermine and subvert the authority of prophetism and with it the cherished traditions of primitive Yahwism" (149).

93. R. W. L. Moberly urges that we ought to "contextualize Micaiah's second vision within the dynamics of Micaiah's attempt to get through to a reluctant king," and consider "that the heavenly court might be revealing the true nature of the earthly court, i.e., that the manipulation, deception, and self-will might belong solely to Ahab and his prophets, and that they are being displayed to Ahab in an ironic and dramatic challenge." "Does God Lie to His Prophets? The Story of Micaiah ben Imlah as a Test Case," *Harvard Theological Review* 96:1 (2003): 1–23, here 22.

So, from whence did the breath of Yahweh derive and which way did it go? As kings ought not to rely on their own (national) capacities, so also those involved in the divine mission ought not to depend on their own resources, certainly not on any weapons of war even if they might be conducive, for a time, for missionary purposes.[94] Yahweh is the main actor in Kings, not only locally or nationally, but beyond. As King Hezekiah later proclaims, "O LORD, the God of Israel, enthroned above the cherubim, you are the God, you alone, of all the kingdoms of the earth" (2 Kings 19:15 ESV). Hence, the *missio spiritus*—the ruahic mission—can only be the mission of Yahweh, and this has to be discerned continually and afresh, as this story unveils. As Yahweh's rule cannot be domesticated, so also the mission of God's breath cannot finally be routinized. The fate of others depends at least in part on our discerning the difference.

Discussion Questions

1. The divine wind in these Former Prophets blows upon political figures, judges, and kings, in particular. Are there any contemporary missional or missiological implications for thinking about mission politically? Why might we need to be cautious about drawing present-day applications from these early experiences of Israel's national life?

2. Adopting a ruahological lens leads, in these Old Testament texts, to noticing references not just to the divine wind but to evil and lying spirits, and these afflict "insiders" (e.g., Saul and Israel's king) not just "others" (pagans or the heathen who need to be converted). How ought we to think missionally or missiologically about evil spirits, without demonizing unbelievers?

3. David's life and work as Israel's king is presented as guided by the divine breath. How do we reconcile that with his biographical details? How might his so-called spirit-led kingship encourage and admonish how we think about our own lives of Christian witness?

---

94. Hence the subtitle of this section calls for a "demilitarization" of mission. I got this idea from Ben C. Ollenburger, "Gerhard von Rad's Theory of Holy War," introduction to *Holy War in Ancient Israel*, by Gerhard von Rad, trans. Marva J. Dawn (Grand Rapids: Eerdmans, 1991), 1–33, here 7; however, Ollenburger is describing the Weberian theory about how the prophet-judges of the pre-monarchic period were "demilitarized" by the kings over the course of the ninth century BCE. Ollenburger refers to Max Weber's *Ancient Judaism*, trans. and ed. Hans H. Gerth and Don Martindale (Glencoe, IL: Free Press, 1952), 101.

3

The Postexilic *Ruah*

Rewriting and Renewing Mission

Introduction

In this chapter we turn to what in the Jewish scriptures is called the Writings, or Ketuvim. Because the divine wind is not referenced in some of these books (e.g., Ruth, Ezra, Esther, Proverbs, Song of Songs, and Lamentations) and because we are following the sequencing of the Christian canon (so that our discussion of Daniel follows in the next chapter with the other prophetic books), this is the shortest chapter in part 1 of this volume. Yet what follows includes disparate forms of material characteristic of the Ketuvim: books following the Former Prophets (treated in the previous chapter), including 1–2 Chronicles and Nehemiah, and books incongruently collected under the unwieldy rubric of Hebrew wisdom and poetic literature: Job, Psalms, and Ecclesiastes (with a further complication related to Psalms, a book of poetry, sitting between two other wisdom texts). We will proceed canonically, however, on the basis that even if some of what is described in these books—for instance, Chronicles and perhaps Job—may have occurred earlier in Israel's history, at least the final and surely the canonical forms of these texts were completed in the postexilic centuries after Israel's return from Babylonian captivity.[1]

---

1. This is agreed upon even among conservative biblical scholars; e.g., Andrew E. Hill and John H. Walton, *A Survey of the Old Testament*, 2nd ed. (Grand Rapids: Zondervan, 2000), 383–401, on the "Formation of the Old Testament Scriptures."

Of greater import for our purposes, however, is the role that these texts in their more or less final form played in the reconstitution and renewal of Israel after the Babylonian exile. The Chronicler, the moniker given by scholars to the author or authors/editors of 1–2 Chronicles, revisits the various histories of Israel found at his disposal (among which might have also been earlier forms of canonical material from Genesis through Kings)[2] from his (or their) vantage point, seeking to reconsider the fate and fortunes of a nation reeling from exilic captivity and now given the opportunity for and seeking restabilization in a context still under the shadow of an imperial regime.[3] From this perspective, Chronicles and Ezra–Nehemiah (usually understood as related) are as much theological reconstructions as they are historical accounts. But if these Writings are reinterpretations and retellings of Israel's story for new generations with new needs,[4] then they also help us ask this missiological question: How might an understanding of these segments of the Ketuvim that describe a colonized Israel, a province under Medo-Persian authority and governance, seeking restoration and renewal amid postexilic pressures and anxieties, help us also imagine the revitalization of Christian witness after the collapse of the classical mission project in our late modern times?

Here is where our exploration of the wisdom and poetic material is apropos. If in the earlier history the focus was primarily insular (see chap. 2 above), the exilic dispersion among the Babylonians and Persians meant that Israel had to understand itself truly among others—other peoples, cultures, and nations.[5] A more cosmic horizon unfolds, one in which the wisdom materials among the earliest (preexilic) Hebrews were retrieved and reappropriated now in a broader ancient Near Eastern context. It is no wonder that sections of these biblical wisdom texts include or are indistinguishable from the wisdom sayings of other cultures since now the chosen people of Yahweh were aliens and strangers among peoples of other "faiths."[6] If Hebrew wisdom seems to come out of nowhere,

2. For more on the various theories regarding how the Chronicler is related to the Deuteronomist and prior histories of ancient Israel, see Donald C. Raney II, *History as Narrative in the Deuteronomistic History and Chronicles*, SBEC 56 (Lewiston, NY: Edwin Mellen, 2003).

3. The basic historical lines of Israel in, through, and after the exile are traced in Iain Provan, V. Philips Long, and Tremper Longman III, *A Biblical History of Israel* (Louisville: Westminster John Knox, 2003), chap. 10.

4. The argument for which is compellingly given in Donn F. Morgan, *Between Text and Community: The "Writings" in Canonical Interpretation* (Minneapolis: Fortress, 1990).

5. See Mary Joan Winn Leith, "Israel among the Nations: The Persian Period," in *The Oxford History of the Biblical World*, ed. Michael D. Coogan (Oxford: Oxford University Press, 2001), 276–317.

6. This is part of the gradual internationalizing of ancient Israelite discourse, as suggested by Ronald E. Clements, *Wisdom for a Changing World: Wisdom in Old Testament Theology*, Berkeley Lectures 2 (Berkeley: BIBAL, 1990), 16–22. For a more in-depth discussion of Hebrew

that may be because it is in some senses derived from everywhere in the ancient world.[7] Further, if in fact the yearnings of such a postexilic people were for the restoration of the earlier monarchy in the face of imperial governance, then it is not only wisdom that is needed but also liturgical renewal; for example, the retrieval of Israel's priestly vocation carried by the Levitical community and reappropriation of its ancient songs (psalms) resounded amid this diasporic people.

Our own pneumatological and missiological perspective thus is led to ask, through the voices heard in these Writings, about if and how the divine wind has been blowing not just among individual outsiders (as we have seen so far in the first two chapters) but also among non-Israelite cultures and traditions.[8] This is an important movement and development. If chapter 2 focuses on the monarchy and its fortunes, this third chapter turns toward postmonarchic Israel, a period of time leading into and out of the Babylonian exile in which Israel realizes that its vocation rests not on military might but on the salvation of God. So, what happens is not that Israel's witness to the nations disappears, but that the fundamental calling of Israel's vocation as priest to the nations is recalibrated now not just *to* but *amid* and *with* the nations.[9] Even the postexilic renewal and restoration[10] unfolds with Israel not being independently reconsolidated from but being intertwined with—ruled and governed by, to be precise—others. Is it possible, then, that the divine wind enables witness by *sendings* (blowings) of various sorts, not all voluntary?

3.1 1–2 Chronicles—Spirit Speaking: Renewing the Call

Compared to his predecessors, the Chronicler writes from a broader, even more universal, postexilic standpoint. Israel's genealogy is situated amid the nations going back to Adam (1 Chron. 1:1),[11] the fame of David extends to

---

wisdom in the ancient Near Eastern context, see Richard J. Clifford, *The Wisdom Literature*, Interpreting Biblical Texts (Nashville: Abingdon, 1998), chap. 2.

7. As intimated by Donald K. Berry, *An Introduction to Wisdom and Poetry of the Old Testament* (Nashville: Broadman & Holman, 1995), 40.

8. I have long been asking these questions vis-à-vis the contemporary theology of religions discussion; see, e.g., Yong, *Beyond the Impasse: Toward a Pneumatological Theology of Religions* (Grand Rapids: Baker Academic, 2003).

9. Michael W. Goheen urges that exile can be understood in terms of the people of God's scattering among the nations; see *A Light to the Nations: The Missional Church and the Biblical Story* (Grand Rapids: Baker Academic, 2011), 60–66.

10. John Goldingay titles his chapter on postexilic theology "Exile and Restoration," in *Old Testament Theology*, vol. 1, *Israel's Gospel* (Downers Grove, IL: InterVarsity, 2003), chap. 10.

11. Gary N. Knoppers, "Shem, Ham and Japheth: The Universal and the Particular in the Genealogy of Nations," in *The Chronicler as Theologian: Essays in Honor of Ralph W. Klein*,

"all nations" (14:17; cf. 29:30), David intends the renown of the temple to reach "throughout all lands" (22:5), and he worships the Lord as exalted over "all that is in the heavens and in the earth" (29:11 ESV). In a real sense, the Chronicler realizes that the prosperity, peace, and fortunes of Israel, the southern kingdom of Judah—these two are synonymous for the Chronicler[12]— indeed the securing of the nation's ideological identity and interests,[13] are tied to that of its neighbors, intricately intertwined with the fate of all the peoples of the earth.

Yet Israel's restoration and renewal, and the destinies of the nations around Israel, are mediated for the Chronicler through the Davidic covenant (1 Chron. 17:3–27).[14] However, it is not primarily the military might of David's armies that secures his rule but the reconstruction of the temple and the restoration of its liturgies through the priesthood. Hence it is the Levites—the priests, singers, musicians, liturgists, temple caretakers, and so on (1 Chron. 6 and 23–26; cf. 9:10–34; 29:1–9)—who are centrally important for this task.[15] Whatever else David might have sought to achieve, from the Chronicler's perspective it is securing the ark and (re)building, dedicating, and worshiping in the temple that are crucial (1 Chron. 13, 15, 16, 22; 2 Chron. 2–7; 29:20–36).[16] This is the Chronicler's vision not only for a renewed Israel but also for its prosperity in the long term: if Israel's kings could not ensure the people's faithfulness before Yahweh then, now that Israel had been given what amounts to a second chance through the Edict of Cyrus allowing return to the land (2 Chron. 36:22–23), the way forward has to be found in repentance from idolatry and unified worship.[17]

---

ed. M. Patrick Graham, Steven L. McKenzie, and Gary N. Knoppers, JSOTSup 371 (New York: T&T Clark, 2003), 13–31.

12. This is because, from the Chronicler's perspective, northern Israel "has been in rebellion against the house of David to this day" (2 Chron. 10:19).

13. See Jonathan E. Dyck, "The Ideology of Identity in Chronicles," in *Ethnicity and the Bible*, ed. Mark G. Brett, BibInt 19 (Leiden: Brill, 1996), 89–116.

14. James D. Newsome Jr., "Toward a New Understanding of the Chronicler and His Purposes," *JBL* 94:2 (1975): 201–17.

15. Kevin L. Spawn urges that it is worship that is at the heart of Israel's renewal in the postexilic context; see "Sacred Song and God's Presence in 2 Chronicles 5: The Renewal Community of Judah and Beyond," *JPT* 16:2 (2008): 51–68.

16. William Johnstone writes, "The primary model of Israel's life turns out to be the life of holiness under the teaching of the Levites, their officiating at the altar and their monitoring of Israel's observance of that holiness." *1 and 2 Chronicles*, vol. 1, *1 Chronicles 1–2 Chronicles 9: Israel's Place among the Nations*, JSOTSup 253 (Sheffield: Sheffield Academic, 1997), 40.

17. Thus Martin J. Selman writes that the Chronicler was "a theological optimist who wanted to bring fresh hope to his people." *1 Chronicles: An Introduction and Commentary*, TOTC (Downers Grove, IL: InterVarsity, 1994), 51; cf. W. F. Stinespring, "Eschatology in Chronicles," *JBL* 80:3 (1961): 209–19.

It is in this context that the four references to the divine breath in the Chronicles are noteworthy, in each case invoking prophetic speech rather than any specific set of spectacular actions. Whereas in Israel's historical narratives the breath of God more often than not inspired toward violence and even war (e.g., chap. 2 above), here the breath coming on Amasai, chief over David's thirty "mighty men," not only enables utterance of words of comfort but even declares to an anxious David instead the contrary of aggression: "Peace, peace to you, and peace to your helpers! For your God helps you" (1 Chron. 12:18 ESV).[18] Similarly, the *ruah Elohim* alights on Azariah, who assures Asa, king of Judah, that Yahweh is a covenant-keeping deity, saying, "Take courage! Do not let your hands be weak, for your work shall be rewarded" (2 Chron. 15:7 ESV). The latter is thus encouraged to lead Israel in a national repentance that results in "rest all around" and peace with the surrounding nations (15:15, 19).

The third instance involves a clarion call in anticipation of war, but in this case the *ruah* Yahweh impels a Levite, Jahaziel, to declare the word of the Lord: "This battle is not for you to fight; take your position, stand still, and see the victory of the LORD on your behalf, O Judah and Jerusalem" (2 Chron. 20:17). The outcome here is the seemingly continuous worship and praise of Yahweh—immediately upon Jahaziel's prophecy (20:18–19), on the day of battle (20:21–22), and after the victory (20:24–26)—and Judah's not engaging in warfare at all but finding the corpses of their enemies strewn all around as they had "helped to destroy one another" (20:23–24).[19] The last reference also involves a priest, Zechariah (24:20), who warns king Joash about his wickedness but unfortunately pays with his life (24:21). Yet two co-conspirators from Ammonite and Moabite backgrounds (Israel's perennial enemies) murder the king soon thereafter (24:25–26),[20] even as the nation is quickly run over by the Arameans. The point is that unlike in earlier references to the wind of God, the postexilic Chronicler comes to

18. Note also that this reference is part of the Chronicler's narrative that all in Israel, even many beyond its official borders—observe the foreigners among David's mighty men: 1 Chron. 11:38–39, 46–47—are being drawn around David's leadership, and that this is itself a prelude to the universal restoration anticipated in the book's genealogies and (proleptically) inaugurated in Solomon's reign (on which more momentarily); see Gary N. Knoppers, *1 Chronicles 10–29: A New Translation with Introduction and Commentary*, AB 12A (New York: Doubleday, 2004), 575–78.

19. It is as if Jahaziel's prophecy was intended to admonish Israel "*not* to fight"; see John R. Levison, *Inspired: The Holy Spirit and the Mind of Faith* (Grand Rapids: Eerdmans, 2013), 134 (emphasis original).

20. "Inexplicably" is how one commentator discusses the referenced feminine forms of the conspirators' forebears; see Steven L. McKenzie, *1–2 Chronicles*, Abingdon Old Testament Commentaries (Nashville: Abingdon, 2004), 319.

associate the divine breath exclusively with prophetic speech and practically dissociates it also from aggressive and violent behavior or activity. Perhaps as important, the fact that these were all four lesser-known individuals, even "nonprofessional" prophets,[21] reflects the more egalitarian character of the divine breath in the postexilic understanding.

At one level, the movement of the divine breath across the narrative of the Chronicles follows a pattern of (1) blessing/testing (Amasai/Azariah), (2) intensification (Jahaziel), and (3) implosion (Zechariah) previously observed in the earlier historical materials (chap. 2 above). At another level, this ruahic arc also suggests that the Chronicler comprehends the work of the divine breath as inculcating "a new commitment, solidarity, and loyalty,"[22] one reflected in the prominence of the Davidic covenant and its culmination in Solomon's reign and temple activities. To the degree that Israel is unfaithful to its God, it is harassed on every side and oppressed by its enemies, even to the point of exile (1 Chron. 2:7; 5:25; 9:1; 2 Chron. 36:21).[23] But within the framework of covenantal faithfulness established with David, the turning of the people to their Lord enables Israel to live into its vocation as light to the nations (1 Chron. 16:8). Solomon's erection of the temple begins to draw the nations into the Israelite sphere as collaborators (2 Chron. 2:3–18), and the temple's ceremonial dedication brings with it a universal invitation that others may also come to worship Yahweh in his holy dwelling place (6:32–33). Thus do the nations of the earth arrive to consult with and pay homage to Yahweh's representative (9:1–28),[24] and Israel's foes become its economic partners (e.g., 2 Chron. 1:16–17; 9:28).[25] The Davidic promise had come to pass, that Solomon "shall be a man of peace. I [Yahweh] will give him peace from all his enemies on every side" (1 Chron. 22:9).[26]

21. Sara Japhet, *I & II Chronicles: A Commentary*, OTL (Louisville: Westminster John Knox, 1993), 717; cf. Nathan MacDonald, "The Spirit of Yhwh: An Overlooked Conceptualization of Divine Presence in the Persian Period," in *Divine Presence and Absence in Exilic and Post-exilic Judaism: Studies of the Sofja Kovalevskaja Research Group on Early Jewish Monotheism*, ed. Nathan MacDonald and Izaak J. de Hulster, FAT 2/61 (Tübingen: Mohr Siebeck, 2013), 2:95–119, here 107.
22. Michael Welker, *God the Spirit*, trans. John F. Hoffmeyer (Minneapolis: Fortress, 1994), 57.
23. Johnstone, *1 and 2 Chronicles*, 1:19–20.
24. Johnstone (*1 and 2 Chronicles*, 1:371) notes that there is "universal recognition of Solomon's reign" following the proper worship of Yahweh.
25. Ralph W. Klein, "Africa and Africans in the Books of Chronicles," *CurTM* 31:4 (2004): 274–80, here 280.
26. For more on Solomon's relationships with other nations, see Ida Glasser, *The Bible and Other Faiths: What Does the Lord Require of Us?* (Carlisle, UK: Langham Global Library, 2005), 96–98. Note that the emphasis of Glasser's theological and missiological argument ultimately is a performative one: the Bible does not give us clear answers to the speculative questions we

Unfortunately, reliance not on Yahweh but on the might of kings and armies continually resurfaces in the second half of the Chronicler's narrative. Whether it is intra-Israelite alliances (2 Chron. 20:35–37) or vassalage with Arameans or Assyrians (16:1–13; 28:16–21), these manifest the infidelity of the house of David. From the Chronicler's postexilic perspective, foreign alliances might be expedient means to political capital, security, and legitimacy, yet dependence on Yahweh is the most assured route toward national renewal and restoration, not to mention toward international harmony and blessing.[27] If Israel was ever going to be the light to the nations, monarchic deeds had to be transfigured by prophetic speech so that the people of God could be the "priestly kingdom and . . . holy nation" (Exod. 19:6) they were called to be.

3.2   Nehemiah—The Spirit from Persia: Reverse Mission?

Reference to the breath of Yahweh appears twice in Nehemiah 9, in the context of his colleague Ezra (Neh. 9:6) and leading Levites (9:4–5) directing the people's prayerful confession (9:5–38) that is central to their cultic worship (including Torah reading and recitation, and penitential ritual) and covenantal recommitment (7:73–10:39).[28] The prayer, which some scholars believe to be a creedal historical-theological psalm of postexilic Judah,[29] recounts Yahweh's historical faithfulness to Israel, even despite the latter's unfaithfulness. Amid the prayer and communal lament, Yahweh's deeds on behalf of Israel are recalled: "You gave your good spirit to instruct them, and did not withhold your manna from their mouths, and gave them water for their thirst" (9:20), and "Many years you were patient with them, and warned them by your spirit through your prophets; yet they would not listen" (9:30). The former's emphasis on Yahweh's breath's instructional activities

---

have about other religions and the salvation of their adherents, but it does urge us to witness to others and, even more importantly, love and serve them in the name of Christ.

27. Gary N. Knoppers, "'Yhwh Is Not with Israel': Alliances as a *Topos* in Chronicles," *CBQ* 58:4 (1996): 601–26; we will return to this theme later (§4.1).

28. For a succinct but expert discussion of this ninth chapter in the broader context of Nehemiah and in relation to Ezra, see H. G. M. Williamson, *Ezra, Nehemiah*, WBC 16 (Waco: Word, 1985), 305–10. For a more thorough study that sees the prayer of confession in Neh. 9 as the "hermeneutical key" and "theological centerpiece" to Israel's postexilic covenant renewal, see Michael W. Duggan, *The Covenant Renewal in Ezra–Nehemiah (Neh 7:72b–10:40): An Exegetical, Literary, and Theological Study*, SBLDS 164 (Atlanta: Society of Biblical Literature, 2001), esp. 298–99; note, though, that Duggan's verse numbering of the Nehemiah text follows the *Biblia Hebraica Stuttgartensia*, which explains the variance from the NRSV.

29. Parallel, for instance, to the psalms discussed in Frank C. Fensham, "Neh. 9 and Pss. 105, 106, 135, and 136: Post-exilic Historical Traditions in Poetic Form," *Journal of Northwest Semitic Languages* 9 (1981): 35–51.

is paralleled in one of the psalms (143:10)—the only two occasions in scripture where the divine wind is qualified as "good"—even as it presumes the distribution of the divine breath to Moses and the seventy elders in Numbers 11:16–30 (see §1.5).[30] Meanwhile, the latter verse (9:30) may be related to a contemporary account, that of the prophet Zechariah in the late exilic period (Zech. 7:12; see §4.8).

Although attributed historically to Ezra (ca. 480–440 BCE) and finalized in the fifth century BCE, there is some indication that the origins of this prayer derive from those left in the land during the late exilic period (Neh. 9:36–37), a time in which, without land, king, or temple, the people of God could draw primarily if not only from their scriptural traditions in order to find spiritual nourishment and encouragement.[31] The "utter shame" of the sixth-century exile followed the people, even into the middle of the fifth century BCE (cf. Ezra 9:7). But by then both the generations that had stayed in the land and those who had returned from exile suffered under heavy taxation and labor burdens (see Neh. 5:14–18). The pressures confronted thus were ethnic/geographical, religious, political, and economic all together—indeed, the survival of a fragile community was at stake. It is in this later context that the prayer is situated: "Those of Israelite descent separated themselves from all foreigners, and stood and confessed their sins and the iniquities of their ancestors. They stood up in their place and read from the book of the law of the LORD their God for a fourth part of the day, and for another fourth they made confession and worshiped the LORD their God" (9:2–3). For the postexilic community, then, the divine breath enabled Torah reception, interpretation, understanding, and practice.[32]

Without minimizing the theological character, orientation, and commitments of the prayer of Nehemiah 9, there is a broader historical backdrop

30. With the important distinction that there is no limitation here as there was in the Numbers episode to the giving of the breath of God to only the seventy elders; see Duggan, *Covenant Renewal in Ezra–Nehemiah*, 213.

31. See Mark J. Boda, *Praying the Tradition: The Origin and Use of Tradition in Nehemiah 9*, BZAW 277 (Berlin: de Gruyter, 1999). An alternative proposal that places this prayer fully in the mid-fifth century—that of Manfred Oeming, "'See, We Are Serving Today' (Nehemiah 9:36): Nehemiah 9 as a Theological Interpretation of the Persian Period," in *Judah and the Judeans in the Persian Period*, ed. Oded Lipschits and Manfred Oeming (Winona Lake, IN: Eisenbrauns, 2006), 571–88, here 584—argues that this ninth chapter "summarizes the whole theological world view of the Judahite community before Ezra" on the basis of the semantic range and polyvalence of vv. 36–37 that allow reference to a benevolent Persian overlord. My missiological reading does not require deciding on the *Sitz im Leben* of this text with such precision.

32. As deftly argued by John R. Levison, *The Spirit in First Century Judaism*, Arbeiten zur Geschichte des antiken Judentums und des Urchristentums 29 (Leiden: Brill, 1997), 194–97.

The Postexilic Spirit
An African Perspective

James Chukwuma Okoye, CSSp, director of the Center for Spiritan Studies, Duquesne University, Pittsburgh, Pennsylvania, USA

The *ruah* of God functions to make the temple-focused *qahal** a veritable "community-in-mission." Levitical singers imbued with this *ruah* as prophets uphold faith, instruct, admonish, predict the success of wars, and lead Israel into war with song and praise (2 Chron. 20). AICs (African Initiated Churches) are churches of *semoya* (Batswana term for spirit) that channel God's *ruah* in ministries of discernment and admonition, unleashing the power of the word, healing, and spiritual combat against the anti-God and anti-human. Even as the human breath is enmeshed with the divine spirit, this breath gives life (Job 33:4), understanding (Job 32:8), and works of power. The divine spirit in African cosmology generally is not imaged as creative breath. The Igbo *chi* derives from *Chi-Ukwu* (Great *Chi*/Creator) as divinely appointed personal destiny; the personal *muǫ* (immaterial spirit) is open to influences from *Ndi Muǫ* (God and immaterial beings) at the level of "seeing" and mystical power for weal or woe.

* *Qahal*: one term for the holy assembly of Israel when gathered for worship or for listening to the word of God.

amid which such confession is unfolding.[33] Nehemiah, who was cupbearer (Neh. 1:11) to Artaxerxes I of Persia, had sought and received authorization from the latter in the twentieth year of his reign (2:1; ca. 445/444 BCE) to return to the Judean/Yehudian province and complete restoration of Jerusalem's walls, to the alarm of the indigenous (Samaritan and other) leaders of the Palestinian region of the time (see Neh. 1–6). The Persian emperor's investment in this mission had to do at least somewhat with securing imperial interests in the region, particularly against the threat of revolt by Egypt, with Greek intervention, precipitated during the seventh and sixth decades of the fifth century BCE,[34] and part of the strategy for this endeavor had to do with

33. For a more political rather than religious sketch of Nehemiah's identity and work, see Morton Smith, *Palestinian Parties and Politics That Shaped the Old Testament*, 2nd ed. (London: SCM, 1987), chap. 6.
34. Details are in Kenneth G. Hoglund, *Achaemenid Imperial Administration in Syria-Palestine and the Missions of Ezra and Nehemiah*, SBLDS 125 (Atlanta: Scholars Press, 1992).

minimizing local incentive to ally with the Egyptians while maximizing loyalty and allegiance to Persian rule. For their part, Nehemiah and his compatriot Ezra took advantage of this opportunity as official representatives of Persian authorities to reconfigure the political infrastructure on the Palestinian ground. In this they succeeded at least through the banning of intermarriage between Israelites and others indigenous to the region (Ezra 9–10; Neh. 13:23–29). Further, they also sought to renew commitment to Yahweh and to the law of the covenant. With these agendas at hand, Ezra's prayer, recorded in Nehemiah 9—not to mention both documents in general, traditionally considered as a unity—does not directly complain about the Persian overlord. The references to the work of the divine wind, in particular, focus on its instructional and admonitional aspects, both directed toward the people of God, not to their engagement with other nations or with the governing authorities.

From a missiological perspective, Nehemiah has emerged as a model missionary, an exemplary strategist who focused on cultural revitalization and national renewal based on the divinely given Torah.[35] Especially evangelicals are captured by his covenantal fervor and political savvy, noting how he seized the opportunity opened up within the imperial regime for missional purposes. From this point of view, evangelists and missionaries can embrace the imperial status quo in exchange for the freedom to practice their religious way of life, in particular its proselyting activities. More to the point missiologically, Nehemiah and Ezra are astute, realizing that their "reverse mission" (from Persia to Jerusalem) appeal to the postexilic Hebrew community had to be disentangled from their state-sanctioned mandates and rooted in the people's historic memory. In this context, when the threats to Nehemiah's work were to be found as much inside the postexilic community, from the "people of the land," as outside it, the focus on the inherited scriptural traditions played a further role of delineating ancestral lines of authority and identity.[36] Thus the prayer of confession drew deeply from the tradition's narratives and attempted

35. E.g., Kenneth Tollefson, "The Nehemiah Model for Christian Missions," *Missiology* 15:1 (1987): 31–55; Getachew Kiros, "The Gates of Jerusalem: Rethinking and Rebuilding Missions in the Light of Nehemiah's Approach," *Missio Apostolica: Journal of the Lutheran Society for Missiology* 21:2 (2013): 236–45, available online at http://lsfm.global/uploads/files/MA-11-13-Online.pdf; and Bob Wielenga, "Renewal and Reconstruction: Holy Writ in Ezra–Nehemiah—A Missional Reading," *In die Skriflig/In Luce Verbi* 47:1 (2013), available online at http://www.indieskriflig.org.za. See also Edward R. Dayton and David A. Fraser, *Planning Strategies for World Evangelization* (Grand Rapids: Eerdmans, 1979), 28, who focus on Nehemiah's managerial gifts.
36. Lawrence M. Wills, *Not God's People: Insiders and Outsiders in the Biblical World* (Lanham, MD: Rowman & Littlefield, 2008), chap. 3, "The Redefinition of We and Other in Ezra–Nehemiah."

to retrieve its cultic and liturgical practices, and the role of the divine *ruah* is emphasized as not only instructing the people but also renewing and celebrating the covenantal identity for present tasks.[37] Only by being reminded about and then reoriented toward living out their historic commitments would there be any hope of bolstering the postexilic community's sense of purpose amid a hostile and antagonistic local political field, not to mention of enabling them to separate themselves from the "defilements" of or with other indigenous groups, whose women they had taken as wives.[38]

Yet from a more specifically postcolonial missiological vantage point,[39] Nehemiah's (and Ezra's) zealousness for ethnic purity can be understood perhaps just as ethnically, economically, and politically motivated—at least as driven also by Persian designs to govern displaced populations according to ethnic groupings[40]—as religiously funded. There were certainly pressures on the postexilic returnees and even threats from the people who had taken up habitation in the land over the course of the exile that impinged on this decision to put away wives married outside the postexilic Yehudite community to the local indigenous peoples (Neh. 10:30). Additionally, there were fears that intermarriage would result in hybridized descendent generations—who were already beginning to lose fluency in the Hebrew language, it should be noted (13:24)—and ultimately in secession of land from Judean ownership that imperiled their long-term survival and fortunes.[41] One might even argue that should Israel cease to be as an ethnic people, so would their priestly ministry and mission to the world also disintegrate. Yet Nehemiah's appeal here (13:26) is not directly to pentateuchal law but to Solomon's disastrous intermarriages. And even if Ezra's rationale (9:11–14) invokes Mosaic authority to declare

---

37. Thus is Neh. 9 the "shared vision of [Israel's] collective history and destiny" set amid the broader declaration and celebration of the people's restored communal identity committed to Yahweh's Torah and temple. Tamara Cohn Eskenazi, "Imagining the Other in the Construction of Judahite Identity in Ezra–Nehemiah," in *Imagining the Other and Constructing Israelite Identity in the Early Second Temple Period*, ed. Ehud Ben Zvi and Diana V. Edelman, LHBOTS 456 (London: Bloomsbury, 2014), 230–56, here 256.

38. For more on these matters, see Anne Fitzpatrick-McKinley, *Empire, Power and Indigenous Elites: A Case Study of the Nehemiah Memoirs*, Supplements to the Journal for the Study of Judaism 169 (Leiden: Brill, 2015), chaps. 8–9.

39. Leo G. Perdue and Warren Carter provide such a reading of the Persian Empire in *Israel and Empire: A Postcolonial History of Israel and Early Judaism*, ed. Coleman A. Baker (London: Bloomsbury, 2015), chap. 4. My own postcolonial optic is focused more on the postexilic Jewish community's efforts to consolidate than on their explicit resistance to the state's pressures.

40. See Hoglund, *Achaemenid Imperial Administration*, 244.

41. Tamara Cohn Eskenazi argues that the call to put away foreign wives is to secure the citizenship rights of Judahite women, so as to build a more egalitarian postexilic community. "The Missions of Ezra and Nehemiah," in Lipschits and Oeming, *Judah and the Judeans in the Persian Period*, 509–29.

such mixed marriages as threatening the purity of Israel, such is indefensible from the letter of the Mosaic and priestly law and stretches the pentateuchal ordinances alluded to beyond their intended scope of applicability.[42] Further, such injunctions were contrary to both preexilic and postexilic practice—there are many documented instances of Israelite intermarriage[43]—and their rigorousness reflects sociopolitical expediency as much as substantive theological consideration.

In fact, missiologically speaking, the prohibition against intermarriage—even the command to break apart existing interethnic marriages—raises questions about Israel's capacity to bear adequate witness to the nations.[44] If in the Christian Testament there is a clear erasure of the boundaries between Jew and Greek (e.g., Gal. 3:28), then the stance advocated by Ezra and Nehemiah perpetuates an us-against-them mentality that exacerbates the chasm through which Israel's priestly mission amid the nations is supposed to unfold.[45] If for Nehemiah and the postexilic community the cultural forms of worship life, even if primarily Davidic in inspiration, are not inessential to true religiosity,[46] then by extension so are the cultural forms of the nations also redeemable for authentic liturgical expression, and such are attained at least in part through ethnic integration rather than by ethnic purification. Unfortunately, the latter themes in scriptural canons such as found here have in their reception history been deployed for nationalistic and anti-migration political ends. To guard against such usage,

42. See Rolf Rendtorff, "The *Gēr* in the Priestly Laws of the Pentateuch," in Brett, *Ethnicity and the Bible*, 76–87, esp. 86–87.

43. See the discussion in J. Daniel Hays, *From Every People and Nation: A Biblical Theology of Race*, NSBT 14 (Downers Grove, IL: InterVarsity, 2003), chap. 4 on intermarriage; thus also does Fitzpatrick-McKinley (*Empire, Power and Indigenous Elites*, 276) write that "perhaps [Nehemiah] should be credited with being the first to use the idea of Mosaic authority (but not specific Mosaic laws) to define the community of Judeans, for elsewhere, in Egypt, among the Judean-Babylonian communities and in Jerusalem and its districts prior to Nehemiah's arrival, no one as far as we can tell, had attempted to impose laws restricting intermarriage."

44. I am revising this chapter in June 2018 when news is headlining that the current US administration is deploying a xenophobic policy of separating children from parents at the southern border in order to deter northward migration from Latin America. Intriguingly, now and over two thousand years ago, religion and migration are intertwined in ways that deeply trouble familial relations and raise probing questions about the witness of the people of God in worlds so politicized. For another discussion of such matters focused on the ancient context, see Herbert R. Marbury, "Reading Persian Domination in Nehemiah: Multivalent Language, Co-Option, Resistance, and Cultural Survival," in *Focusing Biblical Studies: The Crucial Nature of the Persian and Hellenistic Periods—Essays in Honor of Douglas A. Knight*, ed. Jon L. Berquist and Alice Hunt (New York: T&T Clark, 2012), 158–76.

45. Thus are these efforts "to recapture the ancient confidence of long life in the prosperous land" identified as a "program . . . of retrenchment." William A. Dyrness, *Let the Earth Rejoice! A Biblical Theology of Holistic Mission* (Pasadena, CA: Fuller Seminary Press, 1992), 119.

46. E.g., D. J. A. Clines, *Ezra, Nehemiah, Esther*, NCBC (Grand Rapids: Eerdmans, 1984), 31.

then, any reverse missional initiative will need to attend to the leading of the divine breath not only as making palatable the message at the missional site but also as illuminating the forces and agenda at the point of origination, whether clearly imperial or colonial (as was Nehemiah's sending agent).

3.3   Job—The Breath of Life: Anticipating Cosmic Renewal

The book of Job precipitates thinking about sickness and suffering, not mission, at least not usually. There is, however, a minority tradition of Job interpretation that might facilitate our thinking about the missiological implications of the Joban message, in particular its references to the divine breath. Such a reading derives from an allegorical consideration of Job as symbolic of Israel, of his diseased condition as reflective of Israel as oppressed by other nations (Job's ostensive "friends"?), and of his ultimate healing as indicative of Yahweh's promise to deliver his people.[47] As scholarly efforts to date the book have been perennially futile, such a proposal can be at home just as well in the context of the Assyrian devastation of Judah around 700 BCE as amid the exilic community.[48] One scholar urges from this perspective that the significance of the book lies therefore in its breaking away from a covenant of rewards and punishments focused exclusively on a deity-nation toward a more universal perspective of the God-world relation: "The ultimate and deepest concern of the book of Job is with the conversion of the God of Abraham into the universal God of all mankind, a conversion which could occur only after the severance of the partisan tie which bound him [Abraham] to His own treasured people."[49] In that case, Job signals the development of a more centrifugal understanding of Israel's mission vis-à-vis the nations.

The reality, however, is that there is little if any internal evidence linking Job to Israel as a nation,[50] that much more needs to be done to be convincing

47. See, for instance, Charles Lee Feinberg, "Job and the Nation Israel," 3 parts, *BSac* 96:384 (1939): 405–11; 97:385 (1940): 27–33; 97:386 (1940): 211–16. Some contemporary Jews also view Job as a national allegory—e.g., Kevin Snapp, "A Curious Ring in the Ears: Ambiguity and Ambivalence in the Conclusion of the Book of Job," *Conservative Judaism* 53 (2000): 34–50, here 46. Although from the perspective of Job's presumed innocence such an approach may be less sustainable (since Israel's exile was due to its sin), yet Job acknowledged his own limitations and even shortcomings in need of repentance (Job 40:3–4; 42:1–6) even as Israel also recognized its election as undeserved (see Deut. 7:7–8; 9:5).

48. David Wolfers argues for the earlier date in *Deep Things Out of Darkness: The Book of Job—Essays and a New English Translation* (Grand Rapids: Eerdmans, 1995).

49. Wolfers, *Deep Things Out of Darkness*, 70.

50. Francis I. Andersen, *Job: An Introduction and Commentary*, TOTC (Leicester, UK: Inter-Varsity, 1976), 62.

about how the innumerable references to Job's ailments correlate with the nation's calamities, and that the primary and even dominant reception of the book has been on Job as, at least potentially, every *person*, not as a national allegory. Yet this minority report rightly foregrounds the universalistic horizon of the Joban narrative that holds even if read in terms of the singular and personal suffering of the book's namesake. In particular, the God who answers his protagonist from "out of the whirlwind" (Job 38:1; 40:6) is also the one who overcomes the chaos of the world by his wind (26:13).[51] These acts of the divine *ruah* invite consideration of the Joban ruahology against the backdrop of Yahweh's more cosmic work.

It is within this framework that I want to focus on the peculiarity of Elihu as the ruahological or ruahic theologian par excellence in the book of Job. Elihu is "son of Barachel the Buzite, of the family of Ram" (Job 32:2 ESV), a lineage from which we can tell little, like the other characters in the book of Job, except that perhaps even with an Israelite name he may have had connections to Edom (cf. Jer. 25:23; 29:7–8).[52] He speaks thrice of the divine breath in his speech. First, before his audience as a whole, Elihu tells of the divine breath that gives wisdom and understanding to one even as youthful as he (Job 32:6–8).[53] Second, addressing Job in particular (33:1), he mentions the divine wind that both gives life in general and inspires his response to his senior in ways that challenge the latter before the deity (33:4–6). Third, now directed toward Job's friends (34:2), Elihu witnesses to the *ruah Elohim* that sustains creaturely life and flesh in all their precariousness (34:14–15). At least two aspects of Elihu's ruahological references are noteworthy. First, if Job himself claimed to have been enabled by the divine breath (27:3), Elihu emphasizes that the wind of God is not limited to Job but belongs to all human beings, if not all living creatures.[54] Second, Elihu's numerous ruahological

51. For more on Job 26:13 as celebrating Yahweh's "victory over chaos," see Wilf Hildebrandt, *An Old Testament Theology of the Spirit of God* (Peabody, MA: Hendrickson, 1995), 44–45.

52. David J. A. Clines, *Job 21–37*, WBC 18A (Dallas: Word, 2006), 713. If indeed Elihu was an Edomite, then what Diane Bergant says vis-à-vis Job and his interlocutor friends—that "the book of Job also challenges ethnic stereotyping"—is all the more appropriate: the divine wind blows through Elihu despite his not being an Israelite. See Bergant, *Israel's Wisdom Literature: A Liberation-Critical Reading* (Minneapolis: Fortress, 1997), 45.

53. John R. Levison characterizes Elihu, from the Joban text, as full of youthful exuberance, self-centeredness, overconfidence, pride, and triumphalism; see *Filled with the Spirit* (Grand Rapids: Eerdmans, 2009), 18–19, 36, 127. The presence and activity of the divine wind never guarantees the presence of virtues that counter the characteristics seen in Elihu.

54. Commenting on these references to the wind of God, Clines insists that Elihu is referring "to the moment of creation . . . when the divine life force was imparted to all humans without differentiation," and highlighting that "the breath of living creatures is not just their own breath but the breath of God. It is *his* spirit . . . and *his* breath . . . that sustain life" (*Job 21–37*, 726, 774;

citations—amounting to half of the book's explicit references to the wind of God (26:13 and 27:3 are mentioned above; see also below)—set up and anticipate the deity's response from out of the tempest. In effect, the divine answer is mediated by this youthful, ruahic, and charismatic figure.

From a traditionalist perspective, Elihu justifies the doctrine of compensation and retribution, but insists that such unfolds not inexorably following any mechanical calculus but according to God's wisdom and timing. Hence from Elihu's vantage point, Job and his friends erred in attempting to speculate about the *why* of Job's anguish, when in fact God is present (and caring even) amid human affliction intimately as the breath of their lives.[55] So Elihu corrects Job only vis-à-vis the latter's presuming grounds for demanding an account of God, but Job is otherwise correct, over against his friends, about his innocence.

Read missiologically, Elihu's speech in general, and his references to the breath of God in particular, lift up the common humanity of all people, within and outside the covenant with Israel.[56] There are both anthropological and theological implications of this Elihuan or Joban ruahology. Anthropologically, the intertwining of travail with breathing suggests that human suffering unfolds in the spirit, as it were, somehow also affected by the divine wind. Simultaneously, then, human questioning, and the concomitant understanding to any greater or lesser degree, also persists in the spirit, again, carried by the divine breath. So the deepest existential quests are constituted by the enmeshment of the human breath with the divine spirit. To experience pain and to ask, "Why, O God?" are two sides of human life and participation enabled by the wind of God.[57] Participation in the *missio Dei* thus refracted through the mission of the *ruah* thereby invites coming alongside others in prolonged solidarity (like Elihu, unlike Job's "friends") amid whatever grief and tragedy. No human distress is thereby untouched by the *missio spiritus*.

---

emphasis original). See also Rosalind Clarke, "Job 27:3: The Spirit of God in My Nostrils," in *Presence, Power, and Promise: The Role of the Spirit of God in the Old Testament*, ed. David G. Firth and Paul D. Wegner (Downers Grove, IL: IVP Academic, 2011), 111–21.

55. See Larry J. Waters, *The Contribution of the Speeches of Elihu to the Argument about Suffering in the Book of Job: A Study in Narrative Continuity*, SBEC 67 (Lewiston, NY: Edwin Mellen, 2009), 85–86, 237, 261.

56. So "the life-giving spirit (cf. [Job] 27:3; Gen. 2:7) and the wisdom-imparting spirit (Gen. 41:38; Dan. 5:12; Exod. 31:3) are identical [and related to] Elihu's emphasis on sharing a common humanity with Job." Norman C. Habel, *The Book of Job: A Commentary*, OTL (Philadelphia: Westminster, 1985), 451.

57. In this respect, prayer from out of the depths of suffering is deeply ruahic; see here the reflections of pentecostal biblical scholar Rickie D. Moore, *The Spirit of the Old Testament*, JPTSup 35 (Blandford Forum, UK: Deo, 2011), chap. 12, "Raw Prayer and Refined Theology: 'You Have Not Spoken Straight to Me, As My Servant Job Has.'"

Theologically, that every creaturely breath is suffused by the divine wind opens it up to the cosmic scope of the deity's presence and activity. God's justice, as the Joban narrative unfolds, is intensely personal, but universally so. The God whose breath supports Job even amid his sorrow is the same God who cares for the beasts of creation and even for the Behemoth and the Leviathan (Job 38–41). But the flip side of God's universal justice entails that the divine judgment comes upon sinners, ultimately if not also penultimately, just as well "by the breath of God" (4:9 ESV). Paradoxically, then, on the one hand the wind of God gives life, but on the other hand the tempest of God crushes creatures (9:17) and the storms of God blow creatures away (21:18; 27:20–21).[58] Job's original family was struck by "a great wind" (1:19), pressing the point that Job somehow knew his "children [had] sinned, and cursed God in their hearts" (1:5). From a missiological perspective, we can never be certain how the catastrophes and misfortunes of life are derivative from the blowing of the divine wind against creaturely wrongdoing. We can only realize that the capacity to ask this question is itself indicative that the cosmic breath agonizes with us in anticipation of the redemption to come.

3.4 Psalms—Singing amid and to the Nations: The Soul of Mission

Many of the psalms, the songs of ancient Israel, originated in liturgical and cultic settings. It is increasingly recognized, however, that Israel's worship was not for its sake alone but was one way in which it witnessed to the nations.[59] This witness unfolded not just in terms of Israel's naming the nations in its songs but in its singing in the presence of other onlookers and on-listeners (e.g., Ps. 57:9; 108:3), and even in its urging the nations also to sing and praise the Lord with Israel (18:49; 22:27; 47:1; 66:4; 67:3; 86:9; 96:2–3; 100:1; 117:1).[60] Israel's songs and worship, then, are thoroughly political.[61] But none of the

58. Thomas F. Dailey, OSFS, "Theophanic Bluster: Job and the Wind of Change," *Studies in Religion/Sciences Religieuses* 22:2 (1993): 187–95.

59. Roger E. Hedlund, *God and the Nations: A Biblical Theology of Mission in the Asian Context* (Delhi: ISPCK, 1997), chap. 8; cf. W. Creighton Marlowe, "Music of Missions: Themes of Cross-Cultural Outreach in the Psalms," *Missiology* 26:4 (1998): 445–56; Michael Landon, "The Psalms as Mission," *Restoration Quarterly* 44:2 (2002): 165–75; and Alan Ludwig, "Mission in the Psalms," *Logia: A Journal of Lutheran Theology* 23:3 (2014): 11–19.

60. Pss. 2, 29, 33, 66–68, 72, 87, 96, 98, 117, and 145 have been specifically identified as including mission-related themes; see also Walter C. Kaiser Jr., *Mission in the Old Testament*, 2nd ed. (Grand Rapids: Baker Academic, 2012), chap. 4.

61. Gordon H. Matties, "God's Reign and the Missional Impulse of the Psalms," in *Beautiful upon the Mountains: Biblical Essays on Mission, Peace, and the Reign of God*, ed. Mary H.

Singing the Psalms in the Philippines
Witnessing through Laments

Federico G. Villanueva, publications secretary, Asia
Theological Association; general editor, *Asia Bible
Commentary*; Manila, The Philippines

That the spirit enables us to cry, "My God, my God, why have you forsaken me?" in the midst of our suffering is an important and challenging truth, especially in many parts of Asia where the teaching of karma is deeply ingrained. Add to this the emphasis on the sinfulness of human beings and the view that one should never question God, and it becomes almost unthinkable to even ask God, "Why?" This attitude was evident when Typhoon Haiyan— the strongest typhoon recorded in human history—devastated parts of the Philippines. Amid all the debris and chaos, the words "Patawarin mo kami" (forgive us) were posted on the ships driven into the center of the city of Tacloban. Traditionally, God is called "Bathala," who is believed to be one who is so powerful and great that no one dares to question his decrees. The influence of Islam further strengthens this belief. In this context, how can we capture the truth about the *missio spiritus*? The laments of Job and those in the book of Psalms provide a way of appropriating this vision. There is a place for honest questioning and the pouring out of one's heart to God. The divine *ruah* is at work in the lives of God's people not only in their praises and thanksgiving but even in their agony and pain. Lament becomes all the more urgent in the light of our own three-hundred-year experience of colonialism, followed by decades of subjugation under the Americans and the Japanese. The tendency is just to accept our lot and never to utter our pain. But if we allow the groaning of the spirit to be heard in our prayers, then there is hope that the *missio spiritus* will flow once more in our time and world today.

psalms that include explicitly this political-missional dimension are of the five that also refer to the wind-breath of Israel's God.[62]

Schertz and Ivan Friesen, Studies in Peace and Scripture 7 (Eugene, OR: Wipf & Stock, 2003), 17–49, here 42.

62. Exegesis of these five texts is provided by Vince McLaughlin, *Ruach in the Psalms: A Pneumatological Understanding* (n.p.: Xlibris, 2012); for another charismatic reading of the spirit *with* (using the prayers and praises of), *behind* (in the inspiration of), and *in* (the five texts of) the Psalms, see John Goldingay, "The Holy Spirit and the Psalms," *JPT* 27 (2018): 1–13.

The five references to the *ruah* in the Psalter are all traditionally related to King David (see §§2.3–2.4). Psalm 33, which is connected to the preceding psalm that is attributed specifically to David and whose first verse appears as a clear response to the exhortation of the final verse of chapter 32 (v. 11),[63] extols the Lord for many reasons, among which we read, "By the word of the Lord the heavens were made, / and by the breath of his mouth all their host" (33:6 ESV).[64] Such a declaration is made in the presence of "all the inhabitants of the world" (33:8; also 33:14).[65] From these cosmic horizons the psalmist's "ruahology" zeros in on the depths of the human soul:

> Create in me a clean heart, O God,
>   and put a new and right spirit within me.
> Do not cast me away from your presence,
>   and do not take your holy spirit from me.
> Restore to me the joy of your salvation,
>   and sustain in me a willing spirit. (Ps. 51:10–12)

This famous penitential psalm, whose ascription reads, "A Psalm of David, when the prophet Nathan came to him, after he had gone in to Bathsheba" (see 2 Sam. 11–12), highlights the role of the divine breath in sanctifying the thoroughly corrupt and wayward human heart, albeit in ways that involve the latter's responsiveness (repentance and remorse, for instance).[66] Of further

63. As noted by John Goldingay, *Psalms*, Baker Commentary on the Old Testament, 3 vols. (Grand Rapids: Baker Academic, 2006–2008), 1:464.

64. This is in contrast to the winds of the earth that are never neutral but always work as Yahweh's (oftentimes destructive) agent/instrument, account for (the swiftness of) divine movement, function theophanically to arouse wonder, and so on; see Steve A. Wiggins, "Tempestuous Wind Doing Yhwh's Will: Perceptions of the Wind in the Psalms," *Scandinavian Journal of the Old Testament* 13:1 (1999): 3–23.

65. So although "the Lord brings the counsel of the nations to nothing [and] he frustrates the plans of the peoples" (Ps. 33:10), the covenantal character of the Psalm and its specified cosmic dimensions suggest that even here "Israel's 'covenant' is left open for the nations." Norbert Lohfink, SJ, and Erich Zenger, *The God of Israel and the Nations: Studies in Isaiah and the Psalms*, trans. Everett R. Kalin (Collegeville, MN: Liturgical Press, 2000), 116.

66. Even if some weighty arguments suggest that the divine *ruah* here refers not to the divine person but to the "power, the spiritual quality of [divine] holiness" (W. Creighton Marlowe, "'Spirit of Your Holiness' ([*ruah qadeshka*]) in Psalm 51:13," *TJ*, n.s., 19 [1998]: 29–49, here 44), we miss the point if we attempt to adjudicate issues in the Psalter as if through a post-Nicene trinitarian lens. Undeniable is the cry of the psalmist in "aiming at a complete renewal of the volitional centre of the inner being," a renewal that involves human response: "the anthropological spirit has got a counterpart in Jhwh's holy spirit, which is of some relevance to the inner restoration of man." Anja Klein, "From the 'Right Spirit' to the 'Spirit of Truth': Observations on Psalm 51 and 1QS," in *The Dynamics of Language and Exegesis at Qumran*, ed. Devorah Dimant and Reinhard G. Kratz, FAT 2/35 (Tübingen: Mohr Siebeck, 2009), 171–91, here 173

noteworthiness here is that Psalm 51:16 and 51:19 might reflect two different periods, with the latter editorial redaction inserted in anticipation of the postexilic rebuilding of the city walls and temple, in which case herein we find how Israel's prayer also bore later, and thus multiple, witnesses to the nations.[67] The third reference zooms back out not quite to Psalm 33's cosmic horizons but at least to the terrestrial realm of the earth and its many creatures:

> When you hide your face, they are dismayed;
> when you take away their breath, they die
> and return to their dust.
> When you send forth your spirit, they are created;
> and you renew the face of the ground. (Ps. 104:29–30)

Connected to the previous psalm by way of their parallel opening and closing verses (cf. 104:1, 35 with 103:1, 22), and thereby to the Davidic authorship clearly heading Psalm 103,[68] the difference is the earlier song's emphasis on blessing Yahweh of Israel and the latter's praising Yahweh as provider of, over, and for the earth and its various occupants. Consistent with the latter more expansive vista, the praise of Yahweh's providence appears to reflect general knowledge of, or at least participation in a similar ethos with, other ancient Near Eastern and also Egyptian hymns, including but not limited to that of Pharaoh Akhenaten's fourteenth-century-BCE adulation of the sun.[69] Within this broader ancient Near Eastern frame of reference, then, we can further appreciate that the psalm is also structured closely according to the creation narrative of Genesis 1,[70] and if the *ruah* there enables life, then here, in the psalmist's hands, the divine wind energizes and renews the world and its animation (as if in response to the cursed world in Gen. 3).[71] Hence the face, or presence, and breath of Yahweh oversee the deity's joyful and playful providence over the world.[72]

---

and 176. Cf. Goldingay, *Psalms*, 2:135, 140; and Daniel J. Estes, "Spirit and the Psalmist in Psalm 51," in Firth and Wegner, *Presence, Power, and Promise*, 122–34.

67. See Donald Senior and Carroll Stuhlmueller, *The Biblical Foundations for Missions* (Maryknoll, NY: Orbis, 1983), chap. 5, "Israel's Prayer and Universal Mission."

68. Derek Kidner, *Psalms 73–150: A Commentary on Books III–V of the Psalms* (Downers Grove, IL: InterVarsity, 1975), 363–64.

69. See the section "Ninurta, Akhenaton, and Psalm 104" in Neil Forsyth, *The Old Enemy: Satan and the Combat Myth* (Princeton: Princeton University Press, 1987), 55–58; and also Mark S. Smith, *God in Translation: Deities in Cross-Cultural Discourse in the Biblical World* (Grand Rapids: Eerdmans, 2010), 69–76; cf. Goldingay, *Psalms*, 3:182.

70. See Kidner, *Psalms 73–150*, 368.

71. Goldingay, *Psalms*, 3:194.

72. See William P. Brown, "Joy and the Art of Cosmic Maintenance: An Ecology of Play in Psalm 104," in *"And God Saw That It Was Good": Essays on Creation and God in Honor of Terence E. Fretheim*, ed. Frederick J. Gaiser and Mark A. Throntveit, Word & World Supplement 5

The last two references, included within the final set of Davidic psalms (chaps. 138–45), accentuate the omnipresence and salvific efficacy of Yahweh's breath. The former queries rhetorically, "Where can I go from your spirit? / Or where can I flee from your presence?" (Ps. 139:7), and answers "nowhere" (my paraphrase) emphatically.[73] The latter, in the context of calling on Yahweh for salvation from enemies, cries out, "Let your good spirit lead me / on a level path" (143:10). Read together, they suggest that the ubiquitousness of Yahweh's wind enables rescue of the psalmist even in the most treacherous of circumstances, even as the latter's deliverance is ensured and assured by his God's constant accompaniment.

How else might we understand the missiological implications of these ruahological texts? We can probe further into this question by observing at least one way in which the Psalms are structured. The earliest collections of these songs already reflected an intentional effort to replicate the five books of the Torah, particularly in the doxologies that respectively begin Psalms 1, 42, 73, 90, and 107. The final or concluding chapters to the first four units further suggest transitions that may helpfully map the political and international context of these songs: Psalm 41 moves from the rule of Saul to that of David; Psalm 72 shifts from David to Solomon; Psalm 89 shows the covenant with Israel in disarray as if against the backdrop of the eighth-century-BCE Assyrian crisis; and Psalm 106 pleads for a regathering from exile, thus situating this fourth book's songs within that international context.[74] Such transitional seams suggest that the Psalms provide sequential windows into the Davidic covenant, moving from David being under the limelight of Saul's reign (Book 1), through the Davidic reign (Book 2), the period of the divided monarchy (Book 3), and the exilic period (Book 4), and concluding with the postexilic restoration (Book 5).[75]

If the songs of ancient Israel are understood as organized at least in part also around the unfolding of Israel's (Davidic) covenantal self-understanding, which includes its political dimension vis-à-vis the nations, then the ruahological references in four of the five Psalter books confirm that the divine breath

---

(St. Paul: Luther Seminary, 2006), 23–32; and Scott A. Ellington, "The Face of God as His Creating Spirit: The Interplay of Yahweh's *panim* and *ruach* in Psalm 104:29–30," in *The Spirit Renews the Face of the Earth: Pentecostal Forays in Science and Theology of Creation*, ed. Amos Yong (Eugene, OR: Pickwick, 2009), 3–16.

73. See Jamie A. Grant, "Spirit and Presence in Psalm 139," in Firth and Wegner, *Presence, Power, and Promise*, 135–46.

74. Thus do Lohfink and Zenger (*God of Israel and the Nations*, 161) summarize this fourth segment of the Psalms under the heading "The God of Israel's Reign over the World" and invite reading of Ps. 104 in that "global" context.

75. See Hill and Walton, *Survey of the Old Testament*, 347–48.

operates at every level of these relationships. We can see, for instance, that the breath and wind of God blows at the deepest biological and existential depths of the human soul (Ps. 139), at the realms where human beings are most in need of the deity's salvific intervention (Ps. 143), at the level where soiled and perverted human hearts need purification (Ps. 51), in the terrestrial and environmental sphere wherein human creatures are embedded (Ps. 104), and through the entirety of the cosmic domain within which human minds wonder and respond in praise (Ps. 33). The point is that the songs of Israel not only declare to the nations the nature and works of the *ruah* Yahweh but also invite their joining in the chorus of such worship precisely since the divine breath both enables such praise and sustains them and the world they inhabit. As such, these psalms are missionally formative not only for Israel's collective self-comprehension but also for individual Israelites—or those who consider themselves in continuity with the people of God rooted in ancient Israel—who would sing these songs on an international stage and across a multinational world.[76]

3.5   Ecclesiastes—Expiring Breath and Ephemeral Mission?

There are no explicit references to the breath of God in Israel's Wisdom literature outside of Job and Psalms except indirectly at the end of Ecclesiastes.[77] There the Preacher or Teacher (the "Qoheleth" of Ecclesiastes) urges, "Remember your creator" (Eccles. 12:1) while possible, before "the dust returns to the earth as it was, and the breath [*ruah*] returns to God who gave it" (12:7). If, in canonical context, Qoheleth's anthropology and ruahology are consistent with that of the early Genesis narrative (see Gen. 2:7 and 3:19; cf. §1.1 above), in the broader context of Ecclesiastes's major theme, "Vanity of vanities . . . all is vanity" (a phrase that appears as bookends: Eccles. 1:2 and 12:8), the emphasis is also clear: the breath and wind of life comes and goes, and its final expiration from human bodies occurs against the horizon

76. Here I extend in a missiological direction the argument of Jon L. Berquist, "Psalms, Postcolonialism, and the Construction of the Self," in *Approaching Yehud: New Approaches to the Study of the Persian Period*, ed. Jon L. Berquist, Semeia Studies 50 (Atlanta: Society of Biblical Literature, 2007), 195–202.

77. Prov. 1:23 has "Lady Wisdom" (1:20) saying, "I will pour out my spirit [*ruah*] unto you, I will make known my words unto you" (KJV), although *ruah* is translated in English Bibles variously—for instance, as "heart" (NLT) or "thoughts" (NRSV). Further, the connection here is with wisdom, so the ruahological implications are sapiential rather than strictly theological. See for further discussion Lindsay Wilson, "Spirit of Wisdom or Spirit of God in Proverbs 1:23?," in Firth and Wegner, *Presence, Power, and Promise*, 147–58.

of a providential, if yet also apparently distant, deity.[78] The Hebrew triply repetitious *hebel*, which literally means "mist, vapor, breath,"[79] is thus understandable as a breath-like evanescence in which all is transient.[80] In fact, the breath of life here is not just connected to God by way of separation from creatures but is emphasized throughout as fundamentally fleeting: "all is vanity and a chasing after wind" (1:14; cf. 1:17; 2:11, 17, 26; 4:4, 6, 16; 6:9).[81]

Although Qoheleth's ruahology highlights the existential import of not only remembering the creator but also fearing God and keeping the divine commandments (Eccles. 12:13), there may be a national dimension to Ecclesiastes with correspondent missional implications if not applications. That the Preacher is also "king in Jerusalem" (1:1, 12) invites consideration of these teachings as a set of either royal instructions[82] or regal reflections, and the elegiac aspects of the sayings then correlate the ephemerality of human endeavors with national fortunes. In that sense, national projects come and go (2:4–8), national prosperity ebbs and flows (5:12–16), and national regimes arise and fade away (6:1–6; 9:12–18). From this perspective, the decay and desolation of cities (12:3–5) parallels not only the degeneration of aging human bodies and lives but also the demise and decline of nations in defeat and exile.[83] And this remains true even when times are good, during which one has the occasion to be reflective, since one realizes that the comforts of the present are built on the impermanence of the past and will surely fade away.[84] From a missiological perspective, then, the institutions of mission are no less transitory than governments and even empires: when (not if) an or-

78. More precisely, one can recall and remember the creator only while one has the breath of life, but such recollection and remembrance anticipates the end of breath: "to think on one's creator is to think of death, for, as 12.7 says, the life-spirit must go back to the one who gave it." Michael V. Fox, "Aging and Death in Qohelet 12," *JSOT* 42 (1988): 55–77, here 72.

79. Ellen F. Davis, *Proverbs, Ecclesiastes, and the Song of Songs* (Louisville: Westminster John Knox, 2000), 166.

80. For translating "vanity" as "breath-like," see also Kathleen A. Farmer, *Who Knows What Is Good? A Commentary on Proverbs and Ecclesiastes*, ITC (Grand Rapids: Eerdmans, 1991), 146.

81. Arguably, then, one central theological message of this book is that "life so quickly passes." Leo Perdue, *Wisdom and Creation: The Theology of Wisdom Literature* (Nashville: Abingdon, 1994), 207.

82. Perdue, *Wisdom and Creation*, 200–202.

83. This is consistent with the scholarly consensus about a fourth- or third-century-BCE dating for the final form of Ecclesiastes; for extensive argument on reading this text at least in part as national memory, however culturally sedimented, see Jennie Barbour, *The Story of Israel in the Book of Qohelet: Ecclesiastes as Cultural Memory* (Oxford: Oxford University Press, 2012).

84. There are various indicators in the text that Qoheleth reflects in a time of stability and perhaps considerable affluence, almost certainly amid, if not in sustained contact with, the emerging Greek Empire and its attendant Hellenistic culture; see Davis, *Proverbs, Ecclesiastes, and the Song of Songs*, 160.

ganization's vitality departs, it no longer achieves its mission effectively, just as when imperial energy diminishes, it is eventually overtaken. So it is not the mechanisms of missionary undertaking but the message, carried paradoxically by vaporous exhalations that call attention to the one who gifts such breathing to begin with, that counts.

Yet the wisdom traditions of ancient Israel undergird a creation theology that has other possible missiological connections. Most obvious is not only that the "sayings of the wise" (Eccles. 12:11; cf. Prov. 1:6; 22:17; 24:23) are drawn from common human experience but that even Israel's collective traditions are inclusive of the wisdom of surrounding cultures (whether of an Agur son of Jakeh in Prov. 30 or of a King Lemuel in Prov. 31). All of this is suggestive for engagement with wisdom traditions around the world—then, throughout history, and certainly now—vis-à-vis the virtues, the common good, and life in the polis or the public square.[85] Further, these wisdom writings also open up windows into what is recognized as the contemplative side of ancient Israelite spirituality, in particular the brevity of human endeavor as noted by Qoheleth, and this in turn charts dialogical bridges particularly with contemplative spiritual traditions, not least those across the Asian world, even if certainly not exclusively so focused.[86] But if Qoheleth foregrounds a contemplative spirituality that precipitates intercultural and interreligious discussion about the meaning of life in general, it has also not gone unnoticed that its message is strikingly resonant in Buddhist contexts. *Hebel*'s ("mist, vapor, breath") momentariness functions similarly to the Buddhist doctrine of impermanence,[87] and the Preacher's message that life's brevity summons a spirituality of contentment with its simplicities is not too far removed from, and even finds points of contact to engage with, the Buddha's Four Noble Truths, which teach one how to overcome the greed and desire that cause suffering.[88] This is not to say that there are no differences between ancient Israel and historic or contemporary Buddhist traditions, but it is

85. Xinzhong Yao, *Wisdom in Early Confucian and Israelite Traditions* (Aldershot, UK: Ashgate, 2006).

86. See thus also John Eaton, *The Contemplative Face of Old Testament Wisdom in the Context of World Religions* (Philadelphia: Trinity Press International, 1989).

87. Timothy Senapatiratne, "Sri Lankan Reading of Ecclesiastes Informed by Buddhist Texts," *Dharma Deepika: A South Asian Journal of Missiological Research* 18:1 (2014): 5–17.

88. Seree Lorgunpai, "The Book of Ecclesiastes and Thai Buddhism," *AsJT* 8:1 (1994): 155–62, reprinted in R. S. Sugirtharajah, ed., *Voices from the Margin: Interpreting the Bible in the Third World*, new ed. (Maryknoll, NY: Orbis, 1995), 339–48; Michal Solomon Vasanthakumar, "An Exploration of the Book of Ecclesiastes in the Light of Buddha's Four Noble Truths," in *Sharing Jesus Holistically with the Buddhist World*, ed. David Lim and Steve Spaulding (Pasadena, CA: William Carey Library, 2005), 147–77.

to say that Ecclesiastes provides springboards to mission in contemporary Buddhist contexts unlike much of the rest of the Old Testament, much less the Bible as a whole.[89]

The ruahological kernel in the Teacher's words prompts two interrelated thoughts within this missiological horizon. First, mission itself is temporal and in effect passing away, just as the breath of mission eventually returns to the God from which it came. This is not therefore to dispense with mission but to recognize its own penultimacy. More pointedly, the breath of life insists that mission unfolds in and through, and does not exclude, the dust of human embodiment, and hence attentiveness to such divine providence overseeing creaturely transiency bids embrace of the mundane but yet real gifts such breath brings, including but not limited to human work (Eccles. 2:24; 3:22; 5:18–19), mealtimes (8:15; 9:7), and relationships (9:9).

Second, as an extension of the first point, the finitude of creaturely breath compels a missional realism, one that is open to the common world within which human beings meet each other. Qoheleth's matter-of-factness about the passing away of human achievements cautions against any missional triumphalism. Instead, encounter with others unfolds within a common creational matrix, one in which we are invited to learn from and share with others in mutual struggle but also encounter. Ecclesiastes nurtures a calm and patient spirituality in approaching and interacting with others, especially in view of the partial perspectives on truth that all finite creatures possess.[90] Yet commitments toward reciprocity vis-à-vis the passing away of this life unfold amid a transcendent horizon, one that bestows the breath of life toward those who were not in any position to demand such to begin with, and toward which creaturely breaths return from moment to moment in anticipation of a final exhalation. Each missional breath hence can be somber about its announcements and pronouncements, even as it whispers—if only through episodic and intermittent gasps—about the creator beyond.[91]

89. E.g., Kari Storstein Haug, *Interpreting Proverbs 11:18–31, Psalm 73, and Ecclesiastes 9:1–12 in Light of, and as a Response to, Thai Buddhist Interpretations: A Contribution to Christian-Buddhist Dialogue*, Studies in Systematic Theology 10 (Leiden: Brill, 2012).

90. John Prior, "'When All the Singing Has Stopped'—Ecclesiastes: A Modest Mission in Unpredictable Times," *IRM* 91:360 (2002): 7–23.

91. My own pneumatology of interfaith encounter vis-à-vis Eastern wisdom and religious traditions is elaborated in *The Cosmic Breath: Spirit and Nature in the Christianity-Buddhism-Science Trialogue*, Philosophical Studies in Science and Religion 4 (Leiden: Brill, 2012).

Discussion Questions

1. Nehemiah was a kind of "reverse missionary," arriving back to the Israelite homeland (Palestine) from the exilic location, burdened by practical and spiritual, as well as political and religious, concerns and responsibilities. What might his life have to teach us about today's reality of "mission from everywhere to everywhere"?

2. The blowing of the divine wind in the Old Testament Wisdom literature is suggestive for thinking about Christian witness as having creational/cosmic and cross-cultural expansiveness. Might the divine spirit be able to speak through, or even redeem, the wisdom traditions of the world, however that may be defined. If so, how?

3. The psalms reveal Israel singing among the nations. What does it mean for the church to do the same in the twenty-first century? How might such singing be a form of missional witness today?

4

The Breath of the (Writing) Prophets

Centripetal and Centrifugal Witness

Introduction

Having discussed what the Old Testament categorizes as the Former Prophets (Joshua–Kings) in chapter 2, we turn here to the Latter Prophets (*Nevi'im Aharonim*). These include the Major Prophets (Isaiah and Ezekiel, with Jeremiah left out in our account since there are no references to the divine breath in that book) and the Minor Prophets, also known as the Book of the Twelve (from the Aramaic *Trei Asar*). The canonical sequencing may be a bit confusing, however, on two counts. First, our Christian canonical order inserts between Ezekiel and the Twelve the prophecy of Daniel, which the Jewish Tanakh includes under the Ketuvim, or Writings. Second, since the Latter Prophets includes voices from prior to the Babylonian exile, that material included in this chapter may lead to the feeling that we are "going backward" from where we had arrived by the end of the previous chapter.

Things might seem further complicated as we proceed through this chapter because of how we have chosen to treat the book of Isaiah in relation to the Minor Prophets we discuss. Thus, for instance, the ruahological missiology of Isaiah is treated in three sections, corresponding to how many recent scholars analyze the book: into First/Proto- (chaps. 1–39), Second/Deutero- (40–55), and Third/Trito- (56–66) Isaiah. This triad of divisions maps somewhat onto the history of Israel as demarcated by the exile: preexilic (Israel under the Assyrian threat), exilic (the Babylonian deportation), and postexilic (under

Medo-Persian governance).[1] To be sure, these are very rough divisions and far from exact correlations according to the present scholarly consensus as, for instance, Isaiah 32 and 34 seem clearly from the exilic period even as chapter 4 (because of the restoration of Zion indicated) and 48:16 and much of Deutero-Isaiah (because of affinity with 61:1–3) appear to be postexilic.[2]

There are at least two related issues here. First, on the issue of Isaianic authorship, even if initially there was one author (assuming forthtelling capacities are possible for divinely inspired prophets),[3] it is clear that Isaiah's message finally is multigenerational in its relevance to the three contexts associated with the three-part theory.[4] Second, and by extension, the point about First, Second, and Third Isaiah is not to deny the organic interrelatedness of these "parts," but to recognize that the poet(s) and preacher(s) who are referred to in chapters 40–66 of this "book" saw themselves as dependent on, if not also inspired by, the original prophet, reinterpreting, expositing, and applying his teachings in exilic and postexilic contexts.[5] The clincher (at least for me) is that a missiological perspective also supports such a triadic discussion since these historically recognized three sections of the book consistently present Israel's centrifugal witness to the nations as, respectively, prophet, priest, and king.[6] Further, and as important, the triad of contextual spaces inher-

1. "Maps somewhat" speaks to the variety of treatments of specific texts and passages. A recent Jewish scholar urges that Isa. 1–2, 6–8, 10–12, 14, 19, 31, and 36–37 are from the eighth century BCE, but this leaves unresolved the provenance of those other chapters across 1–39. See Shawn Zelig Aster, *Reflections of Empire in Isaiah 1–39: Responses to Assyrian Ideology*, Ancient Near East Monographs 19 (Atlanta: SBL Press, 2017).

2. The periodization for these chapters are acknowledged even by evangelical and pentecostal biblical scholars like Wonsuk Ma, *Until the Spirit Comes: The Spirit of God in the Book of Isaiah*, JSOTSup 271 (Sheffield: Sheffield Academic, 1999), 117, 136–38.

3. As presumed by conservative biblical scholars like Allan A. MacRae, *The Gospel of Isaiah* (Chicago: Moody, 1977), who urges a seventh-century provenance for the entire book.

4. I get the notion of Isaiah's multigenerational relevance from Rickie D. Moore and Brian Neil Peterson, *Voice, Word, and Spirit: A Pentecostal Old Testament Survey* (Nashville: Abingdon, 2017), 184.

5. Thus, the author(s) of chaps. 56–66 drew from the preceding fifty-five chapters, while the author(s) of chaps. 40–55 also retrieved and reappropriated materials from the first thirty-nine chapters; see R. N. Whybray, *Isaiah 40–66*, NCBC (Grand Rapids: Eerdmans, 1981), 39.

6. Robert Martin-Achard, *A Light to the Nations: A Study of the Old Testament Conception of Israel's Mission to the World*, trans. John Penney Smith (Edinburgh: Oliver & Boyd, 1962). The centrifugality of ancient Israel's witness must be underscored as Israel was no "missionary religion" in any classical sense, although this is not to say that gentiles were never welcomed into the Jewish fold; for a cumulative perspective on the scholarly consensus in this regard, see Scot McKnight, *A Light among the Gentiles: Jewish Missionary Activity in the Second Temple Period* (Minneapolis: Fortress, 1991), and, defending McKnight's thesis, Andreas J. Köstenberger and Peter T. O'Brien, *Salvation to the Ends of the Earth: A Biblical Theology of Mission*, NSBT 11 (Downers Grove, IL: InterVarsity, 2001), chap. 3.

ent in this scholarly division also highlights how the ruahic references across the sixty-six chapters of the book can be received in multiple contemporary parallel missiological and sociopolitical situations.

But be admonished: if there is a general development from Proto- through Deutero- and then Trito-Isaiah following the preexilic/exilic/postexilic periodization, then this breaks down in the rest of this chapter. Our discussion of Ezekiel, which comes canonically after Isaiah, takes us back squarely into the exilic period, while turning then to the Book of the Twelve takes us backward (Joel perhaps but Micah surely as a preexilic prophet) and then forward (Haggai and Zechariah as late exilic in some respects but mostly as postexilic texts). It is important to remember, then, that while there is some chronological sequence in this chapter, the following discussion is canonically structured, and our questions are missiological and ruahological rather than strictly historical.

The most important missiological considerations in this chapter pertain to the *otherness* of the nations surrounding Israel. The nations in Isaiah are a complicated aggregate, as agents of judgment on and deliverance of Judah and as those who are being judged themselves simultaneously on the one hand[7] and who are comforted by Yahweh and embraced in Yahweh's worshiping community on the other hand.[8] Even if Ezekiel maintains a more intra-Israel ethnic focus compared to Isaiah,[9] on its own terms, as we shall see, Ezekiel opens up to almost as rich a transnational missiological horizon. Israel's transnational status is also clearly of concern in the four books of the Twelve that we will be looking at in this chapter. The point is that Israel's priestly—and prophetic and regal—witness to, among, and within the nations and their many peoples evolves according to different historical contexts and various international relations.

7. There is a similar conditionality to how the nations fare compared with Israel, both being dependent on how they respond to Yahweh; thus, the great nations and empires "*are not consistently mythologized as evil*. If these empires act in an evil way, it is because an evil king has risen up to perform particular actions that are destructive to Israel" and to fulfill God's judgmental purposes. Lawrence M. Wills, *Not God's People: Insiders and Outsiders in the Biblical World* (Lanham, MD: Rowman & Littlefield, 2008), 39 (emphasis original).

8. John Goldingay, *Isaiah*, NIBC (Peabody, MA: Hendrickson, 2001), 19–20. Generalizations are of course always in need of qualification. Rather than being the pinnacle of thinking about the nations in the Tanakh, Deutero-Isaiah may be more ambiguous (for instance), particularly regarding the nations' punishment and their service to Israel (cf. Isa. 45:14–17; 49:22–26); see Roy F. Melugin, "Israel and the Nations in Isaiah 40–55," in *Problems in Biblical Theology: Essays in Honor of Rolf Knierim*, ed. Henry T. C. Sun et al. (Grand Rapids: Eerdmans, 1997), 249–64.

9. Kenton L. Sparks documents the gulf between later Isaiah and Ezekiel in terms of universalistic versus ethnic Israelite horizons of concerns; see *Ethnicity and Identity in Ancient Israel: Prolegomena to the Study of the Ethnic Sentiments and Their Expression in the Hebrew Canon* (Winona Lake, IN: Eisenbrauns, 1998).

Ruahologically, Israel's Latter Prophets introduce us to what Norman Gottwald once called a "pneumatic realism"—the notion that the nation's seers were, under the inspiration of the divine breath, able to warn about Israel's impending doom and judgment for its reliance on international alliances.[10] Such *pneumaticism*—or more accurately *ruahism*—is thereby not ethereal but material, having real historical effects in the interactions between nations even in the world of *Realpolitik*. On the other side, it is the cosmic work of the divine wind to enact "peace and justice," and this must be transnational rather than for only one among all other nations.[11] May the *ruah* Yahweh that inspired Israel's prophets guide our own missiological reading at this time.

4.1 Isaiah, Part 1—The Justice of the Spirit: Witness amid International Threat

The first thirty-nine chapters of Isaiah, designated by scholars First or Proto-Isaiah, contain about a third of the references to the *ruah* Yahweh even if they cover more than half of the canonical book. The book is named after Isaiah son of Amoz, the eighth-century-BCE prophet who preached during "the days of Uzziah, Jotham, Ahaz, and Hezekiah, kings of Judah" (Isa. 1:1 ESV) and whose life spanned many of the events discussed in these chapters 1–39 (although arguably materials from other time periods are also included). The first unambiguous reference to the "spirit of the LORD"[12] includes three parallel identifiers:

> A shoot shall come out from the stump of Jesse,
>   and a branch shall grow out of his roots.
> The spirit of the LORD shall rest on him,
>   the spirit of wisdom and understanding,
>   the spirit of counsel and might,
>   the spirit of knowledge and the fear of the LORD. (Isa. 11:1–2)[13]

---

10. See Norman K. Gottwald, *All the Kingdoms of the Earth: Israelite Prophecy and International Relations in the Ancient Near East* (New York: Harper & Row, 1964), 358–61.

11. See Michael Welker, *God the Spirit*, trans. John F. Hoffmeyer (Minneapolis: Fortress, 1994), chap. 3.

12. Isa. 4:4, about which I will say a bit more momentarily, is not directly about the *ruah* Yahweh.

13. I will not say more about the final clause, but Lian Sian Mung, "The Charismatic and Non-Charismatic Roles of the Spirit in Isaiah 11:1–5," in *The Old Testament in Theology and Preaching: Essays in Honor of Kay Fountain*, ed. Teresa Chai and Dave Johnson (Baguio City, Philippines: Asia Pacific Theological Seminary Press, 2018), 133–53, notes that the divine breath's non-charismatic endowments include what will enable political engagement and navigation in an ancient imperial context: "the fear of the LORD"; for more expansive discussion, see Hilary

The promise of the restoration of the Davidic covenant here (denoted by the "stump of Jesse"; cf. Isa. 7:1–17; 9:1–7) unfolds in the context of the Assyrian crisis in the last third of the eighth century, in particular the fall of the northern kingdom (the ten tribes) to Sargon II in 721 BCE.[14] On the one hand, the Assyrians were going to be used by Yahweh to judge Israel, particularly for its reliance on its own political and other resources (10:5; 20:4; 52:4). But on the other hand, Assyria itself would be judged by Yahweh and its grand designs ultimately overthrown (10:12, 24–27; 30:31; 31:8). Note here that the Assyrians across the Isaianic narrative, but in particular in Proto-Isaiah, are not objects of mission in any traditional centrifugal sense. Rather, they, like the Egyptian Empire before and the Babylonian and Persian Empires after, are instruments of Yahweh and will be held accountable for their actions that either bless or curse Israel.[15] Against this broader Isaianic background, then, Israel's messiah, the one anointed by the breath of Yahweh, would emerge, full of wisdom, to "decide with equity for the meek of the earth; / and he shall strike the earth with the rod of his mouth, / and with the breath of his lips he shall kill the wicked" (11:4 ESV).

The justice to be meted out and the righteousness to be established (Isa. 11:5) first of all vindicate Israel from the hands of its oppressors and then ensure that "the earth will be full of the knowledge of the LORD as the waters cover the sea" (11:9). Hence the renown of Yahweh's achievements through this Davidic figure also becomes "a signal to the peoples; the nations shall inquire of him, and his dwelling shall be glorious" (11:10). In short, it is exactly through the reassembling of the "remnant" and "outcasts" of Israel and their regathering "from Assyria, from Egypt, from Pathros, from Ethiopia, from Elam, from Shinar, from Hamath, and from the coastlands of the sea," in effect "from the four corners of the [then Assyria-dominated] earth," that has transnational and international significance (11:11–12).[16]

Marlow, "The Spirit of Yahweh in Isaiah 11:1–9," in *Presence, Power, and Promise: The Role of the Spirit of God in the Old Testament*, ed. David G. Firth and Paul D. Wegner (Downers Grove, IL: IVP Academic, 2011), 220–32.

14. Goldingay, *Isaiah*, 83.

15. See further Mary Katherine Y. H. Hom, *The Characterization of the Assyrians in Isaiah: Synchronic and Diachronic Perspectives*, LHBOTS 559 (New York: T&T Clark, 2014), esp. the epilogue.

16. The salvation of Assyria is also forecasted in Isa. 11:16; 19:23–25; 27:13. In fact, in the main, the prophet Isaiah may counsel various responses to the Assyrian threat depending on the circumstances, but the primary message of Yahweh's sovereignty even during this time of Assyrian dominance is consistent (see Aster, *Reflections of Empire*, 319–21). Of Isa. 19:24–25 specifically read against the backdrop of many other Old Testament texts that exclude others from Israel, one scholar notes, "The texts that call for destruction of enemies, avoiding foreigners as impure, and nationalistically reusing the terminology of the 'impure peoples' who

The other Proto-Isaian references to the breath of Yahweh confirm the basic themes found in this text. Looking backward, Isaiah 4:4 refers to the judgment of Jerusalem "by a spirit of judgment and by a spirit of burning,"[17] while looking ahead, Isaiah 28:5–6 refers to the Lord of Hosts' "spirit of justice" that will render a verdict on the disobedient leaders of Israel. This is consistent with the messianic decrees that unfold not via ordinary means: "He shall not judge by what his eyes see, / or decide by what his ears hear" (11:3).

Isaiah 30:1–2 reads:

> Oh, rebellious children, says the LORD
> who carry out a plan, but not mine;
> who make an alliance, but against my will [*ruah*]
>   adding sin to sin;
> who set out to go down to Egypt
>   without asking for my counsel,
> to take refuge in the protection of Pharaoh,
>   and to seek shelter in the shadow of Egypt.

Here the prophet warns Judah against reliance on Egypt to ward off the Assyrian menace.[18] If this were not sufficiently deterrent, Isaiah clarifies: "The Egyptians are human, and not God / their horses are flesh, and not spirit" (31:3). The parallelism is clear that Egyptian might (horses) is no less finite than Egyptian soldiers, neither matching up to the strength of the divine *ruah*.[19]

The point is that if the Assyrians will be displaced by the messianic judgment, then so also is Egyptian power fleeting. And if Egypt will finally be adjudged, as detailed by the oracles in chapters 30–31, then it is Yahweh himself who will raise up a king to "reign in righteousness" and "rule with justice" (Isa. 32:1). More concretely, Israel's restoration to flourishing, the renovation of Israel's moral and social orders, in effect,[20] will happen when "a spirit from

---

were driven from the land cannot be allowed to overshadow or rule out the tremendous hope engendered by a passage such as the last two verses of Isaiah 19." Daniel L. Smith-Christopher, "Between Ezra and Isaiah: Exclusion, Transformation, and Inclusion of the 'Foreigner' in Postexilic Biblical Theology," in *Ethnicity and the Bible*, ed. Mark G. Brett, BibInt 19 (Leiden: Brill, 1996), 117–42, here 141.

17. The construction in 4:4 is "more detached from God," being "so impersonal here that one can [should] say 'a spirit of judgment' or 'burning' as if there were many other functional spirits in Yahweh's court." Ma, *Until the Spirit Comes*, 26 and 181.

18. J. Alec Motyer, *Isaiah: An Introduction and Commentary* (Downers Grove, IL: InterVarsity, 1999), 21.

19. Note then that Isa. 31:3 "articulates, for the first time, that *ruah* is God's essential element." Wonsuk Ma, "The Spirit (*ruah*) of God in Isaiah 1–39," *AsJT* 3:2 (1989): 582–96, here 590.

20. See Christopher J. H. Wright, *Knowing the Holy Spirit through the Old Testament* (Downers Grove, IL: IVP Academic, 2006), 124–26.

on high is poured out on us, / . . . [then] the wilderness becomes a fruitful field, / and the fruitful field is deemed a forest" (32:15).[21] This promise of the *ruah* Yahweh is then preliminarily fulfilled (at least in the final form of the Isaianic text) in Hezekiah's rescue from the hands of Sennacherib at the end of First Isaiah (chaps. 36–39, particularly 37:36–38), although final fulfillment awaits eschatological consummation.[22] The themes of justice and righteousness are highlighted (32:16–17), though, and these fruits of the blowing divine wind are consistent with that wrought by the spirit-anointed messiah.

First Isaiah effectively draws to a close (the Hezekiah chapters, 36–39, excepted) with the final proclamation of judgment on the nations in general (Isa. 34:1–2) and on Edom in particular (34:5–15).[23] Edom comes under prophetic censure around the time of the Babylonian exile chiefly because the Edomites betrayed Judah during the Assyrian peril (2 Chron. 28:16–18) and then later abandoned their Israelite kin to the Babylonians in 587 BCE.[24] The judgment on Edom in this Isaianic passage is itself suggestive of a perspective that regarded Edom as Babylon and hence as subject to the same prophetic fate.[25] So the cruelty of these outsiders—Edomites, Babylonians, the nations at large—will be punished. Yahweh will also exonerate his people, salvaging

---

21. Even if this were an exilic or postexilic text—for the former alternative, see Richard J. Sklba, "'Until the Spirit from on High Is Poured out on Us' (Isa 32:15): Reflections on the Role of the Spirit in the Exile," *CBQ* 46 (1984): 1–17—it fits well canonically here, especially if understood as nurturing Israel's hope amid pronouncement of judgment on the nations (Isa. 13–34). As Sigmund Mowinckel observes with regard to how 32:15–18 is fitted into a tenuous circumstance, "Here too an older Isaiah saying became the starting point for a new supplementary promise of the end of the period of punishment." *The Spirit and the Word: Prophecy and Tradition in Ancient Israel*, ed. K. C. Hanson (Minneapolis: Fortress, 2002), 69.

22. See Walter Brueggemann, *Isaiah 1–39*, Westminster Bible Companion (Louisville: Westminster John Knox, 1998), 219.

23. As Gottwald (*All the Kingdoms of the Earth*, 382–83) notes, total apocalyptic destruction of the nations is rare (e.g., Judg. 5; Ps. 68; Ezek. 38–39; Hab. 3), less common than their subjugation and vassalship under Israel's dominion; even the destructive cosmic judgment of Isa. 64:1–7 is set within a broader context of the renewal of heaven and earth in 65:17–25.

24. If Genesis presents a more full-orbed account of the Jacob-Esau relations, and Deut. 23:7–8 urges Israel to treat Edomites graciously as kin, then the more antagonistic posture was fueled at least in part during the times of the Davidic monarchy when Judah annexed some of Edom's land (see §2.4), and then certainly in developments leading up to the Babylonian exile, not only because Edom forsook Israel during the latter's time of need but also since Edom attempted to enlarge its own borders at the expense of Israel and its banishment from the land (cf. Ps. 137:7; Jer. 49:7–22; Lam. 4:21–22; Ezek. 25:12–14; 35:1–36:15; Joel 4:19; Obad. 11–14; Mal. 1:2–5); see Bradford A. Anderson, *Brotherhood and Inheritance: A Canonical Reading of the Esau and Edom Traditions*, LHBOTS 556 (New York: T&T Clark, 2011).

25. Bert Dicou suggests that Isa. 34 draws on three other long oracles against Edom: Jer. 49:7–22; Ezek. 25:12–14; and Ezek. 35:1–36:15; see *Edom, Israel's Brother and Antagonist: The Role of Edom in Biblical Prophecy and Story*, JSOTSup 169 (Sheffield: Sheffield Academic, 1994), 105.

them, to the very last one, from the clutches of historical erasure: "For the mouth of the LORD has commanded / and his spirit has gathered them" (Isa. 34:16). Yahweh's *ruah* thereby facilitates the return and restoration of the people of God (chap. 35), here a reiteration of the promise of regathering made earlier amid the Assyrian peril (11:1–12), but now in light of the Babylonian conquest and in anticipation of Israel's final redemption (Isa. 40–66).[26]

The ruahology of First Isaiah is clear: the *ruah* Yahweh is on the side of justice, more specifically justice for the people of God vis-à-vis its adversaries. Yet the justice of the divine spirit, while clearly opposed to the intentions of the nations insofar as they were malevolent toward Israel, is not without implications for international shalom. The renewal and reestablishment of Israel will at least be known among the nations, to the ends of the earth. If Proto-Isaiah from this perspective does not support any explicit missionary witness beyond Israel, its acclamation of *ruah* Yahweh's works of justice has implications for all missional endeavors. Aside from admonishing against self-inflated notions based on presumed status as the elect of God, the works of justice cannot finally be self-contained, whether nationally (for the Hebrew prophets) or ecclesially. It is not as if we can be content with divine justice meted on "our" behalf, as if what happens to those who are not of or with "us" has no implications for implementing divine righteousness. Hence, First Isaiah's *ruah* of justice urges reconsideration of the witness of the people of God not as unrelated to divine deliverance from the ferocity of so-called pagan actions but directly amid such rescue. This in effect presses the question of what it means to be the people of God and then to bear witness to others in a conflict-ridden and transnational world.

4.2   Isaiah, Part 2—The Comfort(s) of the Spirit: Witness in a Far Country

If First Isaiah suggests that the justice of *ruah* Yahweh has international implications, then the so-named Second or Deutero-Isaiah, which covers chapters 40–55,[27] delves more deeply into that very space. The generally agreed upon

26. This is the argument of Claire R. Mathews, based on the Esau-Jacob relationship and on Isaiah's (here understood in terms of the final form of the whole book) need to reaffirm the latter's election despite the aggression of the nations, of which Edom is the closest; see *Defending Zion: Edom's Desolation and Jacob's Restoration (Isaiah 34–35) in Context*, BZAW 236 (Berlin: de Gruyter, 1995).

27. Mowinckel (*The Spirit and the Word*, 62) argues that whatever the later redaction history, these sixteen chapters are best understood and read as having "a single prophetic figure as their originator," what the guild has called Deutero-Isaiah.

vantage point here, though, is the Babylonian exile, particularly toward the end,[28] during which the people are hoping for deliverance and amid which the servant of Yahweh (Isa. 42:1; 49:3–6; 52:13; 53:11) is announced as the one through whom such liberation will be achieved. And as First Isaiah prophesied about a Davidic redeemer anointed by the spirit (11:1–2), so also Second Isaiah announces that the liberator is enabled by the *ruah* Yahweh:

> Here is my servant, whom I uphold,
>   my chosen, in whom my soul delights;
> I have put my spirit upon him;
>   he will bring forth justice to the nations. (42:1)[29]

Note, though, that the deeds of the *ruah*-empowered servant accomplish not only salvation for Israel but also justice for the nations, and this is reiterated a few lines later: "He will not grow faint or be crushed / until he has established justice in the earth; / and the coastlands wait for his teaching" (42:4). More controversially, it is indeed through anointing even unbelieving rulers like Cyrus of Persia (45:1) circa 539 BCE that the nations are subdued and Yahweh's will for ending the exile is achieved (Ezra 1:2–4; 2 Chron. 36:22–23).[30]

Herein we are thrust headlong into one of the most contentious aspects of the Deutero-Isaianic chapters: whether or not or to what degree the redemption of Israel includes the salvation of the nations. Are blessings for Israel alone (Isa. 41:11; 42:13; 43:3, 8–13; 47:3; 49:26; 51:22) or for the world (40:5; 42:1–7, 12; 44:5; 45:6, 22–24; 49:6; 51:4–5; 52:10; 55:5)? Is Israel active or passive in its witness to the nations? Are nations subject to Israel or coequal with Israel before God?[31] Part and parcel of the debate, at least from a missiological perspective, is the twice-repeated assertion that Israel is to be "a light to the nations" (42:6; 49:6),[32] particularly in order that Yahweh's salvation

---

28. Leo G. Perdue and Warren Carter suggest the decade of the 540s from internal evidence correlated with known historical developments; see *Israel and Empire: A Postcolonial History of Israel and Early Judaism*, ed. Coleman A. Baker (London: Bloomsbury, 2015), 96.

29. This text is quoted in Matthew's Gospel (see §5.1).

30. See Asher Eder, "King Cyrus, Anointed (Messiah) of the Lord," *JBQ* 23:3 (1995): 188–92; and Ralph W. Doermann, "Cyrus, Conqueror of Babylon: Anointed (by the Lord) or Appointed (by Marduk)?," *Proceedings of the Eastern Great Lakes and Midwest Bible Societies* 7 (1987): 1–16.

31. For orientation to the arguments, see Michael A. Grisanti, "Israel's Mission to the Nations in Isaiah 40–55: An Update," *The Master's Seminary Journal* 9:1 (1998): 39–61.

32. This does not include the parallel assertion in 51:4: "Listen to me, my people, / and give heed to me, my nation; / for a teaching will go out from me, / and my justice for a light to the peoples." Interestingly, in the first instance, the Lord who enables Israel's light or witness to the nations is also the one "who created the heavens and stretched them out, / who spread out the earth and what comes from it, / who gives breath to the people upon it / and spirit to

"may reach to the end of the earth" (49:6; cf. 45:22–23).[33] Yet the scope of the latter is specified in the following verse as involving only the wondrous acknowledgment by the kings of the earth of Yahweh's restorative powers over the destiny of his people:

> Kings shall see and stand up,
>> princes, and they shall prostrate themselves,
> because of the LORD, who is faithful,
>> the Holy One of Israel, who has chosen you. (49:7)[34]

Over the last two generations, then, such qualifications have influenced the disputation about whether Second Isaiah has a nationalistic (Israelite) or universalistic (including the nations) soteriological horizon in the latter direction: any salvation made available to the nations is embedded within their submission to (minimally) or incorporation within (maximally) a restored and renewed Israel.[35]

The other four ruahological references in Second Isaiah do not appear to trouble this trajectory of adjudicating the matter. In the original oracular clarion call to comfort Israel (Isa. 40:1–8), the prophet lifts up the magnanimity

those who walk in it" (42:5). This is reminiscent of the ruahological references in the Wisdom literature (see chap. 3 above).

33. This is emphasized by the earlier writers on Old Testament missiology, including H. H. Rowley, *The Missionary Message of the Old Testament* (London: Carey Southgate, 1955), chap. 3. Martin-Achard encapsulates this message for the Isaianic exilic community: "The ultimate destiny of the world depends on the existence of Israel in the midst of the nations; in living by Yahweh the Chosen People lives for mankind. Such is the missionary outlook that emerges from the oracles of Deutero-Isaiah" (*Light to the Nations*, 31). See also Ronald E. Clements, "A Light to the Nations: A Central Theme of the Book of Isaiah," in *Forming Prophetic Literature: Essays on Isaiah and the Twelve in Honor of John D. W. Watts*, ed. James W. Watts and Paul R. House, JSOTSup 235 (Sheffield: Sheffield Academic, 1996), 57–69; and Ivan Friesen, "Light to the Nations in Isaiah's Servant Songs," in *Beautiful upon the Mountains: Biblical Essays on Mission, Peace, and the Reign of God*, ed. Mary H. Schertz and Ivan Friesen, Studies in Peace and Scripture 7 (Eugene, OR: Wipf & Stock, 2003), 63–74.

34. One of the earliest defenders of Second Isaiah as a positive missionary message to the nations suggests, in light of such presumed qualifications, that "the prophet discerned in moments of high vision the glorious fact that Yahweh's salvation was for all the world, while at other times he sank back to a more traditional and superior attitude towards the Gentiles." Anthony Gelston, "The Missionary Message of Second Isaiah," *Scottish Journal of Theology* 18:3 (1965): 308–18, here 316. Yet that these "more traditional" attitudes are right next to what is called "moments of high vision" invites consideration that the latter ought to be understood in light of the former.

35. If its repeated citation in the literature on the matter since is any indication of whence the discussion has traveled, D. W. van Winkle represents a culmination of thinking up until the mid-1980s, even as he then charts representative pathways forward; see "The Relationship of the Nations to Yahweh and to Israel in Isaiah XL–LV," *VT* 35:4 (1985): 446–58.

of Yahweh (40:9–14) in contrast to the nothingness of the nations (40:15–17) and their idols (40:18–20; cf. 41:21–29; 44:9–20),[36] and in this context makes astonishingly contrasting claims about the *ruah* Yahweh. First the prophet says the breath of God scorches and destroys as certainly as the word of God stands forever (40:7–8), and then he rhetorically asks:

> Who has directed the spirit of the LORD,
>   or as his counselor has instructed him?
> Whom did he consult for his enlightenment,
>   and who taught him the path of justice? (40:13–14)[37]

So if, on the one hand, the wind of God persists as a source of divine judgment,[38] the same breath is also revealed as unparalleled among the deities of the world so that the works of the *ruah* Yahweh thereby are inimitable. Then, as this initial oracle repeats the links between the wind of Yahweh and justice, the next allusion, also in the context of encouraging the exiles amid Babylonian rule, connects to the earlier Proto-Isaianic pronouncement (32:15) about the divine breath's revitalization of the land:

> But now hear, O Jacob my servant,
>   Israel whom I have chosen! . . .
> For I will pour water on the thirsty land,
>   and streams on the dry ground;
> I will pour my spirit upon your descendants,
>   and my blessing on your offspring. (44:1–3)

Although the blast of the *ruah* can blister and destroy (40:7), here the same breath facilitates both the redemption of the people and their restoration to the land from which they are exiled. The final Deutero-Isaianic reference to the *ruah* Yahweh suggests that his servant *and* breath are sent as if in tandem to guide Israel's renewal: "And now the Lord GOD has sent me and his spirit"

---

36. Ironically, it is indeed in exile, when the people are overcome by other nations, that monotheistic commitments emerged in ancient Israel, almost as if to say the exilic experience itself is allowed if not ordained, not by foreign deities, but by the only God, Yahweh of Israel; for more on the superiority of Second Isaiah's monotheism over against the ultimate nonreality of Mesopotamian "summodeism" (the idea of Marduk as including features or characteristics of more local deities), see Mark S. Smith, *God in Translation: Deities in Cross-Cultural Discourse in the Biblical World* (Grand Rapids: Eerdmans, 2010), 177–80.

37. Wilf Hildebrandt, *An Old Testament Theology of the Spirit of God* (Peabody, MA: Hendrickson, 1995), 39–41, comments on *ruah* in this text as referring to Yahweh as creator.

38. Hearkening back to the days of old, for instance at the Red Sea (§1.2); cf. Isa. 11:15; 27:8; and 30:28.

(48:16),[39] so that his people can flourish in their restoration (48:17–19)[40] and that the ends of the earth may know "the LORD has redeemed his servant Jacob!" (48:20). Here Israel's witness to the nations consists in proclaiming Yahweh's redemptive powers over his people and ends ominously for those in Babylon and Chaldea (48:20), not to mention any other international onlookers: "'There is no peace,' says the LORD, 'for the wicked'" (48:22).

In the end, Deutero-Isaiah's ruahology suggests that the salvation of the nations, if actualizable at all even eschatologically, will be subsumed within Israel's restitution.[41] Israel's light ultimately illuminates and signals to the nations (Isa. 49:22) "that I am the LORD; [that] those who wait for me shall not be put to shame" (49:23). If, on the one hand, "all the ends of the earth shall see the salvation of [Israel's] God" (52:10), then, on the other hand, "your descendants will possess the nations" (54:3; cf. 43:3; 45:14; 49:22–23).[42] This is because "the Holy One of Israel is [Israel's] Redeemer, / the God of the whole earth he is called" (54:5). Yet the focus is actually less on the nations and their fate than on God and his people.[43] International blessings are solely an effect of Israel being a magnet to other nations and peoples,[44] even

39. The "me" being either the author of the text or Cyrus the ruler of Babylon referenced by implication in 48:14–15; see Paul D. Wegner, "Isaiah 48:16: A Trinitarian Enigma?," in Firth and Wegner, *Presence, Power, and Promise*, 233–44 (Wegner's answer to the question in the essay's subtitle is *no*, since this text does not address trinitarian issues, even inchoately).

40. As John Goldingay shows, Isa. 48:16, with 48:17, introduces "the divine word in vv. 17b–19"; see Goldingay, *The Message of Isaiah 40–55: A Literary-Theological Commentary* (New York: T&T Clark, 2005), 354.

41. Rikk E. Watts shows that Deutero-Isaiah's ideas about the nations' judgment/salvation, understood as incorporation into Israel, draw from prior literature—for instance, Gen. 12:1–3, which talks not only about the blessing of nations but also about their being cursed if they cursed Abraham's descendants; or the exodus, conquest, and Davidic monarchic narratives, in which there is a place reserved among the people of God for outsiders—except that "what had transpired in a more local setting in the past would now take place on a grander and universal scale." "Echoes from the Past: Israel's Ancient Traditions and the Destiny of the Nations in Isaiah 40–55," *JSOT* 28:4 (2004): 481–508, here 506.

42. Thus, the nations are not only gathered under or into Zion and Jerusalem—on Jerusalem as the "center of salvation for the nations" in terms of being asylum, attracting the nations and their wealth, and hosting the eschatological banquet, see A. de Groot, *The Bible on the Salvation of Nations*, trans. F. vander Heijden (De Pere, WI: St. Norbert Abbey, 1966), 47–64—but the exiles in the far country in effect switch roles with their regents. This would be consistent also with the claim that "the nations" are not homogeneous but refer to those who find themselves related in various ways to the Jewish diaspora; for the latter theory, see D. E. Hollenberg, "Nationalism and 'the Nations' in Isaiah XL–LV," *VT* 19:1 (1969): 23–36.

43. Whybray, *Isaiah 40–66*, 31–32. So, what we take as language of contempt for the nations is "more concerned with glorifying Yahweh," and the submission of the nations, rather than indicating loss of status or humiliation, "can instead mean elevation, the obtaining of wisdom, and substantial blessing" (Watts, "Echoes from the Past," 504 and 506).

44. Goldingay, *Isaiah*, 18–19.

as it is the renewal of Israel that is central for the redemptive fortunes of the world as a whole.[45]

In the exilic context, it is understandable that the prophet's words of comfort would include both vindication from their Babylonian and Persian overlords—projecting Israel's own narrative of lordly domination—and a reversal of fortunes. But there is little in Second Isaiah inviting the witness of the exiles in the alien land, much less to "seek the welfare of the city where I have sent you into exile, and pray to the LORD on its behalf" (see Jer. 29:7). Yet even if this may have been a missed opportunity and the conversion of those outside the covenant was not explicitly stated as a task for the exiles, it is implied within the Deutero-Isaianic vision of the nations drawn into Israel's orbit.[46] Later (apostolic and Christian) readers certainly deployed these texts as justifying if not underwriting mission to the gentiles.[47]

What is less often retrieved is that the light of Israel also witnessed to the justice of the divine *ruah*. If contemporary believers find the comfort of the divine spirit in sustaining their lives during exile or other diasporic circumstances, then they may also want to recall that the works of the divine breath are to enact divine justice in a broken world. And because justice is a relational affair—here also consistent with references to *ruah* in Proto-Isaiah (above)—God's righteousness will involve healing between, rather than only hierarchical subordination of, nations in relationship to the people of God, no matter where the latter find themselves or how nations are aligned. Hence, although from the exilic site the salvation of Yahweh is anticipated as overturning the oppressiveness of imposing (Babylonian-Persian) rule, in reality such deliverance can never merely be a reverse imperialism (under Israelite dominion)[48] but will need to reflect divine righteousness and shalom for both the people of God and all nations.

---

45. See E. John Hamlin, *God and the World of Nations: The View from Babylon as Found in Isaiah 40–55*, The Southeast Asia Journal of Theology Occasional Papers 2 (Singapore: Association of Theological Schools of Southeast Asia, 1972).

46. Andrew Wilson notes that "Deutero-Isaiah universalized the Mosaic covenant to the nations, and in this limited sense, he demanded of them a conversion." *The Nations in Deutero-Isaiah: A Study in Composition and Structure*, Ancient Near Eastern Texts and Studies 1 (Lewiston, NY: Edwin Mellen, 1986), 329.

47. See James A. Meek, *The Gentile Mission in Old Testament Citations in Acts: Text, Hermeneutic, and Purpose*, LNTS 385 (New York: T&T Clark, 2008), chap. 3; Michael F. Bird, "'A Light to the Nations' (Isaiah 42:6 and 49:6): Inter-textuality and Mission Theology in the Early Church," *RTR* 65:3 (2006): 122–31; G. O. Abe, "The Messianic Theology of Deutero-Isaiah: The Challenges of Mission to the Twentieth Century African Churches," *Africa Theological Journal* 18:1 (1989): 61–70.

48. As Smith (*God in Translation*, 225) notes, such a vision of supremacy coming out of the exile "was arguably a form of notional imperialism on the part of a people with no claim or capacity to imperialism of its own."

4.3　Isaiah, Part 3—The Present Promise of the Spirit: Witness Betwixt and Between

Isaiah 56–66, called Third or Trito-Isaiah in the scholarly literature, is now understood by most students of the book to be quite dependent on the preceding fifty-five chapters, in many cases reappropriating them for a postexilic Judahite (Yehudite) or Palestinian community. If Deutero-Isaiah looked forward to deliverance from exile and return to the homeland, it is surmised that the author or authors of Third Isaiah, fresh off their own experience from the imperial center (so to speak),[49] now not only faced the immense task of rebuilding the nation and the city of Jerusalem (Isa. 60:10; 61:4) but also confronted opposition on the ground, whether because of infighting among local religious and other (political) leaders (56:9–12) or because of divisive factions and perceived idolatry among the so-called indigenous groups that had remained and lived in the land through the exilic period (57:1–13). Herein was a set of (persisting) circumstances truly betwixt and between, as the saying goes, in which the Judahites found themselves back "home," but not in a home that was recognizable, certainly not one in which they could comfortably resettle. The parallels here to the situation addressed in Nehemiah (see §3.2) lead us to expect a similar ruahology, and we are not disappointed.

For our ruahological purposes, the most obvious connection to the post-exilic developments unfolded in Nehemiah is the community lament song for divine mercies in Isaiah 63:7–64:11, which not only may have been derived from Palestinian liturgical prayers from the exilic period (like Neh. 9:5–38) but also features signal developments in ancient Israel's understanding of the divine spirit.[50] At one point, there are three distinct appearances of the breath of Yahweh in the midst of recollecting and calling upon the deity's patience and kindness, and they are italicized in this quotation:

> But they rebelled
> 　and grieved *his holy spirit*;
> therefore he became their enemy;
> 　he himself fought against them.

---

49. Brent A. Strawn thus suggests that the authors of this portion of Isaiah may have been envisioning their own *pax Jerusalem* from out of their own experience of the *pax Persica*. "'A World under Control': Isaiah 60 and the Apadana Reliefs from Persepolis," in *Approaching Yehud: New Approaches to the Study of the Persian Period*, ed. Jon L. Berquist, Semeia Studies 50 (Atlanta: Society of Biblical Literature, 2007), 85–116, here 115.

50. On Isa. 63:7–64:11 as a communal lament with exilic provenance but postexilic application, see Walter Brueggemann, *Isaiah 40–66*, Westminster Bible Companion (Louisville: Westminster John Knox, 1998), 228; cf. Whybray, *Isaiah 40–66*, 255–56.

> Then they remembered the days of old,
>   of Moses his servant.
> Where is the one who brought them up out of the sea
>   with the shepherds of his flock?
> Where is the one who put within them
>   *his holy spirit,*
> who caused his glorious arm
>   to march at the right hand of Moses,
> who divided the waters before them
>   to make for himself an everlasting name,
>   who led them through the depths?
> Like a horse in the desert,
>   they did not stumble.
> Like cattle that go down into the valley,
>   *the spirit of the* LORD *gave them rest.*
> Thus you led your people,
>   to make for yourself a glorious name. (Isa. 63:10–14)

Not only is this an unusual cluster of references, but their convergence manifests two distinct achievements. First, a highly elevated view of the *ruah* with divinity, and specifically with the divine holiness, is presented (the latter of which occurs elsewhere in the Jewish canon only in Ps. 51:11).[51] Second, the present fortunes of Israel are interwoven with the founding narratives of the Mosaic covenant via the work of the divine breath (as in Neh. 9), but here as a means of appealing that the same wind of Yahweh manifest in the exodus from Egypt would continue its liberative work vis-à-vis the return from Babylonian exile. These features of the ruahology of Isaiah 63 suggest that herein is the "summit of the book's theology of the spirit."[52]

But if this communal lament seeks to receive inspiration and assistance from the divine breath present at the nation's founding, elsewhere in Third Isaiah the divine *ruah* is promised to accomplish Israel's full restoration "from now on and forever" (Isa. 59:21). In fact, Yahweh says, it is the divine spirit and

---

51. Claus Westermann thus writes, "Taking the three occurrences together and noticing how often the term comes, we realize that this is the first step towards the employment of 'Spirit' in relation to God in which each and all of his acts can be attributed to his Spirit or to God's holy Spirit," even as John R. (Jack) Levison urges, "Isaiah 63 . . . is an indication that an early, high pneumatology . . . existed centuries prior to Paul." See Westermann, *Isaiah 40–66*, trans. David M. G. Stalker, OTL (Philadelphia: Westminster, 1969), 389; and Levison, "The Spirit in the Second Temple Context: An Exegetical Analysis of the Pneumatology of N. T. Wright," in *God and the Faithfulness of Paul: A Critical Examination of the Pauline Theology of N. T. Wright*, ed. Christoph Heilig, J. Thomas Hewitt, and Michael F. Bird, WUNT 2/413 (Tübingen: Mohr Siebeck, 2016), 439–62, here 456.

52. George T. Montague, *The Holy Spirit: Growth of a Biblical Tradition* (Peabody, MA: Hendrickson, 1994), 59; see also Ma, *Until the Spirit Comes*, 135.

word that will remain upon and within Israel perpetually: "my spirit that is upon you, and my words that I have put in your mouth, shall not depart out of your mouth, or out of the mouths of your children, or out of the mouths of your children's children" (59:21). And it is with this promise that the heart of Trito-Isaiah's message of future hope, glory, and salvation is then unfolded.[53] More precisely, the central node of this promise of final restoration hearkens back also to the Davidic or messianic servant of Second Isaiah:

> The spirit of the Lord GOD is upon me,
>   because the LORD has anointed me;
> he has sent me to bring good news to the oppressed,
>   to bind up the brokenhearted,
> to proclaim liberty to the captives,
>   and release to the prisoners;
> to proclaim the year of the LORD's favor,
>   and the day of vengeance of our God;
> to comfort all who mourn. (61:1–2; cf. 42:1–4)[54]

Clearly the message is for the full renewal of Israel and the covenant, beset as these exilic returnees are by a multitude of challenges (see 61:3–11), but imbued from within by the word of Yahweh and set upon from above by his breath.

Still, if the ruahology of Second Isaiah is forged within the tension therein between a nationalistic versus universalistic salvation, the promise of the divine breath in Third Isaiah is decidedly Israel-focused. This is not to say that the nations have been excised from the purview of this last segment of Isaiah. On the contrary, the tension remains that the scope of salvation touches in some way or encompasses the nations (e.g., Isa. 60:3; 61:9; 62:2; 64:2) but will nevertheless be located in Zion,[55] to which gifts from the rest of the world, not to

---

53. For more on the view that Isa. 59:21 should be read with the next few chapters than with the preceding portions of chapter 59, see Goldingay, *Isaiah*, 337–38; cf. Carol J. Dempsey, "From Desolation to Delight: The Transformative Vision of Isaiah 60–62," in *The Desert Will Bloom: Poetic Visions in Isaiah*, ed. A. Joseph Everson and Hyun Chul Paul Kim, Ancient Israel and Its Literature 4 (Atlanta: Society of Biblical Literature, 2009), 217–32.

54. Read from the New Testament perspective of Luke 4:16–19 wherein this text is deployed to launch Jesus's public ministry (see §5.3), Isa. 61 has long been understood as a prominent missiological text; for discussion of this and the broader issues, see Holly Beers, *The Followers of Jesus as the Servant: Luke's Model from Isaiah for the Disciples in Luke-Acts*, LNTS 535 (New York: Bloomsbury, 2015).

55. As Mark Brett notes, the nations find blessing *within* Israel, just as non-Israelites found refuge within the descendants of Abraham who were delivered from Egypt (see Exod. 12:43–49; cf. §1.3); see "Imperial Imagination in Isaiah 56–66," in *Isaiah and Imperial Context: The Book of Isaiah in the Times of Empire*, ed. Andrew T. Abernethy et al. (Eugene, OR: Pickwick, 2013), 169–75.

mention the worship of all creation,[56] are directed (60:3–6; 66:12–13, 18–20). Thus, foreigners will "join themselves to the LORD," but through Israel: "my house shall be called a house of prayer for all peoples" (56:6–7).[57] And there will be new heavens and a new earth, yet they also will be Jerusalem- and Israel-centric (65:17–18; 66:22–23).[58] So if the eschatological preeminence of Zion cannot be ignored, neither should the anticipation be minimized that its salvation is internationally constituted.[59]

Further consideration of this transnational diversity amid Zionist unity is warranted as the spirit-anointed messiah's work in 61:1–4 lies at the midpoint of Third Isaiah. That 61:1–4 is the fulcrum implies not only that chapters 60–62 are at the core of the chiastic or concentric structure of Isaiah 56–66 but also that 61:1–9 is the pivot upon which the visions of the restored Jerusalem turn (60:1–22 and 61:10–62:12), and is the hinge around which the judgment (chaps. 56–59) and redemption (chaps. 63–66) of Yahweh are thereby also achieved to the ends of the earth.[60] Read from this perspective, the blowing of Yahweh's *ruah* has ripple effects far beyond revitalization of the land for the disenfranchised exiles, so that the nations are caught up in Israel's restoration in anticipation of cosmic renewal.[61] So in this respect, yes, the witness

56. This segment of Isaiah "sees God's spirit as being given to worshipers in the temple to refresh their spirits and make worship possible." John D. W. Watts, "'The Spirit' in the Prophets: Three Brief Studies," in *Spirit and Renewal: Essays in Honor of J. Rodman Williams*, ed. Mark W. Wilson, JPTSup 5 (Sheffield: Sheffield Academic, 1994), 84–91, here 90.

57. Thus, the message to this postexilic community is "the liberation and return of the different Judean diasporas," and the nations instead "will receive the negative lot of the reversal of fortunes." J. Severino Croatto, "The 'Nations' in the Salvific Oracles of Isaiah," *VT* 55:2 (2005): 143–61, here 161.

58. For more on Isa. 65:17–25 as "in a certain sense the apex of Old Testament revelation on the election of Israel," see James Chukwuma Okoye, *Israel and the Nations: A Mission Theology of the Old Testament* (Maryknoll, NY: Orbis, 2006), chap. 14.

59. Se-Hoon Jang argues that Isaiah's message is uncompromisingly both monotheistic and particularistic with regard to Israel and Yahweh, but nevertheless universalistic in embracing the cosmos, and thereby invites a posture of tolerance, hospitality, dialogue, and mutuality/reciprocity vis-à-vis people outside the covenant; see *Particularism and Universalism in the Book of Isaiah: Isaiah's Implications for a Pluralistic World from a Korean Perspective*, Bible in History 4 (Bern: Peter Lang, 2005).

60. See John Goldingay, *A Critical and Exegetical Commentary on Isaiah 56–66* (London: Bloomsbury, 2014), 2–3 and throughout the remainder of his introduction. In this regard, while Christopher Wright (*Knowing the Holy Spirit*, chap. 1) is right to identify the "creating spirit" also as the spirit of the "new creation," biblical warrants for such are not relegated only to the New Testament but can be understood in this Trito-Isaianic sense. Later in his fifth chapter, Wright does discuss what he calls the "coming spirit" (Isa. 32; Ezek. 36–37; and Joel 2, the latter of which I discuss below), and in this regard I would argue these texts also can be understood as heralding the spirit of the "new creation" in the Old Testament.

61. Matthew J. Lynch, "Zion's Warrior and the Nations: Isaiah 59:15b–63:6 in Isaiah's Zion Traditions," *CBQ* 70 (2008): 244–63. For more on the importance, even centrality, of the land

of Israel to the nations is centripetal rather than centrifugal, culminating with Zion and Jerusalem.[62] Yet insofar as the work of the messiah involves a comprehensive and holistic restoration that addresses social realities, to that same degree the redemption of Israel through the anointed servant, both in Isaiah 61 and across Isaiah, must include, rather than ignore, righteousness and justice for the nations.[63]

Part of the point is that even now, in this postexilic context, Israel may have gotten a perspective on the wider world within which it was situated, but Israel's vision of Yahweh's spirit both connected Israel to the primordial origins as the people of God and reached out to embrace the nations and even Yahweh's creation. To be sure, the exiles were now back in their homeland, yet they were now also more entwined than ever with the (nations of the) world and its systems.[64] In effect, theirs was a view still in between—after the exile but yet awaiting full redemption. For this people, the divine breath promised the divine presence, even as the wind of Yahweh blew in anticipation of the full salvation to come.

4.4   Ezekiel, Part 1—Transported by the Spirit: Witness Crossing Borders

If the Isaianic prophecies spanned generations if not centuries, the prophecies of Ezekiel seem to be concentrated within his lifetime, perhaps the quarter-century period surrounding the fall of Jerusalem and exile of its leaders to Babylon.[65] Whereas the latter Ezekielian prophecies that mention the divine *ruah* (to be treated in the next section) are focused predominantly on the

---

for postexilic renewal, see George A. F. Knight, *The New Israel: A Commentary on the Book of Isaiah 56–66*, ITC (Grand Rapids: Eerdmans, 1985), 123.

62. Thus "the kingdom does not go out to the nations. The nations come into the kingdom." Dirk H. Odendaal, *The Eschatological Expectation of Isaiah 40–66 with Special Reference to Israel and the Nations* (Nutley, NJ: P&R, 1970), 184.

63. See Elmer A. Martens, "Impulses to Mission in Isaiah: An Intertextual Exploration," *BBR* 17:2 (2007): 215–39; and Steven D. Mason, "Getting a 'Handle' on Holistic Christian Mission: The Contribution of Isaiah 61 as a Discrete Old Testament Voice," *Missiology* 40:3 (2012): 295–313.

64. Thereby inviting a postcolonial consideration; see John Goldingay, "Isaiah 56–66: An Isaianic and a Postcolonial Reading," in Abernethy et al., *Isaiah and Imperial Context*, 151–66, esp. 160–65.

65. Or even more precise, given the dates noted by Ezekiel, from 593 to 571 BCE; however, there is some debate about whether Ezekiel prophesied at least in part from Babylon (if he was one of the exiles carried off) or remained in Jerusalem (if he was one of those left behind); see Dale F. Launderville, *Spirit and Reason: The Embodied Character of Ezekiel's Symbolic Thinking* (Waco: Baylor University Press, 2007), 55–56; and John W. Wevers, *Ezekiel*, NCBC (Grand Rapids: Eerdmans, 1982), 23–24.

people of Israel, the earlier clusters concern more the prophet himself.[66] The following briefly examines three constellations—in chapters 1, 2–3, and 11—while making connections to a few other relevant *ruah* citations in the book.[67]

Ezekiel's first vision involves "something like four living creatures," each with four faces (of a human, a lion, an ox, and an eagle) and four wings (Ezek. 1:5–6, 10), and on four wheels with stunning eye-filled rims (1:15, 18). These are vigorous creatures, each somehow moving "straight ahead; wherever the spirit would go, they went, without turning as they went" (1:12). "Spirit" here, as throughout Ezekiel (except in chapter 37), is anarthrous (used without the article) in the Hebrew, so at the textual level it is unclear whether the spirit of God is being referred to. However, it is reiterated: "Wherever the spirit would go, they went, and the wheels rose along with them; for the spirit of the living creatures was in the wheels" (1:20),[68] as if to say that technological artifacts could be animated by nonmaterial breath.[69] Thus in the broader context of the four creatures as figurative of the majesty and incomprehensibility of the deity, the wheels can be understood simultaneously at multiple levels: meteorologically as wind, as Yahweh's breath, or as Yahweh's life-giving spirit.[70]

If Ezekiel's prophetic call was initiated through this leading vision, he prostrates himself (Ezek. 1:28) and then is addressed by Yahweh (2:1): "And when he spoke to me, a spirit entered into me and set me on my feet; and I heard him speaking to me" (2:2). Ezekiel is told he is being sent to "the people of Israel, to a nation of rebels who have rebelled against me" (2:3) and who "will not listen to you, for they are not willing to listen to me" (3:7). It is within this context that we are informed:

> Then the *spirit lifted me up*, and as the glory of the LORD rose from its place, I heard behind me the sound of loud rumbling; it was the sound of the wings of the living creatures brushing against one another, and the sound of the wheels beside them, that sounded like a loud rumbling. The *spirit lifted me up and bore*

66. For an overview, see John Woodhouse, "The 'Spirit' in the Book of Ezekiel," in *Spirit of the Living God, Part One*, ed. B. G. Webb, Explorations 5 (Homebrush West, NSW: Lancer and Moore Theological College, 1991), 1–22.

67. These categorizations are my own; for alternative assessments, see Daniel Block, "The Prophet of the Spirit: The Use of *RWH* in the Book of Ezekiel," *JETS* 32 (1989): 27–49; and Harold E. Hosch, "*RÜAH* in the Book of Ezekiel: A Textlinguistic Analysis," *Journal for Translation and Textlinguistics* 14 (2002): 77–125.

68. Later Ezekiel recounts similarly, "When they stopped, the others stopped, and when they rose up, the others rose up with them; for the spirit of the living creatures was in them" (10:17).

69. Thanks to John Edmiston for conversation about this connection.

70. James Robson, *Word and Spirit in Ezekiel*, LHBOTS 447 (New York: T&T Clark, 2006), 86–91.

me away; I went in bitterness in the heat of my spirit, the hand of the LORD being strong upon me. I *came to the exiles at Tel-abib, who lived by the river Chebar. And I sat there among them, stunned, for seven days. (3:12–15; emphases added)*

After the week, Ezekiel goes into the valley following the Lord's command, beholds the glory of the Lord, and again falls to his face. And once more: "The spirit entered into me, and set me on my feet; and he spoke with me" (Ezek. 3:24). The connecting thread so far, from the first vision through the prophet's call, is the dynamism of the divine wind or breath that moves the living creatures and also the prophet, long before *Star Trek*–like transporters were conceived.

A third grouping of *ruah* references, occurring in Ezekiel's second vision (chaps. 8–11), about a year after the first one,[71] is consistent about the spirit's vitality. First, Ezekiel reports that "the spirit lifted me up between earth and heaven, and brought me in visions of God to Jerusalem, to the entrance of the gateway of the inner court that faces north" (8:3), in order to unveil the abominations of the people in the temple (8:3–18) and the departure of the divine glory from the sacred site (10:1–22). Next, the spirit "lifted me up and brought me to the east gate of the house of the LORD" (11:1) to prophesy against the leaders who were gathered, typically, at that site (11:1–4). Last but not least, after empowering his indictments of judgment on these leaders (11:5), "the spirit lifted me up and brought me in a vision by the spirit of God into Chaldea, to the exiles. . . . And I told the exiles all the things that the LORD had shown me" (11:24–25). As in the preceding, the divine *ruah* is characterized by movement—in these cases, of the prophet himself.[72] Yet as the prophet's movements are liberated by the breath of Yahweh, so also is the idolatry of Israel as centered in the temple in Jerusalem exposed and judged.[73]

There are both centripetal and centrifugal aspects of Ezekiel's ruahology when considered missiologically within the perspective of Jerusalem having been established by Yahweh "in the center of the nations, with countries all around her" (Ezek. 5:5). With regard to the former, it is important to emphasize that Ezekiel's focus, and that of the divine spirit as well in this connection, is on the scattered people of God. The divine *ruah* moved the prophet here and there—to Babylon or to Jerusalem—but always in relation to either those in exile or the remnant "back home." Hence the fortunes of the prophet and that

71. On the timing, following the reference dates provided in Ezek. 8:1, see Wevers, *Ezekiel*, 66.

72. For more on Ezekiel as being "moved" and "transported" by the spirit, see Hildebrandt, *Old Testament Theology*, 189–90.

73. The ruahic manifestation of God, Moore and Peterson write, "blows away the entire religious and theological system of the Jerusalem temple ([Ezek.] chs. 8–10)" (*Voice, Word, and Spirit*, 214).

of the people are intertwined.[74] So, yes, here is a pressured, fragmented, and threatened "people,"[75] on the one hand needing a sense of reassurance, and on the other hand requiring broader awareness of how to comprehend the unfolding sequence of historical events, in order to come to a fresh appreciation of what it meant to be the people of God away from home and among the nations. Yet it is surely in this context that the divine wind moves on to the chosen prophet, attends to him and his people's situation, is manifest at the various sites where the elect of God are situated, and expresses the divine commitment to remain with them despite both sides of the exilic experience. In fact, the wind of God is first unveiled in relation to the four living creatures, representative of the divine majesty and glory, thereby insisting that as creaturely breath is closer to them than they are to themselves, so also divine breath is with the people of God regardless of the circumstances.[76] It is the awesome, and awful, spirit of the wheels and of the living creatures that moves them, and their prophet, in their sojourn. Hence the glorious Lord is simultaneously the spirit of vivaciousness for an oblivious (for the unrighteous leaders) or weary (for those in exile) Israel, both admonishing and caring for them wherever they are.

But if the Ezekielian spirit exhibits this centripetal character vis-à-vis the people of God, it also expresses a centrifugal trajectory in relation to the nations.[77] Ezekiel's "radical theocentricity"[78] is manifest not only in a spirit-filled set of wheels moving the divine creatures in the opening vision but also

74. See on this point the essay by Rickie D. Moore, "'Then They Will Know That a Prophet Has Been among Them': The Source and End of the Call of Ezekiel," in *Passover, Pentecost and Parousia: Studies in Celebration of the Life and Ministry of R. Hollis Gause*, ed. Steven Jack Land, Rickie D. Moore, and John Christopher Thomas, JPTSup 35 (Blandford Forum, UK: Deo, 2010), 53–65.

75. I derive this description in part from Steed Vernyl Davidson, "After the Nation: Reading Oracles against the Nations amidst the Fragmenting of the Nation-State," in *Concerning the Nations: Essays on the Oracles against the Nations in Isaiah, Jeremiah and Ezekiel*, ed. Else K. Holt, Hyun Chul Paul Kim, and Andrew Mein, LHBOTS 612 (London: Bloomsbury, 2015), 223–38.

76. Pieter de Vries, "The Relationship between the Glory of YHWH and the Spirit of YHWH in Ezekiel 33–48," *JBPR* 5 (2013): 109–27.

77. Our discussion does not dwell on Ezekiel's oracles against the nations—Ezek. 25–32, on which see Paul R. Raabe, "Transforming the International Status Quo: Ezekiel's Oracles against the Nations," in *Transforming Visions: Transformations of Text, Tradition, and Theology in Ezekiel*, ed. William A. Tooman and Michael A. Lyons (Eugene, OR: Pickwick, 2010), 187–207—but proceeds with the realization that the judgments against the nations, like the judgment of Israel, are a precondition for experiencing divine salvation, here again for the nations as much as for Israel.

78. I get this from Christopher J. H. Wright, *The Message of Ezekiel: A New Heart and a New Spirit* (Downers Grove, IL: InterVarsity, 2001), 23, who is himself drawing from the work of P. Joyce, *Divine Initiative and Human Response in Ezekiel*, JSOTSup 51 (Sheffield: JSOT Press, 1989), chap. 6.

Ezekiel's Visions
The Universality of the Spirit's Witness

Amelia Rebecca Basdeo-Hill, lecturer in Old Testament,
Pentecostal Theological Seminary, Cleveland, Tennessee, USA

The Old Testament prophets bring into sharp focus the diverse missiological activities of the spirit, and the universal salvific mission of the spirit clearly emerges from these texts. This universal saving work of the spirit is depicted in the life-giving and healing river that flows out of the new temple in Ezekiel 47:1–12. In other parts of Ezekiel, Yahweh's presence that brings about healing and life is expressed through Yahweh's *ruah* (Ezek. 37). Thus, the river flowing out of the temple may be another expression of the life-giving presence of Yahweh, particularly Yahweh's *ruah*. The river, a symbol of Yahweh's *ruah*, makes available to everyone (Israelites and non-Israelites) Yahweh's soteriological benefits of life, healing, and salvation, demonstrating, therefore, the universal salvific mission of Yahweh accomplished through the giving of the spirit.

in a restored and refurbished temple signifying the dwelling place of Yahweh in the closing revelation (chaps. 40–48). In the latter context, Ezekiel also says, "As the glory of the LORD entered the temple by the gate facing east, the spirit lifted me up, and brought me into the inner court; and the glory of the LORD filled the temple" (43:4–5). Herein once again, we are reminded that if the people of Israel were called to be priests to the nations (see Exod. 19:6), then the temple of Israel, destroyed in 586 BCE, would have to be the central locale around which the world would (eventually) be gathered.[79] Within this sacred space, the divine breath introduces the prophet to "the sound of mighty waters" (43:2), "like the vision that [he] had seen by the river Chebar" (43:3; cf. 3:12). And there came a river, with water "flowing from below the threshold of the temple" (47:1). And "on the banks, on both sides of the river, there will grow all kinds of trees for food. Their leaves will not wither nor

79. More specifically from the prophet's perspective, Israel itself originated from among the nations, and hence its salvation is in that sense bound up with those of its neighbors as well; note the verse, "Thus says the Lord GOD to Jerusalem: Your origin and your birth were in the land of the Canaanites; your father was an Amorite, and your mother a Hittite" (Ezek. 16:3), whose connection to the point here I first made reading Herbert Niehr, "'Israelite' Religion and 'Canaanite' Religion," in *Religious Diversity in Ancient Israel and Judah*, ed. Francesca Stavrakopoulou and John Barton (New York: T&T Clark, 2012), 23–36, here 32.

their fruit fail, but they will bear fresh fruit every month, because the water for them flows from the sanctuary. Their fruit will be for food, and their leaves for healing" (47:12). Significantly, from this river of spiritual life, there would be room for the flourishing of all people, even those otherwise deemed alien to Israel (47:21–23).[80] Hence the movement across the Ezekielian visionary arc is precipitated by the spirit-enabled movement of the wheels and its creatures in multiple directions and culminates in the glorious spirit-filled presence hosting foreigners now incorporated into the people of God.

4.5 Ezekiel, Part 2—Transformed by the Spirit: The Heart of Witness

Ezekiel's famous vision of the valley of dry bones (Ezek. 37:1–14) is both central to the latter part of the prophecy[81] and the most *ruah*-filled passage in the whole Old Testament, as the word appears no less than eleven times. Not only does the wind of Yahweh move the prophet toward the visionary site (37:1)—herein consistent with the transportational effects of the divine *ruah* repeatedly highlighted elsewhere in this book (see §4.4)—but this occasion also in effect foregrounds the brutality and reality of death in relation to the breath of life.[82] On the other hand, it is through stark confrontation with mortality that the Lord promises to give breath and life to the bones (37:5–6), representative here of Israel in exile, and urges the prophet, "Prophesy to the *breath*, prophesy, mortal, and say to the *breath*: Thus says the Lord GOD: Come from the four *winds*, O *breath*, and *breathe* upon these slain, that they may live" (37:9; the five references are italicized). Yahweh concludes with this assurance: "I will put my spirit within you, and you shall live, and I will place you on your own soil; then you shall know that I, the LORD, have spoken and will act, says the LORD" (37:14).[83]

The culminating pledge of this oracle reiterates what is said variously earlier in the book, on multiple occasions. If in the dry bones vision Yahweh acts unilaterally to invigorate Israel, earlier it is said that Israel and its wicked

---

80. See William H. Brownlee, *Ezekiel 1–19*, WBC 28 (Waco: Word, 1986), xxxiv; likely, John's vision on Patmos about the river of life with leaves for the healing of the nations (Rev. 22:1–2) was shaped by images from this prophet overlooking the river Chebar.

81. Pieter de Vries argues that chaps. 34–48 of the book are chiastically structured, rotating around the vision of 37:1–14; see "The Relationship between the Glory of YHWH and the Spirit of YHWH in the Book of Ezekiel—Part One," *Old Testament Essays* 28:2 (2015): 326–50.

82. See Robson, *Word and Spirit in Ezekiel*, 113.

83. See Jacqueline Grey, "Acts of the Spirit: Ezekiel 37 in the Light of Contemporary Speech-Act Theory," *JBPR* 1 (2009): 69–82, and her emphasis here on the central role of Yahweh's *ruah* in transforming Israel.

leaders (Ezek. 11:1–2) will repent and "remove from [the land] all its detestable things and all its abominations" (11:18) before Yahweh's act: "I will give them one heart, and put a new spirit within them; I will remove the heart of stone from their flesh and give them a heart of flesh, so that they may follow my statutes and keep my ordinances and obey them" (11:19–20). Then there is a further call by Yahweh to the exiles to don such new dispositions for themselves: "Cast away from you all the transgressions that you have committed against me, and get yourselves a new heart and a new spirit! Why will you die, O house of Israel?" (18:31). Although these earlier passages include Israel's role in its revitalization, later in the prophecy the emphasis shifts back to Yahweh's autonomous agency, as if recognizing that Israel is unable to repent on its own initiative, much less remain faithful: "A new heart I will give you, and a new spirit I will put within you; and I will remove from your body the heart of stone and give you a heart of flesh. I will put my spirit within you, and make you follow my statutes and be careful to observe my ordinances" (36:26–27). Perhaps this does not discount Israel's contribution (11:18–19) and even essential role (8:31) vis-à-vis its relationship with Yahweh,[84] but there is no denying in the end that the deity will have to take responsibility for implanting the new heart and spirit required for Israel's covenant faithfulness (36:26–27; 37:14).[85]

Yet note also how, ultimately, Yahweh's act of renewal and restoration is to be achieved in order to vindicate the name and holiness of Israel's God among the nations. With a reputation tarnished by Israel's disobedience and sinfulness, Yahweh acts so that "the nations shall know that I am the LORD" (Ezek. 36:23). The "resurrection" of Israel anticipated in the blowing of the divine *ruah* over the valley of dry bones is designed similarly, so that "the nations shall know that I the LORD sanctify Israel, when my sanctuary is among them forevermore" (37:28). And in this same context, in order to triply ensure that Yahweh's purposes are not misunderstood, judgment is declared against Gog and Magog (38:1–39:20), which represent those opposed to God's intentions to bless Israel. Then the promise of the spirit is once again connected to the divine aims to communicate to the nations: "They shall forget their shame . . . when I have brought them back from the peoples and gathered

84. Verena Schafroth does not neglect to comment on these aspects of the references to the new heart and spirit in Ezek. 11 and 18; see "An Exegetical Exploration of 'Spirit' References in Ezekiel 36 and 37," *Journal of the European Pentecostal Theological Association* 29 (2009): 61–77.

85. See John R. Levison, "The Promise of the Spirit of Life in the Book of Ezekiel," in *Israel's God and Rebecca's Children: Christology and Community in Early Judaism and Christianity*, ed. David B. Capes et al. (Waco: Baylor University Press, 2007), 247–59.

them from their enemies' lands, and through them have displayed my holiness *in the sight of many nations*. Then they shall know that I am the LORD their God because I sent them into exile among the nations, and then gathered them into their own land. I will leave none of them behind; and I will never again hide my face from them, when I pour out my spirit upon the house of Israel, says the Lord GOD" (39:26–29; emphasis added).[86] Surely here there is no direct or causal interface between the outpouring of the divine *ruah* and the repentance or salvation of the nations, but there is no overlooking the fact that the salvation of Israel will occur in terrestrial, even cosmic, daylight, observable by the world.[87]

The explicit missiological point to be underscored is that the work of the divine *ruah*, while focused on the internal dimensions of Israel's life before its God, has transnational implications and reverberations. To be sure, like Gog and Magog, the nations are found wanting, and a whole segment of Ezekiel's prophecies explicate this verdict (chaps. 25–32). But even amid these judgments, the nations "shall know that I am Yahweh," a refrain that occurs on over a dozen occasions within these pronouncements, and even more when we read the book as a whole.[88] Hence, the work of the divine breath to renew and restore Israel serves also to salvage its witness to the world, even to redeem Yahweh's cosmic standing. And in Israel's emerging monotheistic view of the world, at least as that was unfolding during the sixth century BCE, it is only a short step from such transnational cognition to the question of how to live before the Lord of the world. The point in the Hebraic mentality is that "knowing," in particular Israel's knowing Yahweh relationally, is not merely intellective but entails worship and obedience, which is exactly why the people of God need the divine breath in their hearts and lives, so that they can live into their vocation in the eschatological temple (chaps. 40–48). Otherwise, the restoration of the temple will not find worthy worshipers, as Israel, and the aliens within the orbit of the sanctuary (47:21–23), may "know" Yahweh only in their heads but not with their hearts.

86. Here the pouring out of the divine *ruah* contrasts with the pouring out of the divine wrath a few chapters earlier (in Ezek. 36:18); for this contrast, see Leslie C. Allen, *Ezekiel 20–48*, WBC 29 (Dallas: Word, 1990), 209.

87. "The pouring out of the Spirit of Yahweh upon his people signified the ratification and sealing of the covenant relationship. It represented the guarantee of new life, peace and prosperity. But it signified more than this. It served as the definitive act whereby he claimed and sealed the newly gathered nation of Israel as his own." Daniel I. Block, "Gog and the Pouring Out of the Spirit: Reflections on Ezekiel xxxix 21–29," *VT* 37:3 (1987): 257–70, here 269.

88. Elmer Martens, "Ezekiel's Contribution to a Biblical Theology of Mission," *Direction* 28:1 (1999): 75–87.

Herein the ruahological underpinnings of Ezekiel's missiology ought not to be overlooked. If the work of the divine spirit is centripetally oriented toward the transformation of Israel's heart, the goal of such activity is the empowering of Israel to live out its witness centrifugally in the eyes of the nations.[89] While in exile, then, it is no wonder that the prophet is repeatedly "transported" back to and from the temple, the symbolic site of Yahweh's presence to the people, so that from the activity and turning of the divine wheels on the living creatures through to the eschatological renovation, the temple is never far.[90] Therefore the divine *ruah* not only gives life back to Israel, effectively birthing Israel's witness to the nations through and out of its death (exile), but also enables sustained obedience on Israel's behalf and attention to the Lord's presence in order to achieve transnational and cosmic renewal with Yahweh at the center. The spirit of Yahweh hence enables divine perception, performs purification, and empowers resurrected life, shalomic (just) community, and divine holiness, all for the purposes of transforming the people of God and renewing their witness. In this case, the ruahology of Ezekiel is no less missiologically relevant to the people of God understood as the body of Christ, even as the latter is recognized as the fellowship of the divine spirit.

4.6 Daniel—The Spirit of Babylon: The Witness of Babel

Our reading of *ruah* in Daniel 4 and 5 could be set off on tangents related to scholarly debates about the historicity of Daniel the seer (as opposed to Daniel being a literary figure)[91] or about the authorship and dating of the book.[92] The latter issue centers on whether the book's two parts—namely,

---

89. Thus does Launderville rightly note that the divine *ruah* transforms Israel into "authentic symbols of Yhwh in the sight of the nations" (*Spirit and Reason*, 348–49); in effect, "when the LORD's Spirit is present in them, they will be able to symbolize properly the LORD's reality" (375).

90. I get this insight from Beate Ego, "Ruah and the Beholding of God—From Ezekiel's Vision of the Divine Chariot to Merkaba Mysticism," in *The Holy Spirit, Inspiration, and the Cultures of Antiquity: Multidisciplinary Perspectives*, ed. Jörg Frey and John R. Levison, Ekstasis: Religious Experience from Antiquity to the Middle Ages 5 (Berlin: de Gruyter, 2014), 153–66, esp. 155–56 and 162.

91. For Daniel's historicity, see William H. Shea, "Nabonidus, Belshazzar, and the Book of Daniel: An Update," *AUSS* 20:2 (1982): 133–49; and Alan Millard, "Daniel and Belshazzar in History," *Biblical Archeology Review* 11:3 (May/June 1985): 73–78; the rejoinder is Lester L. Grabbe, "The Belshazzar of Daniel and the Belshazzar of History," *AUSS* 26:1 (1988): 59–66.

92. Evangelicals—e.g., Joyce G. Baldwin, *Daniel*, TOTC (Downers Grove, IL: InterVarsity, 1978), and Tremper Longman III, *Daniel*, NIV Application Commentary (Grand Rapids: Zondervan, 1999)—remain among those who defend an earlier sixth-century date. I have found the consensus mainstream arguments for a late date in Louis F. Hartman, CSSR, and Alexander A. Di Lella, OFM, *The Book of Daniel*, AB 23 (Garden City, NY: Doubleday, 1978), helpful,

the narratives (chaps. 1–6) and the apocalyptic visions (chaps. 7–12)—derive primarily from the sixth-century exilic context or perhaps are to be situated amid the mid-second-century Maccabean revolt against the Seleucid Empire, with mediating explications of every kind in between. For our missiological purposes, thankfully, these critical issues do not need to be resolved. The *Sitz im Leben* of either the sixth or second century BCE involves Jewish oppression under foreign regimes, and it is within such a context that our missiological interests can be crafted.[93]

What is interesting about Daniel is that all references to the divine *ruah* are from the mouths of unbelieving rulers. In the fourth chapter, Nebuchadnezzar, who ruled over the Babylonian Empire for over forty years (ca. 605–562 BCE), had a second dream that "frightened" and "terrified" him (Dan. 4:5). Although Daniel had successfully identified and interpreted a first dream the king had had (chap. 2), Nebuchadnezzar turned first to his court of magicians, enchanters, and diviners, but "they could not tell [him] its interpretation" (4:7). Then, as Daniel, who appears to have been in the regal lineup,[94] approaches the king, it is as if this jogs the monarch's recollection: "At last Daniel came in before me—he who was named Belteshazzar after the name of my god, and who is endowed with a spirit of the holy gods [which makes sense within the henotheistic or polytheistic Babylonian context][95]—and I told him the dream: 'O Belteshazzar, chief of the magicians, I know that you are endowed with a spirit of the holy gods and that no mystery is too difficult for you.'" (4:8–9). Then, after detailing the dream he had (4:10–17),

---

even almost a generation later. In particular, not only does Daniel's long life span across the whole of the exilic period seem unlikely, but it seems not just unusual but unfathomable that his exalted position within the Babylonian court gives him access to "insider" (read: imperial) perspectives on exilic realities and conditions, and yet there is little comment on the latter, unlike what engrossed contemporaries like Jeremiah and Ezekiel.

93. Thus John E. Goldingay, fully accepting a later date for the book, writes, "The forward projections in Daniel were designed to bring a message that was meaningful to people in the postexilic period." *Daniel*, WBC 30 (Dallas: Word, 1989), xxxix.

94. Even if Daniel is a literary rather than historical character—the reference in Ezek. 14:14, 20 is to another, Ugaritic, Daniel (see Wevers, *Ezekiel*, 91–92)—the protagonist of the biblical book that goes by that name is clearly part of the royal court, a member of the *maskilim* or "the wise" ones (Dan. 1:4), and hence perhaps an antecedent of the wisdom teachers or Hasidim of later Jewish traditions; see W. Sibley Towner, *Daniel*, IBC (Atlanta: John Knox, 1984), 8; and C. L. Seow, *Daniel*, Westminster Bible Companion (Louisville: Westminster John Knox, 2003), 13.

95. "Spirit of the (holy) gods" and "spirit of the (holy) God" are both possible grammatically, but the former is preferred given the narrative arc toward acknowledgment of Yahweh's supreme divinity; see Bob Becking, "'A Divine Spirit Is in You': Notes on the Translation of the Phrase *ruah 'elāhim* in Daniel 5,14 and Related Texts," in *The Book of Daniel in the Light of New Findings*, ed. A. S. van der Woude, BETL 61 (Leuven: Leuven University Press and Uitgeverij Peeters, 1993), 515–19, here 516.

the king invites Daniel's response: "This is the dream that I, King Nebuchadnezzar, saw. Now you, Belteshazzar, declare the interpretation, since
all the wise men of my kingdom are unable to tell me the interpretation.
You are able, however, for you are endowed with a spirit of the holy gods"
(4:18).

The next chapter features two equivalent characterizations of Daniel. The
first is by the queen of King Belshazzar: "There is a man in your kingdom
who is endowed with a spirit of the holy gods" (Dan. 5:11). Then Belshazzar
himself says to Daniel, "I have heard of you that a spirit of the gods is in you,
and that enlightenment, understanding, and excellent wisdom are found in
you" (5:14). The scene was "a great festival for a thousand of [Belshazzar's]
lords" (5:1), at which wine was consumed at least in part through "the vessels
of gold and silver that his father Nebuchadnezzar had taken out of the temple
in Jerusalem" (5:2),[96] when "fingers of a human hand appeared and began
writing on the plaster of the wall of the royal palace" (5:5) the words "MENE,
MENE, TEKEL, and PARSIN" (5:25). When neither the king nor the wise men
of Babylon could comprehend the inscription, the former become "greatly
terrified and his face turned pale, and his lords were perplexed" (5:9). Again,
Daniel interprets the writing and was promptly promoted by Belshazzar to a
position of authority immediately under his own (5:29).

The main thrusts of both stories are consistent with the overall theological
message of the book. Nebuchadnezzar was, in fulfillment of the dream's
message, humbled to the point of acknowledging the sovereignty of Israel's
God as the Most High and the King of Heaven (Dan. 4:34–37), while Belshazzar's kingdom is taken from him, as the interpretation of the handwriting on
the wall prefigured, even that very night (5:30). Within the broader scope of
the book of Daniel, world powers rise and fall, even those that oppress and
attempt to destroy the people of God. Daniel himself is a colonized subject
and thus a target of such efforts, even as he survives the fiery furnace and the
lions' den (chaps. 3 and 6). Nevertheless, the providential plans of Israel's
almighty deity remain in control over creaturely affairs, not least the imperial
mechanisms of this world.

96. "Father" here means ancestor, a well-accepted ancient Near Eastern literary means of
identifying lineage that skips generations. In this case, Nebuchadnezzar is Belshazzar's grand-
father, with Nabonidus being the middle generation who reigned as king from ca. 556–539
BCE, although he had left Babylon by way of a self-imposed exile for more than half of this
time, leaving his son Belshazzar in charge. For a more complete discussion, including how such
circumstances can be understood as providing a historical core to the stories detailed in Dan.
4–5, see Matthias Henze, *The Madness of King Nebuchadnezzar: The Ancient Near Eastern
Origins and Early History of Interpretation of Daniel 4*, Supplements to the Journal for the
Study of Judaism 61 (Leiden: Brill, 1999), 57–73.

From a ruahological perspective, two missiological insights present themselves for our consideration. First, as with Pharaoh in Genesis (see §1.2 above), the divine spirit is recognized by unbelievers to be at work, not just by those who are the non-elect of Yahweh, but by those who are actively lording it over Yahweh's chosen people. To be sure, Nebuchadnezzar, Belshazzar, and the queen in each case cannot do much better than perceive the divine wind in their own polytheistic terms. Nevertheless, such recognition is consistent with the narrative's connections between the divine breath that inspires Daniel's interpretive powers and the message of divine dominion communicated through the stories. The point is that even among the nations, there is the capacity to discern the divine breath and its jurisdiction over the human realm.

The second and related point is that there is a close relationship between the divine and human breath at work in Daniel, a colonized figure who is outside but yet also within the (Persian) imperial regime.[97] Daniel was made "chief of the magicians, enchanters, Chaldeans, and diviners, because [of his] excellent spirit, knowledge, and understanding" (Dan. 5:11–12), even as the evident "spirit of the gods" in him was manifest in terms of his "enlightenment, understanding, and excellent wisdom" (5:14). Earlier we are told that Daniel and his companions, while brought into exile as young persons, were found to be "versed in every branch of wisdom, endowed with knowledge and insight, and competent to serve in the king's palace; they were to be taught the literature and language of the Chaldeans . . . [and] God gave [them] knowledge and skill in every aspect of literature and wisdom" (1:4, 17). While on the one hand it is clear that Daniel's achievements as interpreter of messages from the divine realm derive from the *ruah Elohim*, on the other hand that breath works with, not apart from, his personal learning and capacities. The point to be appreciated is that the potency of the divine spirit does not preclude the efforts of human spirits in their mission contexts.

The irony is that the *ruah Elohim* appears at both the apex (Nebuchadnezzar's repentance and restoration) and denouement (Belshazzar's demise) of the Babylonian Empire, and that this involved the divine spirit's gift of interpretation and comprehension of confusing images and languages.[98] If the original Babel brought about the dispersal of humankind because of their many languages, the translation of and decipherability across languages in

97. See Deborah Appler, "'Digging in the Claws': Daniel 4 and the Predatory Nature of Empire," in *Focusing Biblical Studies: The Crucial Nature of the Persian and Hellenistic Periods— Essays in Honor of Douglas A. Knight*, ed. Jon L. Berquist and Alice Hunt (New York: T&T Clark, 2012), 121–37.

98. This is my ruahological version of what is suggested by Rabbi Dr. Michael Hilton, "Babel Reversed—Daniel Chapter 5," *JSOT* 66 (1995): 99–112.

this Babelian context occurs by the blowing of the divine wind.[99] This itself is another anticipation of the outpouring to come that will enable the communication of God across cultural-linguistic borders.

4.7   The Book of the Twelve, Part 1—The Spirit of Yahweh: Prophetic Witness in Joel and Micah

The Jewish canonical literature has long featured the "twelve prophets" as a collection intended to be read together (alongside the major prophets of Isaiah, Jeremiah, and Ezekiel) and yet in a way that did not compromise the distinctiveness of each voice and message.[100] Although most of the references to the divine *ruah* occur in the latter portions of this Book of the Twelve (see §4.8 below), two are found (one each) in Joel and Micah.[101] Read together and in missiological perspective, these witnesses of the spirit of God highlight judgment and justice, but also anticipate redemption, for both Israel and the nations.[102]

Even though we lack a reliable *Sitz im Leben* for the Joel passage (since there is no consensus about the dating of this book), its canonical location both connects (in the first part of Joel) to the call to repentance in the later chapters of Hosea and segues (in the second half of Joel) into the oracles against the nations that open Amos's prophecy.[103] More particularly, the theme of the day

99. As Donald C. Polaski urges, at the end of empire it is God who reads and writes, unlike the crumbling Babylonian bureaucracy; see "*Mene, Mene, Tekel, Parsin*: Writing and Resistance in Daniel 5 and 6," *JBL* 123:4 (2004): 649–69. These Daniel stories thus "demonstrate the superiority of divinely inspired knowledge over and above the extensive educational training of Mesopotamian scribes and scholars in antiquity." Michael Segal, "Rereading the Writing on the Wall (Daniel 5)," *ZAW* 125:1 (2013): 161–76, here 175.

100. See, e.g., Paul L. Redditt and Aaron Schart, eds., *Thematic Threads in the Book of the Twelve*, BZAW 325 (Berlin: de Gruyter, 2003); and Jason T. LeCureux, *The Thematic Unity of the Book of the Twelve*, Hebrew Canon Monographs 41 (Sheffield: Sheffield Phoenix, 2012).

101. Those wishing for a sort of ruahology of the Twelve might wish to consult Martin Clay, "The Book of the Twelve," in *A Biblical Theology of the Holy Spirit*, ed. Trevor J. Burke and Keith Warrington (Eugene, OR: Cascade, 2014).

102. Interestingly, each of these four prophets that mention the spirit of God are among those minor prophets that "affirm that *some from among the nations have . . . , can . . . ,* or will . . . enter a positive relationship with Israel/Judah and YHWH and so will not be punished in the end," as opposed to a smaller group of others (Obadiah, Habakkuk, Hosea, and Nahum) that do not have anything positive to say about the nations. Daniel C. Timmer, *The Non-Israelite Nations in the Book of the Twelve: Thematic Coherence and the Diachronic-Synchronic Relationship in the Minor Prophets*, BiblInt 135 (Leiden: Brill, 2015), 227 (emphasis original).

103. James D. Nogalski, "Joel as 'Literary Anchor' for the Book of the Twelve," in *Reading and Hearing the Book of the Twelve*, ed. James D. Nogalski and Marvin A. Sweeney, SBL Symposium Series 15 (Atlanta: Society for Biblical Literature, 2000), 91–109, esp. 95–100; and

From Israel to the Nations
The Witness of the Writing Prophets

Lian Sian Mung, instructor of Old Testament, Asia Pacific Theological Seminary, Baguio City, The Philippines

While previous ruahological studies were primarily concerned with the chrono-logical development of the ruahic tradition in the history of Israel, recent scholarship has begun to recognize the fruitfulness of a canonical reading of the ruahic passages within their respective literary contexts. The added missiological consideration of such texts in the final form of these Writing Prophets brings fresh insights to our understanding of the wind and breath of the God of Israel by demonstrating that while the divine *ruah* plays a central role in transforming and restoring Israel (and Zion), the effect of *ruah* Yahweh's work is not limited to the internal dimensions of the people of God, because the ruahic transformation and restoration of Israel (and Zion), accomplished or achieved either directly or through *ruah*-empowered agents, has international and global implications.

of the Lord is not only central to Joel (occurring at least half a dozen times) but may also serve as a unifying thread for the rest of the Twelve.[104] And it is in relationship to this day that the prophet says,

> Then afterward
> I will pour out my spirit on all flesh;
> your sons and your daughters shall prophesy,
> your old men shall dream dreams,
> and your young men shall see visions.
> Even on the male and female slaves,
> in those days, I will pour out my spirit. (Joel 2:28–29)[105]

The lavishness of the divine *ruah* responds at least in part to the plague of locusts that left the people and land desolate (1:2–12). Or put another way:

Barry Alan Jones, *The Formation of the Book of the Twelve: A Study in Text and Canon*, SBLDS 149 (Atlanta: Scholars Press, 1995), 231.

104. Rolf Rendtorff, "How to Read the Book of the Twelve as a Theological Unity," in Nogalski and Sweeney, *Reading and Hearing the Book of the Twelve*, 75–87, esp. 80–83.

105. Mordecai Schreiber, "I Will Pour Out My Spirit on All Flesh (Joel 3:1)," *JBQ* 41:2 (2013): 123–29.

"The promise of the Spirit outpoured will be fully realized only by those whose hearts have been torn open and poured out."[106]

There is surely a sense in which the outpouring of the spirit here provides additional perspective on the day of Yahweh's visitation to Israel (Joel 1:15; 2:1–2, 11), but it is also specifically here that the day of the Lord has cosmic reverberations (2:30–31). More relevant for our purposes, it is through this pivotal text that the attention of the prophet turns from Israel to the nations, and in particular to the judgment that will come upon the nations (3:2, 9, 11–12). From this perspective, following the repentance of the people of God (2:12–14), the arrival of Yahweh's spirit brings about the blessing Israel needs after the plague of locusts even as the outpouring transitions to divine justice exacted upon the nations. Still, transnational judgment is not exclusive of salvation at least from among the nations. As the spirit is given to "all flesh" (2:28), deliverance is made available to "everyone who calls on the name of the LORD" so that "among the survivors [gathered from the nations, it is clearly implied] shall be those whom the LORD calls" (2:32).

The ministry of Micah, on the other hand, is dated in the last third of the eighth century while Israel confronted and then succumbed to the Assyrian threat.[107] Micah claims himself to be *ruah*-filled:

> But as for me, I am filled with power,
>   with the spirit of the LORD,
>   and with justice and might,
> to declare to Jacob his transgression
>   and to Israel his sin. (Mic. 3:8)[108]

Surely the key here is that the *ruah* Yahweh is the spirit of justice, pronounced immediately against the prophets who are leading the people of God astray (3:5), but also against heads of Jacob (the southern kingdom) and rulers and chief of the house of Israel (the northern kingdom), all of whom are oblivious to, ignore, and even "abhor" justice (3:1, 9). It is also Micah who, after indicting the people of God, famously said, "And what does the LORD

106. Moore and Peterson, *Voice, Word, and Spirit*, 232.

107. For historical details, see J. G. Strydom, "Micah of Samaria: Amos's and Hosea's Forgotten Partner," *Old Testament Essays* 6 (1993): 19–32; and Eric A. Mitchell, "Micah—The Man and His Times," *SwJT* 46:1 (2003): 57–76.

108. While some might argue that the *ruah* reference derives from a later, exilic or postexilic redaction—e.g., Elizabeth Achtemeier, *Minor Prophets I*, Understanding the Bible Commentary (Grand Rapids: Baker, 1996), 321—our canonical reading does not require deciding such issues; see also Wilhelm J. Wessels, "Empowered by the Spirit of Yahweh: A Study of Micah 3:8," *JBPR* 1 (2009): 33–47.

require of you / but to do justice, and to love kindness, / and to walk humbly with your God?" (6:8).

Yet the spirit of justice through whom Micah appeals is concerned to expose the transgression and sin of the people of Yahweh so that Jerusalem can be judged (Mic. 3:12) and, through such purging and cleaning, precipitate the day of the Lord and the renewal and reestablishment of Israel. When the latter occurs, as we have already seen in Isaiah (esp. §§4.2–4.3), toward the house of Yahweh, "peoples shall stream . . . and many nations shall come" (Mic. 4:1–2); and nations

> shall beat their swords into plowshares,
>   and their spears into pruning-hooks;
> nation shall not lift up sword against nation,
>   neither shall they learn war any more;
> but they shall all sit under their own vines and under their own fig trees
>   and no one shall make them afraid. (4:3–4)

This is not a minor theme, as Micah's prophecy is pronounced within a universal horizon, addressed to "O earth, and all that is in it" (1:2), even as the salvation of the nations absolutely involves judgment for opposing Yahweh (4:11–13) and the shame that comes with recognition of the vindication of Israel by those who are its enemies (7:7–17). In other words, the justice of God is not only focused on achieving judgment on Israel (and the nations) in order to elicit repentance, but is ultimately designed to establish shalom—peace, harmony, and righteousness—transnationally.[109]

Missiological readings of Joel's ruahology, in particular, are certainly boosted by its citation in the day of Pentecost narrative (Acts 2:17–21),[110] to which we will get later. Taken on Joel's own terms, however, it may be a bit more difficult to comprehend the missiological relevance of his views of the spirit, particularly since the outpouring of the divine *ruah* precipitates the judgments of God internationally. Nations could be warned about the divine judgments unleashable at any moment, such as in Obadiah 15 (this entire prophecy sees the nations as opposed to Yahweh and his chosen nation). It is nevertheless not politically correct today to pronounce such religious verdicts on non-Christian countries (even if this does not hinder contemporary "prophets" from saying that this or that earthquake or tsunami or terrorist act represents divine decrees on present-day

109. So also the contemporary missiological reading of Kosuke Koyama, "The Mountain of the Lord: Micah 4:1–7," *IRM* 77:306 (1988): 194–200.

110. E.g., Larry R. McQueen, *Joel and the Spirit: The Cry of a Prophetic Hermeneutic*, JPTSup 8 (Sheffield: Sheffield Academic, 1995); see also Norberto Saracco, "I Will Pour Out My Spirit on All People: A Pastoral Reading of Joel 2:28–30 from Latin America," *CTJ* 46 (2011): 268–77.

nations!). On the other hand, the missionary message to the nations may also provoke repentance, as it certainly did among the Ninevites (see Jonah), with the possibility of this response forecasted in Joel and Micah as well.

Perhaps the more important missiological implication is to emphasize Micah's spirit of justice as animating the witness of the people of God.[111] The focus among the prophets as a whole (as we have seen), not to mention the Old Testament generally, is that such justice ought to begin within and among the elect of Yahweh. This is the centripetal dimension of mission that starts with Israel, but the centrifugal aspects are palpably present as well.[112] Justice for Micah entails hating evil and loving good, not exploiting the vulnerable (meaning here resisting the powerful!), and being equitable rather than being bribable (Mic. 3:2–3, 9, 11; cf. 1:10–15; 2:1–5, 8–9; 6:9–15). Yes, Micah is stronger on resisting injustices in the abstract and shorter on concrete proposals for enacting righteousness,[113] so contemporary missiology may be inspired by Micah toward justice today but will have to discern how to work for such justice more on our own. But there is no denying that when the spirit comes, there is equity at least in the sense that *all* are included in God's salvation, male and female, young and old alike. Just as important, "slaves" (Joel 2:29) are caught up in the saving day of the Lord, which suggests justice, recompense, and the arrival of an alternative world order that turns upside down the present class-stratified status quo, and this is possible only because Yahweh is "the Lord of the whole earth" (Mic. 4:13).[114] It is toward such a world that the prophets bear witness in the power of the spirit.

4.8   The Book of the Twelve, Part 2—The Spirit of/from the Second Temple: The Transnational Witness of Haggai and Zechariah

If there are only a meager couple of *ruah* references in the first half of the Book of the Twelve, there are four mentions of the divine spirit in Zechariah

111. E.g., Sylvanus G. Bent, "Reflections on Micah: A Passion for Justice," in *Many Voices: Multicultural Responses to the Minor Prophets*, ed. Alice Ogden Bellis (Lanham, MD: University Press of America, 1995), 37.

112. Thus, we can understand that Micah is about "the restoration of Zion as the culmination of Israel's relationship with the nations." Jerry Hwang, "'My Name Will Be Great among the Nations': The *Missio Dei* in the Book of the Twelve," *TynBul* 65:2 (2014): 161–80, here 172.

113. As argued by Itumeleng J. Mosala, "A Materialist Reading of Micah," in *The Bible and Liberation: Political and Social Hermeneutics*, ed. Norman K. Gottwald and Richard A. Horsley (Maryknoll, NY: Orbis, 1993), 264–95; we need not agree with all the details of how Mosala's hermeneutics of suspicion works to appreciate the point I highlight.

114. Mic. 4:13 is taken as being at the center of Micah's theology; see Leslie C. Allen, *The Books of Joel, Obadiah, Jonah, and Micah* (Grand Rapids: Eerdmans, 1976), 253.

alone, and a fifth when including Haggai. At least Zechariah 1–8 derives from about the time of Haggai's prophecy even as, if we accept the dates in these texts (Hag. 1:1; 2:1, 10, 20; Zech. 1:1, 7; cf. Zech. 7:1), Haggai 1–2 through Zechariah 6 come from a six-month period during 520–519 BCE. Three of the five times *ruah* appears concern the rebuilding of the temple, the singular focus of Haggai and the dominant theme of Zechariah's eight visions as recorded in its initial six chapters.

Our prophetic protagonists emerged during a time when the returning Jews "realized that they were residents of a tiny province (or even sub-province) of Judah in a gigantic pagan empire which was supremely powerful politically, militarily, economically, and culturally."[115] In reality, further, Persian governance over this outpost was facilitated by religious centers so that the rebuilding of the temple, in this case, served not just local religious purposes but also imperial requirements. During this period, the works of earlier prophets about Yahweh's overthrow of these foreign powers were less and less convincing as time pressed on, and work on the temple had practically ground to a halt because of a complex set of reasons related to local and foreign dynamics. It is here that Haggai encourages the people and attempts to mobilize convergence of political and religious interests—thus including Zerubbabel the governor of Judah and Joshua the high priest (Hag. 2:2)—to press forward with the rebuilding program: "Take courage, all you people of the land, says the LORD; work, for I am with you, says the LORD of hosts, according to the promise that I made you when you came out of Egypt. My spirit abides among you; do not fear" (2:4–5).

About four months later, Zechariah is given a vision in which an angel says, "This is the word of the Lord to Zerubbabel: Not by might, nor by power, but by my spirit, says the LORD of hosts. What are you, O great mountain? Before Zerubbabel you shall become a plain; and he shall bring out the top stone amid shouts of 'Grace, grace to it!'" (Zech. 4:6–7).[116] This is followed up with two more visions, the latter of which includes four horse-drawn chariots representing the "four winds of heaven going out, after presenting themselves before the Lord of all the earth" (6:5). The black-horse chariot is going to the north country, about which the angel says, "Lo, those who go toward the north country have set my spirit at rest in the north country" (6:8). In this culminating vision, the angel of the Lord announces that international

115. Hartman and Di Lella, *Book of Daniel*, 38.
116. Lyle Story's exegesis of this text concludes that the spirit is "vitally concerned with the establishment and maintenance of civic and Christian [Jewish, to be more precise] life in the broader national community." "Zechariah's Two Sons of Oil: Zechariah 4," *JBPR* 2 (2010): 31–56, here 56.

order has been restored and that Yahweh reigns even in the north country from whence Israel's oppressors—the Assyrians, Babylonians, Medes, and Persians—had repeatedly come.[117]

Almost two years after this night of multiple visions, the word of Yahweh comes again to Zechariah, this time in the context of addressing questions regarding the annual fasts in Israel's liturgical calendar, now arisen in the context of renewed activity within a temple perhaps almost fully restored. Yahweh's response, echoing Micah's message, is that liturgical rites have to be accompanied by acts of kindness, mercy, and justice (Zech. 7:9), and Israel's failure to maintain the latter undermines the religious fasts, as in the days of old before the exile: "They made their hearts adamant in order not to hear the law and the words that the LORD of hosts had sent by his spirit through the former prophets. Therefore great wrath came from the LORD of hosts" (7:12). Yet Yahweh will not persist in anger but will restore Zion, Jerusalem, and Israel so that their fasts may be authentic expressions of piety and justice (8:1–19). The results will echo beyond the borders of Israel: "Many peoples and strong nations shall come to seek the LORD of hosts in Jerusalem, and to entreat the favor of the LORD. Thus says the LORD of hosts: In those days ten men from nations of every language shall take hold of a Jew, grasping his garment and saying, 'Let us go with you, for we have heard that God is with you'" (8:22–23). There is therefore a constancy of *ruah*-inspired messages throughout the prophetic tradition, including the calling of Israel to repentance and the announcement of the people of God being a blessing to others through their covenantal faithfulness.

The final reference to the divine *ruah* in Zechariah occurs in the so-called apocalyptic segment of the prophecy (chaps. 12–14). It is certainly in this context when and where "all the nations of the earth shall come together against" the people of God, and Yahweh "will seek to destroy" and judge them (Zech. 12:3, 9).[118] Then Yahweh says, "I will pour out a spirit of compassion

117. John Goldingay and Pamela J. Scalise, *Minor Prophets II*, Understanding the Bible Commentary (Grand Rapids: Baker Books, 2009), 240; see also Mark J. Boda, "Terrifying the Horns: Persia and Babylon in Zechariah 1:7–6:15," *CBQ* 67 (2005): 23–41; and Max Rogland, "Heavenly Chariots and Earthly Rebellion in Zechariah 6," *Biblica* 95:1 (2014): 117–23.

118. Recall the final part of Joel that announces the judgment of the nations. Judgment against the nations is a major theme in the Book of the Twelve, and this is reflective of the exilic and later Persian period when Israel was weak in the face of great and mighty nations, and thereby in a fundamental sense dependent on God against their overlords; see, e.g., Jakob Wöhrle, "Israel's Identity and the Threat of the Nations in the Persian Period: Reflections from a Redactional Layer of the Book of the Twelve," in *Judah and the Judeans in the Achaemenid Period: Negotiating Identity in an International Context*, ed. Manfred Oeming, Gary N. Knoppers, and Oded Lipschitz (Winona Lake, IN: Eisenbrauns, 2011), 153–72.

and supplication on the house of David and the inhabitants of Jerusalem, so that, when they look on the one whom they have pierced, they shall mourn for him, as one mourns for an only child, and weep bitterly over him, as one weeps over a firstborn" (12:10).[119] This outpouring of the divine *ruah* (echoing Joel from the beginning of the Book of the Twelve) enables the repentance of the people of God that is the necessary precursor to their full renewal, and this in turn will involve both the judgment (12:1–9; 14:1–15) and the salvation of the nations: "Then all who survive of the nations that have come against Jerusalem shall go up year after year to worship the King, the LORD of hosts, and to keep the festival of booths" (14:16; cf. 2:11).[120] This eschatological arrival of the nations to the temple of the Lord that follows judgment is consistent with the prophecy of Haggai: "I will shake all the nations, so that the treasure of all nations shall come, and I will fill this house with splendor, says the LORD of hosts. . . . I am about to destroy the strength of the kingdoms of the nations, and overthrow the chariots and their riders; and the horses and their riders shall fall, every one by the sword of a comrade" (Hag. 2:7, 22).[121]

Here at the end of the Old Testament, the *ruah* instances communicate not just a coherent message across two of the twelve books but also one consistent with earlier prophetic anticipations: that the reconstruction of the temple serves both local and foreign interests (for instance, as a local site through which imperial taxation is implemented) but yet is understood by the prophets as linked with the salvation of the nations. In this postexilic context, the redemption of Israel, in all its complex situatedness amid the nations, begins with the concreteness of its place of worship. The reconstituted temple is central to Israel's witness, as it is only the manifest presence of the Lord symbolized in this edifice that constitutes the city of Zion and the nation of Israel as bearers of the divine name.[122] In other words, the temple is interconnected in this postexilic milieu with the city, the nation, and the international order, and just as there can be no restoration of any without each of the others, so also there is ultimately no witness to the

119. On Zech. 12:10 as part of a prophecy that consists largely of interpretation of older prophets, rather than consisting of new communications by angels prevalent in the earlier part of the book, see Eibert J. C. Tigchelaar, *Prophets of Old and the Day of the End: Zechariah, the Book of Watchers and Apocalyptic*, Oudtestamentische Studiën 35 (Leiden: Brill, 1996), 244.

120. For more on the universal and cosmic scope of Zechariah's redemption, see David L. Petersen, *Haggai and Zechariah 1–8*, OTL (Philadelphia: Westminster, 1984), 114–16.

121. See also Herbert Wolf, "'The Desire of All Nations' in Haggai 2:7: Messianic or Not?," *JETS* 18:2 (1968): 97–102.

122. Because the return of people to the land does not guarantee Yahweh's presence, the promise of the divine spirit in Hag. 2:5 and Zech. 4:6 speaks to "Yahweh's abiding help at the reconstruction of the temple" (Tigchelaar, *Prophets of Old*, 43–44).

nations apart from this cosmic renewal.[123] Similarly, this restoration of Israel involves its purification, and this happens through Yahweh's whirlwind (Zech. 7:14; 9:14).[124]

In short, the centrifugal witness of Israel to the nations is interdependent with its getting its own house in order, and the centripetal movement of the nations to Israel in this context ought to be not so much taken literally as understood to call attention to how Yahweh's glory emanating from the shalom of God's people is a light to the deity's redemptive plans for the world. The missiological message of Haggai and Zechariah, read ruaho-logically, thus eliminates any bifurcation of the centripetal or centrifugal trajectories of Israel's witness, as they are interwoven. From such a missiological perspective, the ongoing breathing of the *missio Dei* involves as much attention to what it means and how to live both as a people of God and as citizens of an imperial order as insisting on going out to evangelize the world.[125] More pointedly, any outward evangelism amid unrighteousness and injustice "within the camp" not only will undermine the mission of God but may incur divine action directed against those who would perceive themselves as missionizers but who are actually more fundamentally in need of repentance and restoration themselves.

Discussion Questions

1. Much of the Old Testament is written from or in response to the Babylonian exile. What are the possible applications for thinking about Christian mission and witness in the third millennium? How might today's migration, refugee, and asylum situations parallel—or not parallel—the witness of the divine breath through Israel's exilic experiences?

2. Micah associates the divine breath with justice. What did that mean and what might that mean now? Is contemporary missiology to be justice oriented? If so, how?

3. The Writing Prophets show Israel's self-understanding forged internationally and transnationally: in relationship to other nations, and in

123. Amid the many negative references to the judgment of nations in Zechariah, redemptive notes regarding those beyond Israel are also sounded: e.g., 2:11, 13; 8:12–13, 22–23; 9:10; see further Paul Nadim Tarazi, "Israel and the Nations (according to Zechariah 14)," *St. Vladimir's Theological Quarterly* 38:2 (1994): 181–92.

124. The Old Testament repeatedly refers to Yahweh's whirlwind as a metaphor for divine judgment; see, e.g., Isa. 29:6; 66:15, Jer. 4:13; Amos 1:4; Nah. 1:3; and Hab. 3:14.

125. Here supplementing Daniel F. O'Kennedy, "Perspectives on Mission in the Book of Zechariah," *Missionalia* 41:3 (2013): 223–30.

particular through exilic and postexilic developments. Compare and contrast such internationalism and transnationalism with modern (colonial) mission. What are the takeaways of such considerations when we think about postmodern and postcolonial mission in dialogue with exilic and postexilic Israel?

Part 2

DIVINE BREATH AND THE CHRISTIAN SCRIPTURES

Pneumatic Witness after Pentecost

5

The Witness of the Evangelistic Spirit

Gospel Mission

Introduction

In arriving now at the second half of the biblical canon, we are on much more familiar pneumatological and missiological terrain. If the divine wind and breath are referred to relatively sporadically throughout the Old Testament, the *pneuma hagios* or related references are much more frequent across the Christian Testament. Further, Christian mission following in the footsteps of the first followers of Jesus is central to the good news of his coming as the spirit-anointed—hence Messiah—representative of the Father, and in that respect the apostolic writings are understandably pneumatological and missiological in ways far more obvious than when reading through the Old Testament. As a result, much of our discussion in this part of the book will be very selective, looking at where pneumatology and missiology most directly intersect. Even there, our engagement with the biblical scholarship on the spirit and on mission will be constrained and circumscribed; far more is available than we will be able to adequately engage. Our only excuse is that, in the first such foray at the nexus of spirit and mission, ours is an opening and exploratory salvo.[1]

Further, given the numerous references to the divine wind or breath in the New Testament, our analysis will be much wider, if less deep, compared

---

1. In my own prior work, I have attended to portions of the New Testament pneumatologically—e.g., in the first and third sections of chaps. 2–11 of my book *Renewing Christian Theology: Systematics for a Global Christianity*, images and commentary by Jonathan A. Anderson (Waco: Baylor University Press, 2014); the following expands such readings in a missiological direction.

with part 1 of this book. What I mean is that we will be covering much more pneumatological ground here in contrast to focusing, as in some sections above, on one, two, or relatively few (compared to the New Testament) spirit references. Nevertheless, our missiological concerns remain. We are interested not only in what the apostolic writers say about the spirit but also in what the missiological implications and explications are, then and now.

Of course, just as the pneumatological and missiological aspects of the Christian writings are more explicit and expansive, so also is the secondary literature on these topics. For instance, if we were lucky to have found some books with references to the divine *ruah* across the Old Testament, there is extensive scholarship on the spirit in the different genres of Christian writing, including those on the Gospels that we are now going to discuss.[2] With regard to missiological literature, we are now seeing not just book-specific discussions but also interrogations representative of the post-mission angst discussed in our introductory chapter.[3] In other texts, specifically Luke and especially Acts, there is too much to consult, and we cannot possibly cite all the existing discussions. Hence, throughout part 2 of this book, our treatment will be more focused, guided by our concerns regarding how pneumatological passages invite fresh consideration of *others*—other nations, peoples, cultures, religions—to whom Jesus's followers are called to bear witness.

This transnational and even political dimension of our discussion is also intensifying in New Testament scholarship. For instance, Jesus's death is certainly a religious matter, but it is also at least a kind of political event, one signaling how first-century Judea was situated within the Roman imperial system.[4] Therefore, as we shall see on the pneumatological front (§5.2), Jesus's exorcisms of evil spirits are not only religious but also arguably political, related to deliverance of people from oppressive socioeconomic and political

2. E.g., an excellent overview is Craig S. Keener, *The Spirit in the Gospels and Acts: Divine Purity and Power* (Peabody, MA: Hendrickson, 1997); other important books on the spirit in each of the Gospels will be referred to as we go.

3. E.g., Mitzi J. Smith and Jayachitra Lalitha, eds., *Teaching All Nations: Interrogating the Matthean Great Commission* (Minneapolis: Fortress, 2014).

4. See, e.g., Richard A. Horsley, *Jesus and Empire: The Kingdom of God and the New World Disorder* (Minneapolis: Fortress, 2002). Those inclined to think the recent assessment of the Gospels and other parts of the New Testament in relation to imperial Rome overemphasizes the latter as a hermeneutical perspective will resonate with the argument of Seyoon Kim, *Christ and Caesar: The Gospel and the Roman Empire in the Writings of Paul and Luke* (Grand Rapids: Eerdmans, 2008), which seeks a via media between the sectarianism of the Johannine Apocalypse on the one side and the accommodationism of the Clementine letters on the other; my own pneumato-theological emphasis is sympathetic to Kim's quest while also not wishing to neglect the fact that these narratives unfold, as Luke puts it (Luke 2:1; 3:1), during the days of ruling emperors and caesars.

conditions.[5] Hence our pneumatological lens is far from being merely spiritual, at least as modernist dualism takes that notion to mean ethereal, immaterial, or otherworldly. Rather, pneumatological missiology is concerned with how the divine breath leads to encounter with *others*, both individual others (as in people of other cultures and faiths) and structural and systemic others (as in other nations, people groups, and social and economic realities).

This chapter focuses on the Synoptic Gospels and St. Luke's sequel book, the Acts of the Apostles. Although canonically the Gospel sequence includes John between Luke and Acts, we have postponed discussion of the Fourth Gospel until chapter 8, preferring instead to engage the writings bearing the name of, or historically associated with, the "school" or community of John all together. There are various downsides and upsides. One of the former is that we will not be treating the Johannine sending by the spirit (John 20:20–22) with the Matthean Great Commission and the Lukan commissioning, not to mention the Markan longer ending, itself full of signs and wonders. One of the upsides is related: we won't need to try to resolve how the Johannine Pentecost is connected to that of Luke. As with our approach so far, each section will try to stay focused on that book and its contents, with minimal cross-referencing unless dictated by the pneumatological references under discussion.

The missiological challenge before us, however, needs to be reiterated. As we are now on much more familiar turf, we might adopt our classical missional spectacles in traversing this literature. The strangeness of Pentecost, however, needs to accompany our rereading of the Gospels and Acts. How might we glean new insight into the call to apostolic witness from what we see in these first-century documents, and how might these be valuable for reconstructing a Christian mission theology—a *missio spiritus* and triunely envisioned *missio Dei*—that adequately engages with the pluralistic postcolonial, post-Western, and post-Christendom others today?

5.1 Matthew—The Spirit of the (First) Gospel: The Messianic Mission to the Nations

Missiologists have already written plenty on the Gospel of Matthew,[6] including on various technical aspects of the Matthean narrative in relation to early

---

5. See Cheryl S. Pero, *Liberation from Empire: Demonic Possession and Exorcism in the Gospel of Mark*, StBibLit 150 (New York: Peter Lang, 2013).

6. E.g., Eung Chun Park, *The Mission Discourse in Matthew's Interpretation*, WUNT 2/81 (Tübingen: Mohr Siebeck, 1995); an overview is Johannes Nissen, "Matthew, Mission and Method," *IRM* 91:360 (2002): 73–86.

Christian mission.[7] Our pneumatological focus, however, invites zeroing in on the heart of this First Gospel, where, in the fourth of six instances in which Isaiah is explicitly cited,[8] the message of the Great Commission (Matt. 28:18–20), rightly seen as the apex of Jesus's mission, is foreshadowed in terms specifically related to the divine spirit:

> "Here is my servant, whom I have chosen,
>   my beloved, with whom my soul is well pleased.
> I will put my Spirit upon him,
>   and he will proclaim justice to the Gentiles.
> He will not wrangle or cry aloud,
>   nor will anyone hear his voice in the streets.
> He will not break a bruised reed
>   or quench a smoldering wick
> until he brings justice to victory.
>   And in his name the Gentiles will hope."
> (Matt. 12:18–21, adapted from Isa. 42:1–4)[9]

Scriptural authority is here drawn on as an apology for Jesus's activities, answering specifically but not only the criticisms of Pharisees and synagogue leaders about his feeding the disciples on the Sabbath and healing on the day of rest (Matt. 12:2, 9–10).[10]

Three points are noteworthy about this text. First, the "justice" that is hereby being manifest by the power of God's spirit to the gentiles (*ethnesin*, or ethnic groups or nations) includes, rather than is distinct from, feeding

7. E.g., Schuyler Brown, SJ, "The Mission to Israel in Matthew's Central Section (Mt 9:35–11:1)," *Zeitschrift für die neutestamentliche Wissenschaft* 69:1–2 (1978): 73–90; Paul Hertig, *Matthew's Narrative Use of Galilee in the Multicultural and Missiological Journeys of Jesus*, Mellen Biblical Press Series 46 (Lewiston, NY: Edwin Mellen, 1998); and Boris Paschke, *Particularism and Universalism in the Sermon on the Mount: A Narrative-Critical Analysis of Matthew 5–7 in the Light of Matthew's View on Mission*, Neutestamentliche Abhandlungen 56 (Münster: Aschendorff, 2012).

8. Matt. 3:3; 4:14; 8:17; 13:4; and 15:7 overtly identify Isaianic authority; these and other texts are discussed in, with our passage being the focus of, Richard Beaton, *Isaiah's Christ in Matthew's Gospel*, SNTSMS 123 (Cambridge: Cambridge University Press, 2002).

9. As Robert H. Mounce indicates, Matthew's version is uniquely his own, not drawn in any direct sense from either the Masoretic Text or the Septuagint; see *Matthew*, NIBC (Peabody, MA: Hendrickson, 1991), 115–16.

10. If Jerome H. Neyrey focuses on the Isaianic quotation in relation to the first part of Matt. 12, then Blaine Charette does so in connection to the remainder of that same chapter. See Neyrey, "The Thematic Use of Isaiah 42,1–4 in Matthew 12," *Biblica* 63 (1982): 457–73; and Charette, "'Speaking against the Holy Spirit': The Correlation between Messianic Task and National Fortunes in the Gospel of Matthew," *JPT* 3 (1993): 51–70.

the hungry and healing the sick, those most vulnerable of groups.[11] From this perspective, justice emerges as central not only to Matthew's Christology but also to the messianic mission so that the reader ought not to be surprised when later it appears as the fundamental criterion demarcating accepted sheep from denounced goats at the last judgment (Matt. 25:31–46).[12] Second, the ministry and mission of Jesus is here, again, divinely certified by the presence of the spirit, previously associated already with his conception (1:18–20), mission (3:11), baptism (3:16–17), and wilderness temptation (4:1) and triumph.[13] Last but not least, although here in the middle section of the book Jesus's mission is still clearly directed toward Israel and exclusive of the gentiles (e.g., 10:5), nevertheless the universal horizons of the divine spirit's mission noted in our quoted Isaianic passage—reiterated twice!—anticipate the more cosmic vision of the resurrected Christ to be lifted up at the end of the book. These last two aspects deserve elaboration.

Ironically, because Jesus told the large crowd that had gathered around his healing powers "not to make him known" (Matt. 12:15–16), Matthew had called on Isaiah's witness to underscore the Messiah's subdued character: "He will not wrangle or cry aloud." Yet the messianic ministry is effectively liberating. From a pneumatological perspective, however, this Matthean citation also invites understanding the messianic mission unfolded in the Gospel as empowered, from beginning to end, by the holy spirit. Now Matthew is certainly not as much of a pneumatological theologian as is Luke (see §5.3), even as there is some evidence about the First Evangelist's overall "ambivalence toward Spirit activity,"[14] perhaps because he is concerned about excesses related to false prophets in the community. Yet we ought not to discount the role of the spirit,[15] especially not when the Old Testament, on which Matthew relies, underscores that the messianic ministry in its full scope is pneumatologically

11. James L. Bailey suggests that the Messiah's mission is marked not only by evangelism but also by the mercy ministry of healing and a vulnerable and self-sacrificial solidarity with those to whom the message is shared. Bailey, "Church as Embodiment of Jesus' Mission (Matthew 9:36–10:39)," *CurTM* 30:3 (2003): 189–96.

12. Emmanuel M. Jacob details how the parable of the sheep and goats is central to Matthean missiology given its theme of discipleship; see "Discipleship and Mission: A Perspective on the Gospel of Matthew," *IRM* 91:360 (2002): 102–10.

13. Matthew's spirit-Christology is explicated further by Blaine Charette, "'Never Has Anything Like This Been Seen in Israel': The Spirit as Eschatological Sign in Matthew's Gospel," *JPT* 8 (1996): 31–51.

14. Leander E. Keck, "Matthew and the Spirit," in *The Social World of the First Christians: Essays in Honor of Wayne A. Meeks*, ed. L. Michael White and O. Larry Yarbrough (Minneapolis: Fortress, 1995), 145–55, here 149.

15. See Blaine Charette, *Restoring Presence: The Spirit in Matthew's Gospel*, JPTSup 18 (Sheffield: Sheffield Academic, 2000).

inspired. More to the point for the purposes of this book, it is the work of God's spirit to enable the mission of Jesus to touch lives in Israel and also to reach far beyond its borders to the nations.[16]

Much effort has been put forward to understand how Matthew's Gospel, generally accepted as written for a Jewish Christian community, nevertheless features a universalistic thread that culminates in Jesus's sending the disciples to "all nations" (Matt. 28:19).[17] Surely the hints and clues about a wider-than-Israel mission are clear when read from this perspective: beginning with the inclusion of four gentile women in Jesus's genealogy (1:3, 5, 6),[18] then involving magi or "wise men from the East" (2:1), and including ministry to a Roman centurion (8:5–13) and a Canaanite woman (15:21–28).[19] Matthew's explicit point is that the Messiah has come about in part through "the nations" and that his ministry has extended beyond Galilee in ways consistent with his commissioning later. If we have seen already and repeatedly throughout part 1 of this book that the Old Testament's largely centripetal conception of Israel in relation to the nations nevertheless does not exclude centrifugal dimensions, so also in this Gospel that retrieves and reappropriates the message of ancient Israel in a christological key do we find a missional address first to Israel as well as an increasing focus throughout the narrative on the gentile peoples and nations. The scriptural witness brought to bear in the middle of Matthew's Gospel, then, urges that we consider this christological and messianic mission also in pneumatological terms: that the story of Jesus cannot be adequately comprehended apart from Yahweh's promise to put his breath on the servant that he has chosen and loved, and with whom he is pleased and delighted.

---

16. See Bitrus A. Sarma, *Hermeneutics of Mission in Matthew: Israel and the Nations in the Interpretive Framework of Matthew's Gospel* (Cumbria, UK: Langham Monographs, 2015).

17. James LaGrand, *The Earliest Christian Mission to "All Nations" in the Light of Matthew's Gospel* (Grand Rapids: Eerdmans, 1999); Martin Goldsmith, *Matthew and Mission: The Gospel through Jewish Eyes* (Carlisle, UK: Paternoster, 2001); Matthias Konradt, *Israel, Church, and the Gentiles in the Gospel of Matthew*, trans. Kathleen Ess (Waco: Baylor University Press, 2014).

Love L. Sechrest explicates the Matthean context vis-à-vis gentiles, in particular the persecution suffered at the hand of gentiles at Antioch combined with the pressure from at least some within the Jewish Christian community to accept gentile believers, and concludes that the Great Commission did not negate the uplifting of Jewish particularity: "What else could one conclude from the exhortation about 'teaching [the nations] to obey everything that I commanded' in 28:20, when 'everything' would surely include Jesus's teaching about doing Torah in 5:19?" "Enemies, Romans, Pigs, and Dogs: Loving the Other in the Gospel of Matthew," *ExAud* 31 (2015): 71–105, here 83–84 (brackets original).

18. See Jason B. Hood, *The Messiah, His Brothers, and the Nations: Matthew 1.1–17*, LNTS 441 (New York: T&T Clark, 2011).

19. Jacques Matthey, "Pilgrims, Seekers and Disciples: Mission and Dialogue in Matthew," *IRM* 91:360 (2002): 120–34.

The Spirit's Witness across the Pacific Rim
Then and Now

K.-K. Yeo, Kendall Chair of New Testament, Garrett-
Evangelical Theological Seminary and Northwestern
University, Evanston, Illinois, USA

"Pneumatology and mission" is the critical lens for this volume, and the scales will fall from our eyes if we use this lens to read and live out the biblical mandates *coram Deo* beyond our own national, gender, religious, linguistic, and political affiliations. As a Chinese Christian born and raised in Malaysia and now serving God's church in the two superpowers (China and the United States), I am often recalled, when reading the Synoptic Gospels and Acts of the Apostles, to ancient Chinese history and cultures. I reflect on how the holy wind (the translation of "holy spirit" in some older Chinese Bibles) has always been at work in *prebiblical* civilizations (e.g., yin-yang and Daoist worldviews), *extrabiblical* philosophical and ethical concepts (e.g., Confucianist, Buddhist), and languages *foreign* to that of the Old Testament and New Testament. *Missio spiritus* is to create the world; to claim it as holy (belonging) to God; to save it from all its brokenness, fallenness, and chaos; and to inspire it to manifest creatively God's glory throughout the world as beauty, flourishing, and truthfulness. Thus the "universalistic thread" motif is God's spirit working out *missio Dei* in the cosmos, from the first point of creation ("in the beginning") to the last point ("eschaton") of consummation.

Such a pneumatological angle further reinforces the trinitarian or, more accurately for our purposes, triune character of the final sending: "All authority in heaven and on earth has been given to me. Go therefore and make disciples of all nations, baptizing them in the name of the Father and of the Son and of the Holy Spirit, and teaching them to obey everything that I have commanded you. And remember, I am with you always, to the end of the age" (Matt. 28:18–20).[20] Whatever the complexities regarding the famous triune formula for baptism inherent in this text,[21] the pneumatological point is multiple: the work of Christian initiation is properly triune (in anticipation of the Nicene

---

20. For a missiological reading of this passage, see Craig S. Keener, "Matthew's Missiology: Making Disciples of the Nations (Matthew 28:19–20)," *AJPS* 12:1 (2009): 3–20.

21. Which I discuss in my *Renewing Christian Theology*, §11.4.

confession but not in any deterministic sense, for us) because the role of the spirit is equally central to that of the Father and the Son; the mission of God is triune because the Son sends the disciples in the threefold name; and the ministry of the gospel in the name of Jesus remains one empowered by the divine breath long ago foretold by the prophets of ancient Israel. So, if in fact some might participate in this messianic mission so that "this good news of the kingdom will be proclaimed throughout the world, as a testimony to all the nations" (24:14),[22] they can do so only on the same basis as the anointed one did: by the power of the divine spirit. Even in his appointing the Twelve in their mission to Israel, Jesus had already foreseen that their witness would extend to "governors and kings," indeed even to the nations of the gentiles amid antagonistic and hostile circumstances (10:17), and he instructed them not to worry, saying, "What you are to say will be given to you at that time; for it is not you who speak, but the Spirit of your Father speaking through you" (10:19–20). It is no wonder that the modern missionary movement has been courageous in the face of steep challenges, perhaps in large part, whether self-understood in pentecostal-charismatic terms or not, because of the work of the holy spirit.

5.2 Mark—The Spirits against the (Second) Gospel: Deliverance Mission amid Empire

Although the Markan version of the Great Commission comes in the so-called longer ending (Mark 16:9–20) that most scholars believe is a later (second-century) addition to the original Gospel text, the reception history of this passage is suggestive of its profound missionary potency for Christian growth and expansion.[23] Yet even if we were to bracket this segment from our considerations, the apostolic sending therein "to the whole creation" (16:15) is consistent with the broader witness of the Second Gospel. It's not just that, reading backward, the Markan apocalypse (13:1–37) also includes the refrain that "the good news must first be proclaimed to all nations" (13:10) before the end will come,[24] or that, earlier in Jesus's cleaning out of the temple,

22. Vicky Balabanski suggests from this passage known as the Matthean apocalypse that the mission to the nations is also understood or understandable "as an eschatological imperative." "Mission in Matthew against the Horizon of Matthew 24," NTS 54 (2008): 161–75, here 161.

23. See James A. Kelhofer, *Miracle and Mission: The Authentication of Missionaries and Their Message in the Longer Ending of Mark*, WUNT 2/112 (Tübingen: Mohr Siebeck, 2000).

24. Willard M. Swartley argues that Mark was "written as a handbook for continuing the Gentile mission begun by Paul," and he sees 13:10 as the center of this message as it culminates in this final part of the Gospel. *Mark: The Way for All Nations* (Scottdale, PA: Herald, 1979),

he retrieves from the prophets Yahweh's pronouncement, "My house shall be called a house of prayer for all the nations" (11:17, citing Isa. 56:7, with echoes of Jer. 7:11). It is also that Mark's Jesus makes multiple forays into gentile territory during his ministry and mission (e.g., 4:35–5:21; 7:24–8:10; 8:13–9:30),[25] and that there are translations of Aramaic/Hebrew expressions provided and numerous uses of Latin loanwords,[26] all of which support the notion of this being a Gospel written for a Roman audience. Hence one could read the declaration in the introduction, "The beginning of the good news of Jesus Christ, the Son of God" (1:1), as being for all the world.[27]

But if our pneumatological point of entry into the First Gospel (§5.1) was from its center, Mark's Jesus from the beginning is announced as the one who "will baptize you with the Holy Spirit" (Mark 1:8). Jesus then is alighted on by the spirit at his baptism (1:10) and then driven "immediately . . . into the wilderness" (1:12). Arguably, Jesus's being led, preserved, and empowered by the divine breath in and through the hostile desert, full of dangerous creatures and even evil spirits, parallels the many ways in which ancient Israel—not to mention Elijah, David, Job, and many others (see part 1)—was redeemed by the divine wind through the wilderness (e.g., Sinai/Moab and the Babylonian exile).[28] After this, there are only three other explicit references by Mark to the divine spirit, all with parallels in the other Synoptic Gospels: explicating the presumed unforgivable sin as blasphemy "against the Holy Spirit" (3:29); underwriting David's witness to the Christ as given "by the Holy Spirit" (12:36); and confirming that the disciples' witness to the nations in the end will also be enabled by the spirit (13:11).[29] There are also references to Jesus's own spiritual discernment: "Jesus perceived in his spirit" (2:8) and "he sighed deeply in his spirit" (8:12). Yet despite the relatively scarce appearances of

203; see also Michael Bird, "Mission as an Apocalyptic Event: Reflections on Luke 10:18 and Mark 13:10," *EvQ* 76:2 (2004): 117–34.

25. E.g., S. Joseph Anthonysamy, *The Gentile Mission in the Gospel of Mark: A Redaction Critical Study of Passages with a Gentile Tendency* (Rome: Pontificia Università Gregoriana, 1995); and Jesper Svartvik, *Mark and Mission: Mk 7:1–23 in Its Narrative and Historical Contexts* (Stockholm: Almqvist & Wiksell, 2000).

26. Lars Hartman discusses Aramaic/Hebrew translations (Mark 3:17; 5:41; 7:11, 34; 14:36; 15:22, 34) and Latin loanwords (4:21; 5:9, 15; 6:27, 37; 7:4; 12:14–17, 42; 15:15–16, 39); see *Mark for the Nations: A Text- and Reader-Oriented Commentary* (Eugene, OR: Pickwick, 2010).

27. David Rhoads, "Mission in the Gospel of Mark," *CurTM* 40:4 (2013): 340–55.

28. John Wright, "Spirit and Wilderness: The Interplay of Two Motifs within the Hebrew Canon as a Background to Mark 1:2–13," in *Perspectives on Language and Text: Essays and Poems in Honor of Francis I. Andersen's Sixtieth Birthday*, ed. Edgar W. Conrad and Edward G. Newing (Winona Lake, IN: Eisenbrauns, 1987), 269–98.

29. I will return to the first and third instances momentarily; regarding the Davidic connection in Mark 12:36, see Emerson B. Powery, "The Spirit, the Scripture(s), and the Gospel of Mark: Pneumatology and Hermeneutics in Narrative Perspective," *JPT* 11:2 (2003): 184–98.

the *pneuma to hagion* (and its variations), the opening presentation invites consideration of the mission of Jesus as charismatically and pneumatically authorized by the divine breath.[30]

Although the blasphemy pericope appears also in other Gospels, Mark's emphasis on Jesus's confrontations with evil spirits deserves mention when thinking missiologically. Again, it is not just that the Markan commission explicitly says that the sent ones "will cast out demons" (Mark 16:17; cf. 6:7), or that Jesus was accused of being possessed by "an unclean spirit" (3:30), but that there are no fewer than four cases of confrontations with and exorcisms of such in this shortest of Gospels (1:23–27; 5:2–13; 7:25–30; 9:17–25).[31] The main point is certainly Jesus's powers over forces of oppression, so much so that "whenever the unclean spirits saw him, they fell down before him and shouted, 'You are the Son of God!'" (3:11). There are obvious implications and applications for a spirit-empowered missionary praxis, not only when considering majority world and indigenous cultural contexts where beliefs in evil spirits remain prevalent,[32] but also in any context where awareness of the demonic and of the systemic destructive effects of the principalities and powers are at work (see also §6.5). Perhaps most obvious is that messianic mission involves deliverance of those oppressed by the devil, and in this regard, it is unsurprising that the longer ending's commission includes the promise that "by using my name they will cast out demons" (16:17). From this perspective, advocates of the renowned power evangelism or spiritual warfare as mission strategies might be up to something in insisting that we ignore these dimensions of contemporary mission to our detriment.[33]

Focusing on evil spirits is certainly not uncontroversial in missiological circles, and we will return to this topic at various moments in the pages to

30. M. Robert Mansfield says, "Mark presents the Holy Spirit as the divine authority who empowered the preaching (word and act) of the historical Jesus and now gives efficacy to the contemporary preaching of the Risen Christ through the same gospel material attributed to the earthly Jesus. . . . We contend that 'Spirit and Gospel' is a permeating, interlocking concept and theme in Mark in which the function of neither component is fully intelligible apart from the other. Gospel demands the inspiration of the Spirit, past and present; the Spirit guides the Christian community through the medium of Gospel into true discipleship and guards against aberration and heresy." *Spirit and Gospel in Mark* (Peabody, MA: Hendrickson, 1987), 5.

31. Whatever the historicity of these accounts, Jesus is at the least remembered as one who cast out evil spirits; see Graham H. Twelftree, *Jesus the Exorcist: A Contribution to the Study of the Historical Jesus* (Peabody, MA: Hendrickson, 1993), §§3.6–3.9.

32. See Dewey Mulholland, *Mark's Story of Jesus, Messiah for All Nations* (Eugene, OR: Wipf & Stock, 1999), who discusses the Markan exorcisms from his decades-long perspective as a missionary to Brazil.

33. E.g., John Wimber and Kevin Springer, *Power Evangelism*, 2nd rev. ed. (Grand Rapids: Chosen, 2009); and Jerry Rankin and Ed Stetzer, *Spiritual Warfare and Missions: The Battle for God's Glory among the Nations* (Nashville: B&H, 2010).

come. Yet what is striking for our purposes at this Markan juncture is that Jesus's repeated incursions into gentile territory involve exorcisms in each and every foray.[34] Hence one way to comprehend these associations is to understand how notions of unholiness and impurity functioned in first-century Palestine, and thus view these episodes as indicative of how local Judeans and Galileans struggled under the over-lording of their Roman colonizers. The casting out of evil spirits in these cases, then, is not just individualistically concerned but has sociopolitical ramifications: mission frees us from the bondages of demons while turning oppressors into neighbors. This last point is an important one, since otherwise such scriptural texts might be read as justifying the demonization of others (political, cultural, or other categories). Read missiologically, the holy spirit empowers the Messiah to deliver those beleaguered by the powers of Satan, and this contrasts forcefully with those who assert, blasphemously, that the former is controlled by the latter (Mark 3:22–30). Hence there are here distinctive practices and strategies designed to transform relationships with outsiders, in this case considered as idolaters.

Prominent in this regard is the deliverance of the by now renowned Gerasene demoniac (Mark 5). Since the episode unfolds during Jesus's first excursion into gentile territory, in this case to the Hellenized territory of the Decapolis (5:20) southeast of the lake of Galilee, the identification of the unclean spirit that drove the man into the mountains (5:5) as "Legion" (5:9) alludes also to the Roman *legio* of "6,000 foot soldiers, in addition to some cavalry and auxiliary troops" that patrolled the region.[35] So even if the demoniac might have been a gentile, his tragic condition also may have been representative of the felt oppression of Roman occupation among the locals.[36] In this respect, the casting out of Legion, especially in and through ridding the area also of the impurities represented in the herd of swine (5:11–13), can be recognized as resisting Roman exploitation and purging spiritual if not also socioeconomic injustices. If "no one had the strength to subdue" the colonial powers before and deliver the people from their "shackles and chains" (5:4),[37] then the Messiah who was sustained by the divine spirit to overcome the

34. Eric K. Wefald, "The Separate Gentile Mission in Mark: A Narrative Explanation of Markan Geography, the Two Feeding Accounts and Exorcism," *JSNT* 60 (1995): 3–26.

35. Roger David Aus, *My Name Is "Legion": Palestinian Judaic Traditions in Mark 5, 1–20 and Other Gospel Texts* (Lanham, MD: University Press of America, 2003), 16.

36. Historical, narrative, and social-psychological analysis is provided by Michael Willett Newheart, *My Name Is Legion: The Story and Soul of the Gerasene Demoniac* (Collegeville, MN: Liturgical Press, 2004).

37. See Ched Myers, *Binding the Strong Man: A Political Reading of Mark's Story of Jesus*, 20th anniv. ed. (Maryknoll, NY: Orbis, 2008), 426–27.

powers of Satan (1:12–13) is the one who can free the subjugated. Perhaps it was beneficiaries of the system who were not as enthused about this assault on their social order that "began to beg Jesus to leave their neighborhood" (5:17).[38] Relevant for us, though, is that the holy spirit of Jesus confronts and dispels the unholy spirits that impair the sick, terrorize the afflicted, and marginalize the displaced.

The bigger Markan picture is that regardless of the powers that be in the present age, "the kingdom of God has come near" (Mark 1:15) through the demon-expelling, miracle-working, and cross-suffering, but also spirit-empowered Messiah, Jesus.[39] If this world's forces of darkness seek to keep human creatures in chains, they are expelled by the good news of the reign of God in the person of Jesus the Christ, the anointed one. If the present life is constituted by enemies within (spiritual) and without (social and political) that keep us antagonistic with others, then the in-breaking of the divine rule by the power of the anointed Messiah saves us from such demons, heals our estrangement, and reconciles us to others. So whereas Matthew's "kingdom of heaven" horizons open up to the nations outside Israel, Mark's "kingdom of God" focus seems also to recognize the need for release from the (Roman) powers within.[40] When the principalities, both cosmic and local authorities, are resistant to the rule of God and demand account from its witnesses, the messianists are encouraged by the second evangelist, "Do not worry beforehand about what you are to say; but say whatever is given you at that time, for it is not you who speak, but the Holy Spirit" (13:11).[41] Are there similar implications and applications for pneumatological mission amid the contemporary nation-state and its glocal manifestations?

38. As is typical of readings of Mark with and against imperial (in this case Roman) power, e.g., C. I. David Joy, *Mark and Its Subalterns: A Hermeneutical Paradigm for a Postcolonial Context*, Bible World (Oakville, CT: Equinox, 2007), chap. 5 on the Gerasene; cf. Simon Samuel, *A Postcolonial Reading of Mark's Story of Jesus*, LNTS 340 (New York: Bloomsbury, 2007), who urges instead that Mark was emergent from a hybridic site between Jewish Palestine and imperial Rome, on the one hand accommodating to but on the other hand disrupting both spaces in carving out and charting the way of Jesus.

39. Lawrence Iwuamadi thus concludes his book: "The content of κηρυσσειν [preaching] during the ministry of Jesus is that *the Kingdom of God is imminent*. On the other hand, the post-resurrection content of the gospel proclamation is the message that *Jesus is the Christ, Son of God*." Iwuamadi, *"He Called unto Him the Twelve and Began to Send Them Forth": The Continuation of Jesus' Mission according to the Gospel of Mark*, Tesi Gregoriana Serie Teologia 169 (Rome: Editrice Pontificia Università Gregoriana, 2008), 252–53 (emphasis original).

40. Scholarship abounds on the fact that *kingdom of heaven* appears only in Matthew in the New Testament, and *kingdom of God* comparatively rarely in the First Gospel; the contrast presented here is my own.

41. See Emerson B. Powery, "The Spirit and Political Dissent: Revisiting Mark 13:11," *JBPR* 2 (2010): 18–30.

5.3   Luke—The Spirit Empowering the (Third) Gospel: Jubilee Mission among the Oppressed

Whereas our pneumatological reading of Matthew began with an Isaianic quotation in the middle of the First Gospel, Luke's Jesus identifies himself with the *ruah*-anointed servant referred to in Trito-Isaiah (§4.3) in order to launch his public ministry.[42] After he went into the wilderness temptation "full of the Holy Spirit" (Luke 4:1)—which the other two synoptic writers also mention—he also, "filled with the power of the Spirit, returned to Galilee" (4:14). Jesus then went into the synagogue at Nazareth and read publicly from the prophet:

> The Spirit of the Lord is upon me,
>   because he has anointed me
>   to bring good news to the poor.
> He has sent me to proclaim release to the captives
>   and recovery of sight to the blind,
>   to let the oppressed go free,
> to proclaim the year of the Lord's favor. (4:18–19; cf. Isa. 61:1–2)

What is important to observe about this passage is that it frames the rest of Jesus's mission (in the next twenty chapters of Luke's Gospel) as messianic.[43] More accurately, as this prophetic text indicates, not only is Jesus's ministry in Luke remarkably multifaceted but the entirety of his mission is also spirit-inspired and spirit-empowered so that it could be said that the spirit is as central a divine character in Luke as is the Messiah who is anointed.[44] It is therefore as the Christ, the anointed one, that Jesus does the work of the Father. For instance, he proclaims a message but also accomplishes life-changing trans-formation; evangelism and holistic mission are thus not mutually exclusive. Further, there is surely the work of spiritual deliverance, even as the Messiah

42. Stanley E. Porter provides a good overview of how Luke uses the scriptures of ancient Israel for his missiological purposes; see "Scripture Justifies Mission: The Use of the Old Testament in Luke-Acts," in *Hearing the Old Testament in the New Testament*, ed. Stanley E. Porter (Grand Rapids: Eerdmans, 2006), 104–26; see also John T. Carroll, "The God of Israel and the Salvation of the Nations: The Gospel of Luke and the Acts of the Apostles," in *The Forgotten God: Perspectives in Biblical Theology*, ed. A. Andrew Das and Frank J. Matera (Louisville: Westminster John Knox, 2002), 91–106.

43. See Michael Prior, *Jesus the Liberator: Nazareth Liberation Theology (Luke 4:16–30)* (New York: Continuum, 1995); for a succinct statement, see Jacques Matthey, "Luke 4:16–30—The Spirit's Mission Manifesto—Jesus' Hermeneutics—and Luke's Editorial," *IRM* 89:352 (January 2000): 3–11.

44. Ju Hur, *A Dynamic Reading of the Holy Spirit in Luke-Acts*, JSNTSup 211 (Sheffield: Sheffield Academic, 2001).

does not neglect physical healing and material liberation.[45] So, on the one side, we see Jesus's ministry include that of delivering those oppressed by evil spirits (e.g., Luke 4:31–37; 6:18; 7:21; 8:2, 26–39; 9:37–42; 10:20; 13:10–17). On the other side, we see Jesus not just healing but also restoring those ostracized to their communities (e.g., 5:12–14; 7:36–50; 17:11–19), restoring livelihood to those without means (e.g., 7:11–17), and acknowledging the humanity and dignity of those otherwise dismissed (e.g., 8:43–58; 10:38–42; 18:1–8; 19:1–10; 21:1–4).[46] Remember, though, that all of these works of Jesus are pneumatically and charismatically charged. As Luke reminds us in his second book: "God anointed Jesus of Nazareth with the Holy Spirit and with power; how he went about doing good and healing all who were oppressed by the devil, for God was with him" (Acts 10:38).[47]

One more aspect of this text deserves additional comment. The declaration of "the year of the Lord's favor" here, as it does in the Isaianic original, refers to the year of Jubilee in the Torah (Lev. 25), one that involved the restoration of land to families and of freedom from servitude to the impoverished.[48] Hence Jesus's concerns over poverty and wealth throughout the Third Gospel (e.g., Luke 12:13–34; 16:1–10; 18:18–30; 19:1–10; 20:45–21:4) are neither aberrational nor to be spiritualized. Rather, they are indicative of the messianic mission's concrete concerns with the flourishing of embodied human beings in real social, historical, economic, and political communities.[49] We shall see momentarily (§5.4) that the earliest disciples, filled with the same spirit that empowered Jesus's work, implemented provisions of the Jubilee mandate that met the needs of the impoverished and also restored an egalitarian sensibility between the haves and the have-nots.

45. On Jesus's "liberation theology" as seen in this passage, see my *The Hermeneutical Spirit: Theological Interpretation and the Scriptural Imagination for the Third Christian Millennium* (Eugene, OR: Cascade, 2017), chap. 8; see also Dario López Rodriguez, *The Liberating Mission of Jesus: The Message of the Gospel of Luke*, trans. Stefanie E. Israel and Richard E. Waldrop (Eugene, OR: Pickwick, 2012).

46. See William J. Larkin Jr., "Mission in Luke," in *Mission in the New Testament: An Evangelical Approach*, ed. William J. Larkin Jr. and Joel F. Williams, American Society of Missiology Series 27 (Maryknoll, NY: Orbis, 1998), 152–69.

47. See Robert P. Menzies, *Empowered for Witness: The Spirit in Luke-Acts*, JPTSup 6 (Sheffield: Sheffield Academic, 2001).

48. See Sharon H. Ringe, *Jesus, Liberation, and the Biblical Jubilee: Images for Ethics and Christology* (Minneapolis: Fortress, 1985); for an overview, see Paul Hertig, "The Jubilee Mission of Jesus in the Gospel of Luke: Reversal of Fortunes," *Missiology* 26:2 (1998): 167–79.

49. E.g., Luke Timothy Johnson, *Sharing Possessions: Mandate and Symbol of Faith* (Minneapolis: Fortress, 1981); John Gillman, *Possessions and the Life of Faith: A Reading of Luke-Acts* (Collegeville, MN: Liturgical Press, 1991); and Thomas E. Phillips, *Reading Issues of Wealth and Poverty in Luke-Acts*, SBEC 48 (Lewiston, NY: Edwin Mellen, 2001).

Although the Lukan Jesus's spirit-anointed mission certainly includes the economic dimension, the messianic message is also expansive beyond that domain. So, on the one hand, the extended prologue to the gospel narrative is clear that the messianic deliverance will have socioeconomic consequences:

> He has brought down the powerful from their thrones,
> and lifted up the lowly;
> he has filled the hungry with good things,
> and sent the rich away empty. (Luke 1:52–53, from Mary's
> Magnificat)

On the other hand, even more prominent in these early chapters of the Third Gospel is that prototypes of the spirit-filled Messiah indicate that God's redemptive work has the nations of the earth in its sights. Thus, Zechariah, the father of John the Baptist, "was filled with the Holy Spirit" (1:67) and intimated as much in his oracle that the work of the coming Messiah would be manifest to the extent that "the dawn from on high will break upon us, / to give light to those who sit in darkness and in the shadow of death, / to guide our feet into the way of peace" (1:78–79). The scriptural allusion in this passage is to an Isaianic text that references "the nations" in relation to Israel (Isa. 9:1).[50] This message is further clarified by John, whose promised spirit-empowered ministry (Luke 1:15) was itself initiated by his mother's being filled with the spirit (1:41).[51] John preached that not only Israel but "all flesh shall see the salvation of God" (3:6; cf. Isa. 40:5). It is John also, under the unction of the spirit, who promises that Jesus, the coming deliverer, "will baptize you with the Holy Spirit and fire" (3:16).[52]

Even before the spirit descends on Jesus at his baptism (Luke 3:22), he comes upon Simeon. In that context, the aged and devout believer and student of Yahweh's promises to ancient Israel heralds:

> My eyes have seen your salvation,
> which you have prepared in the presence of all peoples,

---

50. See Joseph Verheyden, "Creating Difference through Parallelism: Luke's Handling of the Traditions of John the Baptist and Jesus in the Infancy Narrative," in *Infancy Gospels: Stories and Identities*, ed. Claire Clivaz et al., WUNT 281 (Tübingen: Mohr Siebeck, 2011), 137–60.

51. Elizabeth's spirit-filled ministry is unpacked in my *Renewing Christian Theology*, §3.1.

52. The reference here is probably to the Messiah's purifying work—e.g., Archie W. D. Hui, "John the Baptist and Spirit Baptism," *EvQ* 71:2 (1999): 99–115—out of which the witness of the pneumatic people of God goes forth to the nations.

a light for revelation to the Gentiles
and for glory to your people Israel. (2:30–32; cf. Isa. 40:5)[53]

The point is that if Jesus is the paradigm of the spirit-filled life whose ministry (in the Third Gospel) is emulated as such by his followers (in Acts), then the extent of Luke's vista that reaches to the nations is anticipated by the spirit-filled archetypes that inaugurate the messianic mission. And these exemplars indicate that Israel's God is concerned both for the oppressed and marginalized and with the fate of the nations. Luke's account thus reveals Jesus's journey to Jerusalem via detour through Samaria (9:52) and Jesus's sending out the seventy (or seventy-two, in some manuscripts) missionaries (10:1) that implicitly correlate with the seventy nations of the world in the Old Testament (see Gen. 10). Luke's approach contrasts with the explicit prohibition in Matthew (10:5–6) against going into Samaria and being focused only on Israel. Luke is arguably hereby presaging Jesus's post-resurrection and pre-ascension commandment: "Thus it is written, that the Messiah is to suffer and to rise from the dead on the third day, and that repentance and forgiveness of sins is to be proclaimed in his name to all nations, beginning from Jerusalem" (24:46–47).

We will return to the transnational horizon when we look at the book of Acts. For the moment, we need to register the important point that Luke's pneumatological missiology, without taking anything away from how such has been traditionally construed,[54] includes a robust socioeconomic dimension. If the disciples are urged to pray for the coming of God's rule as they are for the gift of the spirit (Luke 11:2, 13), and if the inspired Messiah repeatedly insists that the divine reign is imminent (10:9, 11; 21:31), even "among you" (17:21),[55] then the mission of God's spirit involves nothing less than the healing of sick bodies, the liberation of oppressed lives, and the righteous repair of unjust systems. Jesus's Jubilee mission of inaugurating God's reign is not only precipitated by the spirit but undergirded throughout by the divine wind. And the end of this christic ministry is also the beginning of the charismatic

53. For more on Simeon as a spirit-inspired *reader* of the Jewish Tanakh, see John R. Levison, "The Spirit, Simeon, and the Songs of the Servant," in *The Spirit and Christ in the New Testament and Christian Theology: Essays in Honor of Max Turner*, ed. I. Howard Marshall, Volker Rabens, and Cornelis Bennema (Grand Rapids: Eerdmans, 2012), 18–34; see also Bo Reicke, "Jesus, Simeon, and Anna (Luke 2:21–40)," in *Saved by Hope: Essays in Honor of Richard C. Oudersluys*, ed. James I. Cook (Grand Rapids: Eerdmans, 1978), 96–108, esp. 100–105.

54. See, for instance, John Michael Penney, *The Missionary Emphasis of Lukan Pneumatology*, JPTSup 12 (Sheffield: Sheffield Academic, 1997).

55. As delineated in Derek Morphew, *The Mission of the Kingdom: The Theology of Luke-Acts* (Cape Town: Vineyard International, 2011).

The Synoptic Witness of the Spirit
Bridging Binaries

Simon Samuel, professor of New Testament studies and Christian origins and the principal of New Theological College, Dehradun, India

The witness of the synoptic evangelists in the spirit may be identified in terms of a witness to the Jews and the *Jathis* (*ethne*/nations) in Matthew, to the empire in Mark, and to the oppressed in Luke. In Luke-Acts it is a summons to the nations to Jerusalem and an outreach to the nations from Jerusalem. Matthew's witness in the spirit engages the Jewish self (10:5) and the gentile other (28:19–20). Mark's witness rejects the Jewish cultural nationalism and the Roman colonialism. The Lukan witness confronts the class divide and the geographical, global divide. Thus, *missio spiritus* in the Synoptic Gospels and Acts goes beyond the binary of "self" and "other," the nationalists and the colonialists, the oppressors and the oppressed, the global and the local. It is in the beyondness and the erasure of these binaries that the synoptic writers perceive the *missio spiritus*.

anointing for his followers' participation in God's redemptive mission from of old.

5.4   Acts, Part 1—Pentecost and Mission: From the Ends of the Earth

We have finally arrived at the book that originally and long ago inspired the ideas driving this volume: the Acts of the Apostles. As Acts has always been well known for providing the authoritative account of early Christian growth and expansion from "all Judea and Samaria, and to the ends of the earth" (1:8), it is not surprising that it has also played a key role in the modern missions movement, especially informing how Western churches have strategized about reaching the nations of the majority world with the gospel.[56] Yet insofar as this

---

56. See James K. Mathews, *To the End of the Earth* (Nashville: National Student Methodist Movement, 1959); cf. Doug Priest Jr., ed., *The Gospel Unhindered: Modern Missions and the Book of Acts* (Pasadena, CA: William Carey Library, 1994).

book has also been renowned historically as the Acts of the holy spirit, the signs and wonders of the book have been prominent in contemporary missiology, not least as mediated in and through the modern pentecostal movement.[57] Without discounting the miraculous work of the spirit for the mission of the church, my own approach has been to utilize Acts as a point of entry not only into the writings of Luke but also to the New Testament more generally, somewhat as Romans played such a role for Reformation theology. Our goal is to reconsider the scriptural witness and traditions from a more specifically pneumatological perspective in order to explore more fully the promise of a robustly triunely shaped theology.[58] For our purposes in this book, the goal has been an explicitly triune theology—in the biblical sense, rather than trinitarian in the Nicene sense, it must be remembered—of the *missio Dei*.

Foregrounding the pneumatological lens invites us to go behind the announcement of the spirit's empowering witness (Acts 1:8) that is central to the missiology of Acts and get to the question that this promise was responding to: "Lord, is this the time when you will restore the kingdom to Israel?" (1:6). Attentive readers to the prequel of Acts would have noticed even there the disciples (Luke 24:41), among others already noted as touched by the spirit—for example, Mary (1:54), Zechariah (1:68), and Simeon (2:25)—have been consistently concerned that the messianic mission would redeem Israel. My point is that the restoration of Israel and the witness to the nations are not exclusive dimensions of what we call the triune mission.[59] Luke later records the Jerusalem Council as deliberating in the spirit (Acts 15:28) and connecting, via Israel's prophets, the renewal of Israel with the mission to the gentiles:

> I will rebuild the dwelling of David, which has fallen;
>> from its ruins I will rebuild it,
>>> and I will set it up,

57. E.g., Gary B. McGee, *Miracles, Missions, and American Pentecostalism* (Maryknoll, NY: Orbis, 2010); Julie C. Ma and Wonsuk Ma, *Mission in the Spirit: Towards a Pentecostal/Charismatic Missiology* (Eugene, OR: Wipf & Stock, 2010); and Paul A. Pomerville, *The Third Force in Missions: A Pentecostal Contribution to Contemporary Mission Theology*, 2nd ed. (Peabody, MA: Hendrickson, 2015).

58. For my reading of Acts-Luke—starting with Pentecost and reading Luke from the Acts perspective—see *Who Is the Holy Spirit? A Walk with the Apostles* (Brewster, MA: Paraclete, 2011); such a Lukan hermeneutic for the New Testament is provided in my book *Renewing Christian Theology*.

59. Compare Max Turner, *Power from on High: The Spirit in Israel's Restoration and Witness in Luke-Acts*, JPTSup 9 (Sheffield: Sheffield Academic, 2000); and Michael E. Fuller, *The Restoration of Israel: Israel's Re-gathering and the Fate of the Nations in Early Jewish Literature and Luke-Acts*, Beihefte zur Zeitschrift für die neutestamentliche Wissenschaft und die Kunde der älteren Kirche 138 (Berlin: de Gruyter, 2006).

so that all other peoples may seek the Lord—
even all the Gentiles over whom my name has been called.
(Acts 15:16–17; cf. Amos 9:11–12)[60]

But the discussion in this second half of the Acts narrative can be comprehended as a logical conclusion drawn from the ingathering of those from
among the nations in Jerusalem on the day of Pentecost outpouring of the
spirit.

Much has been written theologically about the Pentecost event.[61] I want
to highlight three elements of the text for the purposes of this volume. First,
this gift of the spirit was promised by the Father (Luke 24:49; Acts 1:4) to
empower witness to the world "about God's deeds of power" (Acts 2:11).
Second, even as Acts 1:8 structures the arc of the narrative so that the spirit-
empowered witness travels from Jerusalem (2:1–5:11) through Judea (5:12–8:3)
and Samaria (8:4–25) and on to the ends of the earth (8:26–28:31), effectively
arriving in Rome (28:11–31), literally the edge of the known world from an
Israel-centered point of view, the initial pentecostal outpouring was given to
"devout Jews from every nation under heaven living in Jerusalem" (2:5). The
list of fifteen nations that follows is a shortened version of the Old Testament
"table of nations" (e.g., Gen. 10; 1 Chron. 1)[62] and thus suggests that the "ends
of the earth" (Acts 1:8), including Rome (2:10), did not need to wait until the
missionaries arrived later to hear the gospel. Rather, in effect, what we have
here is a primordial form of "reverse mission," the unexpected phenomenon
whereby the local Galilean messianists not only proclaim the good news to
the world at their doors but are transformed by the witness that comes in and
through these other languages.[63] As a result, third, the missionary dynamic

---

60. See the discussion of the use of this passage from Amos in James A. Meek, *The Gentile
Mission in the Old Testament Citations in Acts: Text, Hermeneutic, and Purpose*, LNTS 410
(New York: T&T Clark, 2009), chap. 4.

61. Including my own pentecostal theological reflection that pivots on this passage: *The
Spirit Poured Out on All Flesh: Pentecostalism and the Possibility of Global Theology* (Grand
Rapids: Baker Academic, 2005).

62. James M. Scott, "Acts 2:9–11 as an Anticipation of the Mission to the Nations," in *The
Mission of the Early Church to Jews and Gentiles*, ed. Jostein Ådna and Hans Kvalbein, WUNT
127 (Tübingen: Mohr Siebeck, 2000), 87–123.

63. In contemporary missiology, the phenomenon of "reverse mission" describes the re-
evangelization of Europe and North America, which were the senders of missionaries to the
world during the modern mission movement, by migrants from the global South during the
past few decades; see, e.g., Gregory Smutko, "Reverse Mission: Consciousness-Raising in North
America," *Missiology* 7:1 (1979): 117–18. The reality, however, is that these are complicated
endeavors, seen from any number of angles, as delineated by Paul Freston, "Reverse Mission:
A Discourse in Search of Reality?," *PentecoStudies* 9:2 (2010): 153–74.

of the divine spirit is from the beginning transnational and cross-cultural, interweaving the regions, peoples, and languages of the world.[64]

Luke's explanation of the Pentecost event, recorded through Peter's sermon (Acts 2:14–36) drawing from the prophet Joel (2:28–31), underscores not only the worldwide character of the spirit's promised outpouring but also the divine intention to bless "all flesh" (Acts 2:17). There is a comprehensiveness of the human community upon whom the spirit descends: sons and daughters, young and old, "even upon my slaves, both men and women" (2:17–18). Inescapably, then, "*everyone* who calls on the name of the Lord shall be saved" (2:21; emphasis added). And if this were insufficiently clear, Peter later reiterates: "For the promise is for you, for your children, and for all who are far away, *everyone* whom the Lord our God calls to him" (2:39; emphasis added). Shortly thereafter, the healing of the lame man at the Beautiful Gate resulting in his entering the temple, "walking and leaping and praising God" (3:8), hearken messianic and Jubilee tropes from the prophets indicative of the arrival of the promised day of the Lord (see, e.g., Isa. 35:6).[65] This leads Peter to herald repentance of the onlookers "so that times of refreshing may come from the presence of the Lord, . . . the time of universal restoration that God announced long ago through his holy prophets, [and] . . . 'all the families of the earth shall be blessed'" according to the primordial promise to Abraham (Acts 3:20–21, 25; cf. Gen. 12:3). So the point is that the Pentecost outpouring that is intended for every nation and even every person not only ushers in "the last days" (2:17) of the divine redemption but also extends to every generation and to the times of creation's and history's consummation.

Whereas pentecostal scholars usually (expectedly!) emphasize from the Joel message mediated through Peter that the divinely empowered mission unfolds through the spirit's "supernatural" work of visions and dreams, boldness in prophecy, and signs and wonders (Acts 2:17–18),[66] our focus reconnects to the Jubilee message of Jesus in Luke's Gospel and lifts up the liberative work of the spirit that made a material and economic difference in the lives of needy "others." As Luke records, "All who believed were together and had all things in common; they would sell their possessions and goods and distribute the

64. Craig S. Keener, "Why Does Luke Use Tongues as a Sign of the Spirit's Empowerment?," *JPT* 15:2 (2007): 177–84.

65. Note that the Isa. 35 reference here derives from the First Isaiah oracle of judgment on the nations (Isa. 34–35), amid which the divine *ruah*'s redemptive work ensues (34:16); see the earlier discussion in §4.1.

66. See Robert P. Menzies, "Acts 2.17–21: A Paradigm for Pentecostal Mission," *JPT* 17 (2008): 200–218.

proceeds to all, as any had need" (Acts 2:44–45).[67] That important point is restated later when, in the context of the suffering of persecution at the hands of the local religious leaders, the messianists "were all filled with the Holy Spirit and spoke the word of God with boldness [and] the whole group of those who believed were of one heart and soul, and no one claimed private ownership of any possessions, but everything they owned was held in common" (4:31–32). In this milieu, Barnabas, "which means 'son of encouragement,'" is an exemplary disciple because "he sold a field that belonged to him, then brought the money, and laid it at the apostles' feet" (4:36–37) for the sake of the community, while Ananias and Sapphira (5:1–10) are archetypal breakers of the charismatic fellowship in their lying to the spirit (5:3) about their charitableness (overcome as they were by their selfishness).[68] As the spirit had already anticipated through David that the nations and peoples of the world would resist the Messiah's work (4:25–26; cf. Ps. 2:1–2), here the spirit literally contests those individuals who undermined the good news of the Jubilee promise.

Pressing further into "the coming of the Lord's great and glorious" Jubilee day (Acts 2:20), note that the three thousand newly baptized members of the messianic community (2:41) were constituted by local Galileans and those gathered from around the Mediterranean world. Then as they drew into the fold—climbing to five thousand quickly (4:4)—others "from the towns around Jerusalem" (5:16), the cross-cultural dynamics of this apostolic group were further stressed. We get a glimpse into the challenges when we are told that as "the disciples were increasing in number, the Hellenists complained against the Hebrews because their widows were being neglected in the daily distribution of food" (6:1). Evidently there are not only issues of linguistic communication (between Greek-speaking Hellenist believers and Hebrew-speaking Judeans) but also misunderstandings of how to relate the Jewish cultural character of the local messianists with the diverse cosmopolitanism of the burgeoning following that heralded from across the Roman world.[69] Greek-speaking Hellenists "full of the Spirit and of wisdom" (6:3)—note their

67. See also Peter Penner, "Practising Community in the Early Church: A Missional Reading of the Summary Texts in Acts," in *Mission in Context: Explorations Inspired by J. Andrew Kirk*, ed. John Corrie and Cathy Ross (Farnham, UK: Ashgate, 2012), 77–91.

68. Aaron J. Kuecker thus contrasts the other-interestedness—even that which extends across ethnic boundaries—of the messianists with the self-interestedness of Ananias and his wife; see *The Spirit and the "Other": Social Identity, Ethnicity and Intergroup Reconciliation in Luke-Acts*, LNTS 385 (New York: T&T Clark, 2008).

69. See Young Lee Hertig, "Cross-Cultural Mediation: From Exclusion to Inclusion (Acts 6:1–7; also 5:33–42)," in *Mission in Acts: Ancient Narratives in Contemporary Context*, ed. Robert L. Gallagher and Paul Hertig (Maryknoll, NY: Orbis, 2004), 59–72; note that many of

names, including that of Stephen, "a man full of faith and the Holy Spirit" (6:5)—were quickly appointed to leadership roles, giving us a window into how the early believers grappled with intercultural differences.[70] The promised enablement of the spirit to witness to the ends of the earth did not mean that issues of cross-cultural communication were easily navigated. Perhaps just the opposite was true: because the redemptive work of the spirit was intended for the nations, the work remained of forming the people of God as a multicultural, intercultural, and transcultural reality.

5.5   Acts, Part 2—Mission after Pentecost: To the Ends of the Earth

If in the past God had "allowed all the nations to follow their own ways" (Acts 14:16) and "to inhabit the whole earth" (17:26), the Pentecost outpouring was not intended to corral the tribes of humanity into one space but to renew them as one people in fellowship, albeit in and through their many tongues and across their many cultures and regions. So, whereas Acts 1–7 shows how the gathering of the ends of the earth in Jerusalem provided a blueprint for the fellowship of the spirit heralded by many languages, the rest of Luke's narrative unfolds the apostolic witness moving outward from Jerusalem. What are the chief missiological lessons we might gain about spirit-empowered witness to the nations in Lukan perspective?

First, as the messianists "were scattered throughout the countryside of Judea and [into] Samaria" (Acts 8:1) by the persecution,[71] we see that the promised blessing of the spirit (2:38–39) was meant to displace the many unclean spirits that, "crying with loud shrieks, came out of many who were possessed" (8:7) in Samaria. Thus, Peter and John came alongside Philip to pray that the Samaritans would receive the gift of the holy spirit (8:15–17), in this case apparently through the laying on of hands (8:19). The spirit then led Philip to (8:29), and later took him from (8:39), the Ethiopian eunuch on the road to Gaza (8:26). In this case, the ministry of the spirit was to one who was multiply marginalized: as an Ethiopian (from outside the Roman sphere), as the

the chapters in this volume touch on and engage in important ways with themes I am highlighting from Luke-Acts.

70. Elucidating this transcultural motif are, among others, Harold Dollar, *St. Luke's Missiology: A Cross-Cultural Challenge* (Pasadena, CA: William Carey Library, 1996); Glenn Rogers, *Holistic Ministry and Cross-Cultural Mission in Luke-Acts* (n.p.: Mission and Ministry Resources, 1996); and Richard B. Harms, *Paradigms from Luke-Acts for Multicultural Communities*, American University Studies Series VII, Theology and Religion 216 (New York: Peter Lang, 2001).

71. This persecution impels the mission outward from Jerusalem, as accounted by David S. Dockery, "Acts 6–12: The Christian Mission beyond Jerusalem," *RevExp* 87 (1990): 423–37.

national treasurer (with all the benefits but also suspicions pertaining to such positions), and as a eunuch (with all the stigma attached to such effeminate identities in the ancient world—so much so that the eunuch resonated with the Isaianic passage he was reading: "In his humiliation justice was denied him. / Who can describe his generation? / For his life is taken away from the earth" [8:33; Isa. 53:8]).[72] He was then initiated, by baptism (8:26–38), into the messianic story. If Samaria was the first step beyond Jerusalem and Judea, the Ethiopian would continue toward the southern ends of the earth.[73] Yet in both cases, the spirit worked materially upon Samaritan and Ethiopian flesh, through the laying on of hands and through baptism, to deliver them from their oppression.

If the visitation of the spirit on the eunuch brought the apostolic missionaries to the borders where Judea and Samaria opened up to the ends of the earth, then what happens next with Peter's encounter with Cornelius the Roman centurion crosses these boundaries.[74] That it was a huge stride for Peter to even enter into Cornelius's home (Acts 10:27) is forcefully communicated through the thrice-given vision of invitation to consume unclean creatures (10:9–16), through which he came to realize that while it is "unlawful for a Jew to associate with or to visit a Gentile . . . God has shown me that I should not call anyone profane or unclean" (10:28). As it turns out, "while Peter was still speaking, the Holy Spirit fell upon all who heard the word. The circumcised believers who had come with Peter were astounded that the gift of the Holy Spirit had been poured out even on the Gentiles, for they heard them speaking in tongues and extolling God" (10:44–46; cf. 11:15–17; 15:7–9). The combination of the divinely granted vision and the manifestation of the spirit's outpouring upon those previously considered unclean transformed Peter, the spirit-empowered missionary: "I truly understand that God shows no partiality, but in every nation anyone who fears him and does what is right is acceptable to him" (10:34–35).[75] The apostle surely witnesses to the gentiles, but he also experiences a conversion

---

72. Marianne Bjelland Kartzow and Halvor Moxnes, "Complex Identities: Ethnicity, Gender and Religion in the Story of the Ethiopian Eunuch (Acts 8:26–40)," *Religion and Theology* 17:3 (2010): 184–204; see also Anna Rebecca Solevåg, "No Nuts? No Problem! Disability, Stigma, and the Baptized Eunuch in Acts 8:26–40," *BibInt* 24:1 (2016): 81–99.

73. See further discussion of this point in James M. Scott, *Paul and the Nations: The Old Testament and Jewish Background of Paul's Mission to the Nations with Special Reference to the Destination of Galatians*, WUNT 84 (Tübingen: Mohr Siebeck, 1995), 171–73.

74. Vanthanh Nguyen, SVD, "Dismantling Cultural Boundaries: Missiological Implications of Acts 10:1–11:18," *Missiology* 40:4 (2012): 455–66.

75. Denton Lotz, "Peter's Wider Understanding of God's Will: Acts 10:34–48," *IRM* 77 (1988): 201–7.

of heart and mind, through these alien others, to the missionary heart of God.[76]

The mission to the gentiles unfolds in the rest of Acts primarily through Paul's ministry, and this takes a variety of forms. Although the next chapter will focus on the Pauline missiology as found in his letters, it is worth surveying its basic elements noted in Luke's account. Paul does the obvious, such as plant churches, but he also bears witness in constrained settings, such as when he is a prisoner of Rome. Performatively, he works miraculous signs like exorcising evil spirits (Acts 16:16–18), healing the sick (19:11–12; 21:8), and raising Eutychus from the dead (20:7–12). But his spirit-empowered witness also takes the form of a martyr—remember that "witness" in Acts 1:8 is the Greek *martyres*—in enduring persecution and stoning (14:19), and in suffering flogging and imprisonment (16:22–24; 21:30–32). Kerygmatically, however, Pauline evangelism in gentile contexts can be said to be dialogical. With the Lystrans, Paul engages in a form of natural theological reasoning and discussion, appealing to the creator God who cares for human creatures (14:14–18),[77] and with the Athenians, he draws from their own cultural and philosophical sources (17:28).[78] Although some have minimized Paul's dialogical manner given what could be surmised as his turn from the relatively unsuccessful Mars Hill mission (17:32–34) toward a more proclamatory approach at Corinth next (18:1; cf. 1 Cor. 2:1–4),[79] even there his argumentative reasoning was interactive (*dialegomai*; cf. Acts 17:2; 18:4). If Paul is the spirit-empowered witness or martyr for the sake of the gospel, then attention should be on the variety of methods enacted in his mission.

Mission strategies aside, the apostolic witness to the nations was undeniably political, burgeoning from the beginning within the domain in which Caesar, rather than Jesus, was Lord.[80] Hence the arrival of Paul at Rome

76. For contemporary missiological applications in a religiously pluralistic world, see Tony Richie, *Toward a Pentecostal Theology of Religions: Encountering Cornelius Today* (Cleveland, TN: CPT, 2013).

77. See Marianne Fournier, *The Episode at Lystra: A Rhetorical and Semiotic Analysis of Acts 14:7–20a*, American University Studies Series VII, Theology and Religion 197 (New York: Peter Lang, 1997), chap. 5.

78. See Andrew M. Mbuvi, "Missionary Acts, Things Fall Apart: Modeling Mission in Acts 17:15–34 and a Concern for Dialogue in Chinua Achebe's *Things Fall Apart*," *ExAud* 23 (2007): 140–56.

79. As argued by Joseph Pathrapankal, "From Areopagus to Corinth (Acts 17:22–31; I Cor 2:1–5): A Study on the Transition from the Power of Knowledge to the Power of the Spirit," *Mission Studies* 23:1 (2006): 61–80.

80. A fuller discussion is in Yong, *In the Days of Caesar: Pentecostalism and Political Theology; The Cadbury Lectures 2009*, Sacra Doctrina: Christian Theology for a Postmodern Age (Grand Rapids: Eerdmans, 2010), esp. chap. 3.

shows that the Pentecost outpouring is not only upon individual Romans, even Jews and proselytes from Rome (Acts 2:10), but unto the ends of the earth, even of Roman space.[81] Yes, there is a sense in which the mission returned to engage Jews in the capital city, as the more inclusive category of Roman "believers" in 28:15–16 (about which more is said in the next chapter: §6.1) is followed by focused interaction with "the Jews" in 28:17.[82] Yet the overarching trajectory of the spirit-empowered Pauline mission that includes speaking truth to power (e.g., before Felix the governor of Judea and Herod Agrippa) and insisting that the powers act justly (e.g., 16:35–40 in Philippi)[83] is unmistakable: the witness to the gentiles and to the nations at the ends of the earth declares the messiahship of Jesus that undermines if not displaces allegiance to Caesar across the then imperially dominated world.[84] Just as the gift of the spirit had socioeconomic consequences in instantiating, even if preliminarily, the year of Jubilee aspirations of the poor and oppressed, so also does this manifestation of the divine breath have public and political implications for worldly kingdoms, on the one hand heralding the demise particularly of their opposition to the rule of God, but on the other hand drawing them into the orbit of Israel's impending restoration and in that sense anticipating their own renewal within the scope of God's ultimate plans for redeeming the world.

Luke ends his second book as he began it, noting that Paul, in chains (Acts 28:20),[85] was testifying to and proclaiming about the kingdom of God (28:23, 31; cf. 1:3). If the coming of the spirit inaugurates the "last days" (2:17) and heralds "the coming of the Lord's great and glorious day" (2:20), then "every

81. Paul W. Walaskay, 'And So We Came to Rome': The Political Perspective of St Luke, SNTSMS 49 (Cambridge: Cambridge University Press, 2005).

82. Darryl W. Palmer reads this as indicative of Luke's continual concern about the redemption of Israel, yet Mitzi J. Smith compellingly shows how Luke portrays "the Jews" as the "external other" in their rejection of the gospel so that Paul is said thrice to turn to the gentiles (13:46; 18:6; 28:28); see Palmer, "Mission to Jews and Gentiles in the Last Episode of Acts," RTR 52 (1993): 62–73; and Smith, The Literary Construction of the Other in the Acts of the Apostles: Charismatics, the Jews, and Women (London: James Clarke, 2012), chap. 3. See also Robert C. Tannehill, "Rejection by Jews and Turning to Gentiles: The Pattern of Paul's Mission in Acts," in Society of Biblical Literature 1986 Seminar Papers, ed. Kent Harold Richards, Society of Biblical Literature Seminar Papers 25 (Atlanta: Scholars Press, 1986), 130–41.

83. Steve Walton, "What Does 'Mission' in Acts Mean in Relation to the 'Powers That Be'?," JETS 55:3 (2012): 537–56.

84. See Rubén Muñoz-Larrondo, A Postcolonial Reading of the Acts of the Apostles, StBibLit 147 (New York: Peter Lang, 2012).

85. Thus, Christian mission proceeds not triumphalistically but in humility; see, e.g., Gary B. McGee, "Pentecostal Missiology: Moving beyond Triumphalism to Face the Issues," Pneuma: The Journal of the Society for Pentecostal Studies 16:2 (1994): 275–81.

episode of Acts is understood against this eschatological horizon."[86] More concretely, the Pentecost outpouring was a divine response to the entreaties for the reign of God that Jesus urged his followers to pray (Luke 11:2) so that the history of the world now pivots not only on the Messiah's life, death, and resurrection but on the risen Christ's pouring out of the divine breath from the right hand of the Father (Acts 2:33). And if the spirit of this Messiah continues to work to establish the divine rule and kingdom of God even in the present time, then this eschatological reign of God impinges on the kingdoms of this world. No wonder the message of the gospel is not merely missiological but surely in its proclamation also politically subversive. We have in this book been reading the scriptures of ancient Israel from a post-Pentecost perspective, and we now continue to read the rest of the Christian New Testament politically in the wake of this eschatological and pneumatic/charismatic turning point in history.

Discussion Questions

1. What role did exorcism play in Jesus's public ministry? What is the relevance of exorcism or deliverance in the *missio Dei* today? Is this more applicable to non-Western contexts than Euro-American venues—why or why not?

2. The earliest messianic believers were filled with the spirit to bear witness to the ends of the earth and began by selling what they had in order to care for each other's physical and material needs. What are the implications of this communal way of life for Christian witness in the global neoliberal marketplace of the twenty-first century?

3. Christian life and faith proceed not only from the incarnation and resurrection (and ascension) but from Pentecost. Does Christian theology and missiology also derive from such a perspective after Pentecost? What difference does such a vantage point make for the missional theology and praxis?

---

86. Anthony B. Robinson and Robert W. Wall, *Called to Be Church: The Book of Acts for a New Day* (Grand Rapids: Eerdmans, 2006), 24.

6

Pauline Testimony in the Spirit

Apostolic Mission

Introduction

This is the longest chapter of the book for the simple reason that there are ten letters associated with the apostle Paul in the New Testament that mention the spirit (Philemon being the sole exception), and we have opted to treat them all together, even if some are of disputed authenticity among scholars. Although sensitive to those historical-critical issues, by and large our bifocal theological—that is, pneumatological and missiological—perspective is impervious to how these matters are decided. The major challenges for us instead are that proceeding canonically and starting with Romans (since the Pauline epistles are organized by length) means working backward, as it were, from some of the apostle's most mature and latest writings to those at the end that were among the earliest actually written (e.g., the Thessalonian letters).[1] At moments within this sequence we move from an early and indisputably Pauline missive (Galatians), through those most vigorously argued as pseudo-Pauline (e.g., Ephesians and Colossians), to those undeniably (Thessalonians) or questionably (Timothy) Pauline. Our hopes are that sticking with the decision to stay as much as possible on the book or letter under examination without being distracted will keep our pneumatological and missiological

1. These critical questions are taken up in any reputable overview, as in Donald Guthrie, *New Testament Introduction*, rev. ed. (Downers Grove, IL: IVP Academic, 1990).

focus. In order to lay out as coherent a framework as possible for the following discussion, however, the following elements need to be kept in mind.

First, reading Paul missiologically is not only appropriate but perhaps required since, after all, Paul was himself a missionary, if not *the* missionary par excellence of early Christianity.[2] Although there may be some complication about if and how to correlate what we find in the Pauline letters with the missionary ventures and career of Paul as recorded in the book of Acts,[3] by and large we will not be relying on such historical reconstruction. Our theological and missiological commitments mean that these are of secondary concern, even if we are not oblivious to the issues.

Second, if the primary (if not sole) author of the letters to be covered in this chapter is a missionary, then he was also a mission theologian and perhaps a mission pneumatologian par excellence. The latter is a horrible neologism, but if we were to follow Gordon Fee's massive (almost one-thousand-page) book on Pauline pneumatology,[4] then we might agree that, of the New Testament writers, St. Paul would be in the running for being not just *the* theologian of mission but also *the* theologian of the spirit.[5] As we shall see, we will find Paul to be not just a pneumatologian in his mature thinking but one who was from the beginning pneumatologically informed and energized.[6]

Third, if Paul is a mission pneumatologian—that is, articulator of a mission theology that was and is fundamentally pneumatological—then it may also be more accurate to identify him as a paracolonial and pneumatological missiologist. What I am referring to here is that just as there has been a boom of scholarship on Jesus amid and in the wake of the Pax Romana, so also has there been an explosion of studies on Paul as missionary-theologian in that

2. See Eckhard J. Schnabel, *Paul the Missionary: Realities, Strategies and Methods* (Downers Grove, IL: IVP Academic, 2008); cf. Andy Johnson, "Missional from First to Last: Paul's Letters and the *Missio Dei*," in *Missio Dei: A Wesleyan Understanding*, ed. Keith Schwanz and Joseph E. Coleson (Kansas City, MO: Beacon Hill, 2011), 67–74.

3. Rainer Riesner, *Paul's Early Period: Chronology, Mission Strategy, Theology*, trans. Doug Stott (Grand Rapids: Eerdmans, 1998).

4. Gordon D. Fee, *God's Empowering Presence: The Holy Spirit in the Letters of Paul* (Peabody, MA: Hendrickson, 1994).

5. "The Holy Spirit is the driving force of the life of Paul's churches." So says Volker Rabens, "The Holy Spirit and Deification in Paul: A 'Western' Perspective," in *The Holy Spirit and the Church according to the New Testament: Sixth International East-West Symposium of New Testament Scholars, Belgrade, August 25 to 31, 2013*, ed. Predrag Dragutinović et al., WUNT 364 (Tübingen: Mohr Siebeck, 2016), 187–220, here 187; see also Rabens, *The Holy Spirit and Ethics in Paul: Transformation and Empowering for Religious-Ethical Life*, WUNT 283 (Tübingen: Mohr Siebeck, 2010).

6. See Finny Philip, *The Origins of Pauline Pneumatology: The Eschatological Bestowal of the Spirit upon Gentiles in Judaism and in the Early Development of Paul's Theology*, WUNT 2/194 (Tübingen: Mohr Siebeck, 2005).

same milieu.[7] Hence Paul's missionary acts and deeds are first and foremost religious but also should be viewed, at least in part, within the wider political project that was the Pax Romana, even as his pneumatological theology and pneumatological missiology also ought to be critically assessed in that same arena. For our purposes, however, one important difference must be registered: Paul the pneumatologian and missiologist operated assuredly within, if not against, the Roman regime, while we, inhabiting more accurately a late modern context, find ourselves *after* but yet not fully extricated from the effects of colonial modernity.

Last but not least, one of the central themes we will find in the apostle's pneumatological reflections is the overcoming of the alienness between Jews and gentiles, albeit with the preservation of the distinctiveness of these two groups (rather than a supersession of one by the other). This is a crucial matter not only in and for the first-century Christians but also for twenty-first-century missiological concerns, especially as they have to do with the overcoming of Euro-American (white) normativity, and its attending anti-Semitism, enshrined in the logics of colonial modernity.[8] Hence to ask about Christian witness after the collapse of the Enlightenment and Christendom enterprises is to be invited to revisit, with and through Paul, the struggle for comprehending ethnic and racial differences—of Jew and gentile then, and of whites and others today—according to the gospel of Jesus Christ and the gift of his spirit to the world. The missiological question then and now is how to welcome and include the dominant and oppressive other, whether the gentiles of the first century or those who are white in the twenty-first century, in all their particularity and yet allow for and nurture the flourishing of all. That Paul's initial responses—to be rehearsed variously in the pages to come of this chapter—may have been theologically (and pneumatologically) sound does not mean that they were practicable, at least not if the divergence between Jews and gentiles at the end of the first century and the long history of Christian anti-Semitism since are indicators.[9] And for

---

7. One of the first forays being Richard A. Horsley, *Paul and Empire: Religion and Power in Roman Imperial Society* (Harrisburg, PA: Trinity Press International, 1997).

8. In fact, it was the convergence of the long history of anti-Semitism and the discovery of non-European peoples and lands that generated the Christian theology of race in the early modern period; see, e.g., J. Kameron Carter, *Race: A Theological Account* (Oxford: Oxford University Press, 2008), part 1.

9. E.g., Abel Mordechai Bibliowicz, *Jews and Gentiles in the Early Jesus Movement: An Unintended Journey* (New York: Palgrave Macmillan 2013); see also the earlier work by James D. G. Dunn, *The Partings of the Ways: Between Christianity and Judaism and Their Significance for the Character of Christianity* (London: SCM, 1991), even as it has generated vigorous discussion and debate since.

us the challenges to understanding Paul and implementing his vision may be even more steep since he wrote as a marginal Jew to the Greco-Roman majority culture, while many of us who read the Bible today do so from a perspective racialized into white (European and American) dominance.[10] This issue of ethnic otherness may therefore be one of the most important missiological questions of our time, even if the answer now, as before, invites pneumatological perspective.

6.1   Romans—"From Jerusalem and as Far Around as Illyricum": The Breadth and Depth of the Spirit's Mission

Any theological inquiry with Paul ends up in Romans, not least because it is generally recognized as one of the latest and most extensive of his authentic writings, but certainly also because it represents his mature theological ideas. But we begin our Pauline exploration of pneumatological missiology in this first letter that is placed after the Gospels and Acts in the New Testament. And to embark on any discussion of a Pauline pneumatological missiology, even if limited to this letter, is to confront an extensive secondary literature largely on parallel, never-interfacing, tracks: the spirit in Romans or mission in Romans.[11] Our task, however, is to bring these thoroughfares of scholarship together.

For this purpose, we turn first to the end of Romans, relatively speaking. Right before he closes by greeting the members of the Roman congregation

10. In my book *The Future of Evangelical Theology: Soundings from the Asian American Diaspora* (Downers Grove, IL: IVP Academic, 2014), esp. chap. 3, I urge that nonwhites can be whitened as well, and suggest adoption of the marginalized location of diasporic hybridity in order to uncover and resist white Euro-American normativity; see also Willie James Jennings, "Can White People Be Saved? Reflections on the Relationship of Missions and Whiteness," in *Can "White" People Be Saved? Triangulating Race, Theology, and Mission*, ed. Love L. Sechrest, Johnny Ramírez-Johnson, and Amos Yong, Missiological Engagements (Downers Grove, IL: IVP Academic, 2018), 27–43.

11. Elsewhere I have written on the former in terms of "A Pauline Pneumatology of Love," which is the subtitle to chap. 8 of my book *Spirit of Love: A Trinitarian Theology of Grace* (Waco: Baylor University Press, 2012); those interested in the literature on the spirit in Romans can follow up on the footnotes to that chapter. For works devoted to mission in Romans, compare earlier contributions to the discussion—e.g., Arland J. Hultgren, *Paul's Gospel and Mission: The Outlook from His Letter to the Romans* (Philadelphia: Fortress, 1985)—with more recent developments, such as Ksenija Magda, *Paul's Territoriality and Mission Strategy: Searching for the Geographical Awareness of Paradigm behind Romans*, WUNT 2/266 (Tübingen: Mohr Siebeck, 2009). A succinct missiological reading of Romans is by Thomas Schirrmacher, *World Mission: Heart of Christianity: Essays*, 2nd ed. (Hamburg: Reformatorischer Verlag Beese, 2008), 11–20: "Romans as a Charter of World Mission: A Lesson in the Relation of Systematic Theology and Missiology."

and community (Rom. 16),[12] Paul says he wants to visit them (15:22–33) as part of his next missionary trip (15:14–21). To envision this sojourn, Paul clarifies the goal, "that the Gentiles might glorify God for his mercy" (15:9), citing various Old Testament texts in this regard (15:9–12),[13] and concludes, "May the God of hope fill you with all joy and peace in believing, so that you may abound in hope by the power of the Holy Spirit" (15:13).[14] Then, in the next few sentence, he reiterates that he will come in the spirit and authority with which he has written, understood in part as "a minister of Christ Jesus to the Gentiles in the priestly service of the gospel of God, so that the offering of the Gentiles may be acceptable, sanctified by the Holy Spirit" (15:16). Precisely because of this vocational call, Paul presses on, "by the power of signs and wonders, by the power of the Spirit of God, so that from Jerusalem and as far around as Illyricum I have fully proclaimed the good news of Christ" (15:19).[15]

Paul's sense that the gospel "has gone out to all the earth" (Rom. 10:18) is surely consistent with Luke's conviction that the spirit-filled messianists will bear witness to the ends of the earth (Acts 1:8). Remarkably, in this passage toward the end of the letter to the Roman church, Paul thrice connects the expansiveness of his missionary endeavors, including "as far . . . as Illyricum" (which, on the northeastern shoreline of the Adriatic Sea, was even farther than Rome from a Jerusalem-centric viewpoint), with the work of the spirit. And Paul of course was not finished, as he wanted the Romans congregants to send him on to Spain (Rom. 15:28). As he had his sights set from the beginning on "all the Gentiles" (1:5, 13), it makes sense that the arrival in Rome is merely a temporary respite. The apostolic mission would reach to the ends of the Roman Empire and beyond, in all cases carried by the spirit's power.

Yet to spiritualize the spirit and to reduce the gentiles to an "unreached people group"—both tendencies prominent in some Protestant missiological circles—will not do since Paul writes to, and is being read by, those living under

12. For a missiological perspective on Rom. 16, see E. A. Judge, "The Roman Base of Paul's Mission," *TynBul* 56:1 (2005): 103–17.

13. Richard J. Gibson urges that this Pauline vision of mission to the gentiles is based on Isa. 11, in particular the work of the messianic spirit in that passage; see "Paul the Missionary, in Priestly Service of the Servant-Christ (Romans 15.16)," in *Paul as Missionary: Identity, Activity, Theology, and Practice*, ed. Trevor J. Burke and Brian S. Rosner, LNTS 420 (New York: T&T Clark, 2011), 51–62.

14. Richard B. Hays suggests that Rom. 1:4 and 15:13 are pneumatological bookends that justify a Third Article consideration of this letter; see "Spirit, Church, Resurrection: The Third Article of the Creed as Hermeneutical Lens for Reading Romans," *JTI* 5:1 (2011): 35–48.

15. John Knox shows that studies of Paul's theology of mission that begin from this passage go back now over half a century; see "Romans 15 14–33 and Paul's Conception of His Apostolic Mission," *JBL* 83:1 (1964): 1–11. A more practical application of Pauline missiology from this text is found in Steve Strauss, "Missions Theology in Romans 15:14–33," *BSac* 160 (2003): 457–74.

the shadow of imperial Rome. Jew-gentile relations remain no less politically fraught today (arguably things have gotten worse over two millennia), and even in this letter, the apostle struggles valiantly to grapple with how to envision one people of God across what had been until then a sociocultural and political-economic chasm. Thus, the emphasis is that "all, both Jews and Greeks, are under the power of sin" (Rom. 3:9). Yet there is one God over all—thus Paul says, "Or is God the God of Jews only? Is he not the God of Gentiles also? Yes, of Gentiles also" (3:29)—and salvation for all comes through the one person of Jesus Christ (5:12–21). Further, the differences between Jews and gentiles are not erased, even if the latter are grafted into God's redemptive plans for the former (Rom. 9–11).[16] The point is that the mission of the spirit to the gentiles seeks, at least in part, their embrace within the covenant made with Abraham, the "father of many nations" (4:17–18). This has implications for Jew-gentile social relations, while also empowering new, joint messianic witness within the public square (13:1–7). From this retrospective pneumatological and missiological reading of Romans, the logic of the argument can also be understood as such: that the order of Rome is reframed as the cosmic disorder introduced by sin (Rom. 1–3); that divine justice (Rom. 4–8) and mercy (Rom. 9–11) are available to all through Israel and the gospel;[17] and that a new "ethic of solidarity" is made possible for ecclesial life within imperial constraints.[18]

16. For more on the interconnections between Rom. 9–11 and 15, see Scott Hafemann, "Eschatology and Ethics: The Future of Israel and the Nations in Romans 15:1–13," *TynBul* 51:2 (2000): 161–92; cf. also G. R. Beasley-Murray, "The Righteousness of God in the History of Israel and the Nations: Romans 9–11," *RevExp* 73:4 (1976): 437–50; and Caroline Johnson Hodge, "'A Light to the Nations': The Role of Israel in Romans 9–11," in *Reading Paul's Letter to the Romans*, ed. Jerry L. Sumney, SBL Resources for Biblical Study 73 (Atlanta: Society of Biblical Literature, 2012), 169–86.

17. Joshua D. Garroway, discussing Rom. 9–11, argues as part of his broader thesis for a redefinition of Israel as including believing gentiles; see *Paul's Gentile-Jews: Neither Jew nor Gentile, but Both* (New York: Palgrave Macmillan, 2012), chap. 6. Thus, he revises the supersessionist interpretation of the gentiles being spiritual Jews to that which insists on gentiles being literal Jews, on the basis of their being grafted into Israel, so that "faith determines (physical) descent" (157). Garroway also urges that this does not touch Jewish identity and invites gentile Christians to think not that they have replaced Israel (thus undermining gentile triumphalism) but that they are now hybridically Israel: instead of "grace, not race," it is "grace determines race" (139). See also Love L. Sechrest, *A Former Jew: Paul and the Dialectics of Race*, LNTS 410 (New York: T&T Clark, 2009), who opts for a *third-race* reading of Paul that emphasizes racial mixedness or hybridity, both in terms of what we mean by "race" and how we think of "purity"; Christian identity, following Paul, is *transracial* (not post-racial), so every Christian is racially blended in terms of their own personal history transformed by Christ. While the details of these (Garroway's and Sechrest's) arguments might be contested, especially at the semantic level, something like either/both is needed to chart a via media between one- or two-covenant solutions to this perennial but currently urgent theological and missiological question.

18. Neil Elliott, *The Arrogance of Nations: Reading Romans in the Shadow of Empire* (Minneapolis: Fortress, 2008), 150. I utilize Elliott's basic thematic outline for Romans here,

Such a political perspective on the mission of the spirit, however, includes rather than marginalizes classical evangelical concerns. That Paul's concluding thoughts regarding his visit to Rome come "by the love of the Spirit" (Rom. 15:30) is consistent with what he had written earlier, that "hope does not disappoint us, because God's love has been poured into our hearts through the Holy Spirit that has been given to us" (5:5). Thus, the sociopolitical work of the spirit involves the transformation of hearts, calling forth and enabling inhabitation of the life-giving ways of the spirit and rescuing souls from the death-conveying mechanisms of the law (7:6) and the flesh (8:1–16).[19] The spirit's saving work—the *missio spiritus*—includes and involves persons but also recognizes that individuals are members of social groups (Jews or gentiles) and citizens of this or that royal state (Rome in this case).

Further, there is no bifurcation of the mission of the divine breath between empowering adopted sons and daughters to cry, "Abba! Father!" (Rom. 8:15) and enabling them also to groan (8:22–23) "with sighs too deep for words" (8:26). The cries of the children estranged from each other (thus the need for social reconciliation between Jew and gentile) and from God (thus the need for the mediating work of Christ by the spirit) are interwoven with the estrangement between the creatures of this cosmic haven, a fractured "creation [that] waits with eager longing for the revealing of the children of God" (8:19). Thus, the intercessions of the spirit, for and through creatures, anticipate the full (eschatological) healing, salvation, and redemption of the cosmos itself.[20] Not only will we then "know that *all things* work together for good for those who love God, who are called according to his purpose" (8:28; emphasis added), but this epistemic sense will have derived from the ontological reconciliation of all things so that absolutely nothing "will be able to separate us from the love of God in Christ Jesus our Lord" (8:39). The point is that the mission of the spirit to gentiles at the ends of the earth includes divine graciousness toward the very smallest—the souls of pained creatures—and the very largest realities: creation and the cosmos itself.

---

not assuming it is the only grid through which to comprehend the full scope of this letter, but as facilitating missiological perspective, albeit under my own pneumatological hermeneutic.

19. John A. Bertone, *"The Law of the Spirit": Experience of the Spirit and Displacement of the Law in Romans 8:1–16*, StBibLit 86 (New York: Peter Lang, 2005); a more succinct statement is J. Ayodeji Adewuya, "The Holy Spirit and Sanctification in Romans 8:1–17," *JPT* 9 (2001): 71–84.

20. For more on the spirit as the "first fruits" of our "eschatological longing," see Wojciech Szypuła, *The Holy Spirit in the Eschatological Tension of Christian Life: An Exegetico-Theological Study of 2 Corinthians 5,1–5 and Romans 8,18–27*, Tesi Gregoriana Serie Teologia 147 (Rome: Editrice Pontificia Università Gregoriana, 2007), esp. 387–96.

From Western Asia to South Asia
Pauline Witness to the Mission of the Spirit

Idicheria Ninan, professor of New Testament studies, South Asia Institute of Advanced Christian Studies, Bangalore, India

Conventional discussions of the holy spirit and mission have explicated the trinitarian theological basis of mission, in addition to the construction of the *ekklēsia* and its charismatic functions, with reference to both its inward and outward orientations. The donation of the spirit by virtue of the death and resurrection of the Messiah, the spirit's manifestation in the messianic reign, and the construction of "resurrection order life" within the present age constitute the bedrock of the promise and challenge of Pauline mission. Experience of the spirit, as diversely demonstrated in the Pauline corpus, is therefore the very essence of being Christian and becoming Christian. The spirit guarantees the "not yet" and fuller shades of the good news while ennobling the people of God within the life of God. Thus, the fundamental virtues of faith, hope, and love are functions of the spirit of God in the messianic communities. However, these shared and in some cases tradition-specific emphases are in danger of "spiritualizing the spirit" despite the celebration of his role in creation and new creation. This book challenges readers to discover the polyvalent implications of the spirit for the nascent multiracial communities of the Pauline corpus for their witness and service within the Roman Empire. The stories of the Indian church as a "little flock" among majority communities, and reports of increasing religious persecution as the gospel makes inroads into traditional bastions of other faiths, are closer to those of the Pauline communities. The spirit enables us to persevere with joy in the midst of suffering and poverty. Yet becoming the one people of the spirit, transcending traditional barriers of gender, caste, and culture, remains a task that still requires the spirit's reformulation of desires.

Missiologically, the call to witness, to embrace both the opportunity of and responsibility for mission, is thoroughly in and through the spirit. Thus, Paul's exhortation, in turning more specifically to the practical aspects of his message, unfolds spiritually: "I appeal to you therefore, brothers and sisters, by the mercies of God, to present your bodies as a living sacrifice, holy and acceptable to God, which is your spiritual worship" (Rom. 12:1). The Roman response is only possible by grace (12:3), and from that perspective it is that charismatic endowment of God (12:6–8) that embraces our participation in the divine mission.[21] Divine graciousness enables patience in suffering, extension of hospitality to strangers, blessing to our persecutors, peacefulness toward all, love and service to our enemies, and the overcoming of evil with good (12:12–20). These dimensions of spirit-empowered mission are not merely individualistic, as already noted. They extend also to the work of the church as a social body in an imperial world (in Paul's day).[22] As Paul notes in thinking about interpersonal relations undermined by social, class, ethnic, and other distinctions, "For the kingdom of God is not food and drink but righteousness and peace and joy in the Holy Spirit" (14:17). From that vantage point, the mission to the gentiles cannot but be envisioned as extensively as possible as the *missio spiritus*: personally, ecclesially, politically, socially, and cosmically.

6.2 1 Corinthians—"With a Demonstration of the Spirit and of Power": Charismatic Mission in the Flesh

Although Paul's first letter to Corinth is not generally read from a missiological perspective, mission dynamics are not completely absent from this letter. After all, members are urged to maintain community standards of holiness that are in contrast to those of their neighbors (1 Cor. 5:1–6:11): some of the women in the congregation are married to unbelievers (7:12–16); others are encouraged to remain within the social settings they find themselves in when possible (7:17–24); and all are alerted to the possibility, even probability, of unbelievers in their midst and attending their services (14:20–25).[23] Paul also writes in effect as an evangelist and (*the!*) church planter of the Corinthian congregation,[24] and there is plenty of evidence in the letter that this work of establishing new ecclesial communities was being undertaken by others, not

21. See Corneliu Constantineanu, "Reconciliation as a Missiological Category for Social Engagement: A Pauline Perspective from Romans 12:1–21," in *Bible and Mission: A Conversation between Biblical Studies and Missiology*, ed. I. Howard Marshall et al. (Bamberg, Germany: Neufeld Verlag, 2008), 160–79; cf. Constantineanu, *The Social Significance of Reconciliation in Paul's Theology: Narrative Readings in Romans*, LNTS 421 (New York: T&T Clark, 2010), esp. chap. 5.

22. See Daniel Patte, "Thinking Mission with Paul and the Romans: Romans 15:1–33," *Mission Studies* 23:1 (2006): 82–104.

23. Victor Paul Furnish, *The Theology of the First Letter to the Corinthians* (Cambridge: Cambridge University Press, 1999), chap. 3, "Belonging to Christ in an Unbelieving Society"; older texts include W. Gordon Robinson, *The Gospel and the Church in a Pagan World: A Study in I Corinthians* (London: Independent, 1958); and David Ewert, *The Church in a Pagan Society: Studies in 1 Corinthians* (Winnipeg: Kindred, 1986).

24. From passages referred to in this paragraph and other passages, Robert L. Plummer argues that the Corinthians were instructed to be active in evangelism. Plummer, *Paul's Understanding*

least Apollos and Cephas (1:12; also 3:5–9), so that some competitive tension might have existed between those who identified themselves with these apostolic figures.[25] Further, even fairly new churches like Corinth were expected to be missionally oriented in setting aside what they could for weekly collections directed toward other churches (16:1–3). Beyond these ministry actions and mission-related activities, some have sought to read the Corinthian correspondence as a case study of early apostolic contextualization: of proclaiming and adapting the message of the gospel in a Greco-Roman context.[26]

Our own approach, however, is not just missiological but also pneumatological. From this bifocal perspective, two pathways into 1 Corinthians present themselves, one relatively early in the letter and the other more toward the latter segments. The earlier section unfolds within Paul's discussions of the divisions within the community, perhaps perpetuated by those who aligned themselves with the various apostolic endeavors crisscrossing the region, and in this context Paul appeals to the authority of Christ in the power of the holy spirit. This comes together most sharply when he writes, defending his own mission, "I came to you in weakness and in fear and in much trembling. My speech and my proclamation were not with plausible words of wisdom, but with a demonstration of the Spirit and of power, so that your faith might rest not on human wisdom but on the power of God" (1 Cor. 2:3–5).[27] The strand flowing into this claim insisted on Christ crucified as the power and wisdom of God,[28] above the wisdom of the scribes and debaters prominent in the Greco-Roman world, above the signs and wonders central to the Jewish tradition, above the nobility of birth and the estimations of affluential power valued by the broader Corinthian society (1:18–2:2). The thread coming out on the other side reasserts the divine wisdom opposing that of "the rulers

---

of the Church's Mission: Did the Apostle Paul Expect the Early Christian Communities to Evangelize (Milton Keynes, UK: Paternoster, 2006), chap. 3.

25. Michael D. Goulder helpfully identifies some of the factional issues, although framed reductively according to the older (F. C. Baur) thesis regarding oppositional Petrine and Pauline communities. Goulder, *Paul and the Competing Mission in Corinth* (Peabody, MA: Hendrickson, 2001).

26. E.g., Dean Flemming, *Contextualization in the New Testament: Patterns for Theology and Mission* (Downers Grove, IL: InterVarsity, 2005), chap. 6.

27. Much of the scholarship on this text and its broader context/passage has focused on the spirit-flesh binary and sought to locate its contextual milieu; e.g., Birger A. Pearson, *The Pneumatikos-Psychikos Terminology in 1 Corinthians: A Study in the Theology of the Corinthian Opponents of Paul and Its Relation to Gnosticism*, SBLDS 12 (Missoula, MT: Scholars Press, 1973).

28. James A. Davis explicates about the eschatological Christ, crucified-resurrected-ascended, being at the core of the wisdom of the divine spirit in the present age; see *Wisdom and Spirit: An Investigation of 1 Corinthians 1.18–3.20 against the Background of Jewish Sapiential Traditions in the Greco-Roman Period* (Lanham, MD: University Press of America, 1984), chap. 4.

of this age" (2:8) and contrasts the knowledge given by God's spirit with the foolishness of merely human knowledge (2:10–16).[29]

The implications of this line of argumentation seem missiologically dire. Mission work worth engaging in, along this Pauline register, is either wholly spiritual or wholly carnal (e.g., foolish and weak in God's sight); there seems to be no middle ground.[30] Further, the task of rational apologetics seems improbable if not impossible. After all, reasoned disputation is at best ineffective, at worst counterproductive, since what is needed is the gift of spiritual discernment and understanding.[31] Yet how can apostolic mission ensue "not with plausible words of wisdom, but with a demonstration of the Spirit and of power"? If God is free, and if the spirit blows where she wills, it seems impossible to prepare adequately for apostolic mission.

Yet we need to keep in mind that this letter is written not first and foremost to Corinthian missionaries but to those in the community who thought much of their own education (at least learnedness), social standing (nobility), and capacities. Thus, Paul is writing to confront Corinthian believers not primarily with regard to their witness to the world but concerning the overestimation of their own gifts, capacities, and potencies. The latter portion of this epistle on the church as charismatic or spirit-gifted body of believers (chaps. 12–14) confirms this more urgent set of apostolic concerns. In that context, Paul clearly emphasizes that there is *one* spirit (1 Cor. 12:4, 11, 13), who disperses many ministry and mission gifts for the many members of the *ekklēsia*.[32] Against Corinthian elitism, then, "the members of the body that seem to be weaker are indispensable, and those members of the body that we think less honorable we clothe with greater honor, and our less respectable members are treated with greater respect; whereas our more

29. Daniel W. Martin argues that "spirit" in vv. 10, 11, 13, and 14 refers in each case to the divine or holy spirit; see "'Spirit' in the Second Chapter of First Corinthians," *CBQ* 5:4 (1943): 381–95.

30. Gail Paterson Corrington suggests that the dualism Paul sets up between his/Christ's wisdom as *the only* divine wisdom, contesting all other/Corinthian earthly wisdoms, sets him up to out-rival his opponents on a Hellenistic playing field; I might grant this as part of the residue of Paul's rhetorical strategy, but I see Paul's arguments to be more intra-ecclesially conducted than in extra-ecclesial terms. See Corrington, "Paul and the Two Wisdoms: 1 Corinthians 1:18–31 and the Hellenistic Mission," *Proceedings* 6 (1986): 72–84.

31. Simo Frestadius is a bit concerned, on this score, that Paul's pneumatic epistemology here undermines the enterprise of natural theology; see "The Spirit and Wisdom in 1 Corinthians 2:1–13," *JBPR* 3 (2011): 52–70. Some might welcome such a conclusion, although the negative case is difficult to prove in my estimation. Still, for those who want to affirm a chastened form of natural theology, even one spirit-empowered(!), read on.

32. See Heleen Murre-van den Berg, "Bible Study I Corinthians 12—Mission Relationships and Partnership: New Models of Partnership?," *IRM* 91:363 (2002): 583–88.

respectable members do not need this. But God has so arranged the body, giving the greater honor to the inferior member, that there may be no dissension within the body, but the members may have the same care for one another" (12:22–25).[33]

It is along this same line of consideration that Paul expounds on the greatest gift of love (chap. 13), which frames the discussion of prophetic and glossolalic gifts (chap. 14). Extensive space is given to these manifestations surely because their exercise in the Corinthian congregation was getting out of hand, but also perhaps because such phenomena were widespread rather than aberrations amid the spiritism of the first-century Mediterranean world.[34] From that perspective, guidance for discerning the work of the divine spirit was essential, as was the task of bearing comprehensible witness to unbelievers who frequented congregational times and spaces. Missiologically speaking, this is also more helpful since, across the landscape of world Christianity, the most challenging questions are pneumatological, less about the nature of the holy spirit as the third trinitarian person and more about the world of many spirits within which we animate creatures live, move, and have our being.

So the Corinthian problem was neither the absence of charismata (spiritual gifts) nor the unavailability of otherwise qualified and even willing members to carry out the mission of God. Rather, the issue was how those so qualified by a variety of worldly standards and measures were going about the business of the church in a spiritually immature (put kindly) and downright carnal (put honestly) manner.[35] It would be as if a Christian community in the global South were to include multiple former shamans in their midst. How then to discern the comings and goings of many spiritual authorities, at least

33. I develop from this Pauline charismatic ecclesiology a vision of the people of God that is inclusive of people with disabilities and impairments, with radical implications for the church's ministry and mission; see Yong, *The Bible, Disability, and the Church: A New Vision for the People of God* (Grand Rapids: Eerdmans, 2011), chap. 4.

34. Clint Tibbs argues, intriguingly in my estimation, that we ought to read about "the spirit" in this passage less according to post-Nicene trinitarian frames and more according to first-century Mediterranean pre-understandings, which is suggestive of a more amorphous "spirit world" that would have teemed with spiritual beings and realities. See Tibbs, *Religious Experience of the Pneuma: Communication with the Spirit World in 1 Corinthians 12 and 14*, WUNT 2/230 (Tübingen: Mohr Siebeck, 2007); a shorter version of the argument is in Tibbs, "The Spirit (World) and the (Holy) Spirits among the Earliest Christians: 1 Corinthians 12 and 14 as a Test Case," *CBQ* 70 (2008): 313–30.

35. What I call here *worldly* and *carnal* can also be comprehended in terms of the *secular*, or the extra-ecclesial, e.g., where society and church overlap; see, for instance, Andrew D. Clarke, *Secular and Christian Leadership in Corinth: A Socio-Historical and Exegetical Study of 1 Corinthians 1–6* (Milton Keynes, UK: Paternoster, 2006).

according to the sociocultural conventions prevalent in the wider community? Hence, the stark Pauline contrast between divine/spiritual wisdom/activity on the one side and creaturely/carnal learning/effort on the other side may have been overly dualistic in the rhetorical sense, but perhaps was the needed antidote in pastoral perspective.[36]

First Corinthians read pneumatologically highlights that even as worldly a bunch as the Corinthians were inhabited by the divine spirit: "Do you not know that you are God's temple and that God's Spirit dwells in you?" (3:16). Yet this spirituality was not opposed to materiality, for later, in the context of admonishing against fornication and urging the sanctity of marriage, Paul makes a parallel claim: "Or do you not know that your body is a temple of the Holy Spirit within you, which you have from God, and that you are not your own?" (6:19). Hence the point is that the outpouring of the spirit is on corporeal bodies, effectively the new site of the divine breath's presence,[37] even if the sanctifying work of the spirit (6:11) is to deliver animated creatures from their fleshliness and carnality. The cosmic and redemptive life of Jesus was also directed toward becoming and being a, if not *the*, "life-giving spirit" (15:45).

Shifting from pneumatology to missiology, the point is at least that the church's mission will proceed nonetheless, but the question is whether we operate merely according to our own capacities (according to our own conventions of wisdom, strength, and power)—which inevitably then enslave us, actually![38]—or allow the mission of the spirit to guide our efforts. The Corinthian missiology is seductive precisely because we ourselves are attracted by and drawn to those appearances of spirituality that are actually affirmations of our own achievements and accomplishments. We can be very effective according to worldly norms if we have the funds, the marketing slogans, and the numbers that we can concoct in our own wisdom. But if these merely build *us* up, then we need to return to 1 Corinthians to rediscover that our missionary endeavors have been promoted in our flesh, rather than lifting up and pointing to the coming reign of God.

36. A wide-ranging discussion of how Paul's pneumatology as such informs ecclesiological ethics is in André Munzinger, *Discerning the Spirits: Theological and Ethical Hermeneutics in Paul*, SNTSMS 140 (Cambridge: Cambridge University Press, 2007).

37. See N. T. Wright, *Paul and the Faithfulness of God*, Christian Origins and the Question of God 4 (Minneapolis: Fortress, 2013), 711–17, which is a discussion of "The Spirit as the New Shekinah."

38. As argued in an exceedingly self-reflective methodological study by Samuel Hio-Kee Ooi, whose seventh chapter is a rereading of the Corinthian correspondence in light of ancient Chinese notions of power; see *A Double-Vision Hermeneutic: Interpreting a Chinese Pastor's Intersubjective Experience of Shi Engaging Yizhuàn and Pauline Texts* (Eugene, OR: Pickwick, 2014).

6.3 2 Corinthians—"Written . . . with the Spirit of the Living God": The Mission of "Weak" Apologetics

With the exception, perhaps, of Philippians (§6.6), 2 Corinthians gives us as deep a glimpse into Paul the missionary as any of his letters.[39] What appears to have happened, as best as scholars can conjecture with the available literary and other evidence, is that the situation at Corinth had intensified compared to when the first letter was sent (§6.2). Whereas before there may have been some factions in the church that were divided in their loyalties between Paul and other apostolic figures and evangelists,[40] what prompts the writing of this second epistle is Paul hearing from Titus (2 Cor. 7:6) that others were attempting to gain a hearing among the Corinthians: "false apostles, deceitful workers, disguising themselves as apostles of Christ" (11:13). These so-called super-apostles (12:11) were threatening the faith of the community, luring them back toward reliance on the law and the older covenant. Paul's entire letter is written to warn the Corinthians and to defend and reassert his authority.[41] In effect, then, this second missive is an apologetic for his missionary call and activity, particularly in relation to the Corinthian congregation.

What are the pneumatological dimensions, then, of the missiological apologetic? A number of venues can be discerned. First, Paul reminds his readers that they are already apostolically interconnected via the spirit's mission: "You yourselves are our letter, written on our hearts, to be known and read by all; and you show that you are a letter of Christ, prepared by us, written not with ink but with the Spirit of the living God, not on tablets of stone but on tablets of human hearts" (2 Cor. 3:2–3). This means at least that the congregants realize their messianic life and identity in Christ was mediated by his apostolic mission and secured by and through the spirit's work.[42] Paul further clarifies that rather than having to confront these false teachers himself, the message of the gospel now written by the spirit on the lives and hearts of the Corinthians ought to be able to be effective for this task. Hence, the

---

39. Troels Engberg-Pedersen thus notes that 2 Corinthians is a "missionary text." Engberg-Pedersen, *Cosmology and Self in the Apostle Paul: The Material Spirit* (Oxford: Oxford University Press, 2010), 173; see also Ralph P. Martin, "Theology and Mission in 2 Corinthians," in *The Gospel to the Nations: Perspectives on Paul's Mission in Honour of Peter T. O'Brien*, ed. Peter Bolt and Mark Thompson (Downers Grove, IL: InterVarsity, 2000), 63–82.

40. E.g., Harry W. Eberts Jr., "Plurality and Ethnicity in Early Christian Mission," *Sociology of Religion* 58:4 (1997): 305–21.

41. This is "an apologetic letter"; so Frances Young and David F. Ford, *Meaning and Truth in 2 Corinthians* (Grand Rapids: Eerdmans, 1988), 28.

42. Linda L. Belleville discusses these aspects as the credentializing work of the spirit in "Paul's Polemic and Theology of the Spirit in Second Corinthians," *CBQ* 58 (1996): 281–304, esp. 291–93.

spirit promulgates the *missio Dei*, ensuring that the apostolic sending is accompanied by reception and germination of the gospel.

Second, the spirit not only empowers apostolic practice but also ensures translation of the apostolic message. Here we shift from the results to the content of apostolic mission—in brief, the ministry "of a new covenant, not of letter but of spirit; for the letter kills, but the Spirit gives life" (2 Cor. 3:6). It may well have been that some of these newly arriving "apostles" were charismatic and pneumatic figures who accomplished signs and wonders or buttressed their claims with purported dreams and visions. At the very least, they appeared as trying to convince the Corinthians that enjoyment of the benefits of the new covenant in Christ involved adherence to the law of Moses.[43] It is in this context that Paul contrasts life in the spirit written on living bodies with "the ministry of death, chiseled in letters on stone tablets" (3:7). Herein he also indicates that as glorious as was the light on Moses's face when he received the law (see Exod. 34:30–35), it is fading away and incomparable to the permanence of the spirit's glory in the face of Christ. Thus, the apostolic message heralds the truth that while Moses's glory was veiled, "when one turns to the Lord, the veil is removed. Now the Lord is the Spirit, and where the Spirit of the Lord is, there is freedom. And all of us, with unveiled faces, seeing the glory of the Lord as though reflected in a mirror, are being transformed into the same image from one degree of glory to another; for this comes from the Lord, the Spirit" (2 Cor. 3:16–18). If these intruders were preaching about the law and the old covenant, then apostolic proclamation announces the freedom of the spirit and the glory of the new covenant.[44]

Yet the spirit not only enables effective mission practice and ensured truthful mission proclamation but also abides with those on mission through all circumstances. A bit later in the letter, after explicating how all of us now have received "the ministry of reconciliation"—"that is, in Christ God was reconciling the world to himself, not counting their trespasses against them, and entrusting the message of reconciliation to us" (2 Cor. 5:18–19), so that we are also all now "ambassadors for Christ, since God is making his

43. Thomas R. Blanton IV, "Spirit and Covenant Renewal: A Theologoumenon of Paul's Opponents in 2 Corinthians," *JBL* 129:1 (2010): 129–51.

44. Scholars are divided about what exactly the spirit achieves. Scott J. Hafemann argues that the spirit enables encounter with the divine glory, through which liberation and freedom emerge, but Sigurd Grindheim counter-argues that the spirit delivers us from the death grip of the law. My instincts are both-and, so I see no need to choose on this matter. See Hafemann, *Paul, Moses, and the History of Israel: The Letter/Spirit Contrast and the Argument from Scripture in 2 Corinthians 3*, WUNT 81 (Tübingen: Mohr Siebeck, 1995); and Grindheim, "The Law Kills but the Gospel Gives Life: The Letter-Spirit Dualism in 2 Corinthians 3.5–18," *JSNT* 84 (2001): 97–115.

appeal through us" who entreat others to "be reconciled to God" (5:20)—Paul turns to reflect on his missionary sojourns. Along the way, he remarks that "as servants of God we have commended ourselves in every way: through great endurance, in afflictions, hardships, calamities, beatings, imprisonments, riots, labors, sleepless nights, hunger; by purity, knowledge, patience, kindness, holiness of spirit, genuine love, truthful speech, and the power of God; with the weapons of righteousness for the right hand and for the left; in honor and dishonor, in ill repute and good repute" (6:4–8). *Holiness of spirit* is actually, in the Greek, ἐν πνεύματι ἁγίῳ (*en pneumati hagiō*), or "in the Holy Spirit."[45] Remarkably and intriguingly, then, the spirit is present amid the twists and turns of the missionary life, in its ups and downs, at its heights and depths.

The apostle elsewhere reiterates that the missionary calling was practically synonymous with suffering: at the hands of others (even in chains, as noted at the end of the book of Acts; see §5.5 above), amid the unpredictabilities of the natural world, and from any and every hardship (2 Cor. 11:16–29). Not for no reason, then, does Paul embrace his own weakness (10:10; 12:5) while relying on divine strength. Thus also does he receive the divine promise: "'My grace is sufficient for you, for power is made perfect in weakness.' So, I will boast all the more gladly of my weaknesses, so that the power of Christ may dwell in me. Therefore I am content with weaknesses, insults, hardships, persecutions, and calamities for the sake of Christ; for whenever I am weak, then I am strong" (12:9–10; cf. 13:4, 9).[46] The enablement of missionary perseverance, then, is central to the spirit's work, as is the ability to be "on mission" amid the ambiguities and challenges of life.

The spirit thus effectuates the gospel, ensures its liberative truth, and enables missional faithfulness. The spirit is here again the power of the coming reign of God that brings the apostolic mission and message into our ordinary histories. For this reason, Paul writes that the Corinthians (and we, by extension) are secure now and ultimately (eschatologically) in the spirit: "But it is God who establishes us with you in Christ and has anointed us, by putting his seal on us and giving us his Spirit in our hearts as a first installment" (2 Cor. 1:21–22). And to be sure that we did not miss this when times of trouble burden our earthly habitation, he reiterates: "He who has prepared us for this very thing is God, who has given us the Spirit as a guarantee. So we are always confident"

45. See Philip E. Hughes, *The Second Epistle to the Corinthians*, New International Commentary on the New Testament (Grand Rapids: Eerdmans, 1962), 228.

46. Timothy B. Savage, *Power through Weakness: Paul's Understanding of the Christian Ministry in 2 Corinthians*, SNTSMS 86 (Cambridge: Cambridge University Press, 2004).

(5:5–6).[47] Regardless of what assails us, the spirit makes available in our present the future promises of the gospel, both promises made to missionaries and those proclaimed by missionaries to their audiences.

Participation in the *missio Dei* is accompanied and empowered by the spirit, 2 Corinthians surely unveils, but this does not preserve the missionary from the trials and even tragedies of life. In weakness the missioner is strong, hence the missiological apologetic unfolds amid this paradoxical weakness-of-effort. Pauline missiology, refracted through this second Corinthian letter is pre-Christendom, then, and this invites our own post-Christendom appropriation, one that depends not on the machinery of a centralized missionary operation but on the power of the spirit to work in and through the mundaneness of creaturely agents.[48] This is the apologetics born not from eloquence but from the finitude and perishability of "clay jars" (4:7), albeit infused with the spirit.

6.4 Galatians—"Having Started with the Spirit": The Beginning and End of Mission

Turning now to the earlier Galatians allows us to anticipate Paul's mature pneumatological missiology seen in the treatise to the Romans (§6.1 above). Yet there are at least three important differences between these two letters that the scholarly consensus believes to be separated by about (no more than) a decade (Galatians being completed around 49 CE, and Romans perhaps in the mid-50s, certainly by 58 CE). First, the Jew-gentile distinction-and-relationship is adjudicated in the later epistle at the heart of the Roman Empire, whereas the same issue is negotiated in the earlier correspondence away from the center where Rome's imposing shadow stretched, in the region of western Asia more broadly (or Asia Minor, as it was also known then).[49]

---

47. Ralph P. Martin therefore writes that Paul "is seeking to establish the Holy Spirit as *the authentic sign of the new age, already begun but not yet realized in its fullness,* and he is building his case on *the readers' participation in the Spirit as the hallmark of their share in both the new world of God's righteousness and the Pauline apostolate that represents it.*" "The Spirit in 2 Corinthians in Light of the 'Fellowship of the Holy Spirit,'" in *Eschatology and the New Testament: Essays in Honor of George Raymond Beasley-Murray,* ed. W. Hulitt Gloer (Peabody, MA: Hendrickson, 1988), 127 (emphasis original).

48. Inspiration here is from Eddie Gibbs, *The Rebirth of the Church: Applying Paul's Vision for Ministry in Our Post-Christian World* (Grand Rapids: Baker Academic, 2013), 129–30, where he discusses 1–2 Corinthians.

49. The area of Phrygia-Galatia as a whole, where Paul planted churches during his first two missionary journeys (cf. Acts 16:6, 23); see James M. Scott, *Paul and the Nations: The Old Testament and Jewish Background of Paul's Mission to the Nations with Special Reference to the Destination of Galatians,* WUNT 84 (Tübingen: Mohr Siebeck, 1995), 215.

Second, our springboard in Romans was from Paul's laying out his missionary plans to the gentiles (Rom. 15:14–33), whereas Galatians reflects part of
Paul's follow-up missionary work and ongoing struggle with these churches.
Last but not least, in Romans we opted to move from back to front given the
prominence of the spirit mentioned vis-à-vis the gentile mission toward the
end of that treatise, but in Galatians the work of the spirit is at the core of
Paul's argument. What then do we learn about pneumatological missiology
from this shorter letter drafted in the heat of Paul's apostolic mission in the
Galatian peninsula?

The major issue in Galatians is Paul's concern that these western Asian
believers were being misled by a group of teachers who sought to retrieve
Jewish customs and reappropriate the law of Moses, not least the practice
of circumcision (Gal. 2:1–12; 5:2–11; 6:12–15). "Judaizers," as they have
since come to be known, derives from Ἰουδαΐζειν (Ioudaizein), translated
as "to live like Jews" (2:14). This was thus a theological battle concerning
at least justification "not by the works of the law [as with the Judaizers]
but through faith in Jesus Christ" (2:16), a message that Paul had preached
to them "through a revelation of Jesus Christ" himself (1:12). Yet, fundamentally, Paul sees this matter in thoroughly pneumatological terms: "Did
you receive the Spirit by doing the works of the law or by believing what
you heard? Are you so foolish? Having started with the Spirit, are you now
ending with the flesh? Did you experience so much for nothing?—if it really
was for nothing. Well then, does God supply you with the Spirit and work
miracles among you by your doing the works of the law, or by your believing what you heard?" (3:2–5). Attentiveness to and remembrance of the
work of the spirit—pneumatology, in other words—is at the heart of the
Galatian problem.[50]

While we ought not minimize the truth about being justified by faith in
and through the work of the spirit,[51] our missiological focus observes also
that "in Christ Jesus the blessing of Abraham might come to the Gentiles,
so that we might receive the promise of the Spirit through faith" (Gal. 3:14).
The "promise of the Spirit," in other words, not only "redeemed us from the
curse of the law [through Christ's] becoming a curse for us—for it is written,
'Cursed is everyone who hangs on a tree'" (3:13; cf. Deut. 21:23)—but exactly

50. As David John Lull writes, "The Spirit was a primary datum of experience for the
Galatians as Christians." *The Spirit in Galatia: Paul's Interpretation of PNEUMA as Divine
Power*, SBLDS 49 (Atlanta: Scholars Press, 1980), 39.

51. See also Sam K. Williams, "Justification and the Spirit in Galatians," *JSNT* 29 (1987):
91–100; cf. Frank D. Macchia, *Justified in the Spirit: Creation, Redemption, and the Triune
God* (Grand Rapids: Eerdmans, 2010).

therein opened up the covenantal blessings of Abraham to the world (also Gal. 3:8; cf. Gen. 12:3). If the Judaizers sought to turn gentiles into Jews, and in that sense perpetuate Israel's unfaithfulness to the covenant and disloyalty to Yahweh's promise, then the work of the spirit makes possible a fresh heeding of Abraham's exemplary trusting-obedience,[52] and through this venue forms a new Jewish-gentile people of faith: "There is no longer Jew or Greek, there is no longer slave or free, there is no longer male and female; for all of you are one in Christ Jesus" (Gal. 3:28).

The former (old covenant) arrangement divided between Jew and Greek—between the children of Sarah and of Hagar, Paul says moments later (Gal. 4:21–31)—between aristocratic slave holders and their servants, between male and female, so that "while we were minors [underage and under supervision of the law], we were enslaved to the ["weak and beggarly"; cf. 4:9] elemental spirits of the world" (4:3).[53] Not only was the human condition so fractured under the old regime, but those on the various sides were set each against the other: for instance, "the child who was born according to the flesh persecuted the child who was born according to the Spirit" (4:29). But now, "God has sent the Spirit of his Son into our hearts, crying, 'Abba! Father!' So you are no longer a slave but a child, and if a child then also an heir, through God" (4:6–7). In other words, the coming of the spirit has overcome the hostilities on all ethnic-political sides, along each ideological register, both in terms of the self-alienation that exists within each human soul and also at every socio-political-structural and also cosmic or creational level that perpetuates estrangement between human creatures.[54] The message

52. Extended argument of this thesis is provided by Jeffrey R. Wisdom, *Blessing for the Nations and the Curse of the Law: Paul's Citation of Genesis and Deuteronomy in Gal 3.8–10*, WUNT 2/133 (Tübingen: Mohr Siebeck, 2001); see also, via another route (reviewing the motif of Israel's renewal) to similar ends, Rodrigo J. Morales, *The Spirit and the Restoration of Israel: New Exodus and New Creation Motifs in Galatians*, WUNT 2/262 (Tübingen: Mohr Siebeck, 2010).

53. For Clinton E. Arnold, the "elemental spirits" (*stoicheia*) are demonic powers, characterizing "life in the present evil age, especially life under the Torah," so that "embracing Torah means returning to the domain of the powers." "Returning to the Domain of the Powers: *Stoicheia* as Evil Spirits in Galatians 4:3,9," *Novum Testamentum* 38:1 (1996): 55–76, here 57 and 72.

54. Sheila Elizabeth McGinn writes that Galatians's pneumatological eschatology "radically undercuts the contemporary patriarchal and aristocratic social order, whether from a Jewish or Roman point of view. It overthrows the prerogatives of aristocrats, slave holders, and men. It entails rejection of the exclusive monopoly of Jews on the promise of God, and rejection of adherence to the patriarchal social system inherent in Torah observance." "Galatians 3:26–29 and the Politics of the Spirit," *Proceedings of the Eastern Great Lakes and Midwest Bible Societies* 13 (1993): 89–101, here 96. See also Ooi, *Double-Vision Hermeneutic*, chap. 6, which reads Gal. 4:3 and 4:8–9 vis-à-vis a Chinese consideration of the powers that structure both internal human hearts and their political and environmental relations.

of justification through Christ in the spirit, then, not only reconciles hearts to God but also heals the isolation of and hostility between people, whether between Jew and gentile or between the children of Sarah and of Hagar.[55] It is not that the differences between Jew and Greek no longer pertain, but the mission of the spirit means that their enmity is vanquished via "the [new] Israel of God" (6:16).[56]

Our point is not about merely politicizing the *missio spiritus*. After all, the spirit's work is focused on nothing less than Christ crucified (Gal. 2:19; 3:1; 6:12–14), so that it is through the power of the cross that the spirit bridges the gulfs between human creatures.[57] Nevertheless, a merely spiritualized soteriology does not do justice to the heart of this letter to the Galatians. In the abstract, the latter portion of the epistle (5:13–24) urging life in the spirit as opposed to remaining in the flesh could be individualized in any spiritualistic approach. However, when we read these commendations coming from a Jew to Jews and gentiles in Galatia and Asia Minor both struggling for community and well-being in the shadow of Rome, another picture emerges. Thus Paul writes, "If we live by the Spirit, let us also be guided by the Spirit. Let us not become conceited, competing against one another, envying one another. . . . If anyone is detected in a transgression, you who have received the Spirit should restore such a one in a spirit of gentleness. Take care that you yourselves are not tempted. Bear one another's burdens, and in this way you will fulfill the law of Christ" (5:25–6:2). At one level, this explicates the ethical dimension of life in the Spirit, surely what ought to be expected by those bearing the fruit of the spirit (5:22–24).[58] At another deeper level, within

55. Thus, "Jews and nations/Gentiles, 'Sarah' and 'Hagar' together with their multi-ethnic and multi-religious children, can finally dwell together." Brigitte Kahl, "Hagar's Babylonian Captivity: A Roman Re-Imagination of Galatians 4:21–31," *Int* 68:3 (2014): 257–69, here 267–68.

56. Charles H. Cosgrove concludes that Paul "appears to affirm a non-ethnocentric and ironic brand of messianic Jewish nationalism—messianic nationalism because Paul's vision casts the people of Israel in a role of saving service to the world; nonethnocentric because Israel cannot claim credit for this service; and ironic because Israel is an unwitting instrument in God's plan." "Did Paul Value Ethnicity?," *CBQ* 68 (2006): 268–90, here 288. I am not sure that *nationalism* is the best way to frame Paul's ecclesial vision, but the more important sentiment is that the *missio spiritus* transforms "us versus them" into "us and them."

57. Charles H. Cosgrove, *The Cross and the Spirit: A Study in the Argument and Theology of Galatians* (Macon, GA: Mercer University Press, 1988); see also H. Terris Neuman, "Paul's Appeal to the Experience of the Spirit in Galatians 3.1–5: Christian Existence as Defined by the Cross and Effected by the Spirit," *JPT* 9 (1996): 53–69.

58. For more on such a pneumatic ethics, see Hans Dieter Betz, "In Defense of the Spirit: Paul's Letter to the Galatians as a Document of Early Christian Apologetics," in *Aspects of Religious Propaganda in Judaism and Early Christianity*, ed. Elisabeth Schüssler Fiorenza (Notre Dame, IN: University of Notre Dame Press, 1976), 99–114.

the Roman context of Jewish-gentile friction, the spirit-led life Paul is calling for here is an earlier version of the fully mature ethical and pneumatological vision of transnational/ethnic solidarity that we saw in the Letter to the Romans (§6.1).[59] If the "nations"—the Galatians in this case—are the peoples that are imaged as subjugated/captive (conquered and enslaved) under the Pax Romana and forced to conform to its "civilizational" norms, here Paul calls the church to solidarity with these marginalized ethnic others in order to resist oppression and assimilation by the power of the spirit.[60]

The path, obviously, is less one of immediate revolution and more one of subversive patience and of eschatological hope. "For through the Spirit, by faith, we eagerly wait for the hope of righteousness," Paul writes (Gal. 5:5).[61] Yet read bifocally—for example, pneumatologically and missiologically—the Galatian letter catalyzes an ecclesial ethic that instantiates, however inchoately, the relational matrix of the coming reign of God. "If you sow to your own flesh, you will reap corruption from the flesh; but if you sow to the Spirit, you will reap eternal life from the Spirit. So let us not grow weary in doing what is right, for we will reap at harvest time, if we do not give up. So then, whenever we have an opportunity, let us work for the good of all, and especially for those of the family of faith" (6:8–10). Mission thus anticipates in the present—for the "family of faith" in particular but also for the world at large—what the divine rule will manifest in the future, even as the work of the spirit connects human hearts to the church and its way of being and acting in the world. Appropriately, then, in Galatians the spirit is the beginning and end of mission: the starting point for the life of faith normed according to the cross of Christ on the one side, while heralding pneumatically the impending divine reign on the other.[62]

59. This basic idea regarding life in the spirit is present, albeit not as prominently as I might wish, in Walter Bo Russell III, *The Flesh/Spirit Conflict in Galatians* (Lanham, MD: University Press of America, 1997).

60. See also Davina C. Lopez, *Apostle to the Conquered: Reimagining Paul's Mission* (Minneapolis: Fortress, 2008), chaps. 3–4.

61. "There are numerous indications in Galatians which support the view that the gift of the Spirit is an eschatological gift [now but also not yet] and can only be appreciated from this perspective." George Eldon Ladd, "The Holy Spirit in Galatians," in *Current Issues in Biblical and Patristic Interpretation: Studies in Honor of Merrill C. Tenney Presented by His Former Students*, ed. Gerald F. Hawthorne (Grand Rapids: Eerdmans, 1975), 211–16, here 213. Also, the spirit in Galatians is "the eschatological life-giver in [for/of] the new creation." G. K. Beale, "The Old Testament Background of Paul's Reference to 'the Fruit of the Spirit' in Galatians 5:22," *BBR* 15:1 (2005): 1–38, here 20.

62. A parallel reading of this epistle's pneumatology appears in Christopher R. J. Holmes, "The Spirit and the Promise: On Becoming Aligned with the Way Things Really Are," in *Apocalyptic and the Future of Theology: With and Beyond J. Louis Martyn*, ed. Joshua B. Davis and Douglas Harink (Eugene, OR: Cascade, 2012), 219–35.

6.5   Ephesians—"Both of Us Have Access in One Spirit": The Mystery of Mission

Although St. Paul's authorship of Ephesians (and Colossians; see §6.7) has long been disputed by scholars, the Pauline character or influence is also undeniable.[63] Our own canonical reading hence can take the authorial ascription (Eph. 1:1) at face value even if we do not proceed presumptively on this score. Thus, we will generally not take the approach of prior missiological readings of the letter,[64] particularly insofar as some of these are based on correlations with the extensive (over two years) Pauline mission to Ephesus covered by St. Luke (see Acts 19:10; also 19:22).[65] Instead, our pneumatological reading of the Ephesian letter focuses on two related themes, one developing the issue of Jewish-gentile relations that we have already seen (especially in our discussion of both Romans and Galatians) and the other unpacking the cosmic dimensions of this apocalyptic mystery.

What Ephesians also makes clear is Jewish feelings regarding gentiles. Thus, these local believers in Asia Minor were urged, "You must no longer live as the Gentiles live, in the futility of their minds. They are darkened in their understanding, alienated from the life of God because of their ignorance and hardness of heart. They have lost all sensitivity and have abandoned themselves to licentiousness, greedy to practice every kind of impurity" (Eph. 4:17–19).[66] Precisely as outsiders, then, the gentiles were before "aliens from the commonwealth of Israel, and strangers to the covenants of promise, having no hope and without God in the world" (2:12). It is within this context that the claim "Both of us [Jews and gentiles] have access in one Spirit to the Father" (2:18) is even more remarkable. The work of the spirit is surely bound up here also with the work of Christ: "For he is our peace; in his flesh he has made both groups into one and has broken down the dividing wall, that is, the hostility between us. He has abolished the law with its commandments and ordinances, so that he might create in himself one new humanity in place of the two, thus

63. E.g., Max Turner holds that this letter expresses Pauline thought, even if the argument for Pauline authorship is still less easily defensible. "Ephesians," in *A Biblical Theology of the Holy Spirit*, ed. Trevor J. Burke and Keith Warrington (Eugene, OR: Cascade, 2014), 187–97.

64. Going back as far as Edwin D. Roels, *God's Mission: The Epistle to the Ephesians in Mission Perspective* (Grand Rapids: Eerdmans, 1962); see also Hugo H. Culpepper, "Ephesians—A Manifesto for the Mission of the Church," *Review & Expositor* 76 (1979): 553–58.

65. Stelian Tofana, for instance, suggests that the existence of presbyters and bishops at Ephesus, from the Acts account, provide one template for a Pauline missiology or mission praxis. "Paul's Discourse in Miletus to the Ephesian *Presbyteroi* (Acts 20:17–35): A Teaching Pattern for a Successful Mission," *Swedish Missiological Themes* 99:3 (2011): 317–39.

66. Gal. 2:15 calls gentiles "sinners" but otherwise spares the kind of negative description we find here in the next (canonically ordered) letter.

making peace, and might reconcile both groups to God in one body through the cross, thus putting to death that hostility through it" (2:14–16).[67]

Thus, herein we find a triune confession of Christ and spirit as reconciling human alienation and estrangement across what we now know as racial and ethnic lines, one consistent with the doxological greeting opening the letter: "Blessed be the God and Father of our Lord Jesus Christ, who has blessed us in Christ with every spiritual blessing in the heavenly places" (Eph. 1:3). Now, both "marked with the seal of the promised Holy Spirit" (1:13), gentiles and Jews "are no longer strangers and aliens, but [they] are citizens with the saints and also members of the household of God. . . . With Christ Jesus himself as the cornerstone . . . [they] also are built together spiritually into a dwelling-place for God" (2:19, 20, 22).[68] In Ephesians, then, Paul undercuts Jewish ethnocentrism, albeit not superseding the covenant with Israel, in order to promote a more inclusive new people of God.[69] Truly, the *missio Dei* in Christ and spirit have overcome the enmity between Jew and gentile, not erasing their differences but enabling gentiles to "become fellow heirs, members of the same body, and sharers in the promise in Christ Jesus through the gospel" (3:6).

Yet the formation of a new people of God, consisting of those despised by each other before, would not come easily. Paul thus pleads and implores the Ephesians: "Lead a life worthy of the calling to which you have been called, with all humility and gentleness, with patience, bearing with one another in love, making every effort to maintain the unity of the Spirit in the bond of peace. There is one body and one Spirit, just as you were called to the one hope of your calling, one Lord, one faith, one baptism, one God and Father of all, who is above all and through all and in all" (Eph. 4:1–6). What the spirit does in achieving this new people of God is not automated. Rather, the *missio spiritus* involves the empowerment of difficult life together: living in

67. This meeting and coming together of Jews and gentiles has been famously described as "a crossroads in Christian history," which is the chapter subtitle of the doyen of mission history, Andrew F. Walls, *The Cross-Cultural Process in Christian History: Studies in the Transmission and Appropriation of Faith* (Maryknoll, NY: Orbis, 2002), chap. 4, "The Ephesian Moment." For further commentary on this by now almost classic Wallsian theme, see also Emmanuel Katongole, "Mission and the Ephesian Moment of World Christianity: Pilgrimages of Pain and Hope and the Economics of Eating Together," *Mission Studies* 29 (2012): 183–200.

68. Cf. Bertram L. Melbourne, "Ephesians 2:13–16: Are the Barriers Still Broken Down?," *Journal of Religious Thought* 57–58:2–2 (2001–2005): 107–17, with Craig S. Keener, "One New Temple in Christ (Ephesians 2:11–22; Acts 21:27–29; Mark 11:17; John 4:20–24)," *AJPS* 12:1 (2009): 75–92.

69. This is the argument of Tet-Lim N. Yee, *Jews, Gentiles and Ethnic Reconciliation: Paul's Jewish Identity and Ephesians*, Society for New Testament Studies Monograph Series 130 (Cambridge: Cambridge University Press, 2005), crystallized in his fifth chapter.

humility, patience, and forbearance, so that "the whole body, joined and knit together by every ligament with which it is equipped, as each part is working properly, promotes the body's growth in building itself up in love" (4:16).[70] In short, solidarity across ethnicities and cultures involves the *work* of the spirit and the *labor* of love and shalom.

What is of further noteworthiness in Ephesians is the development of the notion that the emergence of a new covenant people including the gentiles is the unveiling of a divine mystery. Barely intimated previously—for example, in Romans the mystery concerned more Israel's temporary rejection of the gospel contrasted with gentile conversion (Rom. 11:25)—here the idea comes into full flowering: "The mystery was made known to me by revelation, as I wrote above in a few words, a reading of which will enable you to perceive my understanding of the mystery of Christ. In former generations this mystery was not made known to humankind, as it has now been revealed to his holy apostles and prophets by the Spirit: that is, the Gentiles have become fellow heirs, members of the same body, and sharers in the promise in Christ Jesus through the gospel" (Eph. 3:3–6). There thus has been a gradual unveiling of this mystery, first and much earlier albeit in an obfuscated manner, to the apostles and prophets. But in this present time, however, and perhaps in a western Asian context rife with magical groups and practices, goddess worship, and the so-called mystery religions,[71] the apostolic mission involves further illumination of this divine mystery: "to make everyone see what is the plan of the mystery hidden for ages in God who created all things; so that through the church the wisdom of God in its rich variety might now be made known to the rulers and authorities in the heavenly places" (3:9–10). The unfolding of this mystery, then, has a cosmic horizon but also involves human creatures. Thus the letter begins, "He has made known to us the mystery of his will, . . . as a plan for the fullness of time, to gather up all things in him, things in heaven and things on earth" (1:9–10; cf. Col. 1:26–27), and we arrive close to its ending at the marriage between man and woman as analogous to the relationship between Christ and the church labeled a mystery (5:32). Hence, we can understand Ephesians as pronouncing the forging of one people who were formerly aliens and strangers as a message also to the heavens, not just for earthlings.

70. This praxis-perspective on mission in the letter is highlighted by Idicheria Ninan, "The Spirit and Mission in Ephesians," in *The Holy Spirit and Christian Mission in a Pluralistic Context*, ed. Roji T. George (Bangalore: SAIACS, 2017), 36–59.
71. See Clinton E. Arnold, *Ephesians, Power and Magic: The Concept of Power in Ephesians in Light of Its Historical Setting*, SNTSMS 63 (Cambridge: Cambridge University Press, 1989), chap. 2.

In other words, the Letter to the Ephesians is concerned both about the ends of the earth and also about the uttermost expanses of God's redemptive mission: the heavenly realm. Christ ascended "far above all the heavens, so that he might fill all things" (Eph. 4:10), and toward that end and from that elevated site and all that it symbolizes, he gave gifts of apostolicity, among other mission and ministry charges (4:11).[72] As participants in this *missio Dei*, then, the Ephesian believers are urged not to grieve and resist but to embrace and be filled with the spirit (cf. 4:30 and 5:18).[73] This enables renunciation of their past paganism (4:17–5:5), fuller inhabitation of their ecclesial koinonia (5:3–20), and mutuality within households and beyond (5:21–6:9).[74] As or more important, this propels participation in the declaration and full realization of the divine mystery to and amid the heavens: "For our struggle is not against enemies of blood and flesh, but against the rulers, against the authorities, against the cosmic powers of this present darkness, against the spiritual forces of evil in the heavenly places" (6:12). The *missio Dei* thereby has cosmic reach: overcoming the principalities and powers of evil and destruction that seek to undermine creation, yet also heralding to the heavenly authorities that the world is being turned right-side up, that the enmity and opposition between and within creation has been healed. If the walls between Jews and gentiles have been surmounted in Christ by the spirit, then the divine reign will continue to manifest through the church in Ephesus and western Asia Minor and extend from there not just to the ends of the earth but also to the edges of the heavens, all the while nurturing creational harmony and differences amid cosmic flourishing.

Reading about the Ephesian letter's concerns with principalities and powers might urge some to embrace a form of contemporary spiritual-warfare supernaturalism believed to be relevant for mission and ministry in majority-world contexts in which indigenous cosmologies feature a plurality of spiritual levels and beings.[75] In global context, a pneumatological-missiological hermeneutic

72. Sunday B. Babajide Komolafe, "Christ, Church, and the Cosmos: A Missiological Reading of Paul's Epistle to the Ephesians," *Missiology* 35:3 (2007): 273–86; cf. Sherron Kay George, "'Joined and Knit Together . . . Each Part Working Properly': A Missiological Reflection on Practices of God's Holistic Mission in Ephesians," *Missiology* 37:3 (2009): 398–409.

73. John Paul Heil writes, "Be filled *in* the Spirit." Heil, "Ephesians 5:18b: 'But Be Filled in the Spirit,'" *CBQ* 69 (2007): 506–16, here 516; see also Gordon D. Fee, "Some Exegetical and Theological Reflections on Ephesians 4.30 and Pauline Pneumatology," in *Spirit and Renewal: Essays in Honor of J. Rodman Williams*, ed. Mark W. Wilson, JPTSup 5 (Sheffield: Sheffield Academic, 1994), 129–56; and James F. Holladay Jr., "Ephesians 4:30: Do Not Grieve the Spirit," *RevExp* 94 (1997): 81–87.

74. See David Liu, "The Work of the Holy Spirit in the Church: A Study of Ephesians," trans. Connie Au, *AJPS* 14:1 (2011): 74–92.

75. Thus, e.g., Kabiro wa Gatumu, *The Pauline Concept of Supernatural Powers: A Reading from the African Worldview* (Milton Keynes, UK: Paternoster, 2008), critiques the African

certainly seeks to be more attuned to the spiritual dimensions of the cosmos as these impinge on and are interwoven within the fabric of human history. What is to be avoided, however, is any gnostic dualism that bifurcates the spiritual and historical realms and is incapable of navigating their dynamic interaction. In the end, the Pauline admonition is that the one Jewish-gentile people of God participate in this spiritual battle *not against* flesh and blood *but as* flesh-and-blood creatures.[76] Materially and concretely, then, believers are exhorted to "take the helmet of salvation, and the sword of the Spirit, which is the word of God. Pray in the Spirit at all times in every prayer and supplication. To that end keep alert and always persevere in supplication for all the saints" (6:17–18). Such *spiritual warfare* involves alertness and perseverance in solidarity with the ethnic/racial, sociopolitical, and cultural other.[77] We will return momentarily to this theme when we read Colossians through this bifocal lens.

6.6　Philippians—Standing in the Spirit: Mission in Chains

With Philippians, indisputably St. Paul's (although written in this case with Timothy: Phil. 1:1), we return to a deeply autobiographical communiqué, one not devoid of apologetic fervor seeking to protect his readers from encroaching opponents, but not as dominated by this task as we saw in 2 Corinthians (§6.3). One of these defensive parries is pneumatologically thrusted: "For it is we who are the circumcision, who worship in the Spirit of God and boast in Christ Jesus and have no confidence in the flesh—even though I, too, have reason for confidence in the flesh" (3:3–4). Here in this section, Paul is comparing his own ethnic Jewish credentials with those of his Judaizing opponents, perhaps a related group to the one that threatened the Galatian churches (§6.4). But the

worldview not because he disagrees with its pluralistic cosmology but because of its occultism that undercuts Christ's supremacy (212–22), all the while urging that the "spiritual, social, political, economic and psychological dimensions of human existence are interlinked and interrelated" (238). The entire thrust of my pneumatological missiology unfolds across the pages of this volume agrees with this latter notion, although in the rest of this chapter I will proceed more cautiously than would global South or majority world conceptualizations of the spirit world, including demonological notions that map straightforwardly onto the Pauline "worldview."

76. Thus, Timothy G. Gombis suggests that the Ephesian call to be filled with the spirit is an invitation to the "church to play their part in being the dwelling place of God on earth." "Being the Fullness of God in Christ by the Spirit: Ephesians 5:18 in Its Epistolary Setting," *TynBul* 53:2 (2002): 259–71, here 271.

77. My own work on the principalities and powers, forged in dialogue with scholars like Walter Wink among many others, is further unpacked in Yong, *In the Days of Caesar: Pentecostalism and Political Theology; The Cadbury Lectures 2009*, Sacra Doctrina: Christian Theology for a Postmodern Age (Grand Rapids: Eerdmans, 2010), chap. 4.

Philippian Witness amid Imperial Rome
The Freedom of the Spirit

Ekaputra Tupamahu, assistant professor of New Testament,
George Fox University, Newberg, Oregon, USA

As both a missionary and a colonized subject, the figure of Paul provides us
with a rich resource to think about Christian mission in the postcolonial world
today. Mission and colonialism can easily be seen as two sides of the same
coin. They are almost inseparable in the eyes of many because, admittedly,
the history of Christian mission has been ingrained in the Western colonial
project. Is it possible to reimagine Christian mission that is not participating
and contributing to colonialism? Can the work of Christian mission be a liberating enterprise? The answer should be yes. However, it requires not only a
fundamental rethinking of the concept of mission itself but also a meaningful
engagement with the experiences of the colonized subjects. An aspect of
such mission can be extrapolated from Paul's conviction of the liberative role
of the Spirit (Phil 1:19). Reading this pneumatology of liberation (or salvation;
Greek *sōtēria*) in light of Paul's struggle with Roman imperialism can give
us ample space to think constructively about Christian decolonial mission.

difference Paul explicates here is that they glory in the circumcision of their flesh
in contrast to authentic messianic trust in Christ by the power of the spirit. It
is from this pneumatic and christic platform that Paul the missionary speaks.

And Paul can write from no other location as his letter emanates from
prison (Phil. 1:7), or some would say from his being secured in Rome (see
Acts 28:14–31; cf. §5.5 above).[78] Although he anticipates that "through
your prayers and the help of the Spirit of Jesus Christ this will result in my
deliverance" (Phil. 1:19), just as important is that "what has happened to
me has actually helped to spread the gospel, so that it has become known
throughout the whole imperial guard and to everyone else that my imprisonment is for Christ" (1:12–13). And on top of this, Christ continues to be
preached in Philippi; whether because these evangelists wish to pick up the
slack left by Paul's absence or to make him jealous, so to speak (1:16–17),

78. The scholarly assessment of the evidence is inconclusive, but the Roman imprisonment
hypothesis makes the most sense; see F. F. Bruce, *Philippians*, NIBC (Peabody, MA: Hendrickson, 1989), 11–16.

"What does it matter? Just this, that Christ is proclaimed in every way, whether out of false motives or true; and in that I rejoice" (1:18). Herein the spirit-guided missionary and evangelistic heart of the apostle comes into full view. Unsurprisingly, then, he urges his readers, "Live your life in a manner worthy of the gospel of Christ, so that, whether I come and see you or am absent and hear about you, I will know that you are standing firm in one spirit, striving side by side with one mind for the faith of the gospel" (1:27). The spirit who is and will be deliverer, even from the chains of imprisonment, is also the one who enables ecclesial fellowship and missionary evangelism, regardless of the physical circumstances of those so filled with her presence.[79]

It is in this context that Paul writes, "If then there is any encouragement in Christ, any consolation from love, any sharing in the Spirit, any compassion and sympathy, make my joy complete: be of the same mind, having the same love, being in full accord and of one mind" (Phil. 2:1–2). Here we find that the mind that Paul commends in the spirit is that of Christ's, specifically that of the crucified and kenotic Christ,

> who, though he was in the form of God,
>   did not regard equality with God
>   as something to be exploited,
> but emptied himself,
>   taking the form of a slave,
>   being born in human likeness.
> And being found in human form,
>   he humbled himself
>   and became obedient to the point of death—
>   even death on a cross. (2:6–8)

This is the famous *kenosis hymn*, or song of Jesus's self-emptying.[80] From the perspective of missiological and evangelistic passion manifest in the first part of this letter, the hymn is meant to be embraced and performed.[81] Readers are called to be singers and then to be living epistles that proclaim, in word and deed, the good news to their community in the selflessness

79. See also Dean Flemming, "Exploring a Missional Reading of Scripture: Philippians as a Case Study," *EvQ* 83:1 (2011): 3–18.

80. For a powerfully provocative reading of Philippians from this kenosis standpoint vis-à-vis East Asian philosophical and cultural traditions and contexts, see John P. Keenan, *The Emptied Christ of Philippians: Mahayana Meditations* (Eugene, OR: Wipf & Stock, 2015).

81. Michael J. Gorman, *Becoming the Gospel: Paul, Participation, and Mission* (Grand Rapids: Eerdmans, 2015); chap. 4 is about (the Philippian) mission as living out the identity and story of Jesus.

of Jesus.[82] If postcolonial readings of this letter are concerned—rightfully so—that assertions of apostolic authority can be understood as paternalistic expressions of power mimicking imperialist and expansionist modalities,[83] the point of the hymn is to encourage mutual edification and reciprocal service, both to ward off a common peril and to carry out the missional task. Paul's objective is not "to infantilize" the Philippians,[84] but to empower, paradoxically through humility and weakness, their mission: to "work out your own salvation with fear and trembling; for it is God who is at work in you, enabling you both to will and to work for his good pleasure" (Phil. 2:12–13).

As 2 Corinthians (§6.3) already informs us that potent mission emerges by the spirit from situations and realities characterized by weakness, so also here mission is achieved, or nevertheless persists, through the cross, even in fetters and restraints.[85] So while Paul is imprisoned, the spirit raises up gospel evangelists as needs arise.[86] There will be those with specific charges in critical circumstances: "I urge Euodia and I urge Syntyche to be of the same mind in the Lord. Yes, and I ask you also, my loyal companion,[87] help these women, for they have struggled beside me in the work of the gospel, together with Clement and the rest of my co-workers, whose names are in the book of life" (Phil. 4:2–3). The spirit has raised up also Timothy and Epaphroditus to represent Paul to the Philippians and vice versa during this time (2:19–30). In other words, the *missio spiritus* moves human agents forward, with or without shackles, through the impediments of life situations.

In fact, Paul recognizes the entire Philippian congregation or community as colaborers with him in the cause of the gospel: "I thank my God every time I remember you, constantly praying with joy in every one of my prayers *for all of you*, because of your sharing in the gospel from the first day until

82. See Jeffrey F. Keuss, *Freedom of the Self: Kenosis, Cultural Identity, and Mission at the Crossroads* (Eugene, OR: Pickwick, 2010), whose kenotic missiology is framed by a trialogue between emergent churches, East Asian aesthetics, and continental philosophy.

83. E.g., Joseph A. Marchal, "Imperial Intersections and Initial Inquiries: Toward a Feminist, Postcolonial Analysis of Philippians," in *The Colonized Apostle: Paul through Postcolonial Eyes*, ed. Christopher D. Stanley (Minneapolis: Fortress, 2011), 146–60.

84. Melanie Johnson-DeBaufre and Laura S. Nasrallah, "Beyond the Heroic Paul: Toward a Feminist and Decolonizing Approach to the Letters of Paul," in Stanley, *Colonized Apostle*, 161–74, here 170.

85. Jim Purves, "The Missional Doxology of the Philippian Hymn," *Baptistic Theologies* 3:1 (2011): 15–30.

86. John P. Dickson discusses Philippians among other Pauline letters in this regard in *Mission Commitment in Ancient Judaism and in the Pauline Communities: The Shape, Extent and Background of Early Christian Mission*, WUNT 2/159 (Tübingen: Mohr Siebeck, 2003), chap. 3.

87. The identity of this "loyal companion" is unknown. Of the three commentaries I consulted, only one—Bruce, *Philippians*, 138—tentatively suggests a name, Luke, although still pleading ignorance.

now" (Phil. 1:4–5; emphasis added).[88] For this reason, then, he exhorts them to live missionally: "Do all things without murmuring and arguing, so that you may be blameless and innocent, children of God without blemish in the midst of a crooked and perverse generation, in which you shine like stars in the world. It is by your holding fast to the word of life that I can boast on the day of Christ that I did not run in vain or labor in vain" (2:14–16).[89] The Greek for "holding fast," ἐπέχοντες (*epechontes*), however, is just as translatable as "holding forth," although the latter seems more consistent with both the immediate context of urging evangelical witness and the broader ethos of the letter about bearing imprisoned and libertarian testimony before the world.[90] Mission extends across space and time, by the spirit, so that the one body with its many members in diverse locations and circumstances witnesses through the exemplary death of the living Christ.

Mission in the spirit, refracted through Philippians, proceeds in the power of the cross. The Acts narrative (16:11–40) tells us about the wondrousness of the deliverance from the jail in Philippi, even if that did not deliver Paul and Silas from flogging and incarceration. Yet in this epistle we hear nothing about signs and wonders, but much about Christian witness following the humiliation of Christ. The Pauline theme of power-in-weakness is consistent across the Pauline Letters and is no less central to a vision of spirit-empowered mission in the Philippian locale.

6.7 Colossians—Loving in the Spirit: Epaphras's Mission within the Mission

A pneumatological perspective applied to Colossians might not seem viable at first glance.[91] It is possible that some of the concerns regarding the mys-

---

88. Alistair I. Wilson, "An Ideal Missionary Prayer Letter: Reflections on Paul's Mission Theology as Expressed in Philippians," in *New Testament Theology in Light of the Church's Mission: Essays in Honor of I. Howard Marshall*, ed. Jon C. Laansma, Grant R. Osborne, and Ray F. Van Neste (Eugene, OR: Cascade, 2011), 245–64; see also Mark J. Keown, *Congregational Evangelism in Philippians: The Centrality of an Appeal for Gospel Proclamation to the Fabric of Philippians* (Milton Keynes, UK: Paternoster, 2008).

89. The major study here is James P. Ware, *The Mission of the Church in Paul's Letter to the Philippians in the Context of Ancient Judaism*, NovTSup 120 (Leiden: Brill, 2005); chap. 6 unfolds the Pauline missiology from this section of Phil. 2.

90. Christoph W. Stenschke, "'*Holding Forth* the Word of Life' (ΛΟΓΟΝ ΖΩΗΣ ΕΠΕΧΟΝΤΕΣ): Philippians 2:16a and Other References to Paul's Understanding of the Involvement of Early Christian Communities in Spreading the Gospel," *Journal of Early Christian History* 3:1 (2013): 61–82.

91. A rather meandering effort, perhaps to be forgiven in light of the obscurity of the spirit in this epistle, is Hendrikus Berkhof, "The Holy Spirit and the World: Some Reflections on Paul's Letter to the Colossians," *Journal of Theology for Southern Africa* 29 (1979): 56–61.

tery religions we saw in the Ephesian letter (§6.5) are present in the Colossian context, and these are pneumatological issues. Thus, the author of the epistle is anxious that his readers are not taken captive "through philosophy and empty deceit, according to human tradition, according to the elemental spirits of the universe, and not according to Christ" (Col. 2:8). Since Christ has "disarmed the rulers and authorities and made a public example of them, triumphing over them in it," the Colossian believers ought not to be caught up in ritual observances (2:15) or carried away by the "worship of angels [and] dwelling on visions" (2:18). Rather, "if with Christ you died to the elemental spirits of the universe, why do you live as if you still belonged to the world?" (2:20).[92] Put another way, dying and being raised with Christ liberates human creatures from the spiritual powers at work against them.[93] From a missiological perspective, attentiveness to this theme suggests that Christ counters and overcomes the cosmic powers and the religious rites and practices propped up by them.[94]

Colossians is definitively more Christ-centered than spirit-occupied. The answer to the Colossian "problem" is the supremacy of Christ. Not only are all things through Christ (Col. 1:16–17), but "in him all the fullness of God was pleased to dwell, and through him God was pleased to reconcile to himself all things, whether on earth or in heaven, by making peace through the blood of his cross" (1:19–20).[95] Read pneumatologically, Colossians, rather than being muted about the spirit, invites consideration of how the spirit exalts Christ, consistent with other New Testament references to the spirit's work. And if this is the case, then "the divine Spirit which is at work throughout the cosmos

92. Clinton E. Arnold discusses the problematic "worship of angels," ritual practices, and philosophical beliefs addressed by the letter. *The Colossian Syncretism: The Interface between Christianity and Folk Belief at Colossae* (Grand Rapids: Baker, 1996).

93. Johannes Nissen discusses the Colossian mission in part as a means of "liberation from tyranny of powers." *New Testament and Mission: Historical and Hermeneutical Perspectives* (Frankfurt am Main: Peter Lang, 1999), 130–31.

94. Thus, Flemming (*Contextualization in the New Testament*, chap. 7) discusses Colossians in terms of the gospel versus syncretism.

95. If the "elemental spirits of the world" (Gal. 4:3, 9) are overcome and "every ruler and every authority and power" is subjected to God the Father (1 Cor. 15:23–28) in the indisputably Pauline letters, here the powers are somehow reconciled to Christ, whose presence and glory already fills the creation, even as in the related missive to the Ephesians, the church is suggested to be participating in the present and eschatological task of Christ's subduing and redeeming of the cosmic powers; see along these lines the argument of George H. van Kooten, *Cosmic Christology in Paul and the Pauline School: Colossians and Ephesians in the Context of Graeco-Roman Cosmology, with a New Synopsis of the Greek Texts*, WUNT 2/171 (Tübingen: Mohr Siebeck 2003), although for our purposes much less depends on his corollary argument that Ephesians depends on and responds to Colossians and that both are pseudo-Pauline.

is none other than the Spirit of Christ."[96] The cosmically enthroned Christ thus becomes the core of the missiological vision of the Colossian letter.[97]

Yet there is *one* explicit reference to the holy spirit in this letter: "This you learned from Epaphras, our beloved fellow servant. He is a faithful minister of Christ on your behalf, and he has made known to us your love in the Spirit" (Col. 1:7–8). Even if some are unsure whether Paul himself authored this letter as indicated in its opening (1:1), it is clear that their experienced intimacy suggested in this description is consistent with how Paul describes Epaphras in the Letter to Philemon, whose authenticity is unquestioned. There Epaphras is identified as "my [Paul's] fellow prisoner in Christ Jesus" and is set off from "Mark, Aristarchus, Demas, and Luke, my fellow workers" (Philem. 23–24).[98] Epaphras's significance in Colossians ought not to be underestimated since his appearance here at the beginning of this letter is followed by reappearance at the end: "Epaphras, who is one of you, a servant of Christ Jesus, greets you. He is always wrestling in his prayers on your behalf, so that you may stand mature and fully assured in everything that God wills. For I testify for him that he has worked hard for you and for those in Laodicea and in Hierapolis" (Col. 4:12–13).

What is clear is that Epaphras bears witness to "your [the Colossian believers'] love in the Spirit." Further, he is not just a "faithful minister" (διάκονος or deacon), but he has been a teacher to "the saints and faithful brothers and sisters in Christ in Colossae" (Col. 1:2), handing on to them truths about faith in Jesus Christ, love for the saints, the hope of heaven, the power of the gospel for the whole world, the fruit of discipleship, and the grace of God (1:3–6). All of this the Colossian believers have "learned from Epaphras" (1:7), who has labored diligently to raise them up in the faith (4:12).[99] The love of and in the spirit, in other words, has been communicated through Epaphras, both from Paul to the Colossians and then again from this community back to an imprisoned Paul (4:18), the letter purports. Put missiologically, the spirit bears interpersonal and interrelational witness through intermediaries—in this case Epaphras—in multiple directions.

96. Vicky Balabanski, "The Holy Spirit and the Cosmic Christ: A Comparison of Their Roles in Colossians and Ephesians, or 'Where Has the Holy Spirit Gone?,'" *Colloquium: The Australian and New Zealand Theological Review* 42:2 (2010): 173–87, here 181.

97. Teresa Okure, "'In Him All Things Hold Together': A Missiological Reading of Colossians 1:15–20," *IRM* 91:360 (2002): 62–72.

98. Thus "beloved fellow servant" (Col. 1:7) and "fellow prisoner" (Philem. 23) are synonymously applied to Epaphras; the only other persons who are so described as intimate colaborers are Andronicus and Junia, "my [Paul's] relatives who were in prison with me" (Rom. 16:7).

99. See Michael Trainor, *Epaphras: Paul's Educator at Colossae* (Collegeville, MN: Liturgical Press, 2008).

Epaphras, clearly a Greek name, perhaps from the Lycan Valley, which included not only Colossae but also Laodicea and Hierapolis, denotes the collegiality of a Jew and a gentile as mutual participants—or as sequential conduits (Paul as elder and Epaphras as younger)—in the mission of the spirit.[100] When we remember that the newly emerging relationship between Jew and gentile has been a central and persisting question in the Pauline missionary endeavor, this becomes of greater rather than marginal import. The truths proclaimed by Paul initially in Asia Minor and now also by Epaphras in the Lycan Valley thus provide a dual vocalization of the new people of God overcoming prior divisions. The Colossians, Jews and gentiles, are told to put aside religious ritual (Col. 2:16–23), practices like fornication and idolatry (3:5), "anger, wrath, malice, slander, and abusive language from your mouth" (3:8), and lying to one another (3:9). In turn, they are called to put on "the new self, which is being renewed in knowledge according to the image of its creator. In that renewal there is no longer Greek and Jew, circumcised and uncircumcised, barbarian, Scythian, slave and free; but Christ is all and in all!" (3:10–11). This message echoes a similar note sounded to other churches in the same region (e.g., Gal. 3:28; §6.4).[101]

The *missio spiritus* is at least in part for the purpose of ensuring that those the gospel touches "may be filled with the knowledge of God's will in all spiritual wisdom and understanding" (Col. 1:9). Yet such spirituality engages the religious fervor and cultic pagan milieu of the Colossian context precisely through being embodied in concrete communities involving Jews and gentiles living with and serving one another. The call is to "bear with one another [and] forgive each other" (3:13); to "teach and admonish one another in all wisdom; and with gratitude in your hearts sing psalms, hymns, and spiritual songs to God" (3:16); and to "do everything in the name of the Lord Jesus, giving thanks to God the Father through him" (3:17). More importantly, such spiritual guidelines were to permeate real-life structural relations, including those organizing marriage life (3:18–19), parent-child interactions (3:20–21), master-slave relations (3:22–4:1), and so on. Regarding external

100. At the end of Colossians, Epaphras (4:12) is set off from Aristarchus, Mark, and Jesus/Justus, "the only ones of the circumcision among my co-workers" (4:11), which is a clear indicator of Epaphras's non-Jewish identity; see also Larry J. Kreitzer, "Epaphras and Philip: The Undercover Evangelists of Hierapolis," in *"You Will Be My Witnesses": A Festschrift in Honor of the Reverend Dr. Allison A. Trites on the Occasion of His Retirement*, ed. R. Glenn Wooden, Timothy R. Ashley, and Robert S. Wilson (Macon, GA: Mercer University Press, 2003), 127–43, here 131.

101. See also John M. G. Barclay, "'Neither Jew nor Greek': Multiculturalism and the New Perspective on Paul," in *Ethnicity and the Bible*, ed. Mark G. Brett, BibInt 19 (Leiden: Brill, 1996), 197–214.

witness, "Conduct yourselves wisely toward outsiders, making the most of the time. Let your speech always be gracious, seasoned with salt, so that you may know how you ought to answer everyone" (4:5–6). The love in the spirit communicated to and from the Colossian community, in other words, trans- formed if not troubled extant cultural hierarchies.[102]

If missionary work involves "completing what is lacking in Christ's af- flictions for the sake of his body, that is, the church" (Col. 1:24),[103] then we might say that the Colossian case involved a Jewish-gentile tag team: Paul and Epaphras (whether synchronically in terms of their real-time collaboration or diachronically in the sense of the latter succeeding the former). Together, then, they exemplified the proclaimed message: "no longer Greek and Jew, circumcised and uncircumcised, barbarian, Scythian, slave and free; but Christ is all and in all." If certain Jews in these first-century messianic circles wanted to preserve Jewish religious privileges in ways that excluded gentiles from the covenantal promises, Epaphras becomes a missionary, pastor, and teacher- educator who crosses ethnic boundaries as a Hellenist Greek in order to urge and encourage inclusivity across religious, class, and other lines. He is part of a Greco-Roman majority working in a hybridic context involving minor- ity citizens (Paul and his fellow Jewish messianists) for their empowerment alongside and with others. Epaphras's lifework of facilitating "love in the Spirit" regardless and across prior commitments remains our missional task and call, no less urgently in global contexts still plagued by ethnocentrism and xenophobia than it was in the crossroads of the Lycan Valley cosmopolis in the first century.

6.8 1–2 Thessalonians—Rejoicing in the Spirit: Mission, Sanctification, and Hope

Our pneumatological-missiological reading of Paul continues by going back to earlier in his life and ministry. With the possible exception of the Letter to the Galatians (§6.4), the Thessalonian letters are among the first of Paul's

102. This is my sympathetic rendition of a work that otherwise employs a hermeneutic- of-suspicion approach to this Pauline text: Marianne Bjelland Kartzow, "'Asking the Other Question': An Intersectional Approach to Galatians 3:28 and the Colossian Household Codes," *BibInt* 18 (2010): 364–89.

103. See John Reumann, "Colossians 1:24 ('What Is Lacking in the Afflictions of Christ'): History of Exegesis and Ecumenical Advance," *CurTM* 17 (1990): 454–61; cf. Hanna Stettler, "An Interpretation of Colossians 1:24 in the Framework of Paul's Mission Theology," in *The Mission of the Early Church to Jews and Gentiles*, ed. Jostein Ådna and Hans Kvalbein, WUNT 127 (Tübingen: Mohr Siebeck, 2000), 185–208.

writings that we have.[104] This allows us to see how ideas developed over time. Two pneumatological motifs present themselves for consideration: the proclamation of the gospel in the spirit and sanctification by the spirit.[105] We will relate these notions to the prevalent theme of parousia as Christian hope that permeates both letters to Thessalonica.

The first letter begins pneumatologically. After the fairly generic salutations, thanksgiving, and prayerful greetings, Paul writes, "For we know, brothers and sisters beloved by God, that he has chosen you, because our message of the gospel came to you not in word only, but also in power and in the Holy Spirit and with full conviction; just as you know what kind of persons we proved to be among you for your sake. And you became imitators of us and of the Lord, for in spite of persecution you received the word with joy inspired by the Holy Spirit" (1 Thess. 1:4–6). Two points are noteworthy up front: first, that the gospel came to Thessalonica not only in word but also by and through the power of the spirit (observed also in Corinthians, for example; §6.2); and second, that the perseverance of these believers during trying times persisted via the joy of the spirit.[106] The powerful coming of the gospel in this city, nevertheless, was in gentleness (2:7), with "labor and toil" (2:9), and as parents might care for their children (2:11–12). In other words, spirit-filled mission occurs not only with signs and wonders or through brilliant oration, but in the mundane efforts of pastoral care and missionary oversight.

What is intriguing is that the coming of the gospel by the power of the spirit also generates gospel witness to the surrounding neighbors: "You became an example to all the believers in Macedonia and in Achaia. For the word of the Lord has sounded forth from you not only in Macedonia and Achaia, but in every place where your faith in God has become known, so that we have no need to speak about it. For the people of those regions report about us what kind of welcome we had among you, and how you turned to God from idols, to serve a living and true God" (1:7–9). In other words, spirit-filled gospel proclamation engenders the spirit-led life and extends the

104. For a summative rationale for considering 2 Thessalonians as authentic and dated shortly after the first epistle was written—both thus around 50–51 CE—see Gordon D. Fee, *The First and Second Letters to the Thessalonians* (Grand Rapids: Eerdmans, 2009), 237–41.

105. E.g., Trevor J. Burke, "The Holy Spirit as the Controlling Dynamic in Paul's Role as Missionary to the Thessalonians," in *Paul as Missionary: Identity, Activity, Theology, and Practice*, ed. Trevor J. Burke and Brian S. Rosner, LNTS 420 (New York: T&T Clark, 2011), 142–57.

106. Note that Nehemiah and Ezra said to a people seeking postexilic renewal in Israel, "Go your way, eat the fat and drink sweet wine and send portions of them to those for whom nothing is prepared, for this day is holy to our LORD; and do not be grieved, for the joy of the LORD is your strength" (Neh. 8:10); see also §3.2.

gospel witness.[107] The Thessalonian believers, like the Corinthians (§6.3), were living epistles and testimonies, and their witness sounded forth even while they suffered persecution from other neighbors who sought to squelch the Jesus message (2:14–16; cf. Acts 17:5–9).[108]

Second, the spirit enables gospel proclamation and spawns the fruits of such endeavors, including the sanctification of those who receive the gospel. In the second half of the first letter, then, Paul writes,

> For this is the will of God, your sanctification: that you abstain from fornication; that each one of you know how to control your own body in holiness and honor, not with lustful passion, like the Gentiles who do not know God; that no one wrong or exploit a brother or sister in this matter, because the Lord is an avenger in all these things, just as we have already told you beforehand and solemnly warned you. For God did not call us to impurity but in holiness. Therefore whoever rejects this rejects not human authority but God, who also gives his Holy Spirit to you. (1 Thess. 4:3–8)

For those who have received the gospel, Christian holiness and purification involves turning away from their prior ways of life, another consistent theme seen across the Pauline Letters. In the sociopolitical, religious-cultural, and historical context of Thessalonica, the ethical norms Paul urges are not in radical discontinuity with those of the surrounding environment, but they are given much more explicit theological warrant.[109] Further, sanctification is a whole-person matter: "May the God of peace himself sanctify you entirely; and may your spirit and soul and body be kept sound and blameless at the coming of our Lord Jesus Christ" (1 Thess. 5:23).[110] Yet its accomplishment is only through the divine spirit: "But we must always give thanks to God for you, brothers and sisters beloved by the Lord, because God chose you as the first fruits for salvation through sanctification by the Spirit and through belief in the truth" (2 Thess. 2:13).[111]

107. James Ware, "The Thessalonians as a Missionary Congregation: 1 Thessalonians 1,5–8," *Zeitschrift für die neutestamentliche Wissenschaft* 83:1–2 (1992): 126–31.

108. Thus, "the Spirit ratifies the proclamation by producing effects." Edgar Krentz, "Evangelism and Spirit: 1 Thessalonians 1," *CurTM* 14:1 (1987): 22–30, here 30.

109. Abraham J. Malherbe, "Ethics in Context: The Thessalonians and Their Neighbors," in *Light from the Gentiles: Hellenistic Philosophy and Early Christianity: Collected Essays, 1959–2012*, ed. Carl R. Holladay et al., 2 vols., NovTSup 150 (Leiden: Brill, 2014), 1:575–96. See also Todd D. Still, "Paul's Thessalonian Mission," *SwJT* 42 (1999): 4–16.

110. Wayne McCown, "'God's Will . . . for You': Sanctification in the Thessalonian Epistles," *Wesleyan Theological Journal* 12 (1977): 26–33.

111. See Victor Paul Furnish, "The Spirit in 2 Thessalonians," in *The Holy Spirit and Christian Origins: Essays in Honor of James D. G. Dunn*, ed. Graham N. Stanton, Bruce W.

Yet holiness of life is not distinct from but intrinsic to missional witness. In fact, pneumatic mission for the Thessalonians involves nothing more than intentional Christ-following. There are no crusades, evangelistic events, or other "attractions" involved, only the life well-lived: "Now concerning love of the brothers and sisters, you do not need to have anyone write to you, for you yourselves have been taught by God to love one another; and indeed you do love all the brothers and sisters throughout Macedonia. But we urge you, beloved, to do so more and more, to aspire to live quietly, to mind your own affairs, and to work with your hands, as we directed you, so that you may behave properly toward outsiders and be dependent on no one" (1 Thess. 4:9–12). Mission according to this pneumatological register therefore involves all-of-life discipleship, with concomitant holiness of behavior and practice that reaches beyond one's community.[112]

If the spirit both saves, through gospel proclamation, and sanctifies, then this happens because of the spirit's outpouring that precipitates the eschatological age in anticipation of the parousia. Both letters to the Thessalonians address this notion of Christ's return as an urgent matter, although neither links the spirit explicitly with this expected event. Yet given the broader New Testament witness to the spirit in connection with the coming divine reign, and given other Pauline indicators about the eschatological character of the spirit's work that we have repeatedly encountered in this chapter, it is appropriate to comprehend the parousia itself "as a pneumatological event."[113] Not to be overlooked is that holiness itself has an eschatological trajectory, so that Paul prays, "May he [the Lord] so strengthen your hearts in holiness that you may be blameless before our God and Father at the coming of our Lord Jesus with all his saints" (1 Thess. 3:13). Such a posture eagerly expects the return of Christ (4:13–18) and remains alert in view of its imminence while living appropriately in its light (5:1–11).[114]

Longenecker, and Stephen C. Barton (Grand Rapids: Eerdmans, 2004), 229–40. Note that this is the only reference to the spirit in 2 Thessalonians, and since it concerns one of the central pneumatic themes in the prior epistle (sanctification), I have decided not to treat these letters separately.

112. "Living a fruitful life in community" is how Volker Rabens puts it in "1 Thessalonians," in *A Biblical Theology of the Holy Spirit*, ed. Trevor J. Burke and Keith Warrington (Eugene, OR: Cascade, 2014), 198–212, here 201; see also Thor Strandenœs, "Completing the Mission: Paul's Application of the Gospel to the Faith and Life of the Thessalonian Converts in 1 and 2 Thessalonians," *Swedish Missiological Themes* 98:1 (2010): 69–98.

113. Andy Johnson, *1 and 2 Thessalonians*, Two Horizons New Testament Commentary (Grand Rapids: Eerdmans, 2016), 314.

114. Charles A. Gieschen, "Christ's Coming and the Church's Mission in 1 Thessalonians," *Concordia Theological Quarterly* 76 (2012): 37–55.

Otherworldly aspirations, however, do not mean this-worldly neglect. This preparedness has both mundane and spiritual dimensions, both personal and communal aspects:

> But we appeal to you, brothers and sisters, to respect those who labor among you, and have charge of you in the Lord and admonish you; esteem them very highly in love because of their work. Be at peace among yourselves. And we urge you, beloved, to admonish the idlers, encourage the fainthearted, help the weak, be patient with all of them. See that none of you repays evil for evil, but always seek to do good to one another and to all. Rejoice always, pray without ceasing, give thanks in all circumstances; for this is the will of God in Christ Jesus for you. Do not quench the Spirit. Do not despise the words of prophets, but test everything; hold fast to what is good; abstain from every form of evil. (1 Thess. 5:12–22)

In other words, living by the spirit in hopes of receiving and welcoming the soon-coming king does not entail sectarian withdrawal from the world. There are practicalities to be attended to for nurturing ecclesial life, and this also has wider social ramifications. As important, there is something about the longed-for eschatological vindication whereby the good that one is (usually barely) holding fast to overcomes, finally and once for all, the evil that stains our lives despite our best efforts to avoid it, and this hope carries with it missional implications.[115] Although this eschatological frame for missiology recedes to the background in the next chapter, such a conception percolates throughout that discussion and will surge back to the forefront in the final pages of this book.

6.9 1–2 Timothy—Admonition by the Spirit: Retrospect and Prospect in Mission

Both writings addressed to Timothy appear to be from Paul at the end of life, perhaps while he is imprisoned in Rome (2 Tim. 1:17; see Acts 28:11–31).[116] Pneumatologically, the spirit appears clearly only once in each epistle.[117] In the

115. C. Timothy Carriker, "Missiological Hermeneutic and Pauline Apocalyptic Eschatology," in *The Good News of the Kingdom: Mission Theology for the Third Millennium*, ed. Charles Van Engen, Dean S. Gilliland, and Paul Pierson (Maryknoll, NY: Orbis, 1993), 45–55.
116. Guthrie (*New Testament Introduction*, 607–49) overviews the arguments against Pauline authorship from historical, ecclesiastical, theological, and linguistic grounds, in each case answering that they do not require negation of the traditional view.
117. "He was revealed in flesh, vindicated in spirit" (1 Tim. 3:16) is easier argued as christological rather than pneumatological, referring to "the spiritual mode or sphere of Christ's

former letter, Timothy is admonished, "Now the Spirit expressly says that in later times some will renounce the faith by paying attention to deceitful spirits and teachings of demons" (1 Tim. 4:1). The other letter also counsels that "in the last days distressing times will come" (2 Tim. 3:1), resulting in godlessness (3:2–9), although the earlier warning is focused on counterspiritual—*demonic* and Satanic, it is averred!—teachings. Interestingly, as we saw earlier in the Letter to the Ephesians (§6.5), combating principalities and powers, a struggle not against flesh and blood per se (Eph. 6:12), nevertheless entails concrete social relations and ecclesial interactions in the Ephesian context, and these linkages remain pertinent in Timothy's case, stationed as he was in Ephesus (1 Tim. 1:3). The spirit's cautions concern turning spiritual vitality on its head to focus on material and carnal concerns like the forbiddance of marriage and abstention from foods (4:3–4). These false doctrines (6:20) foster an oppressive (disembodied) religiosity rather than enable a wholesome (embodied) spirituality.[118]

In 2 Timothy the spirit is associated with the deposit of faith within the hearts and lives of Christ's followers (see also 2 Cor. 3:1–6): "Hold to the standard of sound teaching that you have heard from me, in the faith and love that are in Christ Jesus. Guard the good treasure entrusted to you, with the help of the Holy Spirit living in us" (2 Tim. 1:13–14). Consistent with the earlier exhortation to "guard what has been entrusted to you" (1 Tim. 6:20), the call here to the younger apostolic apprentice is to be *unlike* "all who are in Asia [who] have turned away from me, including Phygelus and Hermogenes" (2 Tim. 1:15). Timothy should step instead into his role as leading minister in Paul's absence (2:1–2).[119] If this work will be difficult and challenging, the spirit is available and indeed within: "I remind you to rekindle the gift of God that is within you through the laying on of my hands; for God did not give us a spirit of cowardice, but rather a spirit of power and of love and of self-discipline" (1:6–7; cf. 1 Tim. 4:14).

Perhaps "all who are in Asia have turned away" from Paul because of the difficulty and contestedness of the mission in that Ephesian and surrounding

---

vindication by God (through his resurrection and exaltation)." I. Howard Marshall, "The Holy Spirit in the Pastoral Epistles and the Apostolic Fathers," in Stanton, Longenecker, and Barton, *Holy Spirit and Christian Origins*, 257–69, here 258. Cf. Brice L. Martin, "1 Timothy 3:15—A New Perspective," *EvQ* 85:2 (2013): 105–10.

118. See also Jerome D. Quinn, "The Holy Spirit in the Pastoral Epistles," in *Sin, Salvation, and the Spirit: Commemorating the Fiftieth Year of The Liturgical Press*, ed. Daniel Durken (Collegeville, MN: Liturgical Press, 1979), 345–68.

119. The sphere of the spirit's work in the pastoral letters concerns ecclesial leadership; so urges Paul Trebilco, "The Significance and Relevance of the Spirit in the Pastoral Epistles," in Stanton, Longenecker, and Barton, *Holy Spirit and Christian Origins*, 241–56.

context (see 2 Cor. 1:8). Later, we will have further opportunity to explore the more expansive area of Asia Minor, including that eastward from Ephesus, since the diaspora Jews of that entire region are the addressees of the letter of 1 Peter (§7.3). For the moment, we can recall the conflictedness of mission in the nearby Galatian and Colossian areas (see §§6.4, 6.7), even as we remember that any missiological theology emergent from Timothy's immediate Ephesian site must also recall what Luke says about Paul's ventures there (Acts 19 and 20:17–38) and anticipate that the spirit's call to this church as such is situated within the broader arc of the final biblical book (Rev. 2:1–7; see also §8.4). Against this broader New Testament backdrop, we will consider two important missiological realities—related to the role of women and the emergence of wealth—in light of the pneumatological admonitions of these letters.[120]

Within the context of the pneumatic warning about "deceitful spirits and teachings of demons," there is a further caution: "Have nothing to do with profane myths and old wives' tales" (1 Tim. 4:7). The latter might have been dismissed or overlooked if not for the palpable concern the author has regarding the women in the congregation and wider community. There is extensive regard for widows, both for their appropriate care and that they lead lives of godliness rather than being idle, gossipers, or busybodies (5:2–16). Readers are commanded to eschew all forms of last-days godlessness, the follow-up letter affirms, which include "those who make their way into households and captivate silly women, overwhelmed by their sins and swayed by all kinds of desires, who are always being instructed and can never arrive at a knowledge of the truth" (2 Tim. 3:6–7). Clearly, there is a local concern both for the behavior of women and for those who might otherwise mislead or take advantage of them, and all of this is certainly part of the broader situation within which Timothy is instructed not to allow women "to teach or to have authority over a man" (1 Tim. 2:12); instead, they will "be saved through childbearing, provided they continue in faith and love and holiness, with modesty" (2:15). Some have conjectured that the prevalence of Artemis as the "great" goddess of the Ephesians, mentioned as such four times in Luke's account (Acts 19:27–28, 34–35), has much to do with the challenges confronted by this young pastor and leader.[121] Surely the historical realities provide perspective

120. One of the very few missiological readings of the Timothean letters is Kevin Salisbury, "Paul's First Letter to Timothy: An Example of Missional Contextualization," *Colloquium* 44:1 (2012): 78–101; our perspective, of course, foregrounds the spirit's work.
121. Sharon Hodgin Gritz, *Paul, Women Teachers, and the Mother Goddess at Ephesus: A Study of 1 Timothy 2:9–15 in Light of the Religious and Cultural Milieu of the First Century* (Lanham, MD: University Press of America, 1991); the historical analysis is relevant, even if the conclusions defending it as normative for the church are less convincing (note: the author

on what otherwise appears as inordinate efforts to constrain the behavior of women. Our own approach reads from the pneumatological notice (1 Tim. 4:1) to the positive principle: "For everything created by God is good, and nothing is to be rejected, provided it is received with thanksgiving; for it is sanctified by God's word and by prayer" (4:4–5). If in Timothy the goal was to undercut deceitful doctrines like marriage forbiddance and foods abstention, the extrapolated missiological guideline affirms the contributions of women as sanctioned otherwise in scripture and receives their spirit-led ministerial and other efforts with thanksgiving and prayer.[122]

These two letters are concerned not only with the women of the congregation but also with what appears to be the congregational members' increasing affluence. There are masters and slaves (1 Tim. 6:1–2), although this is not exceptional across the early Christian communities. What is unique, it seems, is that among these class divisions are both "those who want to be rich" (6:9) and "those who in the present age are rich" (6:17).[123] The former are reprimanded: "For the love of money is a root of all kinds of evil" (6:10); and the latter are invited "to do good, to be rich in good works, generous, and ready to share" (6:18). These commendations are consistent with the exhortation to Timothy, that the ecclesial leader is "not a lover of money" and "not greedy for money" (3:3, 8). Instead, as already indicated, the spirit-filled minister and missionary (2 Tim. 1:14) embodies "the faith and love that are in Christ Jesus" (1:13).[124]

Asking about a Timothean missiology more conventionally will surely lift up the call for good works or deeds spread out in both letters (1 Tim. 2:10; 5:10; 2 Tim. 2:21; 3:17).[125] Our own pneumatological theology of mission, however, notes how the spirit warns against false teachings by providing

---

writes from and to a Southern Baptist Convention context that defends a traditionalist and complementarian account of male headship).

122. As put otherwise, then, we read these texts in ways that encourage "a Christian lifestyle that will maximize the mission witness both outside and within the Church as the believer's [women in this context] responsibility." Royce Gordon Gruenler, "The Mission-Lifestyle Setting of 1 Tim 2:8–15," *JETS* 41:2 (1998): 215–38, here 216.

123. See Gary C. Hoag, *Wealth in Ancient Ephesus and the First Letter to Timothy: Fresh Insights from "Ephesiaca" by Xenophon of Ephesus*, Bulletin for Biblical Research Supplements 11 (Winona Lake, IN: Eisenbrauns, 2015).

124. I have been aided here by Elsa Tamez, whose chap. 1, "The Rich and the Struggles for Power in the Christian Community," connects with her chap. 4, "Criteria for Leadership in the Struggles for Power," in *Struggle for Power in Early Christianity: A Study of the First Letter to Timothy*, trans. Gloria Kinsler (Maryknoll, NY: Orbis, 2007).

125. Chiao Ek Ho, "Mission in the Pastoral Epistles," in *Entrusted with the Gospel: Paul's Theology in the Pastoral Epistles*, ed. Andreas J. Köstenberger and Terry L. Wilder (Nashville: B&H Academic, 2010), 241–67.

alternative practices and by enabling emulation of the person of Jesus. Within the background Ephesian context, such a pneumatological reading also observes how spirit-filled living empowers witness to Jesus amid concrete public spaces crowded by other deities (Artemis in this case) and pressured by other conventions and ideologies (e.g., wealth). As already intimated, then, pneumatic perspectives missiologically understood are not spiritualistic or privitistic but public and political and economic.[126] There must be alignment of the inner spiritual life with the outer public performance. Our next and final Pauline section will clarify the apostle's theology of mission refracted pneumatologically.

6.10 Titus—Renewal in the Spirit: The "Crete-ability" of Mission

Aside from the letter's stipulations that it is from Paul, addressed to Titus, whom the former left at Crete (Titus 1:5), there is little help otherwise about when and from whence the letter was written.[127] And as with the epistles to Timothy, there is only one clear mention of the spirit. In the last part of this document, while urging Titus and his congregants toward good works commensurate with their redemption from paganism and its practices (Titus 3:1–4), the author is drawn to wonderment about Christian salvation: "He saved us, not because of any works of righteousness that we had done, but according to his mercy, through the water of rebirth and renewal by the Holy Spirit. This Spirit he poured out on us richly through Jesus Christ our Savior, so that, having been justified by his grace, we might become heirs according to the hope of eternal life" (3:5–7). Not only is this arguably an excellent synopsis of Pauline pneumatology,[128] it is also a clear articulation of soteriology in a triune direction: of God's saving work accomplished through Christ and the spirit.[129]

126. Coming from another angle, see Greg A. Couser, "'Prayer' and the Public Square: 1 Timothy 2:1–7 and Christian Political Engagement," in *New Testament Theology in Light of the Church's Mission: Essays in Honor of I. Howard Marshall*, ed. Jon C. Laansma, Grant R. Osborne, and Ray F. Van Neste (Eugene, OR: Cascade, 2011), 277–94.

127. Ronald A. Ward, *Commentary on 1 & 2 Timothy and Titus* (Waco: Word, 1974), 227.

128. See Robert W. Wall, "Salvation's Bath by the Spirit: A Study of Titus 3:5b–6 in Its Canonical Setting," in *The Spirit and Christ in the New Testament and Christian Theology: Essays in Honor of Max Turner*, ed. I. Howard Marshall, Volker Rabens, and Cornelis Bennema (Grand Rapids: Eerdmans, 2012), 198–212, here 199.

129. There is also an unfolding triune theology in the letter, beginning with God the truthful savior (Titus 1:2–3), opening up to "our great God and Savior, Jesus Christ" (2:13), and culminating with "God our Savior . . . [who] saved us . . . through the water of rebirth and renewal by the Holy Spirit . . . poured out on us richly through Jesus Christ our Savior" (3:4–6). I observed this

Intriguingly, this sole pneumatological reference in the letter is accompanied immediately by "the saying is sure" (Titus 3:8). It is one of five "faithful sayings" in the Pastoral Letters (the others being 1 Tim. 1:15; 3:1; 4:9; and 2 Tim. 2:11) that are both soteriological and christological.[130] In Titus, however, there is a further contextual element, one registered early on when the author seeks to identify the Judaizing opponents, like those in Galatia (see §6.4), confronted by his protégé. There, in describing these "rebellious people, idle talkers and deceivers" (Titus 1:10), he draws on an islandic folk saying, attributed historically to the mythic Epimenides (sixth century BCE), that "Cretans are always liars, vicious brutes, lazy gluttons" (1:12). This reputed "liar's paradox" is a well-known form of intellectual puzzle since the fourth-century-BCE philosopher Eubulides of Miletus. If a Cretan says all Cretans are liars, can this Cretan be believed or not? Such a saying had become an effective cultural stereotype and may well have prompted the alethic emphases in the letter's salutations, written thus: "for the sake of the faith of God's elect and *the knowledge of the truth* that is in accordance with godliness, in the hope of eternal life that *God, who never lies, promised* before the ages began" (1:1–2; emphasis added). Clearly, the saying by a Cretan that all Cretans are liars is a logically self-defeating one that contrasts with the true deity, who can never lie.[131]

Yet the irony of the saying incorporated into this missional letter is even more effective when we understand the point less as a discursive one about unbelieving untruth and Cretan dishonesty and more as a performative or pragmatic one about Christian truth and believing Cretan ethics and way of life.[132] If these unorthodox unbelievers are "those who reject the truth" (Titus 1:14), then when read in local Cretan context, the point is that, as one

---

trinitarian—or *triune*, consistent with the thrust of our explorations—dynamic through help from Aldred A. Genade, *Persuading the Cretans: A Text-Generated Persuasion Analysis of the Letter to Titus* (Eugene, OR: Wipf & Stock, 2011), who highlights these texts as the doctrinal core of the epistle.

130. See George W. Knight III, *The Faithful Sayings in the Pastoral Letters* (Grand Rapids: Baker, 1979).

131. Logically speaking, at least from a modern perspective, the citation of the liar's paradox is problematic if the letter is pseudonymous, and in that respect, the epistle reads more naturally if authentically Pauline; on the other hand, even if by one of Paul's circle of apprentices, ancient epistolary practices treated authorship not quite as moderns do, and may have been able to deploy such genres for their own exhortative or ideological purposes. For an argument along the latter lines vis-à-vis Titus, see John W. Marshall, "'I Left You in Crete': Narrative Deception and Social Hierarchy in the Letter to Titus," *JBL* 127:4 (2008): 781–803.

132. Anthony C. Thiselton, "The Logical Role of the Liar Paradox in Titus 1:12,13: A Dissent from the Commentaries in the Light of Philosophical and Logical Analysis," *BibInt* 2:2 (1994): 207–23.

scholar puts it, "true doctrine is accompanied by sound living," while "doctrinal error is accompanied by moral corruption."[133] Thus, the author urges
Titus and his parishioners both to heed sound doctrine and to enact moral
and righteous behavior (2:1–10).[134] More to the point, if unbelievers are said
to be untruthful, animalistic, and appetitive (1:12), then "the grace of God
has appeared, bringing salvation to all, training us to renounce impiety and
worldly passions, and in the present age to live lives that are self-controlled,
upright, and godly" (2:11–12). The threefold contrast is unmistakable, with
the threefold virtues, found also in the wider Hellenistic culture, brought
about by divine redemption.[135]

The sociohistorical mission context in Crete has further explanatory power
along two lines.[136] First, the call to moral and sanctified behavior is elaborated
in this letter as pertaining also to household norms, but this time delineated
in terms of age and gender (Titus 2:3–10) rather than in the usual orders
depicted elsewhere in the New Testament (cf. Eph. 5:21–6:9; Col. 3:18–4:1;
1 Tim. 2:1–15; 5:1–2; 6:1–2, 17–19; 1 Pet. 2:18–3:7). The reason might concern the fact that historically, on the island, children were separated by age
and gender for educational purposes and adult males ate together in certain
communal contexts. Second, our pneumatological reference—regarding "the
water of rebirth and renewal by the Holy Spirit"—makes sense also within
the island's Isis cult involving water and washing rituals. In short, the regen-
erative (this being a descriptive rather than technical theological usage) work
of the spirit can be received in this letter as contextually correlated with and
embedded in Titus's missional duties—that is, that of "appoint[ing] elders
in every town" (Titus 1:5).[137]

The larger point is to persuade the messianic Cretans that the work of the
spirit empowers—or ought to empower—their faithful discipleship in ways
that embody the truth of the gospel.[138] If the letter is premised on counter-

133. Reimer Faber, "'Evil Beasts, Lazy Gluttons': A Neglected Theme in the Epistle to Titus,"
WTJ 67 (2005): 135–45, here 141 and 145, respectively; see also Wolfgang Stegemann, "Anti-
Semitic and Racist Prejudices in Titus 1:10–16," in Brett, *Ethnicity and the Bible*, 271–94.

134. See also Abraham J. Malherbe, "Paraenesis in the Epistle to Titus," in Holladay et al.,
Light from the Gentiles, 1:407–30. Paraenesis refers to a style of moral exhortation deployed
by philosophers in the ancient world.

135. Reggie M. Kidd, "Titus as *Apologia*: Grace for Liars, Beasts, and Bellies," *Horizons
in Biblical Theology* 21:2 (1999): 185–209.

136. See George M. Wieland, "Roman Crete and the Letter to Titus," *NTS* 55:3 (2009):
338–54, esp. 340–44 and 349–51 for the two points, respectively.

137. Note also that Crete was known as "the island of a hundred towns." Homer, *Illiad*
2.649, in Wieland, "Roman Crete," 352.

138. This being the rhetorical objective of the letter, as argued by Genade, *Persuading the
Cretans*.

ing the irony of the liar's paradox, then the promise of salvation in Christ is no mere platitude but the trustworthy faithfulness of the spirit's saving and sanctifying work that enables creaturely devotion to good works (Titus 3:8).[139] Part of the contemporary challenge is that in a postcolonial context, truth claims are more often than not expressions of the will to power rather than the correspondence of speech with reality. Missional declarations are as likely to deploy sacred texts to underwrite and authorize so-called "mission" practices that benefit missionaries rather than support those whom missionaries are serving. The truth of the gospel, refracted through the Cretan context, is that the work of the spirit brings about the life of truth. Put alternatively, truth is not abstract but concrete, historic, embodied, and lived out. If Christian mission is to be credible in the present age, those who bear witness must testify in their bodies and not just by their words (1:8, 16; 2:7, 14; 3:1, 14). The message of the gospel in Crete so long ago may have been incredible indeed, and that was because the Cretan disciples of Jesus demonstrated they were not incredulous liars, neither perpetually nor occasionally. The saving work of the spirit thus confirms the promises of God against whatever competing half-truths or untruths.

The last point to be made is that the spirit given by God through Jesus Christ renews and revitalizes human animals also so that they are neither beastly nor gluttonous. Instead, as creatures saved and sanctified by the power of the spirit, they bear witness to "the blessed hope and the manifestation of the glory of our great God and Savior, Jesus Christ" (2:13). Thus, Pauline pneumatology and Pauline missiology are intertwined: the spirit poured out on all flesh in the last days heralds the day of the Lord and its righteousness to the ends of the earth.[140] Put otherwise, the pneumatological connection here is missional just because it is soteriological, and the spirit's saving work has missional implications, even as the spirit's mission is soteriologically oriented.[141] Although isolated on an island off the beaten path, the truth of the gospel resounds because the spirit cleanses, transforms, and animates human lives in the image of God in Christ.

139. This movement from words to actions is one from irony to seriousness, as described by Thomas G. Long, *1 & 2 Timothy and Titus*, Belief: A Theological Commentary on the Bible (Louisville: Westminster John Knox, 2016), 263–67.

140. See Charles L. Holman, "Titus 3.5–6: A Window on Worldwide Pentecost," *JPT* 8 (1996): 53–62.

141. For further exegetical treatment of the pneumatology-soteriology interconnection of this Titus text, see George M. Wieland, *The Significance of Salvation: A Study of Salvation Language in the Pastoral Epistles* (Waynesboro, GA: Paternoster, 2006), chap. 19.

Discussion Questions

1. The theme of power-in-weakness is pervasive in especially the authentic letters of Paul (e.g., Corinthians and Philippians). How might Christian witness emanating from such a posture be different from the colonial versions, and how might it be more effective and representative of the spirit's missional work in our present late modern historical period?

2. The issues concerning Jews and gentiles receive more substantive theological and pneumatological treatment in Romans and Ephesians especially, and we are given personal glimpses into Paul's relationships with gentile believers and coworkers in our discussion of Colossians. What takeaways are available for us in thinking about and practicing Christian witness across ethnic and racial lines in our contemporary, especially North American, culture marked by white (European-American) normativity?

3. Paul is no doubt a church planter and, in that sense, the most exemplary of the earliest messianic missionaries working as a minority (Jewish) person within a majority (Roman) culture, while he also wrote about and reflected upon the spirit-filled life. How might we imitate his theology and practice in order to be faithful witnesses to the gospel two thousand years later in very different imperial contexts?

7

The Witness of the Eternal Spirit

Catholic Mission

Introduction

We have now come to that portion of the New Testament that remains among the most neglected, what since the eighteenth century has been called the Catholic Letters (related to their reception by the church ecumenical in the early Christian centuries),[1] along with the book of Hebrews, which has not necessarily been so overlooked. This relative disregard for the former is perhaps not surprising. On the one hand, the Gospels concern the central person of Christian faith (Jesus Christ), and the letters of Paul cumulatively constitute a large portion of the Christian testament, even as the figure of the apostle himself may have been as formative for the origins of the Christian faith as, if not even more than, Jesus.[2] On the other hand, most of these are among the shortest writings in the New Testament. Yet James, Peter, and John—this is the order in which they appear in Galatians 2:9 and which has long been believed as undergirding the canonical order—were well known as the leading triumvirate of Jesus's disciples, even as Jude was believed to be related to

1. See Ralph P. Martin, *New Testament Foundations: A Guide for Christian Students*, rev. ed., 2 vols. (Grand Rapids: Eerdmans, 1986), 2:329. Thanks to Carl Toney for this reference, including pointing to his own editorial contributions to Ralph P. Martin and Carl N. Toney, *New Testament Foundations: An Introduction for Students* (Eugene, OR: Cascade, 2018).
2. As hinted at by the title of David Wenham's book *Paul: Follower of Jesus or Founder of Christianity?* (Grand Rapids: Eerdmans, 1995), even if the answer, reasoned over four hundred pages of argumentation, affirms the first part of the subtitle rather than the second.

James. But insofar as these name connections have also never guaranteed the popularity of their associated writings, the sheer bulk of the Pauline legacy continues to overwhelm these otherwise comparatively marginal voices.

Still, this chapter will treat the homilies of Hebrews through the Epistle of Jude,[3] the Johannine Letters excepted. Hebrews and the General Letters have historically been discussed together,[4] so that needs little apology. Our discussion, however, will skip over the Johannine Epistles, deferring this to chapter 8 for reasons partly laid out vis-à-vis the Fourth Gospel (see the introduction to chap. 5). Yet gathering even these five documents together poses questions of coherence for this chapter. For one, Hebrews is predominantly theological, while James is pastoral and, more frankly, practical. Second, Hebrews is directly concerned with negotiating Jewish-Christian identity matters, while the others seem to embrace a Jewish-Christian milieu. Third, 2 Peter and Jude are apocalyptic in ways that the others are not. Yet insofar as these writings are concerned with intra-ecclesial matters,[5] they may have much in common.

That Hebrews and the General Epistles are intra-ecclesially focused, however, may raise pointed questions for our purposes. Specifically, if we grant that these are writings devoted to navigating intracommunal issues, they are then not missiological in any traditional sense of this notion, at least not in the way in which the modern missionary movement has understood mission in terms of a sending or going out to an unbelieving world. Yet to argue this way is to assume that the modern missionary paradigm is normative. Instead, why not read these sermons and letters in their missional context at least as self-understood against the first-century Mediterranean backdrop? In other words, why not read James amid its Jewish diaspora realities and 1 Peter as unfolding within the western Asian region as these letters situate themselves? Further, why not read 2 Peter and Jude as missiological exactly in their concerns about how to understand for themselves the meaning of divine judgment on "others" at the end of time? If so, even these apocalyptically dominated letters might be found to have missiological significance, not based on modernist notions of sending and going, but based on apostolic considerations of how to understand the time of the divine spirit in anticipation of the coming judgment.

3. For discussion of these New Testament writings as homilies (except the Petrine Letters), see Ben Witherington III, *Letters and Homilies for Jewish Christians: A Socio-Rhetorical Commentary on Hebrews, James and Jude* (Downers Grove, IL: IVP Academic, 2007), 11–12.

4. E.g., Karen H. Jobes, *Letters to the Church: A Survey of Hebrews and the General Epistles* (Grand Rapids: Zondervan, 2011).

5. For this argument, at least vis-à-vis the Catholic Letters, see J. Daryl Charles, "Interpreting the General Epistles," in *Interpreting the New Testament: Essays on Methods and Issues*, ed. David Alan Black and David S. Dockery (Nashville: Broadman & Holman, 2001), 433–56.

Our question is this: How might we be able to discern afresh missional strategies from adhering to these documents on their own terms, especially as guided by pneumatological motifs, rather than attempting to import our own modern constructions and categories of assessment onto documents from two thousand years ago? I suggest that it is surely the pneumatological lens that helps us to comprehend the missiological praxis of engaging others—cultural, ethnic, and theological others—within and outside the community of faith. At the least, Hebrews and the Catholic Epistles open up to the possibility of reenvisioning Christian witness in a theologically, practically, and temporally informed manner, and this is of relevance not only for the earliest messianists but also for those of us seeking Christian faithfulness in a post-mission era.

7.1 Hebrews—The Spirit Witnesses: Sustaining Mission outside the Gate

The *Sitz im Leben* of Hebrews remains contested and obscure, so it is difficult to discern the contextual circumstances amid which its pneumatological claims were originally read or heard. So when we begin at the literary level, the foremost thing to be said about the pneumatology of this book is that the spirit speaks, first through the scriptures (the Old Testament writings), in order to lead and guide the new people of God into their eschatological rest.[6] Translated missiologically, this means that the spirit's work is to bring about God's promised salvation, at least in the there and then of the anticipated parousia, but also in the here and now of the pilgrimage of history. Let's see how this unfolds.

To begin, on at least two occasions, the spirit is attributed with speaking in and through the writings of ancient Israel. Initially (Heb. 3:7) the spirit introduces the voice of the psalmist in warning the people to hearken to Yahweh's invitation to enter into the promised land of rest or be consigned to the wilderness wandering (3:7–11; cf. Ps. 95:7–11).[7] Later, adopting the same strategy of quoting scripture, but now also explicitly addressing the contemporary audience, "the Holy Spirit *also testifies to us*" (Heb. 10:15; emphasis added), to assure the readers regarding the divine witness to the

6. Thus, we can understand the spirit "as eschatological orator." Martin Emmrich, *Pneumatological Concepts in the Epistle to the Hebrews: Amtscharisma, Prophet, and Guide of the Eschatological Exodus* (Lanham, MD: University Press of America, 2003), 28.

7. Hence, in this text the spirit not only speaks (via scripture) but also acts (to warn!); see Martin Emmrich, "*Pneuma* in Hebrews: Prophet and Interpreter," *WTJ* 63 (2002): 55–71, esp. 56–60.

new covenant (10:15–17; cf. Jer. 31:33–34).[8] These pneumatological references emphasize that the spirit spoke before and now speaks again. Such is an important point for a book that relies so heavily on allusions to and quotations from the Old Testament (a sampling includes Heb. 1:5–13; 2:12–13; 3:15; 4:3, 5, 7; 5:5–6; 6:13–14; 7:17, 21; 8:8–12; 10:5–7, 16–17, 37–38; 12:5–6; 13:6).[9] The present message is thus consistent with and extends from the prior word. That this is the same divine breath further warrants consideration of the spirit's unending nature, whose characterization appears in the middle of the lengthy "word of exhortation" (13:22) in Hebrews: "If the blood of goats and bulls . . . sanctifies those who have been defiled . . . , how much more will the blood of Christ, who through the eternal Spirit offered himself without blemish to God, purify our conscience from dead works to worship the living God!" (9:13–14).[10] It is the spirit's eternality that enables the speaking of the earlier prophetic words, that achieves the ultimate sacrificial salvation of Christ, and that then (and now) brings the people of God into their intended rest.[11]

Second, then, the spirit's guidance into the respite achieved and made available in Christ works with the pilgrimage theme in Hebrews in ways that converge with the letter's missiological strands.[12] Literarily, again, the sojourner theme across the book, culminating in members of the "hall of faith" in the eleventh chapter not receiving what was promised but still searching for and anticipating the promised repose, followed by the call to "run with perseverance the race that is set before us" (Heb. 12:1) toward "the city of the living God, the heavenly Jerusalem, . . . innumerable angels in festal gathering, and . . . the assembly of the firstborn who are enrolled in heaven" (12:22–23), urges consideration of the missionary venture as a trek in search

8. John R. Levison, "A Theology of the Spirit in the Letter to the Hebrews," *CBQ* 78 (2016): 90–110.

9. For more on the spirit and scripture in Hebrews, see Steve Motyer, "The Spirit in Hebrews: No Longer Forgotten?," in *The Spirit and Christ in the New Testament and Christian Theology: Essays in Honor of Max Turner*, ed. I. Howard Marshall, Volker Rabens, and Cornelis Bennema (Grand Rapids: Eerdmans, 2012), 213–27, esp. 222–26.

10. Heb. 9:14 also has been interpreted christologically rather than pneumatologically, as in Joseph F. McFadyen, *Through Eternal Spirit: A Study of Hebrews, James, and I Peter* (London: James Clarke, 1925), 144–46; but see Jeffrey S. Lamp, *The Greening of Hebrews? Ecological Readings in the Letter to the Hebrews* (Eugene, OR: Pickwick, 2012); in chap. 5, "A Whispered Voice in the Choir: Toward an Ecological Pneumatology in Hebrews," Lamp treats 9:14 pneumatologically, although his discussion is less directly focused on the spirit and given more to elaborating on the adjective "eternal" vis-à-vis his environmental theological concerns.

11. See Martin Emmrich, "'*Amtscharisma*': Through the Eternal Spirit (Hebrews 9:14)," *BBR* 12:1 (2002): 17–32.

12. William G. Johnsson, "The Pilgrimage Motif in the Book of Hebrews," *JBL* 97:2 (1978): 239–51.

of eschatological salvation.[13] Theologically, and in parallel venue, missiologists have suggested that the movement throughout the book climaxes "outside the city gate" (13:12), both in terms of Christ's suffering and passion "outside the camp" (13:13) and in his followers' quest for the coming—as opposed to earthly—city (13:14). But there is also a comprehensible countercultural, counter-imperial, and counter-establishment mission of God (as opposed to the mission of colonialism or of Christendom) implicit in this allusion.[14] In the present twenty-first-century context, mission ought to proceed not from the institutional centers of the church but from its margins. It is not just that the poor and oppressed should not merely be the recipients of mission but that the church's mission can be better mobilized apart from the paternalism of a dominant Euro-American-centric missiological imagination.[15] If Christ accomplished his mission outside the gate of the earthly city, then also the spirit will carry out the mission of God today on the edges of the world's structures and conventions, including outside the institutional forms of the church to the degree that such have been domesticated by the world's values and commitments. In this way, the mission of the spirit is to escort the people of God away from death and destruction imposed by this world's mechanisms and toward life and salvation given in Jesus the anointed Messiah.

But, third, it is indeed for this reason that the spirit is not only courier but also admonisher. The spirit does this both positively and, if one wills, negatively. On the one hand, it is through signs, wonders, miracles, and gifts (Heb. 2:4) of the holy spirit that weary travelers are encouraged to "pay greater attention to what we have heard, so that we do not drift away" (2:1). On the other hand, those who have "shared in the Holy Spirit" but then fail to persevere are warned: you will not be able to finish the course (6:4–6).[16] "How much worse punishment do you think will be deserved by those who have spurned the Son of God, profaned the blood of the covenant by which they were sanctified, and outraged the Spirit of grace?" (10:29), the author

13. Nicholas Alexander Venditti highlights the theme of being migrant aliens and strangers in this world as central to the missiology of Hebrews. "The God Who Speaks: A Comparative Study of Mission Paradigms in Hebrews, Vatican II, and Liberation Theologies" (PhD diss., Fuller Theological Seminary School of World Mission, 1998), chap. 10.

14. See Edwin A. Schick, "Priestly Pilgrims: Mission Outside the Camp in Hebrews," *CurTM* 16 (1989): 372–76; cf. David G. Forney, "To the One Outside the Gate: A Missional Approach to Polity," *Journal of Religious Leadership* 5:1–2 (2006): 45–78.

15. Orlando Costas, *Christ outside the Gate: Mission beyond Christendom* (Eugene, OR: Wipf & Stock, 2005).

16. Martin Emmrich writes, "Disobedience was believed to result in the forfeiture of the Spirit's presence" (cf. Acts 5:32, which says that the spirit is "given to those who obey" God). "Hebrews 6:4–6—Again! (A Pneumatological Inquiry)," *WTJ* 65 (2003): 83–95, here 94.

Catholicity and Ecclesiality
The Spirit's Testimony to the Missio Dei

Bitrus A. Sarma, associate professor of biblical studies and provost of ECWA Theological Seminary, Kagoro, Nigeria

The *missio spiritus* is fascinating and unpredictable. We have here a new vista, a missional reading of the Catholic Letters that, given their ecclesiastical nature, represents a significant shift from conventional missiology. Such an uncharted perspective invites us to comprehend mission beyond the modern missionary paradigm of sending and going. A better understanding is that the Catholic Letters can be illuminated by pneumatological motifs and be read in their missional context from their first-century backdrop. Ecclesial, communal, and social witness is possible through the divine spirit. The new missional angle is that these letters present the gospel of grace as well as judgment for those who reject the message of salvation. Similarly, they carry the pneumatological emblem as the spirit "testifies to us" (Heb. 10:15). Therefore, their pneumatological message and missional focus are unmistakable.

demands! These are certainly difficult texts that have exercised interpreters and commentators over the centuries. But if our task at present cannot be to offer up any definitive resolution, it can provide some missiological perspective. If the mission of the spirit is to conduct a fatigued and meandering—even hard-hearted (3:8, 10, 12, 15; 4:7)!—people from the wasteland of history to the promised city "whose architect and builder is God" (11:10), then they need the firmest form of encouragement and exhortation.[17]

But in reality the ancient Israelites were not able to enter into the promised rest—the land of Canaan—on their own, on account of either their conventional (priestly and ritual) framework or their sacrificial offerings.[18] Specifically, the "Holy Spirit indicates that the way into the sanctuary has not yet been

17. The threat is made not by insiders to outsiders peering in but, analogously, by a generous benefactor to his clientele, exhorting them to perseverance; see David A. deSilva, "Exchanging Favor for Wrath: Apostasy in Hebrews and Patron-Client Relationships," *JBL* 115:1 (1996): 91–116.
18. Jason W. Whitlark argues that a more pessimistic anthropology (of the postexilic Hebrew prophets) underlies much of this letter. *Enabling Fidelity to God: Perseverance in Hebrews in Light of the Reciprocity Systems of the Ancient Mediterranean World* (Milton Keynes, UK: Paternoster, 2008), esp. 103–25.

disclosed as long as the first tent is still standing" (Heb. 9:8). Instead, what is
needed is a new covenant, one that works not from without but from within.
Thus, the spirit opens up the way through Christ (9:9–14), weaving this path
into the minds of the people and inserting such into their hearts (8:10). The
author of this letter is here drawing from the prophet Jeremiah (31:31–34),
the same text that, as noted above, is repeated shortly, albeit not warranted
pneumatologically (Heb. 10:15–17). But Jeremiah's contemporary, Ezekiel
(as we saw in part 1 of this book), indicated such a work could only be accomplished by the breath of Yahweh (e.g., Ezek. 36:26–27; see §4.5 above).
So, whereas the mission of God is to reconcile humanity to deity by providing
passageway into the holy of holies—effectively into the divine presence—such
entry is achieved and realized only by the spirit.[19]

But where specifically is the spirit leading? A surface reading of Hebrews
might suggest an otherworldly destination—for example, a "heavenly calling"
(Heb. 3:1), a heavenly country (11:16), or a "heavenly Jerusalem" (12:22). Yet
the gifts of the spirit (2:4) are at work in anticipation of an arriving or "coming
world" (2:5). Hence, carried by the spirit, we participate in the divine mission
by approaching toward (10:22) and "receiving [present tense] a kingdom that
cannot be shaken" (12:28), one in which our possessions are "more lasting"
(10:34).[20] This is not to deny the heavenly character of the divine salvation,
but it is to resist comprehending such in exclusively spiritual or post-worldly
or otherworldly terms. Nevertheless, we cannot persevere in the divine mission
across this eschatological thoroughfare—in this time between the times of the
first and second coming of Jesus—unless we are preserved and empowered by
the spirit.[21] So, while en route, the breath of God accompanies us continuously
beyond the gate and nourishes us exhausted voyagers.

7.2   James—Redeeming the Missionary Spirit:
Wisdom-Work-Witness

The outside-the-gate theme carried over into James is signaled in the first
verse: "James, a servant of God and of the Lord Jesus Christ, To the twelve

19. Jon C. Laansma, "Hebrews and the Mission of the Earliest Church," in *New Testament
Theology in Light of the Church's Mission: Essays in Honor of I. Howard Marshall*, ed. Jon C.
Laansma, Grant R. Osborne, and Ray F. Van Neste (Eugene, OR: Cascade, 2011), 327–46, here 344.
20. See the discussion about "realized eschatology" in Witherington, *Letters and Homilies*,
347–51.
21. Thus, the spirit is "the one whose very presence and reception testifies to the inauguration of the new covenant dispensation." David M. Allen, "'The Forgotten Spirit': A Pentecostal
Reading of the Letter to the Hebrews?," *JPT* 18 (2009): 51–66, here 63.

tribes in the Dispersion" (James 1:1). One of the reputed leaders in the Jerusalem church was James (Acts 15:13; 21:18; cf. Gal. 2:9), and if this is the
same individual whose letter bears that name and that we are reading here,
then he is writing beyond Jerusalem and Judea, beyond Palestine even, to
Jewish followers of Jesus dispersed across the Roman Empire. These would
have once been migrants, now in their second or later generation of existence,
assimilated more or less within just about "every nation under heaven" (Acts
2:5). They are not missionaries in the strict modern sense,[22] but insofar as they
are "brothers and sisters . . . [who] really believe in our glorious Lord Jesus
Christ" (James 2:1), they bear witness, appropriate or not!

There is but a sliver of pneumatology in James, hanging literally by an
interpretive thread. In the broader context of urging these diaspora Jewish
messianists to cease quarreling enviously among themselves (James 3:13–4:3),
James writes, "Adulterers! Do you not know that friendship with the world
is enmity with God? Therefore whoever wishes to be a friend of the world
becomes an enemy of God. Or do you suppose that it is for nothing that the
scripture says, 'God yearns jealously for the spirit that he has made to dwell in
us'?" (4:4–5). Some interpreters argue that since the scripture clearly referred
to in the next verse (4:6) comes from Proverbs (3:34) and does not refer to
the divine breath, the reference here is to the human spirit rather than the
holy spirit.[23] On the other hand, the saying itself is identified as of scriptural
origin, and it connects not directly to the Tanakh but to the apocryphal *Book
of Eldad and Modad*—whose names we recognize from the book of Numbers
(see §1.5)—originally written in Hebrew (ca. 280–79 BCE), even if James is
"quoting" from *The Shepherd of Hermas*, a Greek translation.[24] When the
wider context of countering creaturely enviousness is taken into consideration,
a plausible translation could be "The Spirit [or spirit] God made to dwell in
us abhors envy."[25] The important point for our purposes is the divine interface

22. The few missional readings of James are less systematically missiological than thematic
applications (e.g., Sunniva Gylver focuses on contemporary relevance in Scandinavia in light
of migration from the global South; "Reading James in Oslo: Reflections on Text, Mission,
and Preaching," *CurTM* 41:6 [2014]: 404–11), which is to be expected given the nature of this
paraenesis or collection of ethical sayings within a wisdom frame; I will call attention to other
missional considerations of this document as we proceed.

23. Thus, it could be translated "The [human] spirit, which [God] caused to dwell in us,
inordinately desires." J. William Johnston, "James 4:5 and the Jealous Spirit," *BSac* 170 (2013):
344–60, here 345 (brackets original).

24. For details, see Richard Bauckham, "The Spirit of God in Us Loathes Envy: James
4:5," in *The Holy Spirit and Christian Origins: Essays in Honor of James D. G. Dunn*, ed.
Graham N. Stanton, Bruce W. Longenecker, and Stephen C. Barton (Grand Rapids: Eerdmans,
2004), 270–81, esp. 279–81.

25. Bauckham, "Spirit of God," 278.

with the human spirit: rather than our desires being focused on our neighbors' possessions, our devotion ought to be directed toward God, who, by his spirit or otherwise, in any case intensely wishes for communion with us.[26]

This divine-human spirit interrelation is the basis for the call to humility (James 4:6–10), to which the author segues via the quotation from Proverbs: "But he gives all the more grace; therefore it says, 'God opposes the proud, but gives grace to the humble'" (4:6). Drawing from the Wisdom literature of ancient Israel in this case is consistent with the broader thrust of James's message, especially with his association of wisdom with the dispositions needed to counteract "bitter envy and selfish ambition" (3:14).[27] The overall message of James is thus framed as one in quest of wisdom: "If any of you is lacking in wisdom, ask God, who gives to all generously and ungrudgingly, and it will be given you" (1:5). In other words, alignment of our spirits with the divine, indeed with the holy spirit, puts us on the path of wisdom and enables us to comport ourselves appropriately before God.[28] This is not to pneumatologize wisdom, not least in relation to James,[29] but it is to recognize that to be open to wisdom from above is to be better positioned to be divinely graced with the humility that is part and parcel of the promises of God.

Yet wisdom in James is not first and foremost cognitive but refers to practical know-how, activity, and behavior. Faith is not merely intellectual but involves works (James 2:14–26). This is not, however, to pit faith against works or vice versa, as those in the Reformation tradition might be inclined to do following Luther, who dismissed James as being inconsistent with the Pauline teaching of salvation by grace through faith rather than works. Instead, when we consider that James was writing as a Jew for other Jewish messianists, and especially amid thousands of believing Jews who were "all zealous for the

26. "The sense then is that, like a parent, God jealously and protectively longs for our human heart, for the very spirit that God put in us to be loyal to God." Witherington, *Letters and Homilies*, 515.

27. By extension, if the Wisdom literature of ancient Israel allows for a missional and interreligious dialogue with the wisdom religions of East and South Asia (see our discussion of Ecclesiastes above, §3.5), then the wisdom of James might also provide a bridge for interfaith mission in the present time; along this bridge, travel with Anglican theologian John P. Keenan, *The Wisdom of James: Parallels with Mahayana Buddhism* (New York: Newman, 2005).

28. Mariam J. Kamell correlates the spirit with Galatians and wisdom with James, but in the present context it is also appropriate to connect the spirit and James. See Kamell, "Life in the Spirit and Life in Wisdom: Reading Galatians and James as a Dialogue," in *Galatians and Christian Theology: Justification, the Gospel, and Ethics in Paul's Letter*, ed. Mark W. Elliott et al. (Grand Rapids: Baker Academic, 2014), 353–63.

29. As resisted by William R. Baker, who argues negatively in response to the question in the subtitle of his essay "Searching for the Holy Spirit in the Epistle of James: Is 'Wisdom' Equivalent?," *TynBul* 59:2 (2008): 293–315.

law" (Acts 21:20), then we can accept that, like Matthew, James comprehends messianic discipleship as fulfilling the law (Matt. 5:17).[30] Thus, if the law is perfect (James 1:25), then the task is to "really fulfill the royal law according to the scripture, 'You shall love your neighbor as yourself'" (2:8; cf. Lev. 19:18). Missiologically speaking, to be of messianic faith and to love the neighbor is to meet the needs of the most vulnerable and needy: "Religion that is pure and undefiled before God, the Father, is this: to care for orphans and widows in their distress, and to keep oneself unstained by the world" (James 1:27). This is consistent with the law of Israel that also required care for orphans and widows (e.g., Deut. 10:18; 14:29; 16:11; 24:17–21; 26:12–19), even as such is certainly also central to any missiological reading of James.[31]

The spirit of humility and wisdom is thus also the spirit of missional care for the poor, oppressed, and marginalized. James is particularly exercised about injustices relating to the haves and the have-nots.[32] Messianists ought not to privilege the affluent who are exploiters (James 2:1–7) but to embrace "the poor in the world" that God has chosen "to be heirs of the kingdom that he has promised" (2:5). More specifically, the rich are excoriated, "The wages of the laborers who mowed your fields, which you kept back by fraud, cry out, and the cries of the harvesters have reached the ears of the Lord of hosts. You have lived on the earth in luxury and in pleasure; you have fattened your hearts in a day of slaughter. You have condemned and murdered the righteous one, who does not resist you" (5:4–6). Unlike wealth that rots and gold and silver that corrode (5:2–3; cf. 1:10–11), wisdom and humility enable recognition that our lives are like "a mist that appears for a little while and then vanishes" (4:14), and that therefore our earthly gains are hardly the basis on which our legacies can securely rest. Thus, James warns his readers in no uncertain words: "The Judge is standing at the doors!" (5:9).[33] Messianists are called to be patient and persevering (5:7, 10–11), and indeed, cultivation of such dispositions configures them with the divine spirit who works to draw them to himself.

---

30. For more on James in relation to the law, see Patrick J. Hartin, *James of Jerusalem: Heir to Jesus of Nazareth* (Collegeville, MN: Liturgical Press, 2004), 95–99.

31. Mariam Kamell, "James 1:27 and the Church's Call to Mission and Morals," *Crux* 46:4 (2010): 15–22.

32. See Elsa Tamez, *The Scandalous Message of James: Faith without Works Is Dead*, trans. John Eagleson (New York: Crossroad, 1990).

33. See Stephan Joubert, who focuses on the letter's call to justice and community in "*Homo reciprocus* No More: The 'Missional' Nature of Faith in James," in *Sensitivity towards Outsiders: Exploring the Dynamic Relationship between Mission and Ethics in the New Testament and Early Christianity*, ed. Jakobus (Kobus) Kok, Tobias Nicklas, Dieter T. Roth, and Christopher M. Hays, WUNT 2/364 (Tübingen: Mohr Siebeck, 2014), 382–400.

"God yearns jealously·for the spirit that he has made to dwell in us," James recalls from Israel's earlier literary tradition. Our pneumatological perspective suggests that the divine breath yearns for and calls human breathers in diasporic venue to seek after wisdom and thereby receive the gracious humility that allows faith to unfold in just deeds of ecclesial, communal, and social witness. No slavish adherence to prior traditions, this is rather the living dynamic of response to the ever-whirling breath of God. On our own strength, we will follow our instincts and appetites (James 4:1) rather than respond to the call to receive humility and wisdom; we will look out for our own gain and cater to those who have made it according to the standards of this world rather than live in solidarity with the poor and oppressed; we will perhaps even claim to be of faith but then be powerless to manifest our faith in our lives and deeds. But the divine spirit persists within us, seeking to redeem our wayward lives for the mission of God. Wherever we might find ourselves in a world of migration and diaspora, it is always time to embrace divine wisdom and align our faith with our ways of life in order to bear witness to the Lord Jesus Christ.

7.3   1 Peter—Sanctifying the Suffering Spirit: Mission in Diaspora

The address of this letter begins, "Peter, an apostle of Jesus Christ, To the exiles of the Dispersion in Pontus, Galatia, Cappadocia, Asia, and Bithynia, who have been chosen and destined by God the Father and sanctified by the Spirit to be obedient to Jesus Christ and to be sprinkled with his blood" (1 Pet. 1:1–2).[34] Assuming Peter was martyred in the mid-sixth decade CE as tradition informs us makes it plausible that this letter was written to these churches in western Asia or Asia Minor (what is today the western portion of Turkey) given what we know about how the Christian mission had expanded to that part of the Mediterranean world by that time. More important is that the epistle is addressed not just to Jewish messianists who lived in this region (what is suggested by "exiles of the Dispersion"; cf. also 1:17) but also to gentile followers of Jesus who now found themselves *in* but not *of* the Roman world (identified as "aliens and exiles" called to "abstain from the desires of the flesh that wage war against the soul" later; 2:11).[35]

34. Elsewhere I have considered 1 Peter from a Southeast Asian and Asian American perspective: "Diasporic Discipleship from West Asia through Southeast Asia and Beyond: A Dialogue with 1 Peter," *AsJT* 32:2 (October 2018): 3–21; my comments here are a missiological extension and development of those ideas.

35. Christoph Stenschke focuses on the gentile converts in "Reading First Peter in the Context of Early Christian Mission," *TynBul* 60:1 (2009): 107–26.

Even if there is a fundamental spiritual dimension to such diasporic existence, the sociopolitical and religio-cultural aspects of exilic life ought not to be minimized.[36] The author's characterization suggests that the messianic way of life will be different if not difficult: "But you are a chosen race, a royal priesthood, a holy nation, God's own people, in order that you may proclaim the mighty acts of him who called you out of darkness into his marvelous light" (2:9).

The difficulties come with the suffering experienced by this exilic community. As mentioned repeatedly (1 Pet. 1:11; 2:19; 4:12–13, 19; 5:1, 9), these western Asians were being treated unjustly—"for doing good" even (3:17)!—by their unbelieving neighbors. No doubt the hostilities that these believers were experiencing also provided them with the opportunity, unwelcomed as such might have been, to bear distinct witness to their persecutors.[37] One passage exhorts the recipients of the letter in this way:

> Beloved, do not be surprised at the fiery ordeal that is taking place among you to test you, as though something strange were happening to you. But rejoice insofar as you are sharing Christ's sufferings, so that you may also be glad and shout for joy when his glory is revealed. If you are reviled for the name of Christ, you are blessed, because the spirit of glory, which is the Spirit of God, is resting on you. But let none of you suffer as a murderer, a thief, a criminal, or even as a mischief maker. Yet if any of you suffers as a Christian, do not consider it a disgrace, but glorify God because you bear this name. For the time has come for judgment to begin with the household of God. (4:12–17)

There is a distinctive triune ethos to this passage that makes explicit the missional aspects of suffering and communicates that perseverance in suffering for the sake of Christ to the glory of the Father comes pneumatically, by the spirit.[38]

This brings us back to the initial address of the letter, which specifies in a similar triune manner that the Jesus path toward the Father is achieved by the sanctifying work of the spirit. The spirit of holiness purifies these exilic believers amid the struggles of their diasporic lives always in anticipation of

36. See Shively T. J. Smith, *Strangers to Family: Diaspora and 1 Peter's Invention of God's Household* (Waco: Baylor University Press, 2016).

37. For more on suffering in mission and mission in light of suffering, particularly in 1 Peter, see Andreas J. Köstenberger, "Mission in the General Epistles," in *Mission in the New Testament: An Evangelical Approach*, ed. William J. Larkin Jr. and Joel F. Williams, American Society of Missiology Series 27 (Maryknoll, NY: Orbis, 1998), 189–206, esp. 200–206.

38. Hidalgo B. Garcia, "Missiology: Some Reflections from Asian Contexts," *CTJ* 44 (2009): 94–107.

the coming glory (also 1 Pet. 1:15–16).[39] Thus, the prophets of old foresaw even the salvation of these on the western Asian margins through "the Spirit of Christ [who] within them [the Old Testament prophetic writers] indicated when it [the Spirit] testified in advance to the sufferings destined for Christ and the subsequent glory. It was revealed to them that they were serving not themselves but you [the recipients of this Petrine letter], in regard to the things that have now been announced to you through those who brought you good news by the Holy Spirit sent from heaven—things into which angels long to look!" (1:11–12). In other words, the spirit sanctifies or sets apart the elect people of God for the salvation that is to come. Theirs is "an inheritance that is imperishable, undefiled, and unfading, kept in heaven for you" (1:4), even as they experience trials in the present.[40]

What then is involved in spirit-inspired and spirit-empowered diasporic witness by a marginal group of Jesus followers?[41] In brief, they are exhorted as follows: "Conduct yourselves honorably among the Gentiles, so that, though they malign you as evildoers, they may see your honorable deeds and glorify God when he comes to judge" (1 Pet. 2:12). More expansively put, "For the Lord's sake accept the authority of every human institution, whether of the emperor as supreme, or of governors, as sent by him to punish those who do wrong and to praise those who do right. For it is God's will that by doing right you should silence the ignorance of the foolish. As servants of God, live as free people, yet do not use your freedom as a pretext for evil. Honor everyone. Love the family of believers. Fear God. Honor the emperor" (2:13–17).

Hence, resident aliens ought to be accused, if at all, only for doing good works.[42] It is not that verbal witness is discouraged, but even such ought to be appropriately conducted: "Always be ready to make your defense to anyone who demands from you an account of the hope that is in you; yet do it with

39. Joel B. Green, "Faithful Witness in the Diaspora: The Holy Spirit and the Exiled People of God according to 1 Peter," in Stanton, Longenecker, and Barton, *Holy Spirit and Christian Origins*, 282–95.

40. 1 Pet. 3:18–19 and 4:6 can be read as referring to the spiritual dimension more generally or to life in the holy spirit more specifically, but we do not need to resolve this matter for our missiological purposes. Years ago I devoted three months of undergraduate study to this passage: "Persevering through 1 Peter" (Hermeneutics BI107 thesis, Bethany College, Santa Cruz, California, fall semester 1984); cf. Andrew J. Bandstra, "'Making Proclamation to the Spirits in Prison': Another Look at 1 Peter 3:19," *CTJ* 38 (2003): 120–24.

41. Dan Devadatta begins to respond to this question, albeit not foregrounding the spirit's work as in our treatment. "Strangers but Not Strange: A New Mission Situation for the Church (1 Peter 1:1–2 and 17–25)," in *Confident Witness—Changing World: Rediscovering the Gospel in North America*, ed. Craig Van Gelder (Grand Rapids: Eerdmans, 1999), 110–24.

42. Torrey Seland, "Resident Aliens in Mission: Missional Practices in the Emerging Church of 1 Peter," *BBR* 19:4 (2009): 565–89.

gentleness and reverence. Keep your conscience clear, so that, when you are maligned, those who abuse you for your good conduct in Christ may be put to shame. For it is better to suffer for doing good, if suffering should be God's will, than to suffer for doing evil" (1 Pet. 3:15–17; cf. 2:21).[43] Thus, as already noted, the Christian witness in diaspora on the periphery of society involves the willingness to suffer, even unjustly, for the sake of the gospel.[44]

That the spirit was present among marginalized western Asian believers struggling against antagonistic government officials or other persons is a comforting image for contemporary missionaries working in, for instance, Muslim-majority or other environments in which Christians are found primarily in exile, refugee, or related subgroup categories. In such contexts, it is encouraging to know that one can give testimony to the risen Christ in less aggressive ways, even nonverbally (unless and except when clear opportunities for such present themselves for apologetic witness), and that all one has to do is to allow the sanctifying work of the spirit to produce fruits for the public square.[45] Holiness of life and deed becomes missional and missiological in this arena, so that by patience and, if necessary, suffering, one allows the light of the gospel and of Christ into an otherwise foreboding world.[46]

But what about those of us who live and work in Christian-majority contexts, even if currently in transition toward some kind of post-Christendom milieu? I mean by this question that those of us living in North America, for instance (from where most readers of this book might hail), are diasporic primarily in the spiritual sense and certainly not in the sociopolitical manner. In such a situation, the Petrine commendations amount to a quietism for those whose voices can and do matter in the public square, and, perhaps more problematically, the spiritual focus can be used to legitimize an otherworldly (heavenly indeed, as the author clearly has stated!) orientation that dispenses with engaging with the missional tasks of history, society, and the present world economic order. If, in the time of the writing of this letter, part of the task was to render the good news of Jesus Christ comprehensible to exiles in the western Asian and Hellenistic context and this involved considerations of the spiritual cosmology and worldview inherited from Plato and other

43. On 1 Pet. 3:15 in missional context, see Mark Boyley, "1 Peter: A Mission Document?," *RTR* 63:2 (2004): 72–86, esp. 84–86.

44. George R. Brunk III, "The Missionary Stance of the Church in 1 Peter," in *Mission in Focus: Current Issues*, ed. Wilbert R. Shenk (Scottdale, PA: Herald, 1980), 70–81.

45. E.g., Dean Flemming, "'Won Over without a Word': Holiness and the Church's Missional Identity in 1 Peter," *Wesleyan Theological Journal* 49 (Spring 2014): 50–66.

46. This is the mission of service: Ralph W. Quere, "The AIDS Crisis: A Call to Mission Based on 1 Peter," *CurTM* 14 (1987): 361–69.

Greco-Roman thinkers,[47] then two thousand years later a deepened spiritualization of this message could be used to justify focusing only on human souls, and the resulting neglect of suffering bodies could be unnecessarily fatal, especially as they would have occurred where and while something could have been done about flesh-and-blood injustices in the name of the risen Christ. In short, yes, the spirit perfects fallen human creatures via suffering and thus also lifts up the name of Jesus. But the spirit also empowers through such suffering witness to the justice and glory of God that can make missional—for example, sociopolitical and even economic—differences in the present world.

7.4   2 Peter—Prophetic Spirit: Mission between the Times

We cannot assume as much about this letter since there is no scholarly consensus that the same person who wrote to the diasporic exiles in 1 Peter also wrote this "second" epistle.[48] Not only does that deprive us of a geographic or sociohistorical backdrop for interpreting this document, but the letter's relationship to Jude is also quite unclear, with some arguing not just for the latter's priority but also for 2 Peter's dependence on Jude.[49] We will attempt to proceed as much as possible without being presumptive on any of these issues. Rather, as per our task, we will try to ask how the work of the holy spirit portrayed in 2 Peter sheds light on theology of mission.

The "answer" to the pneumatological question of 2 Peter is this: "No prophecy of scripture is a matter of one's own interpretation, because no prophecy ever came by human will, but men and women moved by the Holy Spirit spoke from God" (1:20–21). But if so, what specifically is the question? Well, up to then, the author sought to lay out the promises and stipulations of the calling, election, and salvation in Jesus (1:3–11).[50] Then he reiterated the authority from which this reminder (1:12–15) ensued: as (putative) eyewitnesses of Jesus's transfiguration (1:16–18), which is consistent with the gospel attestation that Peter, with James and John, was present (Matt. 17:1–8

47. E.g., as delineated by Reinhard Feldmeier, "Salvation and Anthropology in First Peter," in *The Catholic Epistles and Apostolic Tradition*, ed. Karl-Wilhelm Niebuhr and Robert W. Wall (Waco: Baylor University Press, 2009), 203–13.

48. Even evangelical and conservative biblical scholars like Donald Guthrie leave the question open; see Guthrie, *New Testament Introduction*, 4th ed. (Downers Grove, IL: InterVarsity, 1990), 842–43.

49. The arguments for the pseudonymity of 2 Peter and its reliance on Jude are laid out in the introduction to these two books discussed in the latter part of J. N. D. Kelly, *A Commentary on the Epistles of Peter and of Jude* (Peabody, MA: Hendrickson, 1988), esp. 225–37.

50. See Scott J. Hafemann, "Salvation in Jude 5 and the Argument of 2 Peter 1:3–11," in Niebuhr and Wall, *Catholic Epistles*, 331–42, here 341.

and parallels). It is in this context that this letter's only reference to the divine wind occurs, as part and parcel of the author's "prophetic message more fully confirmed" (2 Pet. 1:19). What the spirit authorizes, however, is either "prophecy *as* interpretation" or "prophecy *and*—separately—interpretation," even both.[51] The point in this context is that fruitfulness in the salvation of Christ is central to the spirit-inspired prophetic message handed down now through the apostolic word.

The assurance of this prophetic message is important particularly because of the emergence of "false prophets" and "false teachers" in the midst of the people (2 Pet. 2:1). The bulk of this next portion of the letter is spent warning the readers about their aberrant teachings, envisaging their judgment, unveiling their blasphemies, and elucidating their dishonesties.[52] Although these are not unimportant matters, what is more relevant for us is that the "deceptive words" (2:3) of these persons contrast with "the words spoken in the past by the holy prophets, and the commandment of the Lord and Savior spoken through your apostles" (3:2). In particular, these "scoffers" (3:3) are seeking to undermine the faith of the messianists, saying, "Where is the promise of his coming? For ever since our ancestors died, all things continue as they were from the beginning of creation!" (3:4). In short, the false prophets' claims include the message that the gospel is unreliable since its prophetic understanding has not come to pass.[53]

There is a real sense in which the Christian understanding of prophecy has been tied to certain missional dispositions. In some mission circles, especially wherein premillennial eschatologies are prevalent, the evangelistic thrust of gospel proclamation proceeds on the assumption that time is short, that Christ's return will foreclose opportunities for repentance. In this perspective, missionary efforts are motivated by the concern that those who have not heard have to be given a chance to turn to Christ before the parousia. It is thought that Christ's reappearance precipitates the final destruction, when "the heavens will be set ablaze and dissolved, and the elements will melt with fire" (2 Pet. 3:12). Then the godless, and by implication all who have not turned to faith in the savior Jesus, will be destroyed (3:7), which thus accentuates all

51. See Tim Meadowcroft, "Spirit, Interpretation and Scripture: Exegetical Thoughts on 2 Peter 1:19–21," in *The Spirit of Truth: Reading Scripture and Constructing Theology with the Holy Spirit*, ed. Myk Habets (Eugene, OR: Pickwick, 2010), 57–72, esp. 66–67.

52. Postcolonial biblical scholars are suspicious that the Petrine harangue against these persons can be used in authoritarian contexts to justify exclusion of dissenters; see Cynthia Briggs Kittredge, "The Second Letter of Peter," in *A Postcolonial Commentary on the New Testament Writings*, ed. Fernando F. Segovia and R. S. Sugirtharajah (New York: T&T Clark, 2009), 405–12.

53. Thus, Jerome H. Neyrey rightly reads 2 Peter as an apologetic theodicy for divine providence. "The Form and Background of the Polemic in 2 Peter," *JBL* 99:3 (1980): 407–31.

the more the urgency of evangelistic proclamation. But it is also within such frameworks, then, that the scoffings dealt with by 2 Peter remain pertinent. If the veracity of the gospel is based in part on spirit-inspired prophecy and Jesus's expected imminent return has not eventuated, this is now exacerbated all the more not just by decades of silence, as it was at the time when 2 Peter was written, but by millennia. What then is the basis for preaching repentance in Jesus's name and believing in its reliability in the third millennium?

But is that the only way to read 2 Peter 3 missionally?[54] If prophecy is nothing less than the communication of "men and women moved by the Holy Spirit," then their unfolding occurs also on the divine rather than human time line: "With the Lord one day is like a thousand years, and a thousand years are like one day" (2 Pet. 3:8), the author avers, relying on the psalmist (Ps. 90:4). From this perspective, the spirit who empowers prophetic speech also engenders perseverance in holiness and godliness (2 Pet. 3:11). Specifically, "we wait for new heavens and a new earth, where righteousness is at home . . . [but] while you are waiting for these things, strive to be found by him at peace, without spot or blemish" (3:13–14). Rather than being "cleverly devised myths" (1:16), the gospel calls forth living witnesses into the prophetic truth.[55] The people of God live out the truth by the spirit in contrast to the deceits of the false prophets and teachers.

Hence, it is clear that the Christian dispensation of Pentecost, the time of the spirit's outpouring on all flesh and enabling of flesh to live into the prophetic message of the gospel until the return of the promised Christ, has persisted over two millennia. These times between the times—between Christ's first and second coming—may yet endure for another two millennia, for all we know, but the apostolic response then remains as valid today: "The Lord is not slow about his promise, as some think of slowness, but is patient with *you*, not wanting any to perish, but *all* to come to repentance" (2 Pet. 3:9; emphasis added).[56] Note that the Petrine address to his readers, the more exclusive *you*, opens up to the universal call of the gospel that extends to *all*.[57] Mission in these times between the times may not be able to calculate eschatological calendars, but the need is not for speculations regarding the parousia. Indeed, "it is not for you to know the times or periods that the Father has set

54. The answer is no; see Barbara R. Rossing, "'Hastening the Day' When the Earth Will Burn? Global Warming, Revelation and 2 Peter 3 (Advent 2, Year B)," *CurTM* 35:5 (2008): 363–73.

55. D. Edmond Hiebert, "Directives for Living in Dangerous Days: An Exposition of 2 Peter 3:14–18a," *BSac* 141:564 (1984): 330–40.

56. See Thomas H. Duke, "An Exegetical Analysis of 2 Peter 3:9," *Faith and Mission* 16:3 (1999): 6–13.

57. Karl Kuhn, "2 Peter 3:1–13," *Int* 60:3 (2006): 310–12.

Marginalized Witness and African Resonance
Transformations of the World Order

Randee Ijatuyi-Morphé, provost and professor of biblical studies, ECWA Theological Seminary, Jos (JETS), Jos, Nigeria

Like the Minor Prophets, Hebrews–Jude has been marginalized, but in the *missio spiritus* they are significant for mission from the *margins*—as of *place* and *people*—inspired by the spirit. Canonically, they are climactic, for they recapture the import of Jesus's mission for their contemporary time. Hebrews–Jude is situated "in the last days" of the spirit's outpouring, whose fulfillment Jesus heralded. These writings exploit that theme and uphold a "virtue-mission" for corrupt Roman society. Their emphasis is rooted in Israel's history: God has revealed himself or been encountered almost always "outside the land." In mission, we follow Jesus "outside" the "camp" or "city-gate," amid pagans, Jews, false prophets-teachers, and rulers who oppose the gospel. "To do mission" is to reshape "history, society, and the present world economic order" (§7.3). This is a tested path to transforming Africa and beyond!

by his own authority" (Acts 1:7). Rather, the call is for faithful believers who will "grow in the grace and knowledge of our Lord and Savior Jesus Christ" (2 Pet. 3:18).[58] Thus the holy spirit continues to empower in the present time anticipation of the coming divine reign no matter how near or far off from full realization that might be.

7.5   Jude—Apocalyptic Spirit: The Mission before the Mission

The letter identifies the author only as "Jude, a servant of Jesus Christ and brother of James" and addresses its readers only generically as "those who are called, who are beloved in God the Father and kept safe for Jesus Christ" (Jude 1). If the James referred to is the (half-) brother of Jesus and the author of the canonical letter bearing that name (see §7.2), then Jude is also the (half-) brother of Jesus and the two siblings bookend what tradition has come to

---

58. Nicholas Sagovsky, "2 Peter for the Third Millennium," in *The Unity We Have and the Unity We Seek: Ecumenical Prospects for the Third Millennium*, ed. Jeremy Morris and Nicholas Sagovsky (New York: T&T Clark, 2003), 221–26.

recognize as the Catholic or General Epistles (James, 1–2 Peter, 1–3 John, Jude).[59] Further, since James wrote to Jews "in the Dispersion" (James 1:1), traditionally Jude has also been assumed to be of Palestinian origin, focused on a Jewish readership, although more recently the Hellenistic background of this letter is being noticed. Last but not least, given the historic coupling of Jude and 2 Peter, with many scholars asserting the former's primacy and the latter's dependence (§7.4), it was also historically assumed that Jude wrote for a Jewish Christian audience and that his message was then extended and expanded into the more predominantly Greco-Roman circles characteristic of the western Asian "exiles of the Dispersion" (1 Pet. 1:1) that form the context for the Petrine letters. What is now obvious, to be clarified in the next few paragraphs, is that hard and fast lines cannot be drawn between Jewish and Hellenistic messianic communities addressed by these General Epistles.[60] But it is also undeniable that with Jude we have a minority report on early Christian witness and mission.[61]

Pneumatologically, Jude warns of "worldly people, devoid of the Spirit, who are causing divisions" (Jude 19), and then urges his readers and hearers in the opposite direction: "But you, beloved, build yourselves up on your most holy faith; pray in the Holy Spirit" (v. 20). Put alternatively, the opposing faction threatening the Jude-an (*not* Judean, as in related to or limited by the Palestinian geographic region) community is carnal and fleshly. They are categorically denounced as spiritually bereft despite their claims of having had dreams and revelations (v. 8).[62] Jude, however, exhorts the believers toward a more authentically spiritual praxis.[63] Whatever praying *in the spirit* meant for Jude and his audience, it was also a means of contesting the factiousness menacing that community.[64] On the other side, to pray in the spirit was to work toward, or to allow the holy spirit to bring about, the edification or uplifting

59. See Robert W. Wall, "A Unifying Theology of the Catholic Epistles," in Niebuhr and Wall, *Catholic Epistles*, 13–40, esp. 18–19.

60. Witherington (*Letters and Homilies*, 563–67) discusses what he calls "the Hellenizing of the Holy Land" as part of the background and context for Jude.

61. Catherine Gunsalus González writes of Jude reflecting "minority views." *1 & 2 Peter and Jude*, Belief: A Theological Commentary on the Bible (Louisville: Westminster John Knox, 2010), 211–12.

62. See Rebecca Skaggs, *The Pentecostal Commentary on 1 Peter, 2 Peter, Jude* (Cleveland: Pilgrim, 2004), 154.

63. This flesh-spirit contrast sits well within a Hellenistic environment; so suggests Jörg Frey, "The Epistle of Jude between Hellenism and Judaism," in Niebuhr and Wall, *Catholic Epistles*, 309–29, here 323–24.

64. Rodolfo Galvan Estrada III argues that (naturally) charismatically gifted persons might undermine authentic charismatic spirituality, including spirited-prayer, whose orthopraxy-orthopathy is needed for orthodoxy. "The Spirit in Jude 19–20," *JPT* 25 (2016): 43–57.

of the community of faith.[65] In other words, the spirit empowered both the warding off of communal underminers and the building up and strengthening of this besieged community. Each entailed the other, the author concludes, as those who pray in the spirit would save not just themselves but also their adversaries: "Keep yourselves in the love of God; look forward to the mercy of our Lord Jesus Christ that leads to eternal life. And have mercy on some who are wavering; save others by snatching them out of the fire; and have mercy on still others with fear, hating even the tunic defiled by their bodies" (vv. 21–23).

Like 2 Peter, with which Jude has long been associated, the challengers are false prophets that are as much inside as outside the community. These are "intruders [that] have *stolen in among you*" (Jude 4; emphasis added) even as they continue "feast[ing] with you without fear, feeding themselves" (v. 12). Jude's letter has thus been described as the "acts of apostates,"[66] thus contrasting appropriately with the Acts of the Apostles. There were many charismatic personalities—for example, "they are bombastic in speech, flattering people to their own advantage" (v. 16)—working subversively within this community. Combating these false teachers, then, cannot but ensue in the power of the spirit, in this case directed more internally or intracommunally than outwardly or to outsiders. The Petrine admonition "For the time has come for judgment to begin with the household of God" (1 Pet. 4:17) is also apropos here: that these Jude-ans (readers of the letter) ought to be focused on thwarting such "scoffers [who are bent on] indulging their own ungodly lusts" (Jude 18). The orientation is more toward getting the house in order than reaching out missionally to the wider community. But if the preservation of biblical orthodoxy from heterodox deviation could be understood missiologically—for example, if "contend[ing] for the faith that was once for all entrusted to the saints" (v. 3) could be viewed as involving a missional dimension[67]—then Jude's missional mandate, through prayer by and in the spirit no less, is comprehensible.

One more point ought to be made about these opponents of Jude's ecclesial community that connects back to themes seen early on in Israel's history missiologically construed. Recall that the Noahic flood (Gen. 6–9) was precipitated at least in part by ruahic (in that context) restraint: "My spirit shall not abide in mortals forever, for they are flesh" (Gen. 6:3; see §1.1). This biblical flood

---

65. George T. Montague, *The Holy Spirit: Growth of a Biblical Tradition* (Peabody, MA: Hendrickson, 1994), 312.

66. S. Maxwell Coder, *Jude: The Acts of the Apostates* (Chicago: Moody, 1958).

67. Jude and 2 Peter's foci on orthodoxy is central to the missiological discussion of Andreas J. Köstenberger and Peter T. O'Brien, *Salvation to the Ends of the Earth: A Biblical Theology of Mission*, NSBT 11 (Downers Grove, IL: InterVarsity, 2001), 228–32.

appears metaphorically in the Petrine writings as symbolic of both salvation (being saved like Noah; 1 Pet. 3:20) and destruction (perishing, for which false prophets are predestined; 2 Pet. 2:1, 5). Jude goes behind the Noahic narrative, even deeper into the primeval history, to call to witness "Enoch, in the seventh generation from Adam, [who] prophesied, saying, 'See, the Lord is coming with ten thousands of his holy ones, to execute judgment on all, and to convict everyone of all the deeds of ungodliness that they have committed in such an ungodly way, and of all the harsh things that ungodly sinners have spoken against him'" (Jude 14–15). This "servant of Jesus Christ" is citing from the apocryphal book of Enoch—1 Enoch 1:9 specifically—although the canonical foundation of the Enochic literature derives from the prediluvian portions of the Genesis narrative (Gen. 5:18–24). The point is twofold. First, 1 Enoch is a type of extrabiblical literature focused on apocalyptic themes forged in times of social upheaval and pseudepigraphically linked with authoritative Jewish sources. This quotation thus was used by this "brother of James" to predict the judgment of such ungodly persons who, as the precipitators of crisis in the contemporary community, "pervert the grace of our God into licentiousness and deny our only Master and Lord, Jesus Christ" (Jude 4).[68] Second, the coming judgment brings also with it the opportunity to be aligned with the heroes of old,[69] to pray in the spirit, if one wills, even as saints like Enoch walked with God. The latter element confirms that travail and life in the spirit is warranted for apocalyptic times when the people of God are assailed by forces internal and external.[70] The former point about extracanonical contributions to orthodox mission hearkens back also to many segments of our discussion in the Jewish scriptures that indicate how non-Israelite voices—for example, Pharaoh (§1.2), Balaam (§1.6), Elihu (§3.3), Cyrus (§4.2), and Belshazzar and his queen (§4.6)—were capable of bearing witness by the breath of Yahweh.

The only caution needed here is an extension of what was registered in our discussion of 1 Peter above: that Jude and Enoch, which Jude cites, are both

68. For an introduction to Enoch as part of apocalyptic literature addressing the sense of Jewish oppression during the two centuries before the Christian era, see John J. Collins, *The Apocalyptic Imagination: An Introduction to the Jewish Matrix of Christianity* (New York: Crossroad, 1992), esp. 36–46.

69. Thus, David A. deSilva writes that the flood is a "historic precedent displaying God's response to ungodliness in speech and deed." *The Jewish Teachers of Jesus, James, and Jude: What Earliest Christianity Learned from the Apocrypha and Pseudepigrapha* (Oxford: Oxford University Press, 2012), 109.

70. Although it has been said that "the author of 2 Peter stands out as *the more complete Christian Jewish apocalyptic theologian* in comparison to Jude," I respond that Jude is the more *Jewish Christian* apocalyptic theologian than 2 Peter. Anders Gerdmar, *Rethinking the Judaism-Hellenism Dichotomy: A Historiographical Case Study of Second Peter and Jude*, Coniectanea Biblical New Testament 36 (Stockholm: Almqvist & Wiksell, 2001), 338 (emphasis original).

located marginally amid the dominant regimes of their times. Contemporary missiologies constructed in the Euro-American West, albeit now increasingly shifting toward the periphery because of post-Christendom dynamics, nevertheless are liable to distorted considerations of these texts, particularly if they succumb to the demonization of the community's antagonists so prevalent in apocalyptic literature, Jude included. The reality is that when those with greater political power and leverage demonize those who are sociopolitically in the minority, they have the capacity to further ostracize these already marginal groups. Christian mission propelled by prayer in the spirit, then, ought to resist presuming that such entreating extends uncritically to whatever actions these prayers and their accompanying dispositions might "inspire" vis-à-vis engagement with others deemed outside the community of faith.

Discussion Questions

1. The Spirit leads to rest in the Letter to the Hebrews, and the life of faith is a journey and sojourn toward another (divine) city. How might faithful discipleship understood as "en route," always outside the gate and crossing borders, shape Christian mission in our present post-Christendom and postcolonial milieu?

2. First Peter, addressed to the messianic diaspora in Asia Minor, urges what missiologists call "lifestyle evangelism." How appropriate is such nomenclature, or what else might you want to call what the author recommends? Would that Petrine vision be appropriate and effective today? If so, in what contemporary contexts?

3. The modern missionary movement was based in part on preaching the gospel to those who had never heard it, so that they would be given the opportunity to repent and confess Jesus Christ before the parousia and the end would come. Does your reading of the General Epistles and Catholic Letters support such an eschatological approach to Christian witness? Why or why not?

8

Johannine Paraclete and Eschatological Spirit

Mission for and against the World

Introduction

As we close the scriptural considerations of this book, we come to a collection of writings gathered from across the Christian Testament and therefore out of canonical sequence. Our justification, provided variously before, is that these have been historically associated with John the apostle or at least the community of which he was believed to have been the apostolic head.[1] Although our assessment does not presume that the same John wrote all five of the documents that bear his name,[2] the reception history of these writings and the legacy of their togetherness within and across the various streams of the Christian tradition provide sufficient rationale for reading them together.

Further, our pneumatological and missiological bifocality enhances the connections across what some (a few) might otherwise consider to be vastly

---

1. See, e.g., Raymond E. Brown, *The Community of the Beloved Disciple: The Life, Loves and Hates of an Individual Church in New Testament Times* (New York: Paulist Press, 1978), although his focus is on the Fourth Gospel and the Johannine epistles, less on Revelation as a product of this putative Johannine community.

2. However, for argument that the author in each case is John the son of Zebedee, see Paul A. Rainbow, *Johannine Theology: The Gospel, the Epistles, and the Apocalypse* (Downers Grove, IL: IVP Academic, 2014), 39–51, esp. 50–51.

dissimilar genres.[3] On the former front, the Fourth Gospel provides at least
two pneumatological streams: that regarding the spirit of Jesus in the first
half and that regarding the Paraclete or Advocate in the second.[4] Both are
consistent with the pneumatological references of the Johannine Letters, while
the book of Revelation ups the ante toward what might be called a pluralistic pneumatological vision, one that consists of no less than "seven spirits"
of and from the one who sits on the throne. Thus, reading all these works
together, we receive not only a diversified but also a relatively "high" pneumatology and pneumatological theology, both consistent with the similarly
"high" Christology of the Johannine materials—to the point of a relatively
widespread recognition of Johannine theology as "proto-trinitarian"[5]—and
undergirding as well as extending the many tongues of the spirit manifest
in the Lukan Pentecost.[6] A Johannine pneumatological hermeneutic, then,
allows us to identify otherness not only vis-à-vis the missiological thrusts of
Christian witness but also in the nature and work of the divine wind itself.

From this perspective, however, the pluralistic pneumatology also opens
up to an expansive theology of mission across the Johannine materials. In
fact, in few other places in the Bible is the *world* as a whole as much an object
of divine concern as here.[7] The missiological relevance of this point is obvious, but what may be less obvious from a modernist mission perspective is
that John is relatively less concerned about the salvation of individual souls
than about the redemption and renewal of all things. More pointedly, the
world that God wishes to save is also a world opposed to God. This is most

3. For an overview of these theological loci across this literature, see Rainbow, *Johannine
Theology*, chaps. 6 (the spirit) and 10 (mission).
4. This division of labor is also why I have spread out my discussion over two sections
(§§8.1–8.2). Anthony C. Thiselton elaborates on the two streams in *The Holy Spirit: In Biblical Teachings, through the Centuries, and Today* (Grand Rapids: Eerdmans, 2013), chap. 7.
5. See Andreas Dettwiler, "The Holy Spirit in the Gospel of John from a Western Perspective," in *The Holy Spirit and the Church according to the New Testament: Sixth International
East-West Symposium of New Testament Scholars, Belgrade, August 25 to 31, 2013*, ed. Predrag
Dragutinović et al., WUNT 364 (Tübingen: Mohr Siebeck, 2016), 149–71, here 170.
6. Yet the divinity of the spirit across the Fourth Gospel in particular, and even the Johan-
nine corpus more generally, is not like that of the Synoptics or of Paul in this one regard: "For
John, the activity of the Spirit is decidedly *non-*'charismatic': the Spirit does not manifest itself
through miraculous works at all." Christopher Tuckett, "Seeing and Believing in John 20," in
Paul, John and Apocalyptic Eschatology: Studies in Honor of Martinus C. de Boer, ed. Jan
Krans et al., NovTSup 149 (Leiden: Brill, 2013), 173, quoted in Pedrag Dragutinović, "The
Holy Spirit and the Church in the Gospel of John: A Discourse Analysis of John 20:19–23," in
Dragutinović et al., *The Holy Spirit and the Church*, 129–47, here 146.
7. E.g., Ruben Zimmermann, "From a Jewish Man to the Savior of the World: Narrative
and Symbols Forming a Step by Step Christology in John 4,1–42," in *Studies in the Gospel of
John and Its Christology: Festschrift Gilbert Van Belle*, ed. Joseph Verheyden et al., BETL 265
(Louvain: Peeters, 2014), 99–118.

The Spirit's Witness in John and the Apocalypse
Revelatory Visions and Indian Asian Visualizations

Johnson Thomaskutty, associate professor of New Testament, Union Biblical Seminary, Pune, India

In John, Jesus is endowed with the gift of full spirit (John 1:32–34; 3:34–36; 6:63). As the agent of spirit-mission, he fulfills several divine tasks: guiding people to birth "from above" and to birth of "water and spirit" (3:3, 5); providing eternal spiritual water, revealing God as spirit, and equipping for "worship in spirit and truth" (4:10–24); leading to redemptive-historical quali-fication on the gift (7:37–39); and promising the spirit as "another Advocate" (14:16–26; 15:26–27; 16:7–15). His mission in public (chaps. 1–12) was one of social transformation; his mission in private (chaps. 13–17) was centered on his promise about the *parakletos*; and the resurrected Lord lavishes the spirit on his disciples with an invitation: "Receive the Holy Spirit" (20:22–23). In this way, John creates a literary plot structure in which the mission of Jesus and the work of the holy spirit are aligned together. In sum, the characteriza-tion of Jesus begins and culminates with the endowment of the holy spirit and the mission of God. As an Indian reader, I visualize in John a missional-pneumatology that demonstrates a lot of liberative insights to the contextual realities of the Asian continent.

clearly evidenced in John's Apocalypse, perhaps for obvious reasons, but the missiological significance of this theme has been relatively underexplored. True, Revelation invites anticipation of many souls—from every tribe, tongue, people, and nation—around the eschatological throne of God, but this also involves an upheaval of this world and its imperial systems and conventions in order that all things may be made new.[8] The missiological implications of such an apocalyptic cosmology are profound and will require extensive and intensive engagement before a new theology of Christian witness plausible for a post-mission era will be born.

When read in pneumatological perspective, the Johannine documents invite us to consider missiologically many types of *others*. Again, these run the gamut from those inside or at the margins of the believing community, especially in

8. Very preliminary steps toward this end can be discerned in Stephen D. Moore, *Empire and Apocalypse: Postcolonialism and the New Testament* (Sheffield: Sheffield Phoenix, 2006), chap. 4.

the Paracletic passages and the epistles, to those who are of other faiths. We also encounter the concreteness of the Johannine community, including its seven explicitly named churches in Revelation, all in Asia Minor, against the cosmic backdrop that predominates both the gospel and apocalyptic skylines. Hence, we are here invited in this final chapter of the book, as before, to move back and forth again and again from the particular to the universal so as to be able to "see" the missional "other" from across this spectrum of sites in a dynamic fashion. Our pneumatological optic enhances our capacities, even as our missiological concerns facilitate our efforts.

8.1   John, Part 1—"The Wind Blows Where It Chooses": The Breath and Mission of God

One of the most widely recognized lines in the Bible about the divine breath reads, "The wind blows where it chooses, and you hear the sound of it, but you do not know where it comes from or where it goes" (John 3:8). This appears in the context of Jesus inviting Nicodemus, a leading teacher (3:10), to be born again "of the Spirit" and "from above" and thereby to enter the reign of God (3:3–7).[9] To be reborn spiritually generates the capacity to bear the spirit's fruits (cf. 3:6) since one has taken on the character of the divine wind.[10] Yet it is in this same conversation that Jesus also defines "heavenly things" and "eternal life" (3:12, 15) in relation to his own testimony. He then invites Nicodemus, a Jew, to consider one of the most famous of biblical texts: "For God so loved the world that he gave his only Son, so that everyone who believes in him may not perish but may have eternal life" (3:16). Being born again, being blown into by God's spirit, effectively,[11] is related to receiving the witness of Jesus, and both are meant for enabling the entire world, every single person whether Jew or Greek, to enter eternal life.

Yet if John's Gospel is acknowledged to be quite different from the Synoptics, their consistent testimony is that Jesus is the Messiah, the one anointed by the spirit. In the Fourth Gospel, it is John the Baptist who testifies to Jesus's messianic identity: "I saw the Spirit descending from heaven like a dove, and it remained on him. I myself did not know him, but the one who sent me to baptize with water said to me, 'He on whom you see the Spirit descend and

9. For overall discussion, see Linda Belleville, "Born of Water and Spirit: John 3:5," *TJ*, n.s., 1 (1980): 125–41.

10. Klyne R. Snodgrass, "That Which Is Born from *Pneuma* Is *Pneuma*: Rebirth and Spirit in John 3:5–6," *Covenant Quarterly* 49 (1991): 13–29, here 22.

11. See Annette Weissenrieder, "Spirit and Rebirth in the Gospel of John," *Religion and Theology* 21 (2014): 58–85, here 81.

remain is the one who baptizes with the Holy Spirit'" (John 1:32–33).[12] It is the overflowing of the divine wind that thereby propels the messianic ministry of Jesus: "He whom God has sent speaks the words of God, for he gives the Spirit without measure" (3:34). From this perspective, all that Jesus does and says, including his signs and wonders, or the "I am" sayings (both categories of which include multiple instances), can be understood as empowered by the spirit.[13] By extension, those who believe in and follow Jesus also embark on a path of what might be called "pneumatic transformation,"[14] which culminates in their receiving of the anointing of the divine breath that is given by the Messiah at the end of the book (see §8.2).[15]

Intriguingly, then, John's Gospel imagines the possibility of the entire world having access to and then participating in this messianic community by the spirit. This ought not to be surprising, since the Logos, the Christ, had come into the world to enlighten every person (John 1:9). The other appearances of the divine wind in at least the first half of this Gospel indicate that God is interested in saving not just Jews and the world in general but Samaritans, Greeks, and, by extension, ethnically constituted human creatures more specifically. After the conversation with Nicodemus, Jesus seemingly felt compelled "to go through Samaria" (4:4) and there had a conversation with a Samaritan woman to whom he said, "But the hour is coming, and is now here, when the true worshipers will worship the Father in spirit and truth, for the Father seeks such as these to worship him. God is spirit, and those who worship him must worship in spirit and truth" (4:23–24). Here Jesus clearly undermines the historic divisions between Jews and Samaritans, indicating that all have access to the Father in and through the spirit.

Later, in an exchange with Jews after the feeding of five thousand men, not counting women and children (John 6:5–13), Jesus urged them to seek not just the manna of this world but the "bread of life" (6:48) that is from heaven, in effect his life and his words. He says here, "It is the spirit that gives life; the flesh is useless. The words that I have spoken to you are spirit and life" (6:63). The Jews were focused on Jesus's ethnic lineage—for instance, whether he was "the son of Joseph, whose father and mother we know" (6:42). Jesus

---

12. Cornelis Bennema, "Spirit-Baptism in the Fourth Gospel: A Messianic Reading of John 1,33," *Biblica* 84 (2003): 35–60.

13. W. Boyd Hunt, "John's Doctrine of the Spirit," *SwJT* 8 (1965): 45–65.

14. The thesis of Gitte Buch-Hansen, *"It Is the Spirit That Gives Life": A Stoic Understanding of Pneuma in John's Gospel*, Beihefte zur Zeitschrift für die neutestamentliche Wissenschaft und die Kunde der älteren Kirche 173 (Berlin: de Gruyter, 2010).

15. Thus the thesis of Gary M. Burge, *The Anointed Community: The Holy Spirit in the Johannine Tradition* (Grand Rapids: Eerdmans, 1987).

insisted it was more important that they realized who his heavenly Father was, who had sent him and whose words and eternal life he was communicating.[16]

Not long after, as Jewish leaders were wondering if Jesus would disappear among the Greeks (John 7:35), Jesus proclaims, "Let anyone who is thirsty come to me, and let the one who believes in me drink. As the scripture has said, 'Out of the believer's heart shall flow rivers of living water,'" to which John adds an explanation: "Now he said this about the Spirit, which believers in him were to receive; for as yet there was no Spirit, because Jesus was not yet glorified" (7:37–39). Again, Jesus is now the source of eschatological life from whom all—Jews and Greeks—can drink, through the spirit.[17] And indeed, the Greeks, representing the nations of the world that God so loved, responded, so that even the Pharisaic opponents of Jesus observed, "Look, the world has gone after him!" (12:19). Rather than waiting for Jesus to arrive, "some Greeks" came looking for him and were invited to receive his offer of eternal life (12:20–25).[18]

John's message is that the Word of God came into the world to reveal the Father. In John's own words, "the Word became flesh and lived among us, and we have seen his glory, the glory as of a father's only son, full of grace and truth" (John 1:14). More importantly, the coming of the Word of God from heaven to earth not only lights up the world (1:9; 8:12; 9:5) and "gives life to the world" (6:33) but also saves the world. "Indeed," John records Jesus as saying, "God did not send the Son into the world to condemn the world, but in order that the world might be saved through him" (3:17; cf. 4:42; 12:47). On the one hand, then, it is fair to say that the Fourth Gospel presents something like an incarnational missiology;[19] on the other hand, Jesus saves certainly

16. Thus, Rodolfo Galvan Estrada III argues that in this episode John is contrasting the death-dealing ancestral/ethnic emphases of the Jewish mindset with Jesus's life-giving relationship with the Father; I am grateful to Estrada for sharing with me his thesis—from which I learned a great deal—before its successful defense (acknowledged by his committee as "distinctive"). Estrada, "Ethnicity and the Spirit in John 1–7" (PhD diss., Regent University, 2018), 226–30; an expanded version of his thesis will be published as *A Pneumatology of Race in the Gospel of John* (Eugene, OR: Wipf & Stock, forthcoming).

17. See Joseph R. Greene, "Integrating Interpretations of John 7:37–39 into the Temple Theme: The Spirit as Efflux from the New Temple," *Neotestamentica* 47:2 (2013): 333–53.

18. John A. Davies, "Desire of the Nations: John 12:20–22," *RTR* 69:3 (2010): 151–63.

19. Johannes Nissen, "Mission in the Fourth Gospel: Historical and Hermeneutical Perspectives," in *New Readings in John: Literary and Theological Perspectives*, ed. Johannes Nissen and Sigfred Pedersen, JSNTSup 182 (Sheffield: Sheffield Academic, 1999), 213–31, esp. 229–30; yet Andreas J. Köstenberger resists "incarnational" given Jesus's unique ontological status, and urges instead a *representational* missiology: "The Challenge of a Systematized Biblical Theology of Mission: Missiological Insights from the Gospel of John," *Missiology* 23:4 (1995): 445–64, esp. 453–55.

by revealing the Father through the spirit.[20] There is in that sense a double brokerage unfolded in the Fourth Gospel: the breath of new life given by the spirit invites the world—Jews, Samaritans, Greeks, and anyone else—to receive the words of Jesus through which the eternal life of the Father is given.[21]

So, yes, of course God loves and wants to save the world. Yet as the pneumatic passages in John suggest, the *missio Dei* involves the Father sending the Son and the spirit to—and then through—the tribes, nations, and peoples of the world.[22] While we shall see this thematized explicitly in another Johannine text later, the implications so far, in our focus on this first part of the Fourth Gospel, are that the world is invited to breathe of and through the divine wind and to drink of the spirit's water of life in Jesus. Having done so enables inhabitation in the life and spirit of the Messiah that is simultaneously a participation in the mission of God. The church as the born-again-of-the-spirit-people-of-God is the sent community as Jesus was the one sent by the Father.[23] Such born-again witnesses in turn testify to the bread, light, and life of the world, Jesus, in his words and his deeds, including his laying down of his life.[24] The goal is that all the world's inhabitants can be turned to the Father and worship God in spirit and truth.

8.2 John, Part 2—"If You Forgive the Sins of Any, They Are Forgiven": Paracletic Mission

Yet even if God desires to save the world according to the Johannine witness, the world is resistant to the divine overtures, including to the Son and the spirit that have been sent.[25] The Jews are those who are indicted as most oppositional to Jesus especially in the first part of the Gospel (e.g., John

20. Marianne Meye Thompson, *The God of the Gospel of John* (Grand Rapids: Eerdmans, 2001), esp. chap. 4.

21. Tricia Gates Brown explicates the thesis that the spirit is broker to Jesus, providing access to the Father through the Son; see *Spirit in the Writings of John: Johannine Pneumatology in Social-Scientific Perspective*, JSNTSup 253 (New York: T&T Clark, 2003).

22. *Sending* and *being sent* are central to the missiological reading of the Fourth Gospel in Albert Curry Winn, *A Sense of Mission: Guidance from the Gospel of John* (Philadelphia: Westminster, 1981).

23. Robert Kolb, "Those Who Are Sent: Christ and His Church—Christology, Missiology, and Ecclesiology in the Gospel of John," *Missio Apostolica: Journal of the Lutheran Society of Missiology* 20:1 (2012): 11–15.

24. Howard Baker, "The Place of Mission in Johannine Discipleship: Perspectives from the Motif of Agency," *Journal of Spiritual Formation and Soul Care* 6:1 (2013): 38–45.

25. See Yong, "'The Light Shines in the Darkness': Johannine Dualism and the Challenge of Christian Theology of Religions Today," *Journal of Religion* 89:1 (2009): 31–56, where I take up this theme of the world's resistance in John vis-à-vis another theological locus.

5:16, 18; 6:41–42; 7:1; 8:48–53; 10:31–33; 11:8, 57), including their expelling of messianists from the synagogues (9:22; 12:42; 16:2). But the world that is inclusive of these adversaries of the Lord also neither recognized or knew the Word of God manifest in Jesus nor accepted him (1:10–11).[26] Loving the darkness rather than light (3:19), the world came to hate Jesus the Messiah (7:7). By the time we get to the second half of the Gospel, the world that has persisted in defying the Messiah has also come to detest the messianic community (15:18–19; 16:20), and its inhabitants are now inhibited from seeing or knowing the Father (17:25). Jesus therefore encourages and prays for his followers, that they will be comforted amid the trouble of the world (16:33) and protected from its ruling prince (17:15; cf. 12:31; 14:30).[27]

It is in this context that we can appreciate the role played by the Paraclete or Advocate references in at least the final form of this portion of the book.[28] John sets the scene for Jesus's final words to his disciples before his passion after the evening Passover meal (John 13:1–2) when Jesus washes his disciples' feet (13:3–17).[29] As the disciples are perplexed about betrayers from within their own groups (13:18–38) and confused about knowing the way forward from his anticipated departure (14:1–13), Jesus promises, "I will ask the Father, and he will give you another Advocate [παράκλητον or *parakleton*],[30] to be with you forever. This is the Spirit of truth, whom the world cannot receive, because it neither sees him nor knows him. You know him, because he abides

26. In response to the anti-Semitism of John read off the surface of the text, Lars Kierspel urges that the historical Jewish rejection of Jesus is deployed by the author to explicate the suffering and rejection his followers experience from the world; thus, for readers suffering under Roman persecution, the author uses "the rejection and death of the master by Jews . . . to explain the same experience of his servants through Gentiles." *The Jews and the World in the Fourth Gospel: Parallelism, Function, and Context*, WUNT 2/220 (Tübingen: Mohr Siebeck, 2006), 216.

27. See Clinton D. Morrison, "Mission and Ethic: An Interpretation of John 17," *Int* 19 (1965): 259–73.

28. Hans Windisch argues that the Paraclete sayings are later interpolations woven into a preexistent Johannine text. Windisch, *The Spirit-Paraclete in the Fourth Gospel*, trans. James W. Cox, Facet Books Biblical Series 20 (Philadelphia: Fortress, 1968), 3.

29. Pentecostal biblical scholar John Christopher Thomas shows how the foot washing of the disciples is intricately intertwined with the promised ministry of the spirit/Paraclete in this section of John's Gospel; see *He Loved Them until the End: The Farewell Materials in the Gospel according to John* (Pune, India: Fountain, 2003).

30. Clearly, Jesus himself is understood here as the first Paraclete; another Johannine text— "But if anyone does sin, we have an advocate with the Father, Jesus Christ the righteous" (1 John 2:1)—confirms this notion as prevalent within the community. For more on the personalized character of the Paraclete, consistent with the personality of Jesus, see Stephen S. Smalley, "'The Paraclete': Pneumatology in the Johannine Gospel and Apocalypse," in *Exploring the Gospel of John: In Honor of D. Moody Smith*, ed. R. Alan Culpepper and C. Clifton Black (Louisville: Westminster John Knox, 1996), 289–300.

with you, and he will be in you" (14:16–17).[31] The divine breath will thereby lead them to follow the words of Jesus and love the Father (14:23–24). More clearly put, "the Advocate, the Holy Spirit, whom the Father will send in my name, will teach you everything, and remind you of all that I have said to you" (14:26). Hence there is no need for the disciples to be troubled by the world (14:27) or about their fate as followers of Jesus.

Rather than being fearful in the world, then, the disciples are to take courage and to be emboldened as witnesses to the world.[32] "When the Advocate comes, whom I will send to you from the Father, the Spirit of truth who comes from the Father, he will testify on my behalf. You also are to testify because you have been with me from the beginning" (John 15:26–27).[33] In fact, when the Advocate arrives, "he will prove the world wrong about sin and righteousness and judgment: about sin, because they do not believe in me; about righteousness, because I am going to the Father and you will see me no longer; about judgment, because the ruler of this world has been condemned" (16:8–11). While confronting the world, the Advocate will encourage the disciples: "When the Spirit of truth comes, he will guide you into all the truth; for he will not speak on his own, but will speak whatever he hears, and he will declare to you the things that are to come. He will glorify me, because he will take what is mine and declare it to you. All that the Father has is mine. For this reason I said that he will take what is mine and declare it to you" (16:13–15). In sum, the Advocate or Comforter is sent both directly to the world and indirectly to that arena through the messianic followers as a holy and set-apart community of witnesses.[34] The latter are reminded about and enabled to persevere and flourish in the words of Jesus the Messiah and in this way become a conduit of God's eternal life to the world.

There is a lot of discussion about the coming of the Advocate in the Fourth Gospel since the spirit is promised after the departure of Jesus on the one hand and seems to be given by Jesus at the end of the book on the

31. Thus, the "greater works than these" (14:12) that the disciples are supposed to be able to accomplish in their carrying out the mission of God are enabled by the spirit; so proposes Russell Morton, "John 14:12–21 as Paradigm for the Wesleyan Understanding of Mission," *Wesleyan Theological Journal* 39:1 (2004): 91–103, here 103.

32. George Johnston thus proposes that the Paraclete comforts the believers in their stance amid and against a hostile world; see *The Spirit-Paraclete in the Gospel of John* (Cambridge: Cambridge University Press, 1970).

33. Rodolfo Galvan Estrada III, "The Spirit as an Inner Witness in John 15.26," *JPT* 22 (2013): 77–94.

34. A "*communio sanctorum*," one commentator calls them. Daniel B. Stevick, *Jesus and His Own: A Commentary on John 13–17* (Grand Rapids: Eerdmans, 2011), xi.

other hand.[35] Our own purposes, however, benefit from, rather than are burdened by, this apparent incongruence since the Johannine Pentecost, as it has come to be called, is, consistent with the Lukan Pentecost (above §5.4), first and foremost a missiological event. John puts the giving of the spirit with the reappearance of Jesus to the disciples after the discovery of the empty tomb and describes it in apostolic terms of divine sending on mission: "After he said this, he showed them his hands and his side. Then the disciples rejoiced when they saw the Lord. Jesus said to them again, 'Peace be with you. As the Father has sent me, so I send you.' When he had said this, he breathed on them and said to them, 'Receive the Holy Spirit. If you forgive the sins of any, they are forgiven them; if you retain the sins of any, they are retained'" (John 20:20–23). What is noteworthy in this context is the stark contrast between the persecuted born-again messianists and the Jewish-worldly oppressors that have persisted through the book.[36] Amid this apparently unbridgeable divide, the word of forgiveness goes forth by the power of the divine breath. Whereas at the beginning of the book the Baptist declares, "Here is the Lamb of God who takes away the sin of the world!" (1:29), here toward the end that promise is now carried out by spirit-filled disciples.[37] The power of the gospel message is all the more impressive since the redemptive mission of the forgiveness of sins extends interpersonally from the spirit of Jesus through his followers to a world—Jews, Samaritans, Greeks, and everyone else—that has up to now been impervious to the love of the Father.

To be sure, John is clear that the Father loves the Son (John 3:35; 5:20; 10:17; 15:9) and that Jesus loves the disciples (13:1), but how is the world turned to the love of God? Interestingly, the disciples are commanded to love not the world but one another: "I give you a new commandment, that you love one another. Just as I have loved you, you also should love one another. By this everyone will know that you are my disciples, if you have love for

35. Many of the interpretive disputes are made evident in Cornelis Bennema, "The Giving of the Spirit in John 19–20: Another Round," in *The Spirit and Christ in the New Testament and Christian Theology: Essays in Honor of Max Turner*, ed. I. Howard Marshall, Volker Rabens, and Cornelis Bennema (Grand Rapids: Eerdmans, 2012), 86–104; see also David Crump, "Who Gets What? God or Disciples, Human Spirit or Holy Spirit in John 19:30," *Novum Testamentum* 51 (2009): 78–89.

36. Not to mention the problems of sin afflicting the wider Johannine community (e.g., 1 John 1:8–10; 5:16–28); on this point, see Michael Becker, "Spirit in Relationship—Pneumatology in the Gospel of John," in *The Holy Spirit, Inspiration, and the Cultures of Antiquity: Multidisciplinary Perspectives*, ed. Jörg Frey and John R. Levison, Ekstasis: Religious Experience from Antiquity to the Middle Ages 5 (Berlin: de Gruyter, 2014), 331–41, esp. 339.

37. Craig S. Keener, "Sent Like Jesus: Johannine Missiology (John 20:21–22)," *AJPS* 12:1 (2009): 21–45.

Jews, Greeks, and Samaritans
Salvation for a Multiethnic World

Rodolfo Galvan Estrada III, dean of academic affairs,
LABI College, La Puente, California, USA

Although not often thought of as writing about Christian mission, arguably the Fourth Evangelist invites a bold and new way of thinking about the missiological role of the spirit. The spirit-Paraclete sayings are his way of presenting the spirit's mission for the entire world, and this is unfortunately often missed in scholarship on Johannine pneumatology that has limited the spirit's activity to a revelatory function. The story of the spirit in John is a historic missiological activity that concerns itself with the people of the world—Jews, Greeks, and Samaritans. The world is invited to drink of the spirit, and the born-again anointed believers are encouraged to go forth into a hostile world and demonstrate the love of God. John's Gospel therefore compels one to recognize that the story of Jesus is also one that includes the very movement of the spirit for the world.

one another" (13:34–35; cf. 15:17). Pointedly put, Jesus insisted, "This is my commandment, that you love one another as I have loved you. No one has greater love than this, to lay down one's life for one's friends" (15:12–13). Yet Jesus laid down his life for the world indeed, including his enemies. The disciples were similarly sent by Jesus "into the world" (17:18) in and through the divine breath (20:21) and in that sense were called to witness to the world through love and the laying down of their own lives (cf. 12:25). As spirit-anointed followers of Jesus, then, the disciples bear witness to the love of God by forgiving the sins of their adversaries and by loving each other within as well as those outside the community of faith in the name of the Son and in imitation of his example. Hence, the followers of Jesus will participate in the *missio Dei* by the spirit, and the world will "come to believe that Jesus is the Messiah, the Son of God, and that through believing . . . may have life in his name" (20:31).[38]

38. I can thus accept the broad thrusts of Stephen R. Holmes, "Trinitarian Missiology: Towards a Theology of God as Missionary," *International Journal of Systematic Theology* 8:1 (2006): 72–90, recognizing his Nicene commitments, even if our efforts here are in the direction of a triune (biblically funded) missiological vision.

8.3   1 John—Discerning Missionary Spirit(s): Incarnational Mission

Although the divine breath is mentioned only in the first Johannine letter, we begin with reference to the other two epistles because of their missionary elements. Second and Third John are both concerned with what we might call, at the risk of being anachronistic, "missionaries," visitors from outside to these ecclesial communities. The former warns against deceivers who apparently hold to anti-Christian doctrines or heterodox christological beliefs (2 John 7–9): "Do not receive into the house or welcome anyone who comes to you and does not bring this teaching; for to welcome is to participate in the evil deeds of such a person" (vv. 10–11). The latter, on the other hand, commends hospitality to "co-workers" who, "even though they are strangers to you" (3 John 5–8),[39] can benefit from the support of this congregation in their carrying out the missionary work of the gospel to nonbelievers.[40] To the degree that these three letters are believed to derive from the same community within a reasonable segment of time,[41] we are invited to consider the pneumatology of 1 John in relation to these missionary dynamics in the background of these epistles.

What is clear is that all of this coming and going into and out of the Johannine community has brought about some confusion. If the language of the Paraclete is absent here except as applied to Jesus (1 John 2:1), the work of the Paraclete-spirit in the Fourth Gospel reappears particularly in relation to the discernment of truth. The author warns against antichrists, understood as "the one who denies that Jesus is the Christ . . . [and] who denies the Father and the Son" (2:22). As these have gone out from the community (2:19), there is a need for a divine anointing to preserve the community from error:

> You have been anointed by the Holy One, and all of you have knowledge. I
> write to you, not because you do not know the truth, but because you know it,
> and you know that no lie comes from the truth. . . . I write these things to you

39. Cf. D. Edmond Hiebert, "An Exposition of 3 John 5–10," *BSac* 144 (1987): 194–207. The historical issues behind the welcoming hospitality to missionaries in this short letter are actually quite complicated; for a synoptic glimpse at what is at stake, see Jan Van der Watt, "On Hospitality in 3 John: An Evaluation of the Response of Malina to Malherbe," *Nederduitse Gereformeerde Teologiese Tydskrif* 55:1 (2014): 389–405, esp. 391–95.

40. See also Harry R. Boer, "The Church and Her Missionaries," *The Reformed Journal* 1:1 (April 1951): 13–15.

41. Although no definitive argument relating the three letters has commanded adherence, the scholarly consensus is that these epistles, along with the Fourth Gospel, are "characterized by a 'family likeness' which even extends to matters of style and grammatical construction." Judith Lieu, *The Theology of the Johannine Epistles* (Cambridge: Cambridge University Press, 1991), 99–100.

concerning those who would deceive you. As for you, the anointing that you received from him abides in you, and so you do not need anyone to teach you. But as his anointing teaches you about all things, and is true and is not a lie, and just as it has taught you, abide in him. (2:20–21, 26–27)[42]

Thus, the divine anointing protects believers from the lies of these antichristic persons and messages, not only reminding them of the words of Jesus (as in the Gospel) but also leading them further in discernment of what is true and good.

But if lies are antichristic, then truth is christic. Recall, though, that the christic is the pneumatic, meaning that Jesus is the Christ indeed as messianically anointed by the spirit. Hence, the anointing that leads to truth exposes the lies of antichrists surely by reminding the community about, and aiding the community to participate in, the life of Jesus the spirit-anointed Messiah: "And this is his commandment, that we should believe in the name of his Son Jesus Christ and love one another, just as he has commanded us. All who obey his commandments abide in him, and he abides in them. And by this we know that he abides in us, by the Spirit that he has given us" (1 John 3:23–24). Discernment of antichristic lies and falsehoods plaguing the community therefore is pneumatically or charismatically supported by the spirit through the norm of Jesus as Christ.[43] The elder[44] or author of this letter puts it thus in a lengthy passage that deserves to be reproduced:

Beloved, do not believe every spirit, but test the spirits to see whether they are from God; for many false prophets have gone out into the world. By this you know the Spirit of God: every spirit that confesses that Jesus Christ has come in the flesh is from God, and every spirit that does not confess Jesus is not from God. And this is the spirit of the antichrist, of which you have heard that it is coming; and now it is already in the world. Little children, you are from God, and have conquered them; for the one who is in you is greater than the one who is in the world. They are from the world; therefore what they say is from the

42. For more on the "anointing" (*chrisma*) in relation to the divine spirit, see Frederick R. Harm, "Distinctive Titles of the Holy Spirit in the Writings of John," *Concordia Journal* 13:2 (1987): 119–35, esp. 133–34.

43. See Pheme Perkins, "*Koinōnia* in 1 John 1:3–7: The Social Context of Division in the Johannine Letters," *CBQ* 45 (1983): 631–41.

44. The author of 2–3 John is identified in their initial verses as "the elder," but although this designation is lacking in 1 John, the recipients of this first epistle are addressed as "children," including "my little children" (1 John 2:1), almost a dozen times; see also Peter Rhea Jones, "The Missional Role of ὁ Πρεσβύτερος," in *Communities in Dispute: Current Scholarship on the Johannine Epistles*, ed. R. Alan Culpepper and Paul N. Anderson, SBL Early Christianity and Its Literature 13 (Atlanta: SBL Press, 2014), 141–54.

world, and the world listens to them. We are from God. Whoever knows God listens to us, and whoever is not from God does not listen to us. From this we know the spirit of truth and the spirit of error. (4:1–6)

Recognition of apostolic missionaries and of the apostolic gospel is thus tied to the criterion of Jesus Christ: "what we have seen with our eyes, what we have looked at and touched with our hands" (1:1). Embrace of Jesus in the flesh thereby separates truth from error, divine from false prophets, and the believing community from an antagonistic world.[45]

There is every indication, given these worries about a spiritualized Jesus, that the Johannine community was beset by at least an incipient if not developing form of gnosticism. Such a movement that came into full flowering in the second century emphasized the spiritual dimensions of knowledge and truth and downplayed if not dismissed the importance of the created material world. It was a set of ideas that minimized the importance of Jesus's coming in the flesh and extolled instead a spiritualized piety that the author of 1 John was combating. Hence when it is also written, "By this we know that we abide in him and he in us, because he has given us of his Spirit" (1 John 4:13), the broader context (4:7–21) of retrieving the love of God and love for God—consistent with what we saw above with the message of John's Gospel—emphasizes that this spiritual abiding is also a material and communal one that participates in the divine mission.[46] "Those who say, 'I love God,' and hate their brothers or sisters, are liars; for those who do not love a brother or sister whom they have seen, cannot love God whom they have not seen. The commandment we have from him is this: those who love God must love their brothers and sisters also" (4:20–21). While the divine breath facilitates discernment of "missionary" lives and messages that distort the truth from the incarnational person of Jesus, the same spirit empowers missionary loving according to the life and love of the incarnated Word of God. The Johannine spirit is hence not ethereal but carnal, supremely manifest in and through Jesus and those flesh-and-blood human creatures gathered in and through his name.[47]

45. Gary M. Burge, "Spirit-Inspired Theology and Ecclesial Correction: Charting One Shift in the Development of Johannine Ecclesiology and Pneumatology," in Culpepper and Anderson, *Communities in Dispute*, 179–85.

46. See David Rensberger, "Completed Love: 1 John 4:11–18 and the Mission of the New Testament Church," in Culpepper and Anderson, *Communities in Dispute*, 237–71.

47. R. W. L. Moberly, "'Test the Spirits': God, Love, and Critical Discernment in 1 John 4," in *The Holy Spirit and Christian Origins: Essays in Honor of James D. G. Dunn*, ed. Graham N. Stanton, Bruce W. Longenecker, and Stephen C. Barton (Grand Rapids: Eerdmans, 2004), 296–307.

The final point to be made echoes the Fourth Gospel's pentecostal missiology of forgiveness of sins outlined above (§8.2), although in this first Johannine letter the link is a bit oblique.[48] Toward the end of this missive, the author highlights a pneumatological witness in ostensible relationship to Jesus's death, at least as recorded in the Gospel account: "This is the one who came by water and blood, Jesus Christ, not with the water only but with the water and the blood. And the Spirit is the one that testifies, for the Spirit is the truth. There are three that testify: the Spirit and the water and the blood, and these three agree" (1 John 5:6–8). "Water and blood" is what flowed out from Jesus's side when pierced by a soldier's spear while on the cross (John 19:34), and in this context the spirit witnesses to the veracity of Jesus's death, thus nurturing faith in *this* crucified Son of God for the purposes both of conquering the world (1 John 5:5) and of accessing eternal life (5:11–12). In other words, the emphasis on Jesus's atoning death prominent already in the letter (2:2; 4:10) is consistent with its message of the forgiveness of sins (1:9; 2:12; 3:5–6), and these are extensions, in our framework, of the pneumatologically undergirded declaration of pardon and absolution from transgressions central to the missional sending of the faithful in the Johannine community. For us who are sent on the path of apostolic mission two thousand years later, we can be grateful that faithful Christian witness involves both the spirit's ongoing testimony to the life and death of Jesus and the spirit's unceasing enablement of our forgiving sins—of those within the fellowship of the believing community, of those on its dynamic and fluid margins, and of those also in the world—in his name.

8.4 Revelation, Part 1—"What the Spirit Is Saying to the Churches": Asian Mission(s)

The pneumatological and the regionally and geographically specified come together clearly in the Johannine literature only when we get to the book of Revelation. The opening address specifies, "John to the seven churches that are in Asia: Grace to you and peace from him who is and who was and who is to come, and from the seven spirits who are before his throne, and from Jesus Christ, the faithful witness, the firstborn of the dead, and the ruler of the kings of the earth" (Rev. 1:4–5).[49] Clearly, Paul's missionary journeys took

48. I was helped initially to see this connection by Keith L. Yoder, "Spirit and Atonement in John," *Conversations with the Biblical World* 32 (2012): 151–74.

49. For an introduction to the seven spirits and the divine spirit in Revelation, see F. F. Bruce, "The Spirit in the Apocalypse," in *Christ and the Spirit in the New Testament: In Honor*

him across what in the first century was known as Asia, with a number of the Pauline epistles associated with its cities (e.g., Galatians, Ephesians, and Colossians, with the letters to Timothy also related to the Ephesian site), even as we have already seen New Testament writings such as 1 Peter addressing this region (§7.3). The final book of the Bible is distinctive, however, in speaking not only to these Asian churches in general but also to each of them specifically.

To my knowledge, there has so far been no attempt to read the letters to the seven churches of Revelation missiologically. I propose an Asian theology of mission with the following contours. First, inasmuch as the continent of Asia itself is vast and resists any homogenization, these seven letters also invite a pluralistic missiological imagination informed by the ecclesial witness of the mid to late first-century western Asian context. As there is no one message in this early Christian milieu, so also there remain multiple missional endeavors that ought to characterize an Asian form of mission theology. In the contemporary world, there is not one Asian Christianity; instead there are multiple Asian Christianities (plural).[50] These letters to the seven churches thus show that the unified message of the living Christ in the western Asian context of the late first century yet found a diversity of expressions and manifestations. Second, and by extension of the first point, the Christian witness in any locale is contextually determined. Even within a not-too-extensive region like Asia Minor during the time that the Apocalypse was written, we can see various missional tasks: repentance and exclusion of varying members of and practices from a community in the cases of Ephesus, Pergamum, and Thyatira; being faithful amid persecution for Smyrna; seeking after revitalization for those at Sardis; engaging the Jewish community for Philadelphia; and awakening from outward affluence for Laodicea. Although we might wonder why just these seven churches are mentioned rather than other churches in Asia,[51] the point is that missional faithfulness is congregationally contextual. Different churches in one region, or even in one city, if we are to extrapolate for contemporary purposes, will have distinctive tasks and trajectories. Last but not least, then, the missional word includes both praise and blame, warning and promise.[52] With one exception on each side, the seven churches are lauded for

---

of Charles Francis Digby Moule, ed. Barnabas Lindars and Stephen S. Smalley (Cambridge: Cambridge University Press, 1973), 333–44.

50. E.g., Peter Phan, ed., *Christianities in Asia* (Malden, MA: Wiley Blackwell, 2010).

51. W. M. Ramsay suggests that John's choices of these seven churches were related to his knowledge of their history, geography, topography, natural resources, trade practices, and so on; see *The Letters to the Seven Churches of Asia and Their Place in the Plan of the Apocalypse* (London: Hodder & Stoughton, 1904).

52. The most extensive discussion of these promises is Mark Wilson, *The Victor Sayings in the Book of Revelation* (Eugene, OR: Wipf & Stock, 2007).

their achievements (except Laodicea) and also chastised for their falling short (except Philadelphia). Missional witness thus emerges not from ecclesial perfection but through recognition of shortcomings and the need for repentance.

Everything we have distilled so far about a first-century Asian missiological imagination is also thoroughly pneumatological. This is because the letters to the seven churches are announced at the beginning of Revelation as being from the seven spirits before the divine throne.[53] But it is also because each church is compelled to attend to the voice of the divine spirit: "Let anyone who has an ear listen to what the Spirit is saying to the churches" is the consistent refrain (Rev. 2:7, 11, 17, 29; 3:6, 13, 22).[54] It is the work of the spirit, in other words, to encourage through praise on the one hand and to speak boldly through truth telling and judgment on the other hand. Similarly, the seven spirits before the throne are sent to admonish the people of God and call them to realignment and reorientation of their lives, and to exhort them via divine promises to persist on pathways of repentance and faithfulness. As the visions of the book of Revelation are given through the testimony of Jesus, so are they given through the seven spirits. Assuredly, this apocalyptic unveiling is the result of the combined missions of the Son and the spirit, as was put to the church in Sardis: "These are the words of him who has the seven spirits of God and the seven stars" (3:1). In short, the letters to the seven churches invite a multifaceted and multipronged mission theology and praxis for the present time.

It is also important here to note that Revelation never talks about the *holy spirit* but talks about the divine spirit variously,[55] including in terms of the *seven spirits*. As is well known, the number seven does multidimensional work in the Apocalypse.[56] There are seven churches and their corresponding seven angels,

53. John's being thus arguably a "spirit-ed" ecclesiology; or, as Cullen Tanner says, John's is "Spirit-led ecclesiology": "Climbing the Lampstand-Witness-Trees: Revelation's Use of Zechariah 4 in Light of Speech Act Theory," *JPT* 20 (2011): 81–92, here 91; see also Richard L. Jeske, "Spirit and Community in the Johannine Apocalypse," *NTS* 31 (1985): 452–66.

54. This is one of a number of strategies through which John is pneumaticizing the apocalyptic message; see Ronald Herms, "Invoking the Spirit and Narrative Intent in John's Apocalypse," in *Spirit and Scripture: Exploring a Pneumatic Hermeneutic*, ed. Kevin L. Spawn and Archie T. Wright (New York: T&T Clark, 2012), 99–114. As Kobus de Smidt also writes, "Although quantitatively the Spirit is seldom mentioned, his deeds in Revelation are qualitatively active: so much so that Revelation was realized *in coram Spiritu*." "Hermeneutical Perspectives on the Spirit in the Book of Revelation," *JPT* 7 (1999): 27–47, here 44.

55. Robby Waddell is focused on the spirit in the middle of the book but situates his discussion well amid a more complete pneumatological consideration of the Apocalypse; see *The Spirit of the Book of Revelation*, JPTSup 30 (Blandford Forum, UK: Deo, 2006).

56. See Richard Bauckham, *The Climax of Prophecy: Studies in the Book of Revelation* (New York: T&T Clark, 2005), 7–15, 29–30.

seven stars, seven golden lampstands (Rev. 1:12), seven torches (4:5), seven seals (5:1), seven eyes (5:6), seven trumpets (8:6), seven thunders (10:3–4), "seven thousand people were killed in the earthquake" (11:13), seven plagues (15:1), seven golden bowls (15:7), and seven mountains and seven kings (17:9). As seven is the number of fullness or completeness across the book, the seven spirits are suggestive both of the fullness of the deity's attentiveness to and engagement with the world and of the expansiveness of the deity's presence across and activity amid the world.[57] In anticipating the next part of our discussion of Revelation, the seven spirits of God also contrast with the seven-headed demonic power to come (12:3; 13:1; 17:3).[58] The point is that the divine spirit—seven spirits indeed—is active in accomplishing the final redemption and transformation of the cosmos and creation, beginning with the people of God and the community of the faithful represented symbolically in and through the seven churches.[59]

We begin this final leg of our canonical journey by focusing on what the spirit says to the churches for three missiological reasons. First, mission is concrete historical activity, following after the work of the spirit surely, but always generative from specific sites, even if this takes us to the ends of the earth. The spirit's instigation of mission in Revelation is with *these* seven churches in Asia, and this invites local and particular mission starting points. Even if, as we shall see, the voice of the spirit is intended to resound at the four corners of the earth, Christian mission proceeds from somewhere to somewhere. Second, Christian mission remains pneumatologically inspired and imbued. We can only bear witness to what the spirit continues to say and speak. This mission is consistent with and extends the message and legacy of Jesus's testimony.[60] Such witness, resulting in martyrdom for Jesus and potentially also for those who would speak in his name, can only be carried out by the power of the spirit. Third, then, the Christian witness is eschatological and apocalyptic. It is carried out by frail and finite human creatures, but it announces in the present

57. "The seven Spirits represent the fullness of God's Spirit in the Church's witness to the nations. . . . The Spirit conquers the Church to be God's eschatological people in their prophetic witness, and the seven Spirits enable the Church to fulfill its prophetic ministry to the world, convincing the nations of God's kingship on earth as it is in heaven." Jan A. du Rand, "'. . . Let Him Hear What the Spirit Says . . .': The Functional Role and Theological Meaning of the Spirit in the Book of Revelation," *ExAud* 12 (1997): 43–58, here 56.

58. Bogdan G. Bucur, "Hierarchy, Prophecy, and the Angelomorphic Spirit: A Contribution to the Study of the Book of Revelation's *Wirkungsgeschichte*," *JBL* 127:1 (2008): 173–94, here 182.

59. Hee Youl Lee explicates the pneumatology of the Apocalypse along this narrative arc of messianic warfare and redemption of the cosmos, including its recalcitrant powers/spirits; see *A Dynamic Reading of the Holy Spirit in Revelation* (Eugene, OR: Wipf & Stock, 2014).

60. On the intertwined nature of the mission of Christ and the church, see also Catherine Gunsalus González, "Mission Accomplished, Mission Begun: Lent and the Book of Revelation," *Journal for Preachers* 22:1 (1999): 9–13.

both "what is, and what is to take place after this" (Rev. 1:19). As eschatological, this is the witness in the present of what is both here and yet to come. As apocalyptic, this is an unveiling of the truth of Jesus that exposes the signs of the present (thus warnings) and anticipates what is on the horizon (thus promises). Such witness can only be taken up by the spirit of Jesus.[61]

8.5 Revelation, Part 2—"The Spirit and the Bride Say, 'Come'": Doxological Mission Back to Jerusalem

If at the beginning "a wind from God swept over the face of the waters" (Gen. 1:2), at the end the divine wind speaks:

> The Spirit and the bride say, "Come."
> And let everyone who hears say, "Come."
> And let everyone who is thirsty come.
> Let anyone who wishes take the water of life as a gift. (Rev. 22:17)

Here the bride is the redeemed people of God—the church in the present age—and "the wife of the Lamb" (21:9; also 18:23; 19:7) that continues to invite all creatures into eternal flourishing, peace, and shalom.[62] Does this invitation only echo throughout the present dispensation, prior to the coming down of the new Jerusalem from heaven to earth (21:2), or does the missional summons persist throughout eternity? Regardless of how this question is answered, the solicitation is pneumatologically inflected if not also sustained: the bride's beckoning follows the divine spirit's initiative.

And the bidding of the spirit continues to resound. Note that the book of Revelation is pneumatically organized.[63] The letters to the seven churches

61. Here I put in pneumatological terms what is elsewhere explicated only missiologically: James C. Smith, "Missions in Revelation: Research in Progress," in *Unto the Uttermost: Missions in the Christian Churches / Churches of Christ*, ed. Doug Priest Jr. (Pasadena, CA: William Carey Library, 1984), 70–92.

62. Loren L. Johns emphasizes the rhetoric of "coming" that invites all into a reign of peace. Consistent with other nonviolent readings of Revelation, Johns sees the violence of the book as a prerogative of God (rather than of humans, who hence sin against each other and God certainly by acting violently) and as overcome by the Lamb slain and slaughtered "from the foundation of the world" (13:8). See "Leaning toward Consummation: Mission and Peace in the Rhetoric of Revelation," in *Beautiful upon the Mountains: Biblical Essays on Mission, Peace, and the Reign of God*, ed. Mary H. Schertz and Ivan Friesen, Studies in Peace and Scripture 7 (Eugene, OR: Wipf & Stock, 2003), 249–68. See also Mark Bredin, *Jesus, Revolutionary of Peace: A Nonviolent Christology in the Book of Revelation* (Waynesboro, GA: Paternoster, 2003).

63. Richard Bauckham, *The Theology of the Book of Revelation* (Cambridge: Cambridge University Press, 1993), 115–17.

were given to John by Jesus when he "was in the spirit on the Lord's day" (Rev. 1:10). If this first part of the book (Rev. 2–3) was effectively pneumatically mediated, then so are its other three main sections:

- Chapters 4–16 on the judgments to come are introduced thus: "At once I was in the spirit, and there in heaven stood a throne, with one seated on the throne!" (4:2).
- Chapters 17–20 on the final destruction of the ungodly and the triumph of God are similarly given by pneumatic vision: "So he carried me away in the spirit into a wilderness, and I saw a woman sitting on a scarlet beast that was full of blasphemous names, and it had seven heads and ten horns" (17:3).
- And the majority of the final two chapters (Rev. 21–22) on the new Jerusalem and the new creation are also pneumatically mediated: "And in the spirit he carried me away to a great, high mountain and showed me the holy city Jerusalem coming down out of heaven from God" (21:10).

If Revelation is the eschatological book that unveils not just the narrative of the God of the Alpha and Omega "who is and who was and who is to come" (Rev. 1:8) but also the human story of what has been "seen, what is, and what is to take place after this" (1:19), then the pneumatic structure of this cosmic drama indicates that the *missio Dei* is from beginning to end also the *missio spiritus*. Thereby is the Christian witness to this God in his relating to the world (ruahically and) pneumatically unfolded. Christian mission at and from any time—whether in this time between the times, or even in the eschatological time of the new Jerusalem[64]—is thus empowered and enabled by the spirit.

But the mission of the spirit is not just from any time to any time, but also from anywhere/everywhere to anywhere/everywhere. It is not just that the seer observes the "seven spirits of God sent out into all the earth" (Rev. 5:6), but it is also the case that these final visions concern "the four corners of the earth" (7:1; 20:8). More importantly for our purposes, the final revelation will cause "all the tribes of the earth [to] wail" (1:7), but yet will manifest a cosmic missional ingathering—indeed, of "saints from every tribe and language and people and nation" (5:9).[65] The seer actually beholds a second

64. See Kwame Bediako, "The Ultimate Vision: New Heaven and New Earth—Bible Study on Revelation 21:1–4," *Mission Studies* 5:2 (1988): 32–38.

65. Nestor O. Miguez, "Revelation 5 as a Missionary Text: A Meditation," in *Plurality, Power and Mission: Intercontextual Theological Explorations on the Role of Religion in the New Millennium*, ed. Philip L. Wickeri, Janice K. Wickeri, and Damayanthi M. A. Niles (London:

time "a great multitude that no one could count, from every nation, from all tribes and peoples and languages, standing before the throne and before the Lamb, robed in white, with palm branches in their hands" (7:9).[66] The gospel is proclaimed, after all, "to those who live on the earth—to every nation and tribe and language and people" (14:6). Yet it also means that this proclamation goes forth at the expense of the lives of the faithful: "Here is a call for the endurance of the saints, those who keep the commandments of God and hold fast to the faith of Jesus. And I heard a voice from heaven saying, 'Write this: Blessed are the dead who from now on die in the Lord.' 'Yes,' says the Spirit, 'they will rest from their labors, for their deeds follow them'" (14:12–13).

From this perspective, the Christian mission is *both* from specific times and specific places (see §8.4) to specific times and places *and* from any/every time and anywhere/everywhere to any and every moment and any and every place. Christian witness can and does proceed from every people, tribe, and ethnicity in the various stages of their histories inward and outward. Both the centripetality and the centrifugality seen in the Old Testament *missio Dei* is confirmed throughout the New Testament. Assuredly, the testimony of the faithful can only proceed in such multidirectionality by the power of the seven divine spirits.

From this perspective, the pneumatological missiology of this final book of the canon brings both good news and bad news. On the one hand, the testimony of the saints is carried by the spirit to the end of time and the ends of the earth, and many will hearken; on the other hand, it is unquestionably such witness that also brings about the demise of the faithful. This tension is

---

The Council for World Mission, 2000), 237–49; see also David Rhoads, ed., *From Every People and Nation: The Book of Revelation in Intercultural Perspective* (Minneapolis: Fortress, 2005).

66. Eckhard J. Schnabel writes: "In Rev 5:9 and 7:9 John reminds the Christians who belong to churches in the cities of Asia Minor that they should look beyond their own congregations and realize that there are followers of Jesus in every tribe (φυλή), i.e., in every family clan and in each of the φυλαί of the cities; in every language group (γλῶσσα), i.e., in every tribe and nation who are distinguished by the languages that they speak; in every people (λαός), i.e., in every group connected through cultural bonds and ties to a specific territory, including the populace of the cities and the village people; in every nation (ἔθνος), i.e., in each group of people united by kinship, culture, and common traditions, including foreigners and members of associations. Individual people from all these ethnic, linguistic, tribal, civic, political, and social backgrounds have repented and now worship the one true and living God, . . . [so] people from all ethnic, linguistic, tribal, civic, political, and social backgrounds need to hear the gospel of Jesus Christ." "Early Christian Mission and Christian Identity in the Context of the Ethnic, Social, and Political Affiliations in Revelation," in *New Testament Theology in Light of the Church's Mission: Essays in Honor of I. Howard Marshall*, ed. Jon C. Laansma, Grant R. Osborne, and Ray F. Van Neste (Eugene, OR: Cascade, 2011), 369–86, here 386.

played out in Revelation also vis-à-vis the fate of the nations.[67] On the one side, the redeemed come from the nations, the nations are anticipated to come and worship the Lord (Rev. 15:4), and they are to be found in the new Jerusalem (21:24–26),[68] indeed experiencing healing from the tree (or trees) of life on both sides of the river flowing through the middle of the city (22:1–2);[69] on the other side, the nations are opposed to God (11:18), have become drunk with worldly wine (14:8; 18:3), are deceived by the lies and sorceries of divinely resistant forces (18:23), and will be judged and struck down (19:15; 20:7–9).[70] The nations are opposed to the divine intentions; they are part of the worldly political and economic system of Babylon, clearly representing the Roman Empire in the time of John but remaining symbolic of all worldly governments, economies, and structures that are self-absorbed rather than given to worship of the creator, his Lamb, and the seven spirits around the throne.[71] There is no clearly pronounced salvific universalism, of nations or anything else, in Revelation, regardless of how hard one might look.[72] Instead, there is a tension between a widespread lostness of people and nations in the

67. Thus the "salvation" of the nations and the "damnation" of all that is impure "stand in some tension with one another and are never fully reconciled in the Apocalypse." John Christopher Thomas, "New Jerusalem and the Conversion of the Nations: An Exercise in Pneumatic Discernment (Rev. 21:1–22:5)," in Marshall, Rabens, and Bennema, *Spirit and Christ in the New Testament*, 228–45, here 244. Dave Mathewson also highlights the tension between the nations' judgment and salvation throughout the Apocalypse: "The Destiny of the Nations in Revelation 21:1–22:5: A Reconsideration," *TynBul* 53:1 (2002): 121–42.

68. Justo L. González, *For the Healing of the Nations: The Book of Revelation in an Age of Cultural Conflict* (Maryknoll, NY: Orbis, 1999); see also David Mathewson, "Abraham, the Father of Many Nations in the Book of Revelation," in *Perspectives on Our Father Abraham: Essays in Honor of Marvin R. Wilson*, ed. Steven A. Hunt (Grand Rapids: Eerdmans, 2010), 169–83.

69. The reappearance of what we might imagine as the garden of Eden in the eschatological city is suggestive of how Revelation supports an ecological or environmental theology that anticipates the renewal of creation itself; see, e.g., Micah D. Kiel, *Apocalyptic Eschatology: The Book of Revelation, the Earth, and the Future* (Collegeville, MN: Michael Glazier, 2017).

70. Ekhard J. Schnabel, "John and the Future of the Nations," *BBR* 12:2 (2002): 243–71.

71. Thus, in his insightful work on the nations in Revelation, Allan J. McNicol summarizes: "Until the concluding moments of the book the centre of the fundamental message remains clear. Do not accommodate to the civic and cultural life of the Roman Empire!" Yet "there is no doubt that John is saying that until the end of the age the present power structures will survive. . . . [But] despite the call to be an alternative community to the idolatries of the time, John never advocates that the remnant retreat into sectarian isolation. Instead the communities that confess to follow the Lamb are to stand firm in non-violent resistance to the gods and power structures of the age." *The Conversion of the Nations in Revelation*, LNTS 438 (New York: Bloomsbury T&T Clark, 2011), 120 and 133.

72. Any universalistic implications—argued strenuously, for instance, by Bradley Jersak, *Her Gates Will Never Be Shut: Hope, Hell, and the New Jerusalem* (Eugene, OR: Wipf & Stock, 2009)—are, in my mind, better understood vis-à-vis Israel's salvation history than with reference to the totality of individual persons, much less to the entirety of ethnicities, nation-states, or people groups; see J. du Preez, "Exegetical Notes: People and Nations in the Kingdom of God

world and yet a bountiful harvest from these domains.[73] If there persists an optimism of redemption for history, creation, and its creatures—individuals and corporate entities like peoples and nations—this is not because the world and its nations have any capacity to respond in themselves, but because of the God who rules by his slain and risen Lamb and by the seven spirits that continue to go forth from the divine throne.[74]

This is why the call of the book to the followers of Jesus is first to worship, and only in and through such adoration and adulation of the God of all is witness borne to the world.[75] Intriguingly, the prophetic witness of the divine breath testifies to Jesus by his words in worship: "Then I fell down at his feet to worship him, but he said to me, 'You must not do that! I am a fellow servant with you and your comrades who hold the testimony of Jesus. Worship God! For the testimony of Jesus is the spirit of prophecy'" (Rev. 19:10). Prophetic witness is less what the faithful speak to the world and more how they persevere in worshiping the true God rather than the dragon, the beast, and the beast's image (13:4; 14:9; 16:2). This worship of the living God persists in and through the world's hatred of the Lamb and persecution of his followers, and culminates in the new Jerusalem, where "the throne of God and of the Lamb will be" (22:3). If the primordial creation account enacted the enthronement of God over the temple of creation, then the new creation is unveiled with the divine throne amid the renewed and refurbished Jerusalem into which the peoples, tribes, and tongues of all nations are called to enter.[76] From this perspective, mission happens from any time and anywhere to every time and everywhere in and through worship of the living God in all times and spaces, not just within church services or walled buildings. Human creatures participate in this triune mission in lives of worship before the one true God who sits on the throne.[77]

---

according to the Book of Revelation," *Journal of Theology for Southern Africa* 49 (December 1984): 49–51.

73. Christopher Rowland, "The Apocalypse: Sensitivity to Outsiders," in *Sensitivity towards Outsiders: Exploring the Dynamic Relationship between Mission and Ethics in the New Testament and Early Christianity*, ed. Jakobus (Kobus) Kok, Tobias Nicklas, Dieter T. Roth, and Christopher M. Hays, WUNT 2/364 (Tübingen: Mohr Siebeck, 2014), 401–17.

74. A thorough and fair discussion of the nations is Bauckham, *Climax of Prophecy*, chap. 9.

75. Michael J. Gorman, *Reading Revelation Responsibly: Uncivil Worship and Witness Following the Lamb into the New Creation* (Eugene, OR: Cascade, 2011); cf. Melissa L. Archer, "*I Was in the Spirit on the Lord's Day*": A Pentecostal Engagement with Worship in the Apocalypse (Cleveland, TN: CPT, 2015).

76. For more on the nations in the new Jerusalem, see David Mathewson, *A New Heaven and a New Earth: The Meaning and Function of the Old Testament in Revelation 21.1–22.5*, JSNTSup 238 (Sheffield: Sheffield Academic, 2003), chap. 4.

77. Dean Flemming, "Revelation and the *Missio Dei*: Toward a Missional Reading of the Apocalypse," *JTI* 6:2 (2012): 161–78.

Discussion Questions

1. Jesus prayed for the disciples in part because, though they were in the world, they did not belong to the world (John 17). How does our reading of the Johannine Pentecost and of the spirit's work in the Fourth Gospel shed light on the witness of the disciples, and on our living amid this tension now?

2. The Johannine community featured missionaries coming and going. Revelation features seven churches with various testimonies, some good and others not so much. As we review what the spirit said to and through these various churches about their witness in their time and place, how might we comprehend what the spirit is saying to us about Christian mission in our context?

3. The eschatological invitation of the spirit and the bride in Revelation is to a new Jerusalem, even a new heavens and a new earth. Is there environmental, ecological, and planetary mission for us today? How do we bear appropriate witness that includes this cosmic dimension among the many others?

Concluding
Late Modern "Prescript"

Missio Spiritus—*Triune Witness in a Post-Mission World*

These final concluding pages sketch, in very brief and broad strokes, a "prescript" for Christian witness in a post-mission world. We began this book with a question: Whither Christian witness after the demise of the colonial, modern, and Christendom world that generated the classical mission enterprise? The wager was that a bifocal retrieval of scripture, one guided by observations about the work of the divine *ruah/pneuma* understood from a post-Pentecost perspective and normed teleologically according to interactions and interface with *others*, would be suggestive for the *missio Dei* in the present global context. What follows recapitulates our findings about the witness to the divine breath, extrapolates further for insight into the notion of triune participation in the *missio Dei*, and concludes with some proposals for witness praxis in a post-missionary era.[1]

The Mission of the Spirit

Our pneumatological and ruahological missiology springs off the Pentecost narrative (Acts 2), read backward (through the Old Testament) and forward (to the coming new Jerusalem that will bring together heaven and earth). How

---

1. As these final few pages are summations and constructive elaborations, there will be minimal scholarly references except to other missiological literature, including relevant items from my own body of work in pneumatology and pneumatological theology.

might the *missio spiritus* be characterized in light of our sojourn? I make a number of overarching observations.

First, a pneumatological and ruahological missiology is not merely spiritual or ideational if these are construed in binary terms according to either a Platonic or modernist sense that excludes the material, physical, and historical world. The spirit is, after all, poured out "upon all flesh" (Acts 2:17) and can be heard, felt, and perceived "like the rush of a violent wind" and as if "a tongue rested on" bodies, certainly with bodies and tongues touched and catalyzed to feeling, action, and speech (2:2–4). In other words, the mission of the spirit is not ethereal but carnal, following the incarnation of the (Johannine) Logos as anointed by the divine breath. Hence the *missio spiritus* is embodied and affective and in that sense holistic. The divine wind rustles, hovers, and swoops "over the face of the waters" (Gen. 1:2), touches the created orders and catches the world up in the divine witness. The discernment of the divine wind can be a kind of empirical matter, not in any reductionistic or scientistic sense, but one that recognizes that the spiritual and material are interwoven rather than discrete and compartmentalized.[2]

Nevertheless, and further, the *missio spiritus* does concern the divine wind contesting other winds, and the divine breath blowing against other breaths. Whether against the winds of Baal or in Jesus's exorcisms of demoniacs or in our struggle against principalities and powers, the spiritual battle cannot be reduced to any mere flesh-and-blood entity. It is true that concrete materialities are the means through which our spiritual orientation is distorted, so we are seduced away from our embrace of the divine breath. That was in part why the nations were banned from Israel in the conquest narratives, so that they would not compromise adoration of and commitment to Yahweh. Similarly, the call to sanctification in the holy spirit in the New Testament reminds us that our allegiances must not be on things below but our devotion ought to be divinely directed. Yet amid such spiritual warfare, we must be cautious about demonizing human others: those of other ethnicities, languages, cultures, (dis)abilities, and even religious traditions and sexual orientations.[3] It is one thing to love others with the compassion of the spirit of Jesus; it is another to demonize others different from us, as that undermines the credibility and

2. See Yong, *The Spirit of Creation: Modern Science and Divine Action in the Pentecostal-Charismatic Imagination*, Pentecostal Manifestos 4 (Grand Rapids: Eerdmans, 2011).

3. I will say more in a moment about other faiths. Here I note my efforts to rethink our understanding of impairment and disability, including articulating a more holistic Christian witness *with* people with disabilities rather than only *to* them. See my books *Theology and Down Syndrome: Reimagining Disability in Late Modernity* (Waco: Baylor University Press, 2007); and *The Bible, Disability, and the Church: A New Vision of the People of God* (Grand Rapids: Eerdmans, 2011).

plausibility of our witness. Such modernist dualisms that separate "us" off from "them" are less easily determinable in our postmodern context and situation. Recall that the warrior Amasai, one of David's "mighty men," wields not the sword in his hand but rather witnesses verbally to the shalom of Yahweh (§3.1). Across the scope of the scriptural witness there are *others* from out of which we are called to depart, but the overarching thrust is that of the redemptive blowing of the divine wind that catches us up with others in heralding the divine reign of love to come.[4]

Additionally, the *missio spiritus* involves bearing witness to the truth, specifically to Jesus as "the way, and the truth, and the life" (John 14:6). The divine wind that comes and goes unpredictably (3:8) nevertheless leads to all truth even as that same heavenly breath enables confession of that truth. Such truth is ruahically enscripturated and pneumatically retrieved, as the discussion of 2 Timothy, Hebrews, and the Catholic Letters clearly revealed. Yet, if not more important, the truth is incarnational, embodied in the Logos made flesh, as the Johannine witness repeatedly reminds us, and it is this scandal or "stumbling block" that Christian witness cannot eliminate: "Christ crucified" (1 Cor. 1:23). Just as important, the truth is asserted against those who would seek to compromise the commitments of the faithful internally even as the truth is performed in life and deeds in relationship to those beyond the community externally. In other words, as 2 Peter and Jude demonstrate, the harshest denunciations are reserved not for those without but for the deceits of so-called teachers within and among the believing community that reject this message of Jesus in his life and death.[5] We will return later to explicate what kinds of practices are involved in bearing truthful witness to external others.

Next, the *missio spiritus* is charismatic, especially in the sense of ecstatic and enthusiastic capacities enabled by the divine breath that are not otherwise possible under normal circumstances. The spirit-inspired tongues speaking and verbal witness in Acts are anticipated surely by the spirit-enabled prophesying manifest in ancient Israel, even as the spirit-empowered healings of Jesus and the apostles were also foreshadowed by the spirit-precipitated mighty deeds of the judges and of seers like Elijah and Elisha. On the other hand, not all manifestations of the divine breath are ecstatic or enthusiastic in these senses. Bezalel and Oholiab reveal that the charismata comprehend the mundane and

---

4. See Yong, *Spirit of Love: A Trinitarian Theology of Grace* (Waco: Baylor University Press, 2012)

5. Thus, every post-Pentecost missiology retrieves as appropriate the pre-Pentecost life and witness of Jesus of Nazareth, the one anointed by the divine breath to do good and heal "all who were oppressed by the devil" (Acts 10:38). I demonstrate how Luke is to be read in light of Acts in my *Who Is the Holy Spirit? A Walk with the Apostles* (Brewster, MA: Paraclete, 2011).

the vocational, not just the extraordinary and the situational. It is not just that the "normal" can be imbued with the divine breath but that the extra-normal can also easily spiral out of control (as the cases of Samson and the Corinthian congregation demonstrate).[6] Hence, while we are urged to "strive for the spiritual gifts" (1 Cor. 14:1, tongues and prophecies in this instance), these are to be tempered by love (1 Cor. 13) and mediated by the fruit of the spirit (Gal. 5:22–24).

Put alternatively, spirit-empowered witness according to the Pentecost account (Acts 1–2) is not just boldness to speak but capacity to be martyred for the sake of the gospel. This was Stephen's fate (Acts 7), even as such was modeled in an exemplary manner by the apostle Paul in the witness borne through chains. The Petrine community also persevered in the holy spirit as aliens in a hostile world, suffering as those bearing the name of Jesus. The call to witness and the sending on mission are therefore not an initiation to comfortableness but an invitation to persecution and suffering.[7] The greatest days of the ancient Israelite monarchy, as we have seen, were in reality contrary to Yahweh's admonitions not to desire to be like other nations and their kings, even as the announcement of Jesus as Lord over against Caesar was to renew Israel's messianic witness to the nations rather than restore its political sovereignty. In other words, Christian mission in a post-Christendom and postcolonial world reverts to the marginal witness of ancient Israel in exile or the earliest messianists living on the underside of the imperial Pax Romana.

Missio Dei: Triune Participation

As we have intimated in the introductory chapter, to elaborate on the *missio spiritus* is also to explore the contours of a more robust triunely understood *missio Dei*. The one caveat we introduced there, however, is that in our canonical-missiological explorations we have to walk a fine line between Pentecost and Nicaea. Our interests in theological interpretation incline us toward fully embracing the Nicene articulation of one God in three persons, but our scriptural commitments temper such explicitly trinitarian formulation in favor of the triune witness of the one God of Israel who sends his Son and

6. For an excellent discussion of how pentecostal exceptionalism can be degenerative, see David J. Courey, *What Has Wittenberg to Do with Azusa? Luther's Theology of the Cross and Pentecostal Triumphalism* (New York: T&T Clark, 2015).

7. For the centrality of the theme of suffering in Christian mission, see Scott W. Sunquist, *Understanding Christian Mission: Participation in Suffering and Glory* (Grand Rapids: Baker Academic, 2013).

spirit into the world.[8] In other words, God witnesses in a differentiated way, through his two hands (as indicated already, here following the pre-Nicene bishop Irenaeus). More to the point, to be filled or empowered with the divine breath is to be caught up in this mission of the one God in and through his word and spirit. In this middle section of our closing pages, then, we expeditiously explore the contours of what I call "participation in the mission of the triune God" along five registers.

First, a post-Pentecost missiology is no respecter of persons. "God shows no partiality" (Acts 10:34) in catching up all who are available for recruitment by the divine wind. Peter is evangelist even as the gentile Cornelius is an instrument of divine witness. In the Old Testament, numerous "outsiders" to Israel, unbelievers variously, are mouthpieces of the divine breath: Pharaoh, Balaam, Elihu, Nebuchadnezzar, and Belshazzar, for instance. While the Enoch of the primeval narrative is clearly a so-called holy pagan (Gen. 5:18–24),[9] in the New Testament epistle of Jude, his is clearly an extracanonical "voice" that is nevertheless prophetic. But let us be clear: that God is no respecter of persons does not mean that the holy spirit only speaks through putative pagans. Instead, as the Pentecost narrative makes clear, male and female (e.g., including Belshazzar's queen!), young (e.g., Timothy and Titus) and old, slave (like Joseph and Daniel!) and free—anyone and everyone upon whom the divine breath descends and alights or through whom the divine wind blows is caught up into the *missio Dei* and becomes a witness to the living God.

Second, the *missio Dei* that involves Father-Son-spirit is triadic or communal in the sense of being differentiated and yet harmonious.[10] Hence, the *missio Dei* refracted especially ruahologically and pneumatologically is similarly constituted by unity-in-diversity. We understand this in the New Testament as ecclesial: one body with many members defined by the holy spirit's various and diverse gifts. The seven churches in Asia in the Apocalypse are expressions of this one body of Christ to whom the seven spirits speak and through whom they bear witness to the living God who sits on the throne, even as the

8. In that respect, I am more biblicistic, methodologically speaking, than John G. Flett, whose book is a brilliant articulation of trinitarian missiology: *The Witness of God: The Trinity, Missio Dei, Karl Barth, and the Nature of Christian Community* (Grand Rapids: Eerdmans, 2010). My *triune* mission theology, by contrast, can be read as a halfway point: after Pentecost but anticipating Nicaea, albeit read from a late modern (thus twenty-first-century) vantage point.

9. See Jean Daniélou, *Holy Pagans of the Old Testament*, trans. Felix Faber (London: Longmans, Green, 1957).

10. This is classical trinitarianism, effectively. In this sense, I am riding the fine line between presuming Nicaea and yet also wishing to be more strictly normed by the biblical canon; cf. Yong, *Spirit-Word-Community: Theological Hermeneutics in Trinitarian Perspective*, New Critical Thinking in Religion, Theology, and Biblical Studies (Burlington, VT: Ashgate, 2002), part 1.

other churches throughout Asia and the surrounding regions to whom the author of 1 Peter writes also reflect what it means to bear multivocal witness as exiles "chosen and destined by God the Father and sanctified by the Spirit to be obedient to Jesus Christ" (1 Pet. 1:2). To reiterate the point differently: the *missio spiritus* is a differentiated and pluralistic ecclesial-communal endeavor, reflecting the inner character of the triune God and participating in that interrelational life.

Third, the Father not only embraces the Son and the spirit but also sends them into the world. Hence, the *missio spiritus* is an invitation to participate in this sending even as the *missio Dei* suggests that the creatures sent and those to whom they are sent are different but yet exist together on the same level in the human community.[11] Beyond the ecclesial reality, then, there is a social compass of the *missio spiritus* and *missio Dei*. The church bears witness not just *to* (here, the distinction) but *in* (here, the togetherness) society. Chiefly, I suggest that our post-Pentecost perspective foregrounds the socioeconomic domain: "All who believed were together and had all things in common; they would sell their possessions and goods and distribute the proceeds to all, as any had need" (Acts 2:44–45). While in a sense this was an ecclesial community, the borders or boundaries between church and society or world were porous: "A great number of people would also gather from the towns around Jerusalem" (5:16), and the circle of sharing was fluid and dynamic (4:32–37; 6:1–6). As the Jubilee principle retrieved by Jesus (Luke 4:16–19) suggests, the people of God are to care for the aliens and strangers in their midst, even as the marginal or exilic community of faith is to "seek the welfare of the city where I have sent you into exile, and pray to the LORD on its behalf" (Jer. 29:7). In short, triune mission participates in the interrelational work of the divine life that creates, sustains, and redeems the world and in that respect interfaces with others at and beyond the so-called borders of the believing community.[12]

This leads, fourth, to a discussion of the political dimension of the *missio spiritus* and the *missio Dei*. The socioeconomic and the political are intertwined; this means that there is no *missio Dei* that is not political in some respect. But in what respect, exactly? As the Old Testament narratives unfold, not least in the Micaiah narrative (1 Kings 22; see §2.6) but also throughout the so-called Deuteronomistic history, it does so not in the *Realpolitik*

11. See Yong, *The Missiological Spirit: Christian Mission Theology for the Third Millennium Global Context* (Eugene, OR: Cascade, 2014).

12. My book *In the Days of Caesar: Pentecostalism and Political Theology; The Cadbury Lectures 2009*, Sacra Doctrina: Christian Theology for a Postmodern Age (Grand Rapids: Eerdmans, 2010) is as much a *public theology* involving the socioeconomic domains as it is a *political theology* limited to the world of statecraft, despite the title.

sense in which Israel aspired to be and act like its national neighbors, but in the relational sense in which monarchic Israel nevertheless bore witness to Yahweh's distinctiveness. Further, as the major and minor prophetic voices heralded, Israel was called to rely on Yahweh, not on its own military might or on its alliances with other nations, and even in the postexilic context of renewal and return, Nehemiah, Haggai, and Zechariah show how easy it is to become dependent on imperial backing even in attempting to do the work of the Lord. In all these respects, it is exceedingly difficult to extricate ourselves from political power once gained, and hence also it is practically impossible for a Christendom church to flourish missionally in a post-Christendom time. It is all the more important, then, that the churches of the Euro-American West attend to the witness of those in the majority world, especially those who find themselves as minorities in political contexts dominated by other religious traditions (like Islamic or Buddhist nations). There is a transnational dynamic to Christian witness today, although this ought to be more along the lines of how the earliest messianists navigated the lordship of Jesus vis-à-vis that of Caesar.[13]

Last but not least, then, participation in the *missio Dei* thereby includes a transnational horizon, but one in which the divine breath witnesses to the shalom of the triune reign to come. In that sense, any *Realpolitik*-al engagement ought to be normed by the peace and justice that the prophets—major and minor—witnessed to. The vision of planetary justice heard across Isaiah is resounded when Matthew retrieves the prophetic imagination of the messianic servant that reiterates the divine wind's gusting for creaturely justice. The evangelistic message of justification by grace through faith prominent in the modern missionary endeavor is hereby complemented and filled out with the prophetic kerygma of justice and righteousness so needed for a late modern world replete with injustice. In effect, the canonical call, across both Testaments, is less the verbal proclamation to nations as such than the call to believing faithfulness amid a watching world. In the end, the eschatological achievement of the seven spirits among those who will hear what they are saying and participate in what they are doing is for the nations of the world, constituted via a plurality of tongues, tribes, and languages, to experience

---

13. See my essays "American Political Theology in a Post Age: A Perpetual Foreigner and Pentecostal Stance," in *Faith and Resistance in the Age of Trump*, ed. Miguel A. De La Torre (Maryknoll, NY: Orbis, 2017), 107–14, and "Conclusion—Mission after Colonialism and Whiteness: The Pentecost Witness of the 'Perpetual Foreigner' for the Third Millennium," in *Can "White" People Be Saved? Triangulating Race, Theology, and Mission*, ed. Love L. Sechrest, Johnny Ramírez-Johnson, and Amos Yong, Missiological Engagements (Downers Grove, IL: IVP Academic, 2018), 301–17; cf. Yong, *The Future of Evangelical Theology: Soundings from the Asian American Diaspora* (Downers Grove, IL: IVP Academic, 2014).

healing and flourishing (Rev. 22:2). The impossibility of this task is to be underscored rather than minimized since such renewal and prosperity happens not through political strategy and rhetorical ingenuity but through redemptive fire and apocalyptic destruction.[14]

The Beginning of Mission: A New Witness Praxis for the Third Millennium

Our post-Christendom, postmodern, and postcolonial world, however, might be evolving to becoming a post-nation-state globe. Market forces are uniting even when governments are dividing, but the truth is that the internet is facilitating the emergence of a reality *after* the nation-state in which many virtual others are interacting in a digital global commons. *Others* are now neighbors even if they might be on the other side of the planet. In these final pages, I chart the future of Christian witness in our post-mission global and electronic context in the form of practices.[15] The following witness practices seen throughout both testaments are commended.

Worshipful witness. The witness of the church is supremely transcendental, directed to God, rather than horizontal, directed to others. Others are observers, of course, but what they are observing is worshipful witness: the church daily meeting together, breaking bread, praying, and praising God (Acts 2:46–47). In the Old Testament, both pre- and postexilic, Levites like Jahaziel led Israel in singing and worship, and the Psalms are the record of Israel's singing and worshiping amid the nations, even as in the New Testament the call is for messianists to worship the one who is on the throne, and the slain Lamb on the right hand, in anticipation of the redemption of the nations.[16] And, intriguingly, it is undoubtedly in this stance of worship that the witness of the people of God is most palpable and potent: "And day by day the Lord added to their number those who were being saved" (Acts 2:47), as Christian worship was manifest not only in the singing but in the loving and caring for one another. Christian witness in a postcolonial, postmodern,

14. I am completing a pneumato-theological/missiological commentary on the Apocalypse: *Revelation*, Belief: A Theological Commentary on the Bible (Louisville: Westminster John Knox, forthcoming in 2020).

15. The shift from theory to practice is crucial in our postmodern context; see, e.g., Terry C. Muck and Frances S. Adeney, *Christianity Encountering World Religions: The Practice of Mission in the Twenty-First Century* (Grand Rapids: Baker Academic, 2009); and David E. Fitch, *Seven Practices for the Church on Mission* (Downers Grove, IL: InterVarsity, 2018).

16. For more on doxological worship as the culmination of the church's missional practice, see Yong, *Renewing Christian Theology: Systematics for a Global Christianity*, images and commentary by Jonathan A. Anderson (Waco: Baylor University Press, 2014), chap. 12.

and post-Christendom context is perhaps most effective when the church worships the living God as part of and central to faithful living in the world.

Neighborly witness. The witness of ancient Israel was to care for the alien and stranger in their midst, even as the witness of the first followers of Jesus as Messiah was to live blameless lives before and around their unbelieving neighbors. As repeatedly observed in the New Testament letters (Paul's and Peter's certainly, but not limited to these), the call was for gospel truth to be lived out or interpersonally embodied and communally incarnated before a neighboring/watching world. Such might also be considered a form of *sanctified witness*, wherein it is the holiness of the people of God that sets them apart—toward the divine (in their worship, for instance)—so that they are first *seen* as living differently rather than *heard* as preaching to the lost. In a digital world, of course, such human community, sociality, and relationality are being reconfigured electronically. The letter writing of the New Testament evidences that long before the arrival of the computer, human relations were epistolarily mediated already, even if that did not exclude incarnational dynamics.[17] The key now, however, is that human nature is being digitally remediated so that we will need to continually revisit neighborly and sanctified witness in an electronically constituted world.

Collaborative-dialogical witness. This witness practice concerns our exchanges with others, discursive, digital, and otherwise. More broadly, Christian witness is collaborative, by which I mean interpersonal, reciprocal, and interactive, not one-directional.[18] Think here about Paul in relationship with Timothy and Epaphras, and their relations with others also. If modernity developed hierarchical modalities of operation, postmodernity or late modernity introduces flat or horizontal networks of relationality.[19] Within such horizontality, human interrelationality discursively parsed then prioritizes not monologue but dialogue, all the more intensified in an electronically mediated globalism. Modernist construals of Acts 1:8 have been reductive to the activity of proclamation, whereas, as we have seen, the apostolic witness was as much if not more in deed than in word. Hence, we have to

---

17. See Yong, "Incarnation, Pentecost, and Virtual Spiritual Formation: Renewing Theological Education in Global Context," in *A Theology of the Spirit in Doctrine and Demonstration: Essays in Honor of Wonsuk and Julie Ma,* ed. Teresa Chai (Baguio City: Asia Pacific Theological Seminary, 2014), 27–38.

18. For more on collaborative mission, see chaps. 34–38 in Mike Barnett and Robin Martin, *Discovering the Mission of God: Best Missional Practices for the 21st Century* (Downers Grove, IL: IVP Academic, 2012).

19. Our late modern and post-denominational ecclesial networks thus can be seen as anticipated in the New Testament church; see Andy Lord, *Network Church: A Pentecostal Ecclesiology Shaped by Mission,* Global Pentecostal and Charismatic Studies 11 (Leiden: Brill, 2012).

reorient even our preaching as dialogical rather than monological.[20] It is not that evangelism and the call to conversion are no longer apropos, but that such invitations are dialogically situated in a late modern world. Ironically, perhaps, revisitation of Israel's witness to the nations enables an alternative vision of mission engagement than that bequeathed by modernity, one whose "function is that of witness as opposed to proselytizer."[21] Ancient Israelite wisdom, reappropriated in James, exhibits conversational mutuality with other wisdom traditions, so that the preaching of Qoheleth resonates in a late modern world of many faiths. In effect, then, Israel's exile opens up to an intercultural relationality that anticipates the many tongues of Pentecost and the many tribes and languages worshiping before the throne in the end.[22] The conversion of others happens, not in any unidirectional manner that makes "them" to be "us," but in the sense of a mutual transformation that draws us into the presence and activity of the divine breath. In short, our postmodern and postcolonial context has foregrounded the reemergence of the many voices, and effective witness in the power of the spirit and as participating in the *missio Dei* in this digital and incarnational milieu is both collaborative and dialogical.

Forgiving witness. The Johannine Pentecost most clearly announces this practice that, as highlighted above, is directed not only to other believers but also to an unbelieving world. Forgiving witness not only pronounces to the world that its inhabitants can be in right relationship with God but also that messianists will not hold against others the sins they (messianists) have suffered. In a postcolonial world, how can those on the underside of modern history participate in forgiving witness of those from the oppressor Euro-American nations except by the power of the holy spirit? As important, how can members of the colonial and Christendom mission enterprises find revitalization in the *missio spiritus* via repentance of their former ways and through participation in the incarnational mission of Jesus the anointed Messiah and through emulation of Paul the "weak" apostolic apologist? Similarly, in an interdependent and interconnected late modernity, how can global citizens participate in the *missio Dei* except through a shalomic forgiveness, one that enacts righteousness and justice in anticipation of the coming

20. As I argue in my "Proclamation and the Third Article: Toward a Pneumatology of Preaching," in *Third Article Theology: A Pneumatological Dogmatics*, ed. Myk Habets (Minneapolis: Fortress, 2016), 367–94.

21. John N. Oswalt, "The Mission of Israel to the Nations," in *Through No Fault of Their Own? The Fate of Those Who Have Never Heard*, ed. William V. Crockett and James G. Sigountos (Grand Rapids: Baker, 1991), 85–95, here 94–95.

22. As I urge in Yong, *The Dialogical Spirit: Christian Reason and Theological Method for the Third Millennium* (Eugene, OR: Cascade, 2014).

reign of God?[23] This is not to further dominate those who have been sinned against, nor to justify perpetuating oppressive (colonial) mission practices, but to experience the redemptive wind of God through confession, repentance, and forgiveness.

Sojourning witness. Finally, though not conclusive (this is just a "prescript," not any final script), the *missio spiritus* involves a *witness on the way.* The ancient Hebrews were called to bear priestly witness even in the desert, certainly while in exile, and also in the postexilic flux of imperial domination, even as the apostolic believers bore witness decisively in and through their diasporic journeys to the ends of the earth. This is also another way of denoting that Christian witness in a post-mission era is as it has always been: dynamic, partial, fragmentary, and eschatological, seeing "for now . . . in a mirror, dimly" (1 Cor. 13:12), awaiting full unveiling in the Lamb that rides on a white horse. As such, Christian witness is hybridic, constituted by interaction with others that continuously brings people close and transforms "us" and "them."[24] Gone are the pretensions of a modernized version of a "white" gospel; vanquished are the colonial renditions of a European-American mission; exposed are the Christendom accounts of a politicized ideology. Instead, Christian witness in a late modern time after the end of mission resorts through the Pentecost message to the forms and expressions of a marginalized people of God, both ancient Israel and the ecclesial body of Jesus. Witness unfolds in humility, resting in the power of the triune deity, and carried by the holy spirit that rests upon many bodies, inspires many languages, and works through any creature open to the divine blowing.[25] Come, holy wind! Breathe into us a new Pentecost!

Discussion Questions

1. At the end of this book, when thinking about Christian mission and witness *after Pentecost*, what are the two or three main ideas that have

23. The multidimensionality of spirit-empowered forgiveness is mapped in Martin William Mittelstadt and Geoffrey W. Sutton, eds., *Forgiveness, Reconciliation, and Restoration: Multidisciplinary Studies from a Pentecostal Perspective* (Eugene, OR: Pickwick, 2010).

24. See Yong, "From Every Tribe, Language, People, and Nation: Diaspora, Hybridity, and the Coming Reign of God," in *Global Diasporas and Mission*, ed. Chandler H. Im and Amos Yong, Regnum Edinburgh Centenary Series 23 (Oxford: Regnum, 2014), 253–61.

25. See my "Apostolic Evangelism in the Postcolony: Opportunities and Challenges," *Mission Studies* 34:2 (2017): 147–67, and "The Church and Mission Theology in a Post-Constantinian Era: Soundings from the Anglo-American Frontier," in *A New Day: Essays on World Christianity in Honor of Lamin Sanneh*, ed. Akintunde E. Akinade (New York: Peter Lang, 2010), 49–61.

been impressed upon you and that you feel are valid to continue to ruminate upon and perhaps even pursue?

2. According to this text, who gets to participate in the *missio Dei*? If we are believers, is it really possible that we can be deepened in our participation in the *missio Dei* through interacting with others to whom we are directing witness, even evangelism and mission? How so?

3. The many tongues of Pentecost open up through this book to many witnesses and mission practices. What are two or three forms of witnessing practice that you feel would be appropriate expressions of the spirit's gifts to you? What about your church, congregation, or community: does it have two or three dominant gifts through which it bears witness to others?

Scripture Index

285

Subject Index

Abiram, 54
Abner, 74
Abraham, 33–34, 42, 63,
    128n55, 174, 186, 198–99
    descendants of, 36, 124n41
Abrahamic covenant, 33n27, 52
Absalom, 74, 83n85
Achaia, 215
Achtemeier, Elizabeth, 144n108
Adam, 89
Adonijah, 74
aesthetics, East Asian, 209n82
affectivity, 4, 274
affluence, 36, 108n84, 190, 221,
    236, 264
African Initiated Churches, 95
Agur, 109
Ahab, 78, 80–85
Ahithophel, 74
Akhenaten, Pharaoh, 105
alien. See foreigner
alien, resident, 239
alienation, 199, 203
Allen, David, 233n21
Allen, Leslie, 137n86
Allen, Roland, 10, 13
Alter, Robert, 75n56
Amasai, 91–92, 275
Ammonites, 70, 76n63, 77,
    83n85, 91
Amnon, 74
Amorites, 60
Anderson, Bradford A., 119n24
anointing, 261
    messianic, 74–77
anthropology, 101, 107, 232n18
antichrist, 261
anti-election, 52
anti-imperialism, 78n70
anti-migration, 98
anti-Semitism, 183, 256n26

apocalypse, 228, 247, 248
    Markan, 162
    pneumatic, 265n54
apologetics, 191, 194–97, 282
apostle, 194, 195
apostolicity, 205
Aram, 75n59, 76, 83, 91, 93
Aristarchus, 212, 213n100
Arnold, Clinton E., 199n53,
    211n92
Artaxerxes, 95
Artemis, 220, 222
Asa, 91
ascension, 12, 78, 180
Asherah, 80–81
Ashkelonites, 67
Ashley, Timothy R., 46n61
Asia, 103
    Christianities, 264
    south, 188
    western, 188, 204, 228, 237,
    239–40
Asia Minor, 197, 219–20, 237,
    248, 252
Assyria, 93, 106, 113, 117–20,
    144, 148
Athenians, 178
atonement, 263
Auld, A. Graeme, 67n29
Ausloos, Hans, 57n1
authorship
    Davidic, 105
    Isaianic, 114
Azariah, 91–92

Baal, 59, 78–82, 274
Baasha, 83
Babel, 141–42
Babylon, 58, 124, 130, 132,
    148, 163
    captivity, 87, 113, 120, 125

empire, 117, 139, 141
exile, 61, 85, 88–89, 113, 121,
    123, 127, 150
Bailey, James L., 159n11
Baker, William R., 235n29
Bal, Mieke, 64n22
Balaam, 46–50, 55, 247, 277
Balabanski, Vicky, 162n22
Balak, 46–50
Barbour, Jennie, 108n83
Barré, Michael L., 46n62
Basdeo-Hill, Amelia Rebecca,
    134
Baskin, Judith R., 47n65
Bathsheba, 74
battle, 60, 274
Bauckham, Richard, 10n30
Baur, F. C., 190n25
Beale, G. K., 201n61
Beaton, Richard, 158n8
Becking, Bob, 139n95
Beers, Holly, 128n54
behavior, 224, 235
Belshazzar, 247, 277
Belteshazzar, 139–41
Ben-hadad, 83n87
Benjamites, 65
Bergant, Diane, 100n52
Bezalel, 41, 275
binarism, 41, 52, 171, 274
    spirit-flesh, 190n27
blessing, 7n17, 25, 33, 34,
    46–48, 51, 76, 82, 93, 105,
    121, 124, 128n55, 144, 148,
    176, 189, 198–99, 203
Block, Daniel I., 52n80, 71n43,
    74n54, 131n67, 137n87
Book of Eldad and Modad, 234
Book of the Twelve, 113, 115,
    142–51
borders, 130–35, 248
Bosch, David, 6